Irish Villages

Irish Villages

Studies in Local History

Karina Holton, Liam Clare
& Brian Ó Dálaigh

EDITORS

FOUR COURTS PRESS

Set in 10.5 pt on 12 pt Bembo for
FOUR COURTS PRESS LTD
7 Malpas Street, Dublin 8, Ireland
e-mail: info@four-courts-press.ie
http://www.four-courts-press.ie
and in North America by
FOUR COURTS PRESS
c/o ISBS, 920 N.E. 58th Avenue, Suite 300, Portland, OR 97213.

A catalogue record for this title
is available from the British Library.

ISBN 1–85182–766–8

Printed in England
by MPG Books, Bodmin, Cornwall.

Contents

Abbreviations

CSORP	Chief Secretary's Office Registered Papers
DED	District Electoral Division
Griffith, *Valuation*	Richard Griffith, *Primary Valuation of Ireland* (1848–64)
HC	House of Commons
IFC	Irish Folklore Commission
JRSAI	*Journal of the Royal Society of Antiquaries of Ireland*
Lewis, *Dictionary*	Samuel Lewis, *A topographical dictionary of Ireland* (2 vols with atlas), (London, 1837).
MS(S)	Manuscript
NAI	National Archives of Ireland
NLI	National Library of Ireland
OS	Ordnance Survey of Ireland
PRONI	Public Record Office of Northern Ireland
RCBL	Representative Church Body Library
RD	Registry of Deeds, Dublin.
RLFC	Relief Commission Records
TCD	Trinity College, Dublin.
UCD	University College, Dublin.
VO	Valuation Office, Dublin.

Preface

These essays, like their predecessors in *Irish Townlands* (Dublin, 1998) and *Irish fairs and markets* (Dublin, 2001), have their origins in the MA course in Local History offered by the Department of Modern History at NUI Maynooth. Graduates of this course have been meeting regularly since 1994 to share ideas about local history and to undertake studies on topics of interest to students and practitioners of local history.

Our contributors wish to thank Professor Vincent Comerford and his colleagues in the Department of Modern History at NUI Maynooth for their encouragement and assistance, and are particularly indebted to Dr Raymond Gillespie for his generous and unfailing support. They wish also to thank the directors and staffs of NUI Maynooth Library, National Library of Ireland, Royal Irish Academy, Registry of Deeds, the Public Record Office of Northern Ireland and the National Archives of Ireland for their assistance.

The editors would like to express their gratitude to Michael Adams for his continued support in publishing this series and to his staff at Four Courts Press for their dedication, professionalism and courtesy during the publication process.

The editors would also like to thank the contributors for their patience and understanding over the long and sometimes arduous editorial process.

Introduction

While villages have typified the settlement pattern of the Irish countryside over many centuries there is no typical Irish village. Villages differ according to their principal economic activity. In rural districts cattle rearing, cereal growing or vegetable gardening may be the principal activity. In other areas industrial activities such as milling, textiles or peat production underpin a village economy. The predominant economic activity of the hinterland will, by and large, dictate the shape and lay-out of each settlement. Villages in cattle-rearing areas tend to have wider streets and open spaces to accommodate the regular cattle fairs. In regions where tillage is predominant, settlements have narrower streets and market squares to facilitate the buying and selling of agricultural produce on market days. Agricultural activity does not exhaust the range of possibilities for village foundation: Lucan in west Dublin and Lisdoonvarna in county Clare owe their modern existence to the discovery of spa wells at their sites. In Ulster the linen industry spawned such mill villages as Derryaghy and Sion Mills. The coming of the railways in the nineteenth century gave rise to the villages of Limerick Junction and Enfield, county Meath. The Curragh, county Kildare, grew up around an army camp. In the late eighteenth century Robertstown developed as a stopping place on the Grand Canal. Centres catering for travellers had hotels and transport facilities so that visitors could be accommodated before proceeding on their journeys. Villages, therefore, are denoted by their diversity rather than their similarities. Every settlement, however, must have a secure commercial dynamic; otherwise it cannot prosper. A wide variety of villages have been chosen for our current study: medieval villages of the Pale, plantation settlements of the seventeenth century, landlord villages of the eighteenth century and fishing and industrial centres of the nineteenth and twentieth centuries.

CHRONOLOGY

The Norman incursion in the late twelfth century provided the impetus for the foundation of large numbers of villages in Ireland. Manorial villages developed in the hinterland of the larger walled towns of the Pale and the fertile lowlands of eastern Ireland. These nucleated settlements clustered around the twin foci of castle and parish church and are represented in our study by the priory village of Kilmainham and the twin villages of the Kill and the Grange at Clonkeen in south Dublin. The Kill and the Grange were manorial settlements attached to the extensive estates of the Convent of the Holy Trinity, later Christchurch Cathedral. Kilmainham grew in the shadow of the Hospitaler Priory of St John and was a strategic outpost on the western approaches to Dublin. While the vil-

9

lages of the Pale were greatly affected by the rupture of the Reformation and by the changes wrought in land ownership by the Cromwellian conquest, many nonetheless continued in existence into the modern period, albeit much reduced in size and altered in function. The experience of the Pale was different from the general pattern of villages in the countryside where ruined medieval churches and castles are today the only reminders of the existence of the once numerous pre-Reformation village settlements.

In the early modern period a new wave of village settlement began. The Tudor government, anxious to spread the ideas of the Reformation and to secure the lands of Ireland, began to plant the countryside with loyal English subjects. Settlers with capital and farming skills would improve agriculture and hasten economic development; incoming merchants would expand commerce and give new vitality to urban life. Sixmilebridge is an example of a settlement founded during the plantation period. In the early seventeenth century the earl of Thomond invited large numbers of English and Dutch merchants to settle on his estates in county Clare. The earl established Sixmilebridge and revitalised the older centres at Ennis and Kilrush. In county Kildare two attempts were made to introduce English settlers into the ancient settlement of Carbury but both attempts failed because of the opposition of the Dublin administration. Carbury would have to await the intervention of its landlord in the eighteenth century before it would flourish as a village settlement.

The majority of modern villages have their origins in the eighteenth and nineteenth centuries. Landlords, anxious to develop the economic potential of their estates, were instrumental in founding hundreds of new villages throughout the country and in renewing older foundations. The lost opportunity of revitalising Carbury was realised in the eighteenth century when the Colley-Pomeroy family promoted renewed development there. In the 1730s the Ievers family of Sixmilebridge built a market house and fostered the commercial development of the village. The arrival of the Lowry family in east Tyrone in the mid-eighteenth century was the catalyst for the foundation of the village of Pomeroy.

The extension of the road network into the remoter regions of the west was a crucial factor in the establishment of new settlements in Connacht as the market economy followed in the wake of the new roads. In the 1790s the Mayo landlord, John A. Knox, leased out lands around Ballycastle which led to the commencement of urban development there. By comparison, Cloone, county Leitrim, was less well catered for. The settlement had survived in attenuated form long after its famous monastic foundation had vanished. In 1821 Cloone had a population of 279 persons. In east Galway the landlord, William McDermott, set up the village of Williamstown on his lands in the early nineteenth century as a focus for the economic development of that area.

The new commercial climate in the second half of the nineteenth century gave rise to a situation where settlements could be established without the need to depend on agriculture for their basic survival. In this collection Portlaw, county Waterford, stands in stark contrast to the other villages, being an industrial settlement founded by the entrepreneurial Malcolmson family; it was a company village where the paternalistic Malcolmsons provided housing, schools and health care for their employees. Similarly, Kilmore Quay is exceptional, having had no external stimulus for its foundation but was established on the initiative of the local people. The village initially grew up around a fishing pier on the south Wexford coast and subsequently developed as a holiday resort.

ENTERPRISE

Trade is essential for village survival. To prosper villages need to interact with the larger urban settlements. Typically, villages acted as local centres where the surplus of the countryside was collected before being brought to the nearest town. The distinction between town and village is easily defined. Villages were settlements where fairs were held, whereas towns were centres where markets operated. While most villages held well-attended livestock fairs, not a single village in our study operated a successful market over a sustained period of time. For markets to operate in villages they needed continuous landlord intervention and investment. In Sixmilebridge markets functioned in the second half of the eighteenth century but only with the aid of the landed proprietor. Once landlord support was withdrawn the markets inevitably failed. In Ballycastle markets operated from the 1830s. However, the village did not succeed as a market centre but rather as a venue for livestock fairs. The village was hosting up to twelve fairs per year by the end of the nineteenth century. In 1837 Cloone was holding nine fairs annually, which were among the principal fairs in county Leitrim. Williamstown, county Galway, is a good example of landlord-led enterprise. The proprietor William McDermott set up markets in his fledgling settlement in the 1820s, which achieved local success for a period but failed to survive the catastrophe of the Great Famine.

In establishing or improving settlements landlords were motivated by economic considerations. Villages were a reliable way of increasing income as higher yields could be had from renting houses and adjoining parks than letting land directly for farming. Sometimes the principal role of the proprietor was to facilitate or stimulate urban improvement through others. Many operated at arm's length through agents or leaseholders. At Ballycastle the landlord, John Knox, resided in county Wicklow while the village's principal leaseholders developed the building plots and set the houses and gardens to incoming tenants. However, it was the landlord rather than the leaseholders, who financed the construction of infrastructure such as streets, squares and market houses. The provision of these symbolised the right of the landlord to regulate affairs and to share in the profits of the local economy. Other investments might include expenditure on schools, dispensaries or churches as happened under the Malcolmsons at Portlaw. Tenants were unequal partners in the enterprise; they were responsible for maintaining their properties and paying the annual rents. Yet they had a clear vested interest in landlord improvement as it enhanced the value of their holdings and improved their standard of living.

While all villages had the common trades of carpenters, bakers, blacksmiths etc. few could boast industrial enterprises. The industries that did emerge were inevitably of small scale and related to agricultural production. Milling occurred in Sixmilebridge where oil and woollen mills operated on the Ogarney river. In Carbury a flourmill flourished and in Ballycastle a sawmill did service. The creamery became the principal village enterprise of Pomeroy in the twentieth century. Commercial brewing and distilling of grain are absent from all our settlements presumably because of their small size. Kilmore Quay displays a unique form of local enterprise in the development of the fishing industry despite calamitous storms and the destruction of its half-completed fishing pier. Portlaw also differs from the other settlements and is a prime example of commercial enterprise, where textiles were produced on an industrial scale for international markets. Many settlements failed to reach their full potential as illustrated by Williamstown, where the landlord failed to have the railway routed through the village or at Sixmilebridge where enterprise remained unrealised.

Settlements have a tendency towards inertia, towards continuing in existence even after economic failure. Occasionally external forces such as the impact of local enterprise or external investment alter their inertial state. Villages may become towns where the enterprise is particularly successful. Those failing in enterprise decay and cease to be settlements of commercial significance, becoming instead merely hamlets or groups of houses. Williamstown might have progressed to the status of a market town were it not for the trauma of the Famine, as would Portlaw were it not for the economic collapse of the Malcolmson Company. Sixmilebridge might be said to have temporarily breached the barrier between village and town when its mills were flourishing and its markets functioned, but the bypassing of the settlement put an end to whatever commercial ambitions it may have had. Villages could not generate the volume of trade necessary to sustain a regular market and villagers clearly lacked the capital and entrepreneurial expertise to establish large-scale industrial enterprises. Consequently, few settlements successfully made the transition from village to town.

Despite the tendency of settlements to remain on their original sites, the relative mobility of villages needs also to be borne in mind. The investment required for infrastructure tended to tie villages to specific locations. There has been a parish church in Carbury since the twelfth century. The village of Cloone has persisted on the same site for over fourteen hundred years. However, villages can and do move. Villages migrate to new locations for a variety of economic and social reasons. There are four examples of 'moving villages' in our collection – two where the functions of the villages were transferred from one place to another and two where the original villages decayed and were replaced by new settlements on adjacent sites. In the early nineteenth century Kilnalag, county Galway, decayed as nearby Williamstown developed and expanded on a greenfield site. The locality did not need and could not support two centres of commerce. In the longer term only one could survive. This was Williamstown whose owner displayed more enterprise and invested more resources than the neighbouring proprietor. When the local fishing industry prospered in Kilmore Quay, following the building of the fishing pier, a new community settled in the coastal village. The population of the inland village of Kilmore declined and services, which were previously centred on the old village, moved to Kilmore Quay. The Kill and the Grange at Clonkeen existed as two separate villages on their original sites for nearly a millennium. Around 1800, however, the two moved to entirely different locations. By then the old manorial organisation was long decayed and as the *raisons d'être* of the original settlements – one spiritual the other commercial – had disappeared, so too had their villages. Two new settlements with similar names developed quite independently as groups of cottages on patches of surplus land close to their former locations, and subsequently developed into viable villages.

RELIGION AND EDUCATION

Churches are generally the most prominent and ornate buildings found in Irish villages. With their weekly services, family celebrations and annual feast days, churches provide spiritual sustenance for the people. They foster a strong sense of community and stand at the heart of every village. It is a moot point whether a village could exist without a church. A settlement without a place of worship would lack coherence and be a mere collection of houses. Indeed, one could define a village as a group of houses gathered round a church. Villages of course are much more than this. However, commercial activity apart, it is the church that has traditionally provided the main focus for village life in Ireland.

In plantation or landlord villages Protestant churches tended to occupy the central positions, while the Catholic churches, which were built later, were relegated to the outskirts. In Sixmilebridge a Protestant place of worship was built adjacent to the market place prior to 1641, while the first Catholic church, when it was eventually built in 1812, was located on the village periphery. A site for the Protestant church was set aside in Ballycastle as early as 1780, whereas the Catholic church was not built in the village until 1827. In Carbury, the Protestant church dominated the village physically and metaphorically. When the Catholic chapel was built, it was located some two miles west of the village at Derrinturn. A settlement gradually accreted around the new church attracting services such as a public house, school, post office and shops. The new settlement grew and prospered while the old centre stagnated. The experience illustrates the extraordinary pulling power of a church as a focus of settlement.

Irrespective of religious affiliation education was an essential component of village life. Informal schooling in the form of 'hedge schools' existed in all districts prior to the establishment of a formal system of education. However, hedge schools have left little trace in the historical record. Formal schooling does not appear in any of our essays until the setting up of the Protestant Charter Schools in the 1730s. The Charter school movement, the attempt to raise the children of the Catholic poor as Protestants, was a dismal failure as the example of Carbury clearly illustrates. A more benevolent and non-denominational type of schooling was provided by the Malcolmsons at Portlaw. There a high standard of adult education was provided for the workers in their spare time. If the example of Sixmilebridge can be taken as an indicator, denominational education was entrenched in rural villages before the setting up of the National Schools in the 1830s. Separate Catholic and Protestant schools operated in the village, although prior to the intervention of the parish priest, there was a high level of attendance among Catholic children at the Protestant school. Despite the oft-expressed hope at the time of the establishment of the National School system that primary schooling in Ireland would be non-denominational, by the end of the nineteenth century denominationalism was the norm. In the 1890s it was the nuns of the Sisters of Mercy, rather than lay teachers, who were invited to teach at the new girl's primary school in Kilmore Quay. Denominationalism continues to the present day as an integral part of our educational system.

COMMUNICATIONS

Good communications are essential if a community is to thrive. Commercial success and ultimately population levels depend on the quality of the communications network. Roads enabled villages to engage with the larger urban centres. Roads also facilitated the export of local produce while at the same time permitting the importation of manufactured goods into rural areas. Along with improved commercial contacts, new roads allowed better social and cultural interaction between communities and facilitated the spread of ideas and new technologies.

Kilmainham was situated on the ancient *Via Magna*, the main artery from Dublin to the west, while Clonkeen lay on the '*Via Regia*', the principal route down the east coast of Ireland. Both settlements were easily accessible and benefited from the constant toing and froing of traffic to the capital city. Visitors from the west sought accommodation at the priory of Kilmainham. The arch-bishop of Dublin lodged at Clonkeen on his visitations to the parishes of his dio-cese. Clonkeen, in addition, acted as a transit point for agricultural produce being channelled into Dublin. Proximity to the main highways was not always bene-ficial. Both settlements suffered at the hands of marauding armies. The com-munity of Clonkeen endured the regular depredations of the Wicklow Irish, whereas Kilmainham priory had its great barn burnt by the forces of Silken Thomas during the Geraldine revolt of 1534. Proximity to Dublin could also be a disadvantage in commercial terms, as the city attracted traders and merchants to the detriment of the smaller settlements on the periphery. Both Clonkeen and Kilmainham were too close to the city to maintain their own separate fairs and markets.

In later centuries roads were constructed by the institutions of central and local government. Whether built by parliament, grand jury or landlord, roads were a critical factor in the development of inland villages. An act of parlia-ment in 1733 authorised the building of the turnpike road through Sixmilebridge to Limerick. Under the authority of the Mayo grand jury, engi-neers Nimmo and Killaly undertook the development of the road network in the Ballycastle area. Williamstown had been relatively remote until its land-lord, William McDermott, petitioned to have the Bianconi car pass through the village to meet the Galway-Dublin mail coach. This resulted in accom-modation being made available for travellers in lodging houses in the village. New roads were built throughout the west of Ireland during the Famine years. The survival of villages often depended on accessibility to food supplies from the larger centres of population.

In the absence of roads, isolated coastal communities were sometimes sup-plied by sea. In north Mayo, before the development of the road network, pro-visions were transported by sea from Sligo to Ballycastle. Communication by water could be a considerable advantage to settlements. Small river craft trans-ported goods from the Shannon estuary up the Ogarney river to Sixmilebridge. The river Clodiagh, a tributary of the Suir, acted as a conduit for raw cotton imported through Waterford and transported upriver to Portlaw. Kilmore Quay depended on the sea for its prosperity and fish, and lobsters caught off the Wexford coast were transported by sea to the Dublin markets.

Railways made a significant impact on the villages through which they passed. They generated increased commercial activity and provided employment, while at the same time opening up remote communities to the outside world. Carbury, Kilmore Quay and Sixmilebridge all benefited in varying degrees from the devel-opment of the railway. The initial success of the rail system led to calls for its expansion. Many believed that commercial success would inevitably follow the development of the railway – an expectation that was not always fulfilled. Plans for a rail connection to Williamstown never came to fruition. Suggestions for the extension of the rail line which served Carbury through Edenderry to Limerick in the 1890s were not acted upon. By the 1930s, road transport had begun to overtake rail, and railway companies reduced their services. The effect is best observed in Pomeroy, where government refusal to upgrade the rail line led eventually to the closure of the railway, resulting in a major body blow to the Tyrone village.

In the twentieth century the emergence of the motorcar as a popular means of transport brought about huge changes in village life. Villages, hitherto isolated and self-sufficient, became satellite settlements of larger towns. The novelty of the car is discussed in Austin Stewart's essay on Pomeroy where, in 1932, the motor trials for the Ulster International Motor Rally were held. Motor transport allowed individuals greater freedom of movement. As car ownership became widespread city dwellers and townspeople tended to move from the larger urban centres to the more intimate village communities. The new inhabitants reflected the changing habits of the population. With motorcars people could reside in rural districts while commuting to work over long distances. The function of smaller settlements has changed with the result that today many of our ancient villages have become mere dormitory settlements around the larger towns and cities.

After surveying the many kinds of villages that populate the Irish countryside, one is inevitably struck by the recent origins of many of our smaller settlements. Compared to the European experience village creation in Ireland was weak. At the time of the setting up of the parish system in the twelfth century, every parish was required to build a parish church. One might expect that in time these parish churches would have become the core element of a village system throughout the island. That this did not happen was due principally to the religious cleavage in the sixteenth century and the Cromwellian conquest of the century following. These events resulted in the ruin and desolation of our parish churches and explains the need for the creation of a whole new village network in the eighteenth and nineteenth centuries. Village life represents one of the many hidden Irelands that have yet to be recovered by local historians. What this collection of essays reveals is that villages have been a crucial mechanism in facilitating the social and economic changes that have permeated the Irish countryside over recent centuries.

The Kill and the Grange of medieval Clonkeen

LIAM CLARE

In the course of the twentieth century the south county Dublin communities of Dean's Grange and Kill of the Grange have lost their separate identities as distinct villages in the all-embracing advance of urban sprawl. It is not widely known, however, that neither of the modern villages so engulfed, are located on their original sites, nor that each settlement was in existence for hundreds of years before being given its current name.

FOUNDATION OF THE KILL AND THE GRANGE

The kill, or church of Clonkeen, is thought to have been founded some 1300 years ago while the grange or farm of Clonkeen is known to have been in existence for at least 900 years.[1] Both of them attracted settlements which survived for centuries. These settlements were villages in the sense of clusters of permanent or semi-permanent dwellings, grouped around one or more institutional buildings, having a community life and a corporate function – in one case spiritual, the other secular.[2]

Beneath to-day's covering of concrete and tarmacadam, manicured lawns and specimen trees, we can visualise ancient Clonkeen as being in a wide flat valley, its sides rising gently towards the ridges of Rochestown Avenue on the east and Brennanstown, Brighton and Torquay Roads on the west. The detailed topography of the past can be filled in by placenames, many of which were referred to in early deeds but are now defunct. The 'Clon' of Clonkeen indicates a wet pasture or 'a fertile clearing surrounded by an expanse of bog' typical of the location selected for so many monastic settlements.[3] This description of the lower ground was reinforced by an extinct name – Cloonahaskin (*Cluain na heascann*, the 'meadow of the eel') – and by a surviving name – Monaloe (*Móin*

1 Elizabeth O'Brien, 'Churches in south-east county Dublin, seventh to twelfth century' in Gearóid Mac Niocaill and Patrick F. Wallace (eds), *Keimelia: studies in medieval archaeology* (Galway, 1988), p. 521; Charles McNeill (ed.), *Calendar of Archbishop Alen's register* (Dublin, 1915), p.28.   2 For similar definitions see Anngret Simms and Patricia Fagan, 'Villages in county Dublin' in F.H.A. Aalen and Kevin Whelan (eds), *Dublin city and county: from prehistory to present* (Dublin, 1992), p. 80.   3 Alfred P. Smyth, *Celtic Leinster* (Dublin, 1982), p. 30.

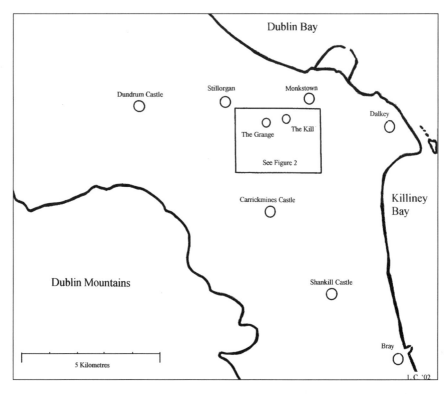

Figure 1 South county Dublin showing the location of the Kill and the Grange of
Clonkeen (see Figure 2 for detail of the area outlined).

na ló, 'the moor of the water') – both of which imply damp or marshy ground.[4]
Parts of the higher lands were separately named Tullachan (*Tulachán* 'the little
hill') and Dromin (*Dromainn,* 'the ridge'), and their ancient vegetation is also
described by names like Kalgach (*Colgach,* 'thorny place') Drinaghmore
(*Draighneach Mór,* 'thorny place'), Creaghanagarulogh (perhaps *Creathán na
ngarbhloch,* 'the marshy ground at the rough place') and Drissyfield (from *Droiseach,*
'brambly'), all indicating thorny, rough overgrown ground – in contrast to the
'caoin' element of Clonkeen which indicated a smoother, more even, ambience
in the valley below.[5] The natural appearance of the landscape would of course

4 Cloonahaskin, RD 556–313–369953 (dated 1803); Monoloe, letter dated 31 August 2001
to author, from placenames branch, Dept of Arts, Heritage, Gaeltacht and the Islands; verbal
advice of Pádraig Ó Cearúill, placenames branch.   **5** Telachkain, Dromming and Kalgach,
M.J. McEnery and Raymond Refaussé (eds), *Christ Church deeds* (Dublin, 2001), no. 6;
McNeill, *Alen's register,* p.80 (AD 1180); Drinaghmore and Creaghanogarulogh, RCBL
C6.3.1.1, map (AD 1638); Drisseyfield, RD 827–404–556539 (AD 1827); verbal advice of Pádraig
Ó Cearúill, placenames branch.

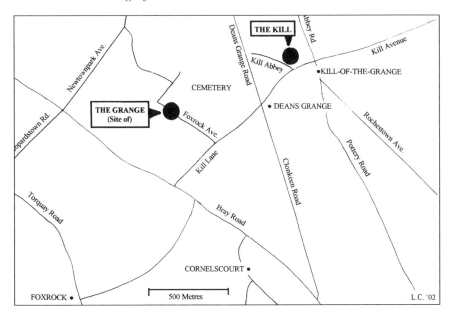

Figure 2 Clonkeen area showing locations of the Kill and the Grange of Clonkeen
(see also Figure 1).

have been altered by early farming practices, commencing with the lower most fertile lands, those which were already clear of undergrowth and persistent weeds, and gradually extending to areas newly cleared of woodland and scrub. The environmental setting of ancient Clonkeen can therefore be summarised as a fertile low-lying area, constrained by two ridges covered by forest, thicket and heath.[6]

The church of Clonkeen, situated on the eastern side of the valley, is believed to have been founded in the late seventh century. The evidence for its early establishment includes the presence of a *bullán*, a carved stone and two stone crosses on the site, as well as a fragment of an enclosure bank. The crosses and carved stone were removed in recent times and the enclosure bank was obliterated in the course of a housing development. The transfer to Clonkeen of the cult of St Fintan, a sixth-century abbot, of Clonenagh, county Laois, is also indicative of an early foundation.[7] The remains of the enclosure and of the *bullán*, together with records of a well now covered over, are evidence of the establishment of an associated settlement. The ruined stone church on the site is thought to have been constructed at a later date, around the tenth or eleventh centuries.[8] The dedication to St Fintan was not formally documented in legal deeds until 1504, although two St Fintans of Clonkeen (in counties Laois and Dublin) are recorded

6 Nancy Edwards, *The archaeology of early medieval Ireland* (London, 1990), p.52.   **7** O'Brien, *Churches*, p. 521.   **8** Ibid., pp 504–24.

in the martyrology of Tallaght, around 830.[9] The phenomenon of the association of the cult of St Fintan with the cult of St Brigid, is apparent in this area
which has many dedications, ancient and modern, to St Brigid.[10]

A grange was located on rising ground one kilometre to the west of the kill.
The word 'grange' (literally a store-house for grain) was often used to describe a
farm, particularly a farm owned by the church. The first documentary record of
the existence of a grange at Clonkeen was in a deed prepared around 1230.
However, Clonkeen itself is mentioned in a document dated 1202, which lists
the lands in south county Dublin which had been donated by benefactors to the
pre-Anglo-Norman Convent of the Holy Trinity (now Christ Church Cathedral).
The donors' names pointed to the benefactors being of both Gaelic and Norse
origin, and the motivation for such donations of lands would have been primarily religious.[11] The grange of Clonkeen would become the home farm and the
administrative centre for the entire holding – a swathe of some 2,500 acres (1,000
hectares), which stretched from the foot of the Three Rock Mountain at
Murphystown to the sea at Shanganagh, and is approximately represented by the
three civil parishes of Kill, Tully and Killiney. The neighbours of the grange lands
were also church institutions: the lands of Shankill and Rathmichael to the south
were in the possession of the archbishop of Dublin, while Clonkeen's neighbours
to the north, at Monkstown, were the monks of St Mary's Abbey.[12] Saint Mary's
Abbey was held for some time by the Cistercians who were renowned as leading promoters of a new commercial farming, and this must have set a high standard for agriculture generally in the south county Dublin. Holy Trinity directly
managed the home farm at Clonkeen, but the outlying lands were let out. The
rents secured from these holdings, payable in cash, in goods or in service, were
applied for the benefit of the Holy Trinity community.[13]

Most documentation up to about 1600, did not distinguish between the twin
villages, but referred to them jointly as Clonkeen – using a variety of spellings.
However, they were named separately in a rent roll dated 1326 as Grangetown (Villa
Grangie) and Churchtown (Villa Ecclesie), and after 1539 as shall be seen, they were
referred to as 'the Dean's Grange' (or simply 'Dean's Grange') and 'Kill-of-the
Grange' respectively. They will be referred to below as 'the Grange' and 'the Kill'.[14]

9 McEnery, *Christ Church deeds*, no. 379; Richard Irvine Best and Hugh Jackson Lawlor (eds),
Martyrology of Tallaght from the book of Leinster and ms 5100–4 in the Royal Library Brussels (London,
1931), pp 15 and 42.   10 Letter, P. Ó Riain, 20 March 2000, to author pointing out parallel
cults.   11 McEnery, *Christ Church deeds*, no. 44; McNeill, *Alen's register* p. 28; McEnery, *Christ
Church deeds*, no. 220.   12 Jocelyn Otway-Ruthven 'The medieval church lands of south
county Dublin' in J. Watt, J.B. Morrall, F.X. Martin (eds), *Medieval studies presented to Aubrey
Gwynn S.J.* (Dublin, 1961), pp 54–73; James Mills, 'The Norman Settlement in Leinster –
the cantreds near Dublin', in *JRSAI*, iv (5th series), 1894, pp. 161–3.   13 Frank Mitchell,
Shell guide to reading the Irish landscape (Dublin, 1986), p. 173; F.E. Ball, *A history of county
Dublin* (Dublin, 1979 reprint), i, pp 2–3.   14 James Mills, *Account roll of the priory of the Holy*

One issue to be addressed is whether the populations of these settlements were living as villagers in two small centralised communities or were scattered throughout the townlands in each case. While the conventional wisdom with regard to Anglo-Norman manorial settlements was that they were centralised, this nuclear model has been challenged by McNeill at least in Ulster conditions.[15] In Clonkeen, however, the existence of labour-intensive demesne farming and of labour-intensive tillage rather than stock-raising, would support the existence of nuclear settlements. Moreover, this evidence is reinforced by the presence of English settlers at Clonkeen who were under constant threat, living in 'fear of the Irish', and therefore likely to congregate together for mutual protection. And again, the two communities were both living in well-established settlements, located in an area which had for long been under cultivation, rather than in recently-cleared marginal land. A rent roll of 1326 (see below) confirms the nuclear settlement model.[16]

ANGLO-NORMAN ADMINISTRATION AT CLONKEEN

While documentary records for Clonkeen only commence with the Anglo-Norman invasion, we can surmise from other research, that even prior to that event, cattle-raising was a major occupation of the villagers, providing dairy products in summer and meat all the year round. Cattle were typically grazed on upland common pasture during the grass-growing months, and left to winter on the uncut hay and the cereal stubble of the lower lands. A variety of cereals was also grown, on long, straight, narrow, ploughed strips of land.[17] In 1169 the Anglo-Norman invasion began, and soon their leaders were in control of the province of Leinster. King Henry II granted large tracts of land throughout the province to the Anglo-Norman lords, but the two cantreds (pre-Anglo-Norman territorial units) now forming south county Dublin (including Clonkeen) and north county Wicklow were not so allocated.[18] Despite this, the influence of the Anglo-Normans on the Clonkeen area was comprehensive. The European-wide manorial system with its military, economic, social and judicial implications was introduced here and this affected church-owned estates as well as the lands held by the Anglo-Norman leaders. A manor house was established under the Anglo-Norman system of government at Clonkeen, the prior of the Holy Trinity Convent became the lord of the manor, and the new milieu involved changes in social structures, changes in land tenure and changes in agricultural practices. Inevitably some displacement of the indigenous inhabitants occurred,

Trinity, Dublin, 1337–1346 (Dublin, 1891), pp 195–6. **15** T.E. McNeill, *Anglo-Norman Ulster* (Edinburgh, 1980), referred to in Kieran Denis O'Conor, *The archaeology of medieval rural settlement in Ireland* (Dublin, 1998), pp 41–71. **16** Mills, *Account roll,* pp 195–7. **17** Edwards, *Archaeology,* pp 56–64; Mitchell, *Irish landscape,* p. 160. **18** Mills, *Cantreds,* p. 161

though it is unlikely that the entire native population was expelled by the new-comers, either in this area, or indeed in any other manorial estate. The indige-nous leaders were, nevertheless, replaced with a new aristocracy.[19] At the end of the thirteenth century it is estimated that over 50 per cent of the population on manorial estates generally were English, and this estimate appears to have been applicable to Clonkeen in 1326.[20]

One of the characteristics of the newcomers was their propensity for the maintenance of written records, and the earliest known deed relating to Clonkeen, is dated 1179, only ten years after their arrival in Ireland. In this deed, Pope Alexander III confirmed to Holy Trinity Church, the lands of Clonkeen, which provided income 'for the canons' table'. An extensive collection of deeds was maintained by the administrators of Holy Trinity, and by their successors at Christ Church, but these perished in the Four Courts conflagration of 1922. Fortunately, a calendar had been made of documents extant in the mid-1880s, and this has now been published in full, up to 1699.[21]

The establishment of the manor house at Clonkeen, gave one of the villages an added importance as an administrative and judicial centre. But *which* village? One commentator, James Mills, while not choosing definitively, seems to opt for the Kill, while Francis Elrington Ball, although referring to the manor and manor court as being located at Kill-of-the-Grange, appears to accept that the Grange was the centre.[22] There is in fact overwhelming documentary evidence that the village of the Grange was chosen for the new roll as the centre of the manor: the Grange became a larger village than its neighbour; the account roll for 1348 shows that the chamberlain or house steward, as well as the bailiff or land steward, and the tradesmen were all resident at the Grange rather than at the Kill; unlike the Kill, the Grange had a slated castle at the time of the Civil Survey in 1665; a lease in 1561 refers to 'the manor town and fields of the Grange of Clonkeen'; a contract was placed in 1574, for fish to be supplied to the Grange (not the Kill), whenever Clonkeen was visited by the dean; a rental dating from around 1633 referred to the mensal lands separately from the Kill farm.[23]

Besides a cluster of small cottages, the village of the Grange when at its zenith, would have incorporated the manor house or prior's house as well as a haggard, a grange, a cow byre, a kiln house, and ancillary buildings such as bake-house and workshops. There was a reference to a mill – an important facility for any manor – at Clonkeen, but having regard to the local topography, this is unlikely

19 S.J. Connolly, *The Oxford companion to Irish history* (Oxford, 1998), pp 343–4; Canon C.A. Empey, 'Medieval Knocktopher: a study in manorial settlement – Part 1' in *Old Kilkenny Review*, ii, no. 4, 1982, p. 339; A.J. Otway-Ruthven, *A history of medieval Ireland* (London, 1980 edition), pp 114–15. 20 Mills, *Account roll*, pp 195–8. 21 McNeill, *Alen's register*, p. 3 22 Mills, *Account roll*, pp 194–5; Ball, *County Dublin*, i, pp 47–9. 23 Mills, *Account roll*, pp 195–7; Robert C. Simington (ed.), *The Civil Survey, vii, County of Dublin* (Dublin, 1945), pp 265–6; McEnery, *Christ Church deeds*, nos. 1271, 1341, 1512.

to have been in either village, perhaps being located on the Glaslower stream near the present Brewery Road.[24] In common with other medieval institutions, in the absence of universal literacy – and indeed of writing materials – a formal, solemn place for the making of bargains and payments was needed. Consequently the Grange had 'the holy stood'[25] for this purpose, just as Limerick and many other towns had their 'nail' for paying of bills and dues ('paying on the nail'), or as the Holy Trinity priory itself had the 'Rood (crucifix) of Christchurch' on which contracts for loans could be sworn.[26] There is no evidence of military defences around either village, despite the continuing threats and insecurity arising from their proximity to the hostile mountainous area. The absence of defences may be accounted for by the archaeological evidence only now being unearthed, indicating that Carrickmines Castle, just a short distance away, was between the thirteenth and the seventeenth centuries, a very extensive military facility, capable of supporting a large force of men in times of military threat. And there is no evidence of a market or a fair being patented or held at the Grange, except for one nineteenth-century manuscript map. This shows a former wide section of what is now the national road, the N11 which lay opposite the site of the Grange, marked both 'fair green' – and also 'galloping green'.[27]

The prior of Holy Trinity, as lord of the manor, held courts at the Grange, redressing misdemeanours and nuisances, perhaps levying small fines for affrays and assaults, and settling property disputes. In practice he delegated this task to one of his canons who was appointed as his seneschal. The seneschal was required to visit each manor attached to the priory, a few times a year, and during these visits he would enquire into matters dealing with rents, services, customs, manorial property (such as lands, woods, meadows, pastures, waters, mills ...), and administer justice. The seneschal also supervised the resident bailiff or land steward.[28] The larger tenants had included in their tenancy agreements, a responsibility to render 'suit of court', as one of their services to their lord, the prior.[29] As suitors they were expected to declare and rule on what had, and what had not, been ancient 'custom and practice' within the manor. They depended on their collective memories for their knowledge of previous decisions and of accepted practices. The system of mental records has resulted in the absence today of any detailed knowledge of manorial courts. This customary court system relied on neither the king's law (common law), canon law or merchant law; it was a completely independent, though parallel code of local law.[30]

---

24 Mills, *Account Roll*, pp 55–87 and 152–3. **25** Stood or stud, an upright post. **26** McEnery, *Christ Church deeds*, no. 1242; P.W. Joyce, *English as we speak it in Ireland* (Dublin, 1977 edition); James Lydon's introduction to Mills, *Account roll* (1996 edition), p. xv. **27** NLI, map 21F53 (70), (n.d. – possibly 1836) – this was at the entrance to the present Westminster Park, about a kilometre south of the present Galloping Green. **28** Ball, *County Dublin*, i, p. 48; Mills, *Account roll*, p. 143. **29** McEnery, *Christ Church deeds* nos. 646, 554. **30** *Oxford companion*, pp 343–4; Empey, 'Knocktopher part II' in *Old Kilkenny Review*, ii, no. 5, 1983, pp 447–50.

Much of the regulation of activity by local courts generally, resulted from the existence of rights of *commonage*. While there are few surviving documentary references to common rights at Clonkeen, the commons at Drumin, at Drinaghmore, at Tipperstown and at Monnelough are specifically mentioned, as are commons of pasture generally.[31] There is also a record of an area of commonage from which clay could be extracted.[32] It is therefore likely that other typical forms of commonage such as gathering of firewood, cutting of turf, fishing, fowling, rights of way, quarrying and so on, were also in existence at Clonkeen, just as they were in other manors. In 1348, the manor courts brought in an income of 13*s*. 2*d*. from fines and fees.[33]

The relationships between the population and the lord of the manor was of the essence in the manorial system, and each individual relationship depended on the relevant form of tenure. Because most of the church lands in Ireland were free of the obligation to provide military service to the king as was customary in the case of lands held by the church in England, the manor of Clonkeen was less militarised than manors held by knights' fee.[34] However, some tenants, as shall be seen in the case of Robert Haketh, had a duty to assist the lord in defence when called on, and certain defensive activities were based at the Grange. Large parcels of land were let to tenants by the townland, for example Ballybrennan (Brennanstown) and Balytypur (Tipperstown), and these were paid for by cash rents and by service. The balance of the land, the demesne lands, were managed directly from the Grange. Some smaller farmers held a few acres within the demesne lands, also paying for them in cash or service, and there is evidence of cottagers who held no land at all.[35] There is little direct evidence of numerous small strips being allotted to particular tenants within large open fields, as is found on the archbishop's estates in Dalkey, Rathcoole or Saggart.[36] However, many of the other elements of agricultural organisation typically found in Anglo-Norman manors are also evident in Clonkeen – commons of pasture, bulk leasing of townlands outside the demesne, service provided by both large and small tenants at sowing and at harvest, paying of 'a custom ridge in harvest' as rent, suit of court by tenants, the lack of boundary fences or ditches (even between townlands), and so on – so it is not unreasonable to conclude that the common approach to strip ploughing also was present. There is no evidence at Clonkeen, of there ever having been burgage tenants, who typically held narrow strip holdings, or of betaghs (serfs inherited by the Anglo-Normans from their Gaelic pre-

---

31 McEnery, *Christ Church deeds*, no. 1635; NLI, MS 100, Materials for the history of county Dublin including extracts of original documents, *c.*1200–1800. See footnote 112; McEnery, *Christ Church deeds*, no. 386; RCBL, C6.1.17, p.9, lease 1 May 1559. 32 Mills, *Account roll,* p. 174. 33 Mills, *Account roll,* p. 55. 34 *Oxford Companion,* pp 343–4; Kenneth Milne (ed.), *Christ Church cathedral Dublin, a history* (Dublin, 2000), p. 81. 35 Mills, *Account roll.* 36 J. Otway-Ruthven, 'Organisation of Anglo-Irish agriculture in the middle ages', in *JRSAI,* lxxxi, 1951, pp 6–8.

decessors), living on the manor, though the townland of Ballybetagh a couple of kilometres away, above the Scalp, indicates their presence in the general area.[37]

Few details of leases survive from the period prior to 1600, but a lease dated 1352 to Robert Haketh in respect of the Balytypur lands, indicates the rent and nature of the service required from the larger tenants in manorial times:

> the tenement of Balytypur for sixteen years, rent thirty shillings for the first eight years, and forty shillings after. Lessee covenants to plough lessors' land of Clonken for one day at the winter sowing, and for another day at the spring sowing; to reap the corn there with one man for one day in autumn; to cart it with a wagon for one day, or for two days with one cart, or for one day with two carts; to give the prior and Convent the customary 'stadabolle' of beer, equal to two gallons, whenever he brews, and to do suit of court at Clonken when summoned; not to sublet the premises or any part thereof, unless to a kinsman, without the consent of the lessors; that lessors on death of lessee during term may have a heriot or half a mark at their pleasure; lessee to attend and aid lessors in counsel, service and assistance at any place in the county of Dublin lessee may be required, but at the expense of lessors, and to maintain the premises in good condition.[38]

It will be noted that the level of service was not too burdensome, being merely aimed at supplementing regular labour at peak periods, nor was it something which had to be done personally. Payment of a toll on brewing was commonplace for tenants of manors generally. The custom of providing a heriot, or best beast on the demise of the tenant evolved from the tradition of lords of manors lending horses to their knights, returnable on the knights' deaths. Again the requirement to attend the lessor anywhere in county Dublin, is a reflection of the link between land tenure and military service. The existence of these and similar provisions in leases, implies that the Grange enjoyed a considerable level of administrative importance and witnessed a substantial level of administrative activity.

While the Grange was engaged in secular administration, the development of the Kill was also under way. The church or convent of the Holy Trinity in Dublin had been founded around 1030 and the Kill of Clonkeen, together with the farmlands of the district was bestowed on Holy Trinity, by 'Donogh son of Donald the Gross' (Donnchad Mac Domnaill Remair) about the year 1088.[39] This transfer of control brought the Kill firmly under the influence of the twelfth-century reformers who were beginning to implement the administrative initia-

37 McEnery, *Christ Church deeds*, no. 1406, 646, 1490; *Oxford companion*, pp 62–3, 45–6. **38** McEnery, *Christ Church deeds,* no. 646. **39** James Kelly and Dáire Keogh, (eds), *History of the Catholic archdiocese of Dublin* (Dublin, 2000), pp 35–6; McNeill, *Alen's register,* p. 28; McEnery, *Christ Church deeds,* no. 364 (c); Milne *Christ Church*, p.28; *Oxford companion*, pp 555, 44, 31.

tives of Pope Gregory VII. The Benedictines, one of the new radical orders, controlled Holy Trinity from 1085 until 1100 when they were ousted in ecclesiastical infighting. However, St Laurence O'Toole, himself a radical, introduced another reforming order, the Arrousian Augustinian canons in the 1160s, and their influence was soon brought to bear on the older monasticism of the Kill. While any devotional or liturgical changes introduced there by the new management are not recorded, the reformers propensity for church building may indeed be reflected at Clonkeen.[40] Archaeologists date the nave portion of the stone church building, (the sole surviving structure of either village), as 'tenth or eleventh century' or 'earliest, eleventh century', and the chancel extension as 'the Anglo-Norman period', both within the age of reform.[41]

In addition, it was most likely that during this period (after the second synod of Cashel in 1171–2), the church achieved a new status – that of a parish church, staffed by a priest, serving a defined area and financially supported by tithes, which was a reforming development encouraged by the Augustinians. This enabled it to survive while some other local pre-Anglo-Norman churches such as Kilbogget disappeared without trace. Indeed, in the thirteenth century the nearby chapel of Carrickbrennan appears to have brought under the aegis of Clonkeen.[42] Yet the enhanced church structure and its new parochial status, could not socially offset the combined effects of the demise of the earlier monastic settlement, and the 'pull effect' of the centralised manorial activity at the Grange across the valley. It remained the smaller of the two settlements.

The first documentary evidence for a local parish structure financed by income from lands and tithes appears in a confirmation by Pope Alexander III dated 20 April 1179 of the possessions of the diocese of Dublin, of its church and of its canons. However, only four city churches are specifically named as *parish* churches in the document.[43] The deed establishing St Patrick's as a cathedral in 1219, designates Clonkeen as a prebend (a parish whose dues and tithes would provide income) for its treasurer. It is recorded as paying forty marks in 1327 – just before it was restored to Holy Trinity.[44] With regard to tithes, the account roll of 1344 referred to above, details the employment of collectors and watchmen of tithes at Clonkeen and the delivery of payments in the form of crops (great tithes). Almost 50 per cent of the corn received into the haggard came from tithes of the surrounding areas. Small tithes, payable on lambs, calves, wool, etc. were also accounted for. Some payments were made in cash. An

40 *Oxford companion*, pp 554–5; Milne, *Christ Church*, pp 34–5, 44–5 and 56–7.   **41** O'Brien *Southeast churches*, pp 515 and 511; Christiaan Corlett, *Antiquities of old Rathdown* (Bray, 1999), pp 46–7.   **42** *Oxford companion*, pp 554–5, 426–7; Mark Hennessy, 'The priory and hospital of New Gate: the evolution and decline of a medieval monastic estate', in W.J. Smyth and Kevin Whelan (eds), *Common ground – essays on historical geography of Ireland* (Cork, 1988), p 47; Ball, *County Dublin*, i, p. 68; McEnery, *Christ Church deeds, nos.* 51–3.   **43** McNeill, *Alen's register*, p.3   **44** McNeill, *Alen's register*, pp 42, 47, 79; McEnery, *Christ Church deeds*, nos. 44, 51–2.

attached valuation of the monastery's possessions dated 1304 calculates the tithes due (£6 2s. 8d.) on the total value of the 'goods profits and rents' within the manor of Clonkeen. Tithes regularly feature in documents relating to Clonkeen for centuries following; individual leases specify payments of tithes – great and small – payable to Holy Trinity.[45]

LIFE IN FOURTEENTH-CENTURY CLONKEEN

In common with the other Anglo-Norman communities in Ireland, it is likely that Clonkeen had passed its zenith of power and influence by the end of the thirteenth century, and suffered declining fortunes during the succeeding centuries. It has been argued that the Anglo-Normans attracted tenants to their new estates in Ireland, by offering through professional 'locators', easier tenures than existed in England. In Clonkeen there is no evidence of extended rent-service from any – even the smallest – tenants; just a few days per year at peak periods. This may reflect the difficulty of retaining the population on the manor lands. Due to limited customary service it was necessary to employ a regular staff of paid tenants. In 1344, no less than 471 of the 562 days of labour recorded in Clonkeen, was carried out by paid service and only 91 by customary service. The migration to Ireland in the twelfth and thirteenth centuries can be seen as reflecting the general European-wide growth of population, a situation which was reversed in the fourteenth century when areas of Ireland were reported as lying waste and uncultivated for lack of tenants.[46] The Black Death and other tragedies which affected Europe, were also felt in county Dublin, but it was the constant wars and the accompanying insecurity, as well as economic uncertainty, which put most pressure on many tenants to depart. The only surviving series of rents payable within the Clonkeen manor, relates to the townland of Balytypur (Tipperstown), and is shown in Table 1.

These rents were based on ever-shorter leases, which indicates a continuous and dramatic decline. Subsequent deeds for larger tracts of land, which include Tipperstown, show a further decline to the sixteenth century. Tithes being a tax on agricultural income, suffered from the same pressures as rents.[47]

The absence of peace and security in south county Dublin in 1294, is clearly illustrated by new taxation plans which note that the manor and church of Clonkeen 'cannot sustain the charges', and that nearby Carrickbrennan, and the vicarage of Bray were also deemed worth nothing 'on account of war'.[48] When the Anglo-Normans had taken over the ownership of the coastal lands south of

45 Mills, *Account roll*, pp 68–9, 78–81, 55, 79, 201. **46** Otway-Ruthven, *Organisation of agriculture*, pp 9–10; Otway-Ruthven, *Medieval Ireland*, p. 109. **47** McEnery, *Christ Church deeds*, nos. 554, 646, 701, 738, 921, 1271, 1410. **48** McEnery, *Christ Church deeds*, no. 150.

Dublin into Wicklow, the O'Byrnes and O'Tooles and O'Nolans remained in
the interior, and from the high ground of the Dublin and Wicklow mountains
they launched frequent attacks on the fertile lands below. Clonkeen was unlucky
enough to be situated in that unhappy territory, the *marches* or borderland area,
where the antagonists joined battle. For about a hundred years after the Anglo-
Norman invasion, the Irish had remained subdued, and had been held in check
by the invaders' superior military technology, but some years before the taxation return of 1294 was prepared, a period of war commenced which would last
some 350 years. In 1279, the archbishop's manors at Shankill and near Tallaght
were returned as waste 'on account of the war with the Irish'. In 1300 Shankill
lay fallow; in 1311 the lord of Bray could take nothing from his wood on account
of robbers and war. Although Clonkeen is not specifically mentioned in these
cases, the descriptions of the wasting of the neighbouring settlements could not
have left its inhabitants unaffected.[49] And the tenants of Clonkeen had something more on their minds than fear of the Irish in 1318, when Dublin was pan-
icking, with Edward Bruce camped at Castleknock, and threatening to attack.
Rumours no doubt were percolating through to Clonkeen from the sister granges
of Glasnevin and Gorman, via the priory in the city. South county Dublin had
already been 'robbed burned and destroyed' by Scots and Irish enemies and there
had been a recent famine. The Clonkeen villagers must therefore have celebrated
their relief when the Bruce army changed direction and moved away from
Dublin, to target their destruction at Leixlip, Naas, and to the south.[50]

Table 1 Variations in rents payable in respect of the townland of Balytypur
(Tipperstown).

Year	Amount of Rent
1320	16s rising to 46s. 8d.
1326	46s. 8d.
1352	30s. rising to 40s.
1366	20s. rising to 26s. 6d.
1379	20s.
1436	5s.

Nine years later in 1326 and 1327, both Shankill and Tallaght were in ruins.[51]
In 1338, the prior the seneschal and other leaders were seen visiting Clonkeen

49 Myles V. Ronan, 'Anglo-Norman Dublin and diocese' in *Irish Ecclesiastical Record,* xlv,
Jan–June 1935, p. 161 and xlvi, July–December 1935, pp 263 and 498; Anngret Simms, H.B.
Clarke, Raymond Gillespie (eds), *Irish historic towns atlas, no. 9, Bray* (Dublin, 1998), p.1. **50**
Goddard Henry Orpen, *Ireland under the Normans, 1216–1333* (Oxford, 1920), iv, pp 188–90;
Otway-Ruthven, *Medieval Ireland*, pp 238–9. **51** Ball, *County Dublin*, iii, pp 6 and 84.

Figure 3 Dublin mountains as seen from near Carrickmines Castle, 2.5 km from Clonkeen. For centuries, the mountains were watched with apprehension 'through fear of the Irish'.

'with horses armed for making muster and to keep ward', indicating that the Grange and the Kill of Clonkeen were used as a staging post for the area, under the direction of the prior, the lord of the manor. Robert Haketh's tenure, referred to above, required him to attend such musters. Armour was also manufactured at the Grange – 'In greaves (shin armour) bought and made for the use of Walter, brother of the Prior, at Clonkeen, 8*d*.'[52] In 1355 wards were placed, among other places, at Bray, Carrickmines and Dundrum

> ... in defence of the king's faithful people there ... against the hostile attacks of Obryn, Otothill, Onolan and their accomplices ... who were daily invading the marches ... and committing homicides, depredations, burnings and other crimes ...[53]

and in 1358, it was proposed that lords would personally live in their peripheral estates, to ensure their defence.[54]

The population and prosperity of Clonkeen, were probably already in decline by the years 1326 and 1344, in respect of which there are detailed documents which give an insight into living conditions in the Grange and the Kill. A rent

52 Mills, *Account roll*, pp 12, 13 and 18.   **53** Philomena Connolly, *Irish exchequer payments records, 1270–1446* (Dublin, 1998), p. 472.

roll survives for 1326, listing outlying farms of the manor of Clonkeen, including Cornelscourt, Murphystown, Stillorgan, Tipperstown, Carrickmines,
Brennanstown, Tully, Killiney and a small part of Dalkey. These were leased as
units in return for cash rents, with an additional requirement to carry out specific 'customary work' at planting time and during the harvest. One requirement read 'He shall work in harvest for three days – and shall do divers other
works with ploughs, carts or cars which are worth by the year eight shillings'.
The home farm was also mentioned under the names of Churchtown (Kill-of-
the-Grange) and Grangetown. The rental listed 12 tenants living in 'the town
of the Church' and 35 living in 'the town of the Grange'. Allowing a multiplier
for family members they were sizeable settlements for the time, perhaps 150
people in Grangetown and 50 in Churchtown.[55] Based on rents payable and a
conversion factor for medieval acres, two of the tenants in the Kill appear to
have had tenures of over 50 statute acres and three had more than 12; one tenant
at the Grange had over 100 acres and another four had in excess of 20 each. Most
of the rest, however, had a just a few acres and there were 21 small plot-hold-
ers or cottagers who had no land at all. These included the bailiff, the chamberlain, two smiths, and a weaver at the Grange, and the clerk at the Kill. See
Table 2.

Table 2 Number and size of holdings in Churchtown (the kill) and Grangetown (the grange) *c.*1326.[56]

Statute acres	less than 1	1–5	5–10	10–20	20–30	50–60	over 100	Total no. of tenants
Churchtown	4	1	2	3	—	2	—	12
Grangetown	21	4	2	3	4	—	1	35

The great majority of surnames of major tenants of outlying townlands are
English rather than Irish – name such as Gregory Taunton, Peter Howell (the
Howells later became Walshs), Robert Fitz Stephen, Gilbert Begg, Sir Ralph,
John the Whyte, Maurice Howell, David M'Nebury, John Milis and John
Kandale. It is harder to identify the backgrounds of the villagers. The 'Grange-
town' residents included Nicholas Obrode, Eva the widow, Thomas the smith,
Hugh the white, Stephen Olyng, John the white, Robert Whyte, John the bailiff,
Johanna the weaver, Cecelia Frankan, Peter Thegg, Adam Dromsalan or Gibbe,
Roger Bellyngs, Ralph Kenedy, Hugh Rodypakke, Walter Fadd, Henry Bossard,
John Manahan, Walter Kylheel, John Ercedekne, Richard Cathelan as well as
many others, while 'Churchtown' has a similar list. Some cottagers at the Kill

54 Ronan, 'Anglo-Norman Dublin', in *IER*, xlvii, January–June 1936, pp 36–7. **55** Mills,
Account roll, pp 194–8. **56** Ibid., pp 194–8, 211.

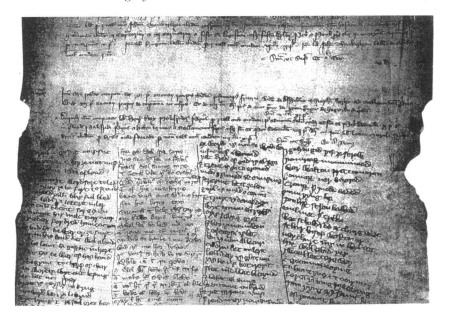

Figure 4 Reproduction of portion of the original manuscript known as the account roll of the Priory of the Holy Trinity (1337–46). The original was destroyed in the Four Courts fire in 1922.

paid a yearly rent of 2*d.* and a hen for their cottages; those at the Grange paid 3*d.* with 'the usual services'.[57]

From accounts kept by the bailiff, we know a lot about life at Clonkeen in 1344. From these, we can extract, as earlier historians have done, a picture of a fourteenth-century working farm in this area.[58] There was an absolute predominance of tillage, the main crops being wheat and oats, although barley, peas and beans were also grown. There were few animals mentioned, but there were some sales of wool, and of sheep's hides which had been received from the grange at Glasnevin. There were also a few references to hogs, including a man casually employed to keep the prior's pigs from his neighbours' crops; there were some references to working horses and oxen, and the employment of a cow- and lamb-keeper.[59] Under the Anglo-Normans' system of agriculture, we would have expected considerable pasturing of cattle as one element of a three-year rotation. The absence of stock has also been noted about this time on the estates

---

57 Ibid., pp 194–8 and 211; McEnery, *Christ Church deeds,* no. 570.   **58** Francis Elrington Ball, James Mills, Jocelyn Otway-Ruthven, George Otto Simms (see following notes).   **59** Mills, *Account roll,* various pages but mainly pp 55–87 and 172–5; Mills, 'Tenants and agriculture near Dublin, etc.', in *JRSAI,* xxi, 1890–1, pp 61–3; Ball, *County Dublin,* i, p. 49; G.O. Simms, *Tullow's story* (Carrickmines, 1983), pp 26–8; Otway-Ruthven, *Organisation of agriculture,* pp 10–11.

of other county Dublin manors.[60] This raises the question of why so little stock was mentioned: were the cattle driven off by the Irish or were their numbers reduced to pre-empt loss, having regard to the vulnerability of Clonkeen to cattle-rustling because of its location near the edge of the 'subdued area'?

Certain details of the farming year can be extracted from the accounts, such as the construction and repair of ploughs, the construction of carts and of wheel-less sledges or cars, the supplying of food to 28 ploughmen providing 'customary service' in lieu of rent, the reaping of corn by 88 men on 5 August, 1344 and by smaller numbers on different days until the harvest was in on 4 September. The paid labourers were not fed. Those workmen who were supplied with food received baked wheaten bread and freshly brewed ale, made mainly from oatmeal but with a small amount of wheat added. Bread and ale was the staple diet, but it is not clear whether the unskilled men consumed ale or had to drink water. As recorded earlier, the manorial mill was probably located outside the village of the Grange, but to-day's older residents remember a quern stone lying near the site of the Grange and this was subsequently brought to a garden on Kill Lane. This implies some grinding of corn within the village itself. The importance to the settlement of the grange barn or haggard, is apparent from the amounts of wheat, oats and other cereals received from harvesters as tithes, and from the miller as tolls. These were reissued, as seed for planting, as bread for ploughmen, to the cellarer in the priory as raw material for brewing, as gifts, as food, as direct payments or for sales, as compensation for injury and as provender for horses. Only the bailiff's table had meat – except on Sundays – but skilled men, like a carpenter were allowed to join his table for supper. One of these, John Punchard, seems to have been a jack-of-all-trades, being mentioned in various sections of the accounts as brewer, as baker, as carpenter and as thresher. And Little Stephen the doorman also sat at the top table, though he may have been the bailiff's son. Special reception arrangements were made for the visits of the prior and of the archbishop; the prior came on inspection or administrative visits, or perhaps for a change of scene from the overcrowded, unhealthy, inner city; the archbishop stopped along the way before proceeding to the important defended outpost of Dublin diocese at Newcastle, county Wicklow. The accounts show the purchase of wine, herrings and almonds, in anticipation of the visits of the prior and archbishop and their retinues.[61]

At the harvest, the reapers were followed in employment by winnowers, by two men threshing, by stackers in the haggard, by a woman binding sheaves and by men forking the stacks. There is also a reference to the gathering-in of the tithes, which were a levy of 10 per cent on agricultural income. These were mainly paid in the form of crops, by outlying tenants in Tully, Killiney,

60 Ronan, 'Anglo-Norman Dublin' in *IER*, xlvii, January–June 1936, p. 29.   **61** Mills, *Account roll*, various pages but mainly pp 55–87 and 172–175.

Loughlinstown and Rochestown, and the giving of gratuities to the tithes collectors is recorded, as is the employment of security men to guard the crops collected. Security was a perennial problem as might be expected, and there is a record of a payment to two men for watching the tops of the mountains for two nights 'through fear of the Irish'.[62] There are many other general details from around the Grange like the employment of a carpenter to repair the carts, the employment of a cooper to mend the vessels, and the repairing by tradesmen of the kiln-house, the cow house, and the grange itself. Not all the craftsmen were from the village. Robert Taloun, a carpenter, bought timber in Glencree and built the new cow-house, but his name had not appeared in the rent roll of some years previously. A grant of bread is recorded in the accounts, presumably as compensation to William Frankan, 'for healing his head which was broken when the cow-house fell'.[63] Among the items sold from the farm, was clay for the making of earthenware pots. Mills refers to a map dated 1684, since destroyed, which shows a commons of Kill marked 'Polloughs' 'a place of holes' located on exactly the spot occupied in Mills' time by the Kill of the Grange pottery. This pottery finally closed around 1970, after at least 300 years on the site.[64] Wool and hides as well as turf, were also sold from the Grange.[65]

The Grange had a full-time staff. The bailiff (the chief official on the site) worked to the seneschal at the priory, between the latter's visits from the city. There were also a sergeant, a carter, four ploughmen, a door keeper, a malt drier, a baker/brewer and a cow and lamb herd. Numerous casuals were also employed. It is worth noting that tradesmen erected or repaired buildings with timber, wattle, hurdles, and with thatching for the roofs. These premises were not permanent structures and although a stone and slated castle was built on the site at some stage, there is no record of the finding of any foundations when the site was redeveloped some forty years ago without any archaeological excavation.[66]

To summarise, there was a well-organised farm business based at the Grange, with directly managed tillage and some pasture, with a number of skilled residents, some well maintained buildings and equipment, an attention to logistics – particularly in connection with the coming of visitors – a concern with security, and a general self-sufficiency within the community with regard to food, clothing and tools. However to avoid an idealised view of life in a manorial village, Canon C.A. Empey's description of the likely conditions in a similar contemporary settlement, the manor of Knocktopher, should be noted: 'in this chaotic muddle of dykes, defensive works, houses, domestic buildings and cattle sheds, men, women, children, cattle, rats and lice, shared a muddy, foul-smelling condominium'.[67]

62 Ibid. **63** Ibid. **64** Interview with the late Patrick Collins, last owner of the pottery; newspaper cutting dated 4 March 1970, from unnamed local newspaper. **65** Mills, *Account roll*, various pages but mainly pp 55–87 and 172–5. **66** Ibid. **67** C.A. Empey, 'Knocktopher part I', p. 332.

The villagers of 1344 had already gone through a stressful period of famine in 1331, and an arctic winter in 1338, but if they thought that things could only get better, they had not anticipated the arrival in Ireland in August 1348, of the Black Death. Having swept through Europe, the 'scourge of God' arrived in Ireland through Drogheda and *either* Howth *or* Dalkey, killing off one Dubliner in every three.[68] There is no specific documentary evidence of the impact of this plague on Clonkeen, however there is much circumstantial evidence. The lice which carried the plague were in turn carried by rats, and consequently the granges to which rats were attracted were locations of high risk. Maria Kelly in *A history of the Black Death in Ireland,* states that there was a high mortality rate in priories and abbeys throughout Europe especially in Cistercian abbeys and Augustinian priories, because of their grain stocks. Again, as noted above, the villages of Clonkeen consisted of thatched buildings constructed with wattle and mortar; these harboured rats within walls and roofs. The inhabitants themselves were particularly susceptible to disease: wars, famines and cold winters must have had their effect on peoples' general health and resistance to disease, reinforced by the limited amounts of meat in their diets. The only precise figures for mortality in a county Dublin settlement is in respect of Colemanstown near Newcastle Lyons, where it was claimed that 16 out of 19 tenants had died.[69] But as the villagers of Clonkeen were based midway between Dalkey and the city, within an hour's walk of each, and had close contacts with both – and particularly intercommunication with the priory in the city centre, it is reasonable to construe that they too must also have been decimated by the plague.

Given the small scale of the settlements at Clonkeen, any significant loss of population would have seriously threatened their very viability. Furthermore, within the next generation, four further plagues, which reduced the city population by a further 20 per cent, and which had entirely impoverished the king's demesne manors in county Dublin, must also have been economically and socially devastating at Clonkeen. In addition, it increased the vulnerability of the coastal inhabitants against the Irish in the hills, who because of their rural environment escaped the worst depredations of the disease.[70]

CONTINUED THREAT FROM THE MOUNTAINS

In 1402 the O'Byrnes were repulsed at Bloodybank (now Sunnybank) outside Bray, but conditions generally around Dublin were still very difficult.[71] The

68 Ronan, 'Anglo-Norman Dublin', in *IEP* xlvi, July–December, 1935, pp 595–6; Aubrey Gwynn, 'The Black Death in Ireland', in *Studies*, 24, 1935, pp 25–42; Otway-Ruthven, *Medieval Ireland*, pp 268–9; *Oxford companion*, pp 47–8. **69** Maria Kelly, *A history of the Black Death in Ireland* (Stroud, 2001), pp 30–4, 78. **70** *Oxford companion*, pp 47–8; Kelly, *Black Death*, pp 27–34. **71** *Bray Atlas*, p. 1.

interaction of the effects of war, famine, and disease with economic conditions in the area are illustrated by the prior of Holy Trinity applying in 1426, in respect of its property generally, for a reduction of taxes. He did this on the grounds of ruin of its buildings, unjust and hostile occupation, destruction of its lands, possessions and rents, the dearth – that is, food scarcity – of the year, and the mortality of men and animals.[72]

In 1487, the coastal area of south county Dublin, including the twin settlements at Clonkeen, was deemed to be within the safer *machaire*, rather then the less stable *marches* region. However by 1504, 'the vill of Churchton and the grange of Clonkeen' were again deemed as being in the *marches* area, the outer or buffer zone of the Pale. The word 'pale' is derived from the Latin word for a stake, and it indicated the area *behind* a palisade or paling. The boundary of the Pale around Dublin, varied from time to time, as the administration's military fortunes ebbed and flowed.[73] As late as 1599 Carrickmines was attacked and burned and 'the prey of that town' taken away.[74]

Clonkeen's borderland position and its susceptibility to attack has left behind a heritage of castles and tower houses in the surrounding area. As early as the thirteenth century, there were fortified castles at Shankill and at Dundrum, while Carrickmines, half an hour's walk from the Grange, was recorded as being heavily defended at various dates during the course of the fourteenth century.[75] Tower houses, smaller and less heavily defended, were dotted around the district, their construction being boosted in 1429, by the introduction of a building grant or subsidy of £10 per castle. Again, in 1537, state assistance was suggested to enable castles to be built towards the territory of the O'Tooles 'who most noyeth (trouble) about Dublin'.[76] Including those now demolished or incorporated into more modern buildings, there were tower houses at Shanganagh, Pucks Castle, Lehaunstown, Loughlinstown, Brennanstown, Cornelscourt, Kilgobbin, Murphystown and Dean's Grange. Rob Goodbody of Rathmichael Historical Society has reported the finding of a portion of the pale ditch only a few kilometres from Clonkeen, at Ballyogan, uncomfortably close to the settlers.[77]

As well as external threats to the peace, there were also internal disputes. In 1482, bonds were lodged with the prior of the Holy Trinity, by the Harolds, the Walshes, the Lawlesses and the Godmans – the leading families of south county Dublin – as an assurance that John Walsh, of Stillorgan would keep the

72 Ronan, 'Anglo-Norman Dublin' in *IER*, xlvii, January–June 1936, p. 460.   **73** McNeill, *Alen's register, pp* 251, 256.   **74** F.E. Ball, 'The Castle of Carrickmines and its history' in *JRSAI*, xxxi, 1901, p. 198; Ernest Atkinson (ed.), *Calendar of state papers, Ireland, 1599–1600* (London, 1899), p. 63.   **75** Kathleen Turner, *If you seek monuments* (Rathmichael, 1983), (no. 64); *Archaeology Ireland*, iii, no. 4, p. 136; Ball, *County Dublin*, i, p. 99, pp 25–32.   **76** F.E. Ball, 'Rathmichael and its neighbourhood' in *JRSAI*, 32, 1902, p. 124; John D'Alton, *The history of county Dublin* (Cork, 1976 edition), p.458.   **77** Rob Goodbody, *On the borders of the Pale* (Bray, 1993), pp 29–30.

peace.[78] There were also boundary disputes. In 1508, the prior of Holy Trinity won a legal battle with St Stephen's Leper Hospital over a boundary at Ballitipper which divided their respective properties of Leopardstown and Clonkeen. Evidence had been heard by an official of the metropolitan court, of carts bringing the tithes from the disputed lands to the grange of Clonkeen, and of Clonkeen tenants having common of pasture there. This was not the end of the dispute however, and a century later an arbitrator finally determined the boundary, and directed that the inhabitants of Leopardstown should make a ditch to delineate the division.[79]

THE REFORMATION AND ITS EFFECTS ON CLONKEEN

In 1539/40, the church of Clonkeen again came under new administration. In the course of the previous year, as part of Henry VIII's general policy, the suppression of the Convent of the Holy Trinity, in common with other monasteries in Ireland, was under consideration by dissolution commissioners. However, there was such a popular resistance in the city on the basis of its central civic, even national role – a resistance led by its leading citizens – that the proposal could not proceed. As a compromise, the cathedral was 'returned to its original condition' of a secular cathedral rather than an institution run by a religious order.[80] The individual dignitaries and vicars choral would be allocated lands to support their positions. The description, 'the Dean and Chapter' replaced 'the Prior and Convent' on formal deeds. The prior, Robert Paynswick, alias Castell, became the first dean, and the members of the community became members of the chapter. The dean (and his successors), received 'for his dignity', the lands of Clonkeen. Henceforth the Grange of Clonkeen was to become known as 'The Dean's Grange'. His allocation also included the Kill of Clonkeen.[81]

The ideological effect of these changes on the church at Clonkeen came slowly. In early post-reformation years, the church in Dublin contained both Catholics and Protestants. Even some sixty years on, the new ideology had reached to just a few English officials and settlers, while the populace, generally ignoring the theological debates, pursued their traditional spirituality under the guidance of clergy from their own stock who spoke their own language. Such clergy were supported by a wealthy, alienated, Catholic laity, who controlled education, and who often retained the right to appoint parish clergy.[82] In Clonkeen, two parishioners, both named James Goodman, lost a court battle as early as 1552, over whether they or the dean should elect the minister, or 'parish clerk'. From the Christ Church point of view at least, the issue may not have

78 McEnery, *Christ Church deeds,* nos. 332, 333.   **79** McEnery, *Christ Church deeds,* nos. 386, 1490.   **80** Milne, *Christ Church,* pp 165–6.   **81** McEnery, *Christ Church deeds,* no. 431.   **82** Alan Ford, *The protestant reformation* (Dublin, 1997), pp 23–30; Kelly, *Diocese,* pp 115–16.

Figure 5 Ruins of the Kill, *c*.1875.

been an ideological one, as the duty of finding a curate was subsequently delegated to three lessees of Dean's Grange land (one of whom, was Sir John Hore, the chaplain).[83] By the late 1580s the Catholic elite began to shun the existing church institutions and to establish new, alternative structures; for example, in the Clonkeen area they provided venues for Mass in their homes or on their properties at Monkstown and at Carrickmines.[84]

The church at Kill began to lose its congregation. The effects of local reaction to the new order can be gauged from the reports of two visitations. At the time of the royal visitation of 1615, only 13 churches, including Saint Fintan's, were in repair in the Bray deanery, compared with 28 in 1531. By 1630, the numbers attending service at the Kill did not exceed 24. It could have been worse; in nearby Tully it was recorded that 'There is not one in the parish that reporteth to church to hear divine service.' Along with other churches in the area, the Kill had been 'uncovered in the late storms'.[85]

The last in the line of curates at Clonkeen was recorded in the 1640s, and the building was reported ruinous in the Commonwealth period (1649–60). The parish of Kill, along with the parishes of Dalkey, Killiney, Tully, Stillorgan and Kilmacud, was amalgamated with Monkstown. The local mass-venues, already

83 McEnery, *Christ Church deeds,* nos. 445, 1271. **84** Kelly, *Diocese,* pp 117–23. **85** 'Royal visitation of Dublin' and 'Visitation of Dublin' in *Archivium Hibernicum,* viii, new series, 1941, pp 1, 44, 85 and 86.

referred to, were not located in the Kill; however, in 1704 the Revd Richard Murphy was returned as parish priest of Kill.[86] This is the only reference to a possible post-reformation Catholic presence at the Kill, but it is likely to have referred to the district rather than to a parish centre. Perhaps because of the close connection in the post-reformation period between Clonkeen and Christ Church, perhaps because of the predominance of English immigrants in the population over lengthy periods, there is little evidence of traditional popular religious practices in the locality. Exceptions are: a reference of pilgrims from Wexford visiting a holy well Tobberbawn, in Kill of the Grange townland, of people praying as they performed stations by walking around Saint Brigid's cross at Tully and of the lighting of bonfires on 'St Peter and Paul's day' at Stillorgan.[87]

The falling into ruin of the church removed the central feature of the Kill settlement. Moreover, back in 1539, with the division of the community's land among the individual dignitaries and their successors, the whole approach to property management changed, with more leasing and less direct management of land.[88] In the case of the Kill, the lands (apart from a small reservation for the curate), were first leased out in 1592. Reference is made in one summary of that deed to 'every tenant with garden plots' (another summary reads '*if* the tenants … shall sow any garden plot'). Both imply, (one more strongly than the other), the continued existence of a grouped settlement at that date.[89] At the time of the 1660 poll tax return (use a multiplier of three to estimate total population), the inhabitants of the townland, not just the village, numbered around 45. This is only slightly higher than the 12 families in the Kill who were recorded in the 1326 rental, but at least it indicates the continuation of a community there despite the wars and the upheavals.[90]

The reconstitution of Holy Trinity Priory in 1539 had as much of a long term effect on the Grange as it had on the Kill. As recorded above, the lands of Clonkeen were allocated to the dean and to his successors, 'for his dignity', so the Grange of Clonkeen became the Dean's Grange. The transfer of the cathedral's properties from a corporate body to individual accounts held on trust for successive office holders, had an effect on the way they were managed, as they introduced into decision-making, considerations of personal effort as well as personal profit and reward. A trend can be seen in the Clonkeen area, from direct

---

86 Ball, *County Dublin*, i, pp 69 and 42–3. **87** W.F. Wakeman, in *Evening Telegraph Reprints No. 4 – Old Dublin, 2nd series*, p. 17; Folklore Department, University College Dublin, schools' folklore project, files 799/132, 799/95. **88** Milne, *Christ Church*, p. 166. **89** McEnery, *Christ Church deeds*, no. 1406; Raymond Gillespie (ed.), *The first chapter book of Christ Church Cathedral, 1574–1634* (Dublin, 1997), p. 80. **90** Séamus Pender (ed.), *Census of Ireland – circa 1659* (Dublin, 1939), p. 381; William J. Smyth, 'Society and settlement in seventeenth century Ireland: the evidence of the '1659 census', in Smyth and Whelan (eds), *Common ground*, p. 56; W.J. Pilsworth, 'Census or poll tax?' in *JRSAI*, lxxiii, 1943, pp 22–4; Brian Gurrin, *Pre-census sources for Irish demography* (Dublin, 2002), pp 73–5.

management of lands, to the leasing of property in large parcels, for long periods.[91] Such leasing, was inhibited by general legislation after 1635. The purpose
of the ecclesiastical land act of that year was to protect both religious institutions
and future ecclesiastical office-holders against alienation of land, either through
negligence, or for the benefit of the current incumbents. Long leases of ecclesiastical property, often of 61 years, had become commonplace, and the 1635 act
limited such leases in future to 21 years for land and 40 years for urban property.
Most relevant to the administration, specifically, of the lands of Dean's Grange,
the legislation precluded any leasing of demesne lands (as Dean's Grange was),
or residences currently used by ecclesiastical office-holders.[92] The leasing out of
the lands other than the mensal lands of Dean's Grange, had the effect of reduc-
ing the administrative role of that village.

There had already been for some centuries, a gradual, undocumented change
from paying tithes by delivering produce to the grange to paying directly in cash;
the leasing out of the tithes themselves, started shortly after the reformation at
Christ Church.[93] An undated eighteenth-century newspaper cutting shows Christ
Church publicly offering 21-year leases of the tithes on a variety of properties,
which indicates the total change of policy relating to tithes.[94] For the purpose
of this essay however, the most important points are that the change from payment in goods to cash payments seriously reduced the role of the Grange, and
that tithes, being a proportionate tax (in this area on agricultural output), fluctuated directly with production and were therefore affected by the same negative influences that were squeezing the local economy.

In addition, the old manorial system was gradually giving way to commercial estate management. Payment by service or goods was being superseded by
cash rents, and the small plots held by labour-service were rapidly being replaced
by large leasehold farms worked by almost landless labourers.[95] The development of agricultural management generally in the period after the plantations,
which was a commercialised and scientifically-based agriculture, required con-
solidation of plots and enclosures of fields. Many old nucleated villages, the foci
of open-field systems, were abandoned or began to decay.[96] There are references
in Clonkeen deeds to developments such as the making of ditches, the planting
ditches with trees, and the existence of 'parks', all of which suggest the enclosure of lands; there are also references to the implementation of 'covenanted
improvements' reflecting the break-up of the out-dated manorial farming. All
these factors combined to reduce the personal commitment of successive deans

91 McEnery, *Christ Church deeds,* no. 431; Milne, *Christ Church,* pp 166, 180–3; McEnery,
Christ Church deeds, nos. 1271, 1406. **92** *Irish Act 10 & 11 Charles I, session 4 cap. 3, An act for
the preservation of the inheritance rights and profits of lands belonging to the Church and persons ecclesiastical.* **93** McEnery, *Christ Church deeds,* nos. 1271, 1377. **94** Mills, *Account roll,* pp 55, 59,
68, 78, 80–1, 200, 202; NLI, MS 101. **95** Mitchell, *Irish landscape,* p. 180. **96** F.H.A. Aalen,
Man and the landscape in Ireland (London, 1978), p. 161.

to their south county Dublin lands and to diminish the importance of the Grange as an administrative centre. Indeed the Grange itself was leased for 61 years in 1561 (though surrendered after seven years) before legal restrictions on leasing were introduced.[97]

The obligation imposed on a joint lessee of tithes of the 'Kill of the Grange of Clonkeen', Gerald Fitzsymon, to do suit of court at both 'courts leet and baron of the lordship of the Dean's Grange' in 1686, indicates that the manor courts of Dean's Grange survived to the end of the seventeenth century.[98]

1641 AND AFTER

In autumn 1641, in common with the rest of Ireland, south county Dublin was in upheaval. The Anglo-Irish were in a quandary as to whether they should support the king who distrusted Catholics, or alternatively join the Catholic Irish. They chose the latter option. The months of lawlessness which followed the rising, had a serious impact on the Grange and the Kill. In subsequent depositions, which may have been exaggerated, John Brackenbury a resident of the Grange, submitted a bill for compensation, claiming robbery and destruction of goods, stock, equipment and corn by the rebels, to a value of £733. John Smithson, minister at the Kill, listed his household goods, cash, garden produce and poultry lost in a raid and then added that his wife was abducted, stripped of her clothes and brought by horse first to Stillorgan and then to Powerscourt where she was hanged with her maid. In both cases culprits were named – the local Anglo-Irish gentry, the Goodmans, Barnwalls, Woolverstons and most of all the Walshs. Indeed, during the winter of 1641/2 the south county Dublin was in rebel hands, under the Walshs' leadership.[99] To counter this rebellion, on 12 February 1642, Lord Lambert marched out from Dublin and it was reported that he routed 1,000 rebels at Dean's Grange, killing 100 of them. Whatever the actual extent of the defeat, the rebels remained in the district but were overwhelmed on 26 March following, when the centuries-old bastion, Carrickmines Castle, was besieged, captured, and demolished. All those in the castle, said to be some 300 men women and children, were put to the sword.[1]

This essentially ended the rising in the south county, although a partisan report exists of four residents, Christopher Archpoll, Murtagh Bredon, 'the good wife of the house' and another, watching for rebels from the roof of the castle at Dean's Grange after sunset on the evening of 23 May 1642, and seeing a lone rebel, a former servant of John Brackenbury, approaching with a musket, taking

97 Otway-Ruthven, *Organisation of agriculture*, p.8; McEnery, *Christ Church deeds*, nos. 1490, 1189, 1691.   **98** McEnery, *Christ Church deeds*, no. 1861.   **99** Dermot Kennedy, *The battle of Deansgrange, 1642* (Foxrock, Co. Dublin, 1986).   **1** Dermot Kennedy, *The siege at Carrickmines Castle – 1642* (Foxrock, Co. Dublin, 1989).

up a firing position in a ditch and calling for an 'English captain' to come out. While the incident itself was a minor one, it demonstrates the continuing edginess of the residents.[2] Exactly seven years and four months later, on 23 September 1649, Cromwell led his 9,000-strong army down the high road to Wicklow and Wexford, now the N11, which passes within a hundred metres of the Grange. But Cromwell controlled his troops on that march and there was no evidence of looting there.[3]

From the fifteenth century onwards, apart from these incidents during the 1641 period, both the Kill and the Grange cease to figure significantly in the written record. The 1635 act, as noted above, precluded the leasing of the lands of Dean's Grange (now represented by Dean's Grange, Galloping Green South, Foxrock, Waltersland and Glebe townlands), as this property was the dean's demesne or mensal lands.[4] However, the surrounding townlands could be, and were leased out. A lack of engagement with the property by successive deans also becomes apparent. As early as 1639, only four years after the imposition of the limitations on leasing, the authorities in Christ Church had prepared a bill for parliament seeking authority to abandon the Dean's Grange as the deans' demesne, mensal or inalienable lands. They wanted to substitute as their demesne, their property at Simmonscourt, Ballsbridge, on the grounds that Dean's Grange was inconvenient and distant from the city. This bill was never passed, but it showed a lack of commitment to the manor at Clonkeen.[5] Eventually in 1792, the dean of the day secured an act of parliament enabling the mensal lands of Dean's Grange to be reduced from about 500 acres to 126 and authorising him to lease the remaining property. The selection of the lands to be retained as the dean's mensal lands was made on financial, rather than on heritage or sentimental considerations. The Grange itself was leased out and became subdivided. The portion which they retained as mensal lands in compliance with the enabling act was that section of the property which they considered to contain the least valuable land at that time. These lands constituted the present townland of Foxrock, some 40 per cent of which was then rough pasture. Their method of leasing the excess land subsequently caused legal problems which were eventually overcome by another special act of parliament in 1811. By then, the dean was merely a medium sized land-owner in the area.[6]

---

2 Royal Society of Antiquaries of Ireland, scrapbook of F.E. Ball, prepared after publication of his *History of county Dublin*, i, p. 74 (Extract in scrapbook from manuscript TCD F 2 3, p.141). **3** James Scott Wheeler, *Cromwell in Ireland* (Dublin, 1999), pp 90–2; Williem Farrand and Williem Storck, map – *The half-barony of Rathdown in the county of Dublin*, [Down Survey map, 1655/7], reproduced by Ordnance Survey Office Southampton, 1908, (1927 reprint). **4** *Irish Act 10 & 11 Charles I*, referred to (incorrectly as Charles II) in preamble to *51 Georgii III cap. 181*. **5** RCBL, C6.5.8.24. **6** OS name books Dublin County, iii, K–O, p.117, in NLI, Ir2942 o 3; *51 Geo. III, cap. 181*, (map referred to in preamble no longer available but area selected can be deduced by elimination).

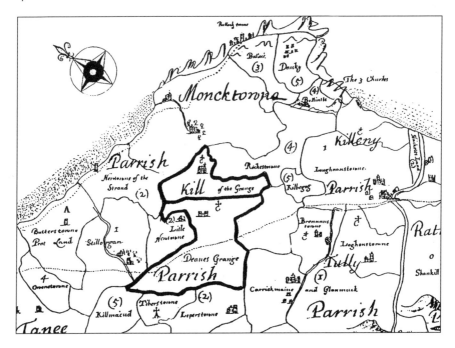

Figure 6 Extract from Down Survey map of the half-barony of Rathdown (*c.*1654),
highlighting the townlands of Deans Grange and Kill of the Grange. Most boundaries
are still identifiable on the ground, being 'set in stone' as boundaries between housing
estates or along roads.

Some records remain to chronicle the decline in the status of the Grange. The
Civil Survey of 1654 recorded a slated castle, a small orchard and a garden at the
Grange together with buildings valued £50. There was as much land under pasture as there was arable land within the townland (200 acres of each), which contrasted with the adjoining townlands where arable land predominated.[7] The moor-
land around Foxrock, and the boggy land by the Clonkeen stream, probably
reduced the proportion of arable land, but there was still a large area of labour-
intensive tillage. The Down Survey of 1656/7 confirms that the land was profitable and that the castle was in repair.[8] This castle with its outhouses has been
stated to have been 'partly repaired and partly rebuilt from the ground in the reign
of James I' (1603–25).[9] The 1660 poll tax return showed a total of 69 taxpayers
for the whole townland, one of the largest settlements in south county Dublin,
and if the multiplier of three is again applied, the figure represents a total population of about 200, compared with some 45 at the Kill. The lack of progress with

---

7 Simington, *Civil Survey*, pp 265–6.   **8** Down Survey parish maps with terriers, of County
Dublin, copied by Daniel O'Brien in 1786/7, NLI Ms 714, (Microfilm P.7382).   **9** NLI, MS
100, Revd John Lyon, Materials for the history of county Dublin.

regard to the plantation by immigrants of the south county during the 500 years since the Anglo-Norman invasion, is highlighted by the fact that 87 per cent of the population were returned as Irish. The principal Irish surnames within the half-barony were the same as to-day's predominant names – Doyle, Byrne, Cavanagh, Kelly, Murphy, Toole, Walsh and Cullen or Callan.[10] One further document survives from this period, the hearth money rolls of 1663, a tax on fire-places. Dean's Grange had only one house which had two hearths, and 14 which had only one, whereas in Stillorgan, James Wolferston's house had seven hearths, and Walter Cheevers had six hearths at Monkstown. This roll is another sign of the decreasing importance of Dean's Grange. After the land upheavals of the seventeenth century, the bigger houses in the south county were now in the possession of tenants with New English names like Harstone, Killcott, Stelly, ffaringdell, Bullard, Swayne, Evans, Brockenbery, Merry, ffloyd, and Swinfield. The Anglo-Norman families – Walshs, Lawlesses and Godmans – had lost their wealth and influence.[11] The statutory restrictions on leasing of the demesne lands resulted in a lack of documentation of their history from the mid-seventeenth to the start of the nineteenth century. But some alternative sources of evidence can be found. John Rocque's map of 1756 shows a considerable village of Dean's Grange. Austin Cooper who in the 1780s described in his notes the antiquities – mainly the castles – of county Dublin, completely ignored it, even though he recorded the existence of 'the remains of a mean old castle' with adjoining cabins at Cornelscourt, as well as other decrepit castles occupied by peasants or used by farmers.[12] In the late eighteenth century, the Revd John Lyon stated that the castle was by then 'totally demolished except for a few low walls'.[13] John Taylor notes the settlement in his 1815 map of the environs of Dublin, but William Duncan's map of 1821 disregards it. Finally the site is ignored in the first Ordnance Survey map of the area in 1843. The old village was by now abandoned. However, in Taylor's 1815 map, the Clonkeen Road had appeared for the first time, and a new village of Dean's Grange subsequently began to grow on the strip of surplus land left over between the boundary of the townland, and the line of the newly constructed road. But there is no apparent connection between the old and the new villages.[14]

The Kill also fades away. The poll tax of 1660, as indicated above, showed a population of about forty-five. The hearth money roll records only one house

---

10 Gurrin, *Irish demography*, pp 73–5. **11** 'Hearth money rolls' in *Journal of County Kildare Archaeological Society*, xi, (1930–33), pp 462–4. **12** John Rocque, *Carte topographique de la Comte de Dublin, 1760,* (Edition published by Harry Margary, Lympre Castle, Kent, n.d., c.1985); NLI, M 772/3, transcription of Austin Cooper's notes; unsorted original notebooks now at NLI, Accessions 4841. **13** NLI MS 100, John Lyon, materials for the history of county Dublin – described in the Hayes Catalogue as early nineteenth century, but Lyon died in 1790 aged 88. **14** John Taylor, *Taylor's map of the environs of Dublin* (Dublin, 1816), (edition of Phoenix Maps Dublin, 1989); William Duncan, *Map of Dublin* (Dublin, 1821); *OS Co. Dublin, 6″ sheet 23,* revised to 1843.

with two hearths in the townland, which appears to be the house constructed on the Kill farm after its leasing in 1590.[15] Cooper refers only to a ruined church beside the gentleman's residence. Rocque's map does not clearly show any village. A Longfield estate map dated 1814 shows a group of buildings around the present Kill Abbey, but these may have been merely the out-offices of the 'gentlemen's residence'. As in the case of Dean's Grange, by the time that the first Ordnance Survey sheet was published in 1843, a cluster of new cottages had sprung up a few hundred metres away from the ruins of the old church, and these cottages formed the basis of to-day's Kill of the Grange. Significantly however, the new village was located, not in the townland of the Kill itself, but in a tongue of another townland Woodpark (formerly part of Rochestown) which protrudes into the Kill. Like the new Dean's Grange, it developed in the early nineteenth century and was confined to two small triangles left over between the site of the new Rochestown Avenue and nearby property boundaries. As in the case of its sister village, there is no direct connection between the old and the new villages of Kill of the Grange.[16]

The ruins of the church pin-point the location of the first Kill village, but where exactly was the site of the old manor and grange? Most of the buildings were constructed of timber and wattle, though there was also a slated castle. The castle may have been removed for building materials, just as the erratic boulders which were once scattered all over the south county area, were cleared and utilised for this purpose. Moreover, the development of the general area started in 1949, before the commencement of systematic archaeological assessments of sensitive sites. Yet there are clues. Francis Elrington Ball stated that extensive remains of medieval buildings were remembered by the Revd Maxwell H. Close.[17] Ball's scrapbook of notes and correspondence contains statements that the ruins were opposite the entrance of the cemetery, and in addition that they appeared on the earliest ordnance sheets but were no longer visible. In fact two small buildings appear on those sheets but they are absent from subsequent editions.[18] Plotting onto an Ordnance Sheet, the location of Dean's Grange as shown on Rocque's and Taylor's small scale and less accurate maps, we find that the Grange was located near the shops on Foxrock Avenue. In this area, various

---

15 Hearth money rolls, pp 462–4; McEnery, *Christ Church deeds,* no. 1406.   **16** Cooper, notes; Rocque, *Compte de Dublin;* Lease map surveyed by John Longfield in 1814 (copy supplied to writer by Land Commission); *OS county Dublin, 6" sheet 23,* 1843; NLI Map, 16 G 42(13), A survey of Rochestown, County Dublin, for John Mapas Esquire, 1787 and NAI, 1130/1/9/iii Map attached to lease, 28 May, 1811, compared with Griffith's valuation and reference map for Woodpark townland, 1848.   **17** Maxwell H. Close, 'The former abundance of granite boulders in the S.E. neighbourhood of Dublin' in *Irish Naturalist,* vi, 1897, pp 29–33; Ball, *County Dublin,* i, p. 47.   **18** Ball, scrapbook i, p. 74, and post-publication notes i. A file containing evidence as to the exact location of the medieval settlement is being prepared by the writer for lodgement with the Gilbert Library, Dublin.

householders have reported finding pieces of pottery when their gardens were being cultivated for the first time, although none of these were preserved. The shards of pottery may, however, date from a later period when the contents of ashpits were regularly spread over their lands by local farmers. Near the top of the cemetery in a particular location, animal bones, burnt stones, and a quantity of seashells, oysters and cockles, have been found. So, in summary, an approximate location can be defined as being 'close to the shops at Foxrock Avenue'.[19] See Figure 2.

CONCLUSION

In the long history of Clonkeen, two villages grew up around two institutions, a church and a grange or home-farm. However, after a short period of peace and prosperity, centuries of war ensued, reflecting national developments, and this conflict impinged heavily on the valley because of its borderland location between the mountains and the populated area around the city. The effect of changes originating at the Reformation at Christ Church, resulted in both a change of management, and a change of management style at Clonkeen, which combined to undermine the traditional role of the villages. In general, settlements tend to continue in existence because there is generally some measure of economic continuity; in Clonkeen there was a complete disruption of role. By the early 1800s people were still living in communities in the area but not in the Grange or the Kill: they lived in villages such as Cabinteely, Cornelscourt and Newtownpark and in *new* settlements at *new* locations close to the medieval settlements. These new villages, or rather the groups of houses built to utilise peripheral pieces of land, provided a nucleus on which to build communities with new commercial and social functions. The new villages with their add-on developments have never become fully balanced settlements with a full range of consumer services, though there are now plans to convert Dean's Grange into a major business and commercial centre. In the meantime, the Grange Pharmacy, the Grange Motors, the Grange Pub and indeed St Fintan's Villas and the Clonkeen Road will be a continuing reminder to future generations that as well as a mundane suburban present the area had a memorable, eventful past.

19 Midden close to graves in Deans Grange cemetery, St Paul's section, graves Z 43/44, and V,W,X,Y, 50 and up.

Kilmore Quay, county Wexford, 1800–1900

RITA EDWARDS

Kilmore Quay (*Cé na Cille Móire*, quay of the big church) is a small fishing village in the barony of Bargy, in the parish of Kilmore in southeast Wexford. It is situated opposite the Saltee Islands on the townlands of Crossfarnogue and Nemestown. By the early nineteenth century, Crossfarnogue and Nemestown together with the townlands of Mulrankin, Tomhaggard and Kilturk had been incorporated into the Roman Catholic parish of Kilmore[1] (Figure 1). The name Crossfarnogue derives from *Cros Fearnóg,* cross of the alder. The name Nemestown, however, is more difficult to translate and may be derived from the family name of one of the early Anglo-Norman or Cromwellian settlers to the area. Kilmore Quay takes its name from the village of Kilmore, which is situated three miles inland. The village is named after the medieval parish of Kilmore, the ruined church of which is located on the nearby townland of Grange. Situated, as Kilmore is, on the main road from Wexford Town to Kilmore Quay, it is likely that the inland village (which in the nineteenth century became known as Kilmore Upper), developed around the new Catholic chapel – 'a spacious building, erected in 1803, adjoining which, a house for the priest has been lately built.'[2] Archaeological surveys indicate signs of early settlement in this area. While they cannot be seen from the ground, aerial photographs show cropmarks of a circular enclosure near the church in the townland of Grange and a second site in the townland of Sarshill.[3] While the translation of Sarshill is uncertain, Ballask means *Baile Easca,* townland of the marsh.[4]

During the Famine decade there was a definable movement of population from Kilmore Upper and the neighbouring townlands of Sarshill and Ballask to the coast. In 1841, Kilmore Upper contained 35 houses with a population of 212 and the townland of Nemestown on the coast (part of the future Kilmore Quay) was returned with 40 houses, containing a population of 249. The 1840 Ordnance Survey map of the coastal area shows a linear arrangement of dwellings flanking a road stretching northeast from a small harbour, overlooked by a coastguard station and a national school in the neighbouring townland of Chapel, one mile from Crossfarnogue and Nemestown (Figure 2). In the census of 1851 it was noted that Kilmore Upper 'does not now contain 20 houses, its present

1 S. Lewis, *Topographical dictionary of Ireland* (London, 1837), ii, p. 187. 2 Ibid. 3 Michael J. Moore, in P. David Sweetman (ed.), *Archaeological inventory of county Wexford* (Dublin, 1996), pp 71, 128. 4 For translations of townland names see Séamus S. de Vál, 'Townland names', in Brendan Culleton (ed.), *Treasures of the landscape* (Dublin, 1994), pp 216, 188.

Figure 1 Map of southeast Wexford from Samuel Lewis, *Atlas of Ireland* (London, 1837), also showing civil parish of Kilmore and Crossfarnogue Point.

population has therefore merged into that of the townlands of Crossfarnogue and Nemestown.' During the following decades the population of Kilmore Upper continued to decline and by 1901, its population was returned with the adjoining townlands of Sarshill and Ballask. In 1911 the census authorities referred to the coastal village as 'Kilmore Quay Town.'[5]. In the revised edition of the Ordnance Survey map in 1902, the settlement of Kilmore Quay contained additional houses, a lifeboat station, an improved harbour and at the centre of it all was St Peter's Catholic chapel (Figure 3). Today, people living in the area speak of going 'up' to the Village and 'down' to the Quay.

External forces ultimately determine the growth or decline of a village. Where Kilmore Quay is concerned, given its geographical location, the village would probably have developed at Crossfarnogue and Nemestown at some stage during the nineteenth century. However, between 1841 and 1851, the movement of people to the coast accelerated its growth and development. While county Wexford did

5 *Censuses,* 1841–1911. For comparative purposes, the population figures for Kilmore Upper and the Quay area have been amalgamated with their adjoining townlands. The reason for the anomaly in the figures for the Quay between 1901 and 1911 is ascribed to the fact that a number of houses, which were returned in the rural portion of the townlands of Crossfarnogue and Nemestown in 1901, were included in the newly named Kilmore Quay Town in 1911.

Figure 2 OS map 1840, not to scale. (Courtesy of map library, Trinity College, Dublin.)

not suffer as much as other parts of the country during the Famine period between 1841 and 1851, its population nevertheless declined by 11 per cent. However, where the parish of Kilmore was concerned, the population rose from 4,761 to 5,071 – an increase of 7 per cent during that same period.[6] One of the reasons for this movement of people can be attributed to the fact that when the potato crop failed, this area provided alternative sources of food. In the early years of the Famine, as the acreage planted with potatoes throughout the parish declined, crops of turnips and oats were planted and harvested instead.[7] Where the coastal area was concerned, rabbits and wildfowl from Ballyteigue Burrow and Ballyteigue Lough and fish both from the Lough and the sea were available. The Lough, an extensive area of water, which stretched from the lower end of Ballyteigue Burrow to Bridgetown, a village a few miles north of Crossfarnogue and Nemestown, gave substantial employment in fishing and commercial trading.[8] There was also a small pier at Crossfarnogue, lying in the shelter of Forlorn Point, which had been built by local fishermen, their friends and neighbours in 1795.[9]

6 *Census*, 1851.   **7** NAI, Parish Constabulary Returns, RLFC 4/31/57, 1 June 1846.   **8** John Power, 'A lake that stretched to Bridgetown' in Hilary Murphy (ed.), *Kilmore Parish Journal* (1975–76), pp 24–5 (henceforth cited as *KPJ*).   **9** *Appendix to first report commissioners of inquiry on state of Irish fisheries, 1836*, HC 1837, [77], xxii, p. 177.

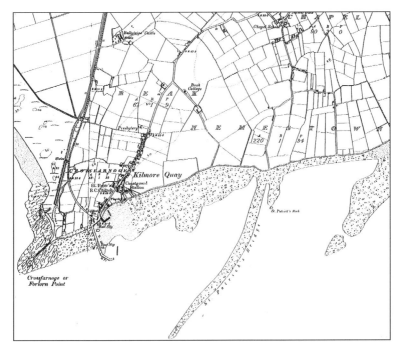

Figure 3 OS map 1902, not to scale. (Courtesy of map library, Trinity College, Dublin.)

Table 1 Census of population – Kilmore Upper, Sarshill and Ballask, 1841–1911.

Year	Kilmore (Upper)	Sarshill	Ballask	Total	Percentages
1841	212	115	211	538	100
1851	–	119	201	320	60
1861	–	117	144	261	49
1871	145	103	41	289	54
1881	184	72	–	256	48
1891	103	82	49	234	44
1901	–	86	89	175	33
1911	–	109	82	191	36

INHABITANTS

For generations the inhabitants of this part of county Wexford had a reputation for being an industrious, thrifty and law-abiding people.[10] However, in spite of

10 Arthur Wollaston (ed.), *Arthur Young's Tour in Ireland, 1776–1779* (London, 1892), i, pp 85–6;

their reputation for being a 'peaceable' people, a number of them became involved in the 1798 Rebellion and their names are remembered in the parish to this day.[11] In the late eighteenth century, the lands at Crossfarnogue, Nemestown and adjoining townlands were in the possession of the Bruen family, whose main residence was at Oak Park, in county Carlow. Ballyteigue Castle, west of Crossfarnogue, was leased to Dr John Henry Colclough. Colclough, a Protestant, aged 30 in 1798, was a member of the United Irishmen, who, it is said, reluctantly took part in the insurrection. Following capture, he was subsequently hanged on Wexford Bridge on 28 June 1798.[12] Another local man who took part in the fighting was John Barry, a native of Nemestown, who fell at the battle of Ross on 5 June.[13] The French travel writer, De Latocnaye, gives a first hand account of the state of Ireland on the eve of the rebellion in *A Frenchman's walk through Ireland, 1796–1797.* Where Wexford was concerned, he noted that there were sporadic outbreaks of agrarian unrest in the area and he was aware of the tension and undercurrents of violence that existed throughout the countryside. De Latocnaye drew many parallels between what he had experienced in France prior to the Revolution in 1789 and what he saw happening in Ireland. 'From complaints and claims, the peasants come to threats, and from threats to the execution of things threatened,' he wrote.[14]

Table 2 Census of population – Kilmore Quay, Crossfarnogue, Nemestown, 1841–1911

Year	Kilmore (Quay)	Crossfarnogue	Nemestown	Total	Percentages
1841	–	–	249	249	100
1851	–	313	171	484	194
1861	308	27	162	497	200
1871	411	–	36	447	180
1881	317	–	117	434	174
1891	269	–	102	371	149
1901	90	49	186	325	131
1911	208	10	75	293	118

In his *Statistical survey of County Wexford* published in 1807, Robert Fraser commented on the culture of silence that had descended on the countryside in

Robert Fraser, *A statistical survey of county Wexford* (Dublin, 1807), pp 6, 55; Jacob Poole, in William Barnes, (ed.), *A glossary with some pieces of verse of the old dialect of the English baronies of Forth and Bargy, county of Wexford* (London, 1867), p. 3. **11** See Richard Roche, *Here's their memory – a record of the United Irish in Co. Wexford in 1798* (Wexford, 1997); 'Our parish's role in "ninety-eight"', in *KPJ* (1979–80), pp 33–4. **12** Art Kavanagh and Rory Murphy, 'Colclough' in *The Wexford gentry* (Bunclody, 1994), i, pp 76–7. **13** *KPJ* (1979–80), p. 33. **14** De Latocnaye, *A Frenchman's walk through Ireland, 1796–97* (trans. from French, John Stevenson, Belfast, 1917), pp 55–6.

the aftermath of the rebellion. He wrote that he hoped that nothing would ever again induce the people in the county 'to leave their fields and their ploughs' and that 'as sudden and general was the rising of the inhabitants ... in the month of May, no less sudden and general was the return by these people in July following, to their industry and their homes (for houses, thousands had none) ... by the beginning of the harvest, order as far as related to the insurgents was perfectly restored'.[15]

Because of their blend of Irish, Norse and Norman blood, the people of southeast Wexford have long been regarded as ethnically distinct from the inhabitants of the rest of the county. In particular, the barony of Bargy, together with its neighbouring barony, Forth have been collectively described as 'the English colonies.' When the Anglo-Normans landed in Bannow Bay in 1169, they brought with them their own language and customs. With regard to language, an old dialect known as Yola, survived in the baronies until the middle of the nineteenth century. Colonel Solomon Richards, a Cromwellian officer, who in the seventeenth century wrote an account of this region for Sir William Petty, said that, 'whoever hath read old Chaucer, will better understand the ... dialect than either an English or Irishman that never read him though otherwise a good linguist'.[16] Martin Parle, an old man who lived in the barony of Forth near Carnsore Point and who died in the mid 1860s was said to have been the last speaker of the dialect.[17] The famous Kilmore Christmas carols, which are still performed annually in the parish, are an important link with this traditional past. According to tradition, the leader of the singers has always been a member of the Devereux family.[18] The surname Devereux, formerly d'Evreux, was the name of one of the most powerful Anglo-Norman families in the county.[19]

Another custom, which is thought to have been introduced from England in the twelfth century is the art of mumming. Traditionally, a mummer is one who acts or performs in a mime or play. In modern times the plays are always in verse and the main theme often deals with the age-old battle between good and evil. Wexford mumming appears to be different to that which takes place in other parts of the country in that the highlight of the play is an intricate sword dance. In his chronicle, *The banks of the Boro*, written about events which occurred between 1817 and 1818, the nineteenth-century writer Patrick Kennedy, gives details of *Dhroghedy's march* which 'we had the good fortune to see ... performed in a complete fashion on the borders of the barony of Bargy'. At the time, the custom had almost died out. Described as 'a stirring, but apparently confused spectacle', but when the music was good and the dancers kept

15 Fraser, *Statistical survey*, pp 55–6. **16** Herbert F. Hore, 'An account of the barony of Forth, in the county of Wexford, written at the close of the seventeenth century', in *JRSAI 1862–3*, (Dublin, 1864), p. 86. **17** Poole, *A glossary*, p. 19. **18** Kevin Danaher, *The year in Ireland* (Cork, 1972), p. 243. **19** Edward MacLysaght, *The surnames of Ireland* (9th ed., Dublin, 1999), p. 81.

time, it 'strongly interested and excited the lookers-on'.[20] During the last fifty years, there has been a revival of the mumming tradition throughout the country, especially in southeast Wexford. A nineteenth-century manuscript entitled, 'The Forth and Bargy Mummers' Play', previously in the possession of Jack Devereux of Kilmore Quay, a fisherman and former leader of the Kilmore carol singers, has been recorded in *Folklore of county Wexford*. [21]

An even older custom associated with religious practice, which has survived since pre-Norman times, is that of the laying of wooden funeral crosses by members of the deceased's family at selected sites on the way to the graveyard. It is believed that it originated with Irish pilgrims returning from Santiago de Compostella, who observed the rite where Charlemagne's soldiers died at the battle of Roncesvalles in AD 778.[22] When the old Grange graveyard closed and a new cemetery opened in 1953, the custom continued.

During his travels through southeast Wexford, De Latocnaye, in addition to commenting on the 'singular language', of the people of Forth and Bargy, also commented on their dwellings which were 'more cleaner and more comfortable than those of the other inhabitants and they are also so much more clean in person that they appear quite a different race'.[23] Men wore a short coat, waistcoat, trunk breeches and a round narrow brimmed hat. The women's attire consisted of a short jacket and a petticoat bordered at the bottom with one, two or three rows of ribbons.[24] This custom appears to have been simply a matter of style or decoration. On other occasions it is thought that the bands were added for practical purposes, for example, for disguising hemlines when a garment had been altered.[25] For many years the people of the baronies lived as a closed society marrying among themselves. The reason why the 'colony' with its own language, customs and traditions survived for so long in this part of county Wexford has been ascribed to the relative isolation of the area. The story is told of a woman who one day wandered to the top of nearby Forth Mountain. It was said that she got such a shock when she saw how vast the world was outside her own place that she vowed never to leave home again.[26]

AGRICULTURE

The majority of the population in the baronies depended on agriculture for their livelihoods and at the beginning of the nineteenth century, especially along the

---

20 Patrick Kennedy, *The banks of the Boro – a chronicle of county Wexford* (new edition published Enniscorthy, 1989), pp 216–17. **21** See James Parle, *The mummers of Wexford* (Wexford), 2001); Diarmaid Ó Muirithe and Deirdre Nuttall (eds), *Folklore of county Wexford* (Dublin, 1999), pp 49–59. **22** Jacqueline Sidney, 'Funeral crosses', in *KPJ* (1996–97), pp 37–9. **23** De Latocnaye, *A Frenchman's walk*, p. 55. **24** Fraser, *Statistical survey*, p. 140. **25** Conversation with Clodagh Doyle, National Museum of Country Life, Turlough Park, Castlebar, Co. Mayo, 9 October 2002. **26** Poole, *A glossary*, pp 2, 4.

coast, holdings were divided into small farms of between five and twenty acres. In parts of the parish of Kilmore, where alternate crops of barley and beans had been sown for generations, 'the land [was] constantly in a state of great fertility'. Competition for land was great and this in turn, ensured that rents remained high.[27] As was the custom throughout Ireland at that period, whenever children married, the holdings were further subdivided. However, according to the Devon Commission that was appointed by the government in November 1843 to examine the law and practice relating to occupation of land in Ireland, this custom had by then almost ceased in Forth and Bargy.[28] When Arthur Young visited the area thirty-five years earlier, he commented on the primitive methods used by the farmers at the time. Cattle were scarce and a few sheep and one or two cows were normally kept for family use.[29] Later it was recorded that small farmers, who were unable to keep a cow, kept a few ewes for their family and then sold the lambs in autumn to sheep farmers from county Wicklow.[30] Pigs, on the other hand, were seen everywhere and were often let loose on the shore in order to forage for fish, seaweed and other offal.[31] However, the fact is that the people of the baronies had lived on and tilled the land for generations and were well adapted to making their living from the soil. By the early nineteenth century, it was noted that 'in some districts of county Wexford, the system of fallowing has long been abolished [with] intermediate crops of beans, between their corn crops, immemorially practised and their ground [being] laid down in good heart with clover and grass seeds. This improved state of agriculture is practised with considerable attention in the baronies of Forth and Bargy.'[32] The introduction of clover and grass seeds gave more summer and winter feeding, thus enabling the farmer to increase his stock. This in turn, provided more manure for the land, which in turn improved the production of grain.

In spite of, or maybe, because of smaller holdings, the majority of the inhabitants of Forth and Bargy worked hard and were able to achieve a good standard of living. Their houses were described as 'decent' and the poorest cabin was well built and covered with thatch. Even the animals were well housed and carts and cars were all stored in their respective sheds. The countryside was a hive of industry, with people constantly at work digging marl from pits, drawing limestone on 'miserable' roads over great distances, dredging wet and oozy mud from beds of rivers and tending to their land and animals. Given their proximity to the seashore, they also used the resources of the sea to fertilise the land. In addition to drawing sand, people were seen out day and night in all weather, (even during winter storms) dragging uprooted seaweed from the surf. Women, in addition

27 Ibid., p. 3; Fraser, *Statistical survey*, p. 53. **28** *Minutes of evidence royal commission of inquiry on state of law and practice in respect to occupation of land in Ireland (Devon Commission)*, iii, HC 1845, [657], xxi, p. 488. **29** Wollaston, *Arthur Young's Tour*, p. 86. **30** *Devon commission*, 1845, xxi, p. 476. **31** Wollaston, *Arthur Young's Tour*, p. 88. **32** Fraser, *Statistical survey*, p. 50.

to working at home industries, did all kinds of agricultural work, except ploughing. And what was most unusual at the time, they received the same rates of pay
as men.[33] Fraser recorded this custom of equal pay between the sexes in 1807
and later in 1836 it was noted that male labourers were paid 8*d.* a day and that
'women and children are generally employed, the former getting 8*d.* a day, the
latter 4*d.* per day ... but when disengaged, they work on their own lands, women
during the harvest get 1*s.* per day if they reap'.[34] In 1836, when government officials visited farmer Thomas Devereux's house at Nemestown, they 'found the
interior of this little establishment a perfect model of neatness and industry. A
very old woman was making lace, by which she contributed 3*d.* per day to the
resources of the family [while] another was plaiting straw for hats and the man
was engaged in his garden.'[35]

One of the reasons put forward for this constant round of activity is that there
were few middlemen in the district and that those who held land were secure
in their leases and consequently had no hesitation in working hard to improve
their holdings. The belief was that industry brought its own reward and a certain intolerance towards the unemployed and idle was evident, in that, if a beggar
appeared in the district he was passed on from house to house until eventually
he arrived in another barony.[36] The Devon Commission was informed in 1844
that the smallest quantity of land of reasonable quality that a farmer in southeast
Wexford would need to support himself and an average family, would be in the
region of ten to fifteen acres. However, in parts of Forth and Bargy near the
coast, there were farmers who were capable of supporting their families 'in great
comfort and comparative respectability on [farms] even as low as five acres – but
of course that is by very great industry.'[37]

FISHING

In addition to being noted for its agricultural produce, county Wexford is also
a noted maritime county, but at the beginning of the nineteenth century there
were very few villages along the coast. Nevertheless, Fraser noted in 1807 that:

> on the southern and eastern coasts there are numerous assemblages of
> people at every creek, where there is shelter for a boat, who derive their
> subsistence partly from little holdings of land, but chiefly from the sea,
> and all that is wanted to raise these poor people to prosperity and wealth,
> is to form small harbours to shelter their boats and afford them the means

33 Ibid., pp 55, 141.   34 *Supplement to appendix (D) first report royal commission for inquiry into
the condition of the poorer classes in Ireland*, HC 1836, [36], xxxi, p. 141.   35 *Appendix to first
report ... state of Irish fisheries*, 1837, xxii, p. 178.   36 Fraser, *Statistical survey*, pp 79, 141.   37
Devon commission, 1845, xxi, p. 479.

of a safe retreat in the event of sudden storms … two very small harbours have been indeed formed, one at Fethard and another at a place called Cross Faranogue in the Bay of Ballyteigue, this last being best adapted to carry on the fishing.[38]

At the time there were about 20 boats and less than 100 men at Crossfarnogue fishing from 'an inadequate' little harbour, mainly for lobsters, which larger boats carried to the Dublin market. Due to inadequate facilities, fishing took place during the summer months only.

For many people, access to land and sea could mean the difference between a reasonably comfortable existence and subsistence living. In the 1830s, a fisherman and a native of the district named John Whitty had no land and lived in miserable conditions. Without access to land, he was often 'hard up' when fish were scarce, a situation 'which would never be the case if there was shelter for boats.' The above- named Thomas Devereux was also a fisherman and boat-owner and 'although no fisherman without a bit of land, can ever lay hold of the world, yet the sea is his estate, and if there was only a pier built at Kilmore, sufficient to give shelter to the boats, Thomas Devereux would not envy the King of England.'[39] There were then 27 open sail-boats, employing 108 men, and 46 row-boats, employing 276 men fishing off Crossfarnogue.[40] In a short period of thirty years there was an increase of 53 boats and over 300 men involved in fishing. Throughout the years the men were criticised for being unskilled and conservative, where fishing was concerned. One of the reasons given for this observation was that they never used long lines. However, they were not tardy in following the fish wherever they might be. During the herring season when the weather was bad, the fishermen were often seen transporting their boats overland some thirteen miles from Crossfarnogue, to a more suitable launch point near Wexford town.[41]

In addition to fish, coal was also landed at Crossfarnogue. Given that there were few trees in the area, furze had long been used as an alternative fuel. Known locally as *sceach*, the furze, which was cut every three years, was extensively planted in small fields throughout the baronies. When times were difficult, the poor used the tenderest part of the bush for feeding their cows and horses. By the mid 1840s, while it was still used for fencing, as land became more valuable, the furze fields or 'nooks' were gradually disappearing.[42]

According to the 1851 census, while Kilmore Upper contained less than 20 houses in that year, the two townlands of Crossfarnogue and Nemestown contained 71 houses.[43] These figures are similar to those listed in Griffith's Primary Valuation, which in the mid 1850s listed 40 households in Crossfarnogue and a

38 Fraser, *Statistical survey*, p. 22. **39** *Appendix to first report … state of Irish fisheries*, 1837, xxii, p. 178. **40** Ibid., p. 183. **41** Ibid., pp 176–7. **42** *Devon commission*, 1845, xxi, p. 476. **43** *Census*, 1851.

further 39 in Nemestown. By then, Crossfarnogue, in addition to its pier, contained a shopkeeper and a carpenter, both named James Rashford, a second shopkeeper and fisherman named James Monahan as well as Edward Meadows, who worked for the Ballast Board. The inhabitants of Nemestown included Nicholas Moran, a smith, and Matthew Meyler, who was in charge of the coast guard station. John Murphy operated a forge in the townland of Ballyteigue. Nicholas Power operated a second forge in Chapel, which also contained the local national school, a windmill and a kiln in the name of Mary Murphy.[44]

COAST GUARD

For a short period in the early part of the nineteenth century a coast guard station had been placed on the Great Saltee Island in order to prevent smuggling.[45] Over the years, the role of the coast guard gradually changed with increased emphasis being placed on assisting vessels in distress, the operation of life saving equipment and the taking in charge of wrecks. By 1847, at the request of Sir James Dombraine, the inspector general of the Royal National Lifeboat Institution, a lifeboat was placed under the control of the coast guard in the area. The service seems to have been discontinued for some years, possibly due to problems associated with maintenance and repair. However, due to local pressure, in 1884 the RNLI re-established the lifeboat station, supplying a thirty-foot, ten-oared self-righting boat called the *John Robert* that was housed in a newly-built station house in Nemestown.[46]

Prior to the invention of navigational aids, travel by sea was potentially dangerous and where southeast Wexford was concerned, there were no warning lights for shipping between Hook Head and Wicklow Head. Ballyteigue Bay, lying west of Crossfarnogue and extending fifteen miles from Hook Head to the Saltee Islands is enclosed on all sides by rocks and shallow waters. Once a ship found its way into this bay, it had little chance of reaching safety. During the winter of 1806 eleven vessels were wrecked on the coast with many bodies washed ashore. Vessels plying their trade through St George's Channel often mistook the light on Hook Head for Eddystone lighthouse on the English coast and instead of reaching Plymouth Sound, the captain of many a vessel found himself in Ballyteigue Bay ending up being grounded in shallow waters, or being wrecked on one of the numerous rocks in the bay.[47] In the early 1830s the civil engineer and hydrographer, Alexander Nimmo, was commissioned to chart St George's Channel, identifying many of the dangerous rock formations along the

44 *Griffith's primary valuation of Ireland, Co. Wexford* (1853), pp 250–1, 253–4.   **45** *Parliamentary gazetteer of Ireland* (Dublin, 1845), p. 202.   **46** John Power, 'Coastguard double rescue', in *KPJ* (1989–90), p. 22; Hilary Murphy, 'Coastguard station', in *KPJ* (1994–95), pp 29–30.   **47** Fraser, *Statistical survey*, pp 27–8.

Wexford coast. In his survey he mentioned Crossfarnogue and mapped the already well-known 'narrow ridge of large stones, called St Patrick's Bridge, [which] extends northward in a curve from little Saltee to the mainland, with only 7 to 10 feet on it at low tide'.[48] By then, two new warning lights had been erected on the southeast coast – one on Tuskar Rock, north-east of Carnsore Point and a second on a floating lightship off Coningbeg Rock, south of the Saltee Islands, both of which helped to minimise danger to shipping.

However, while improved safety features helped to prevent numerous and appalling shipwrecks, some continued to occur. In December 1833 a vessel of 500 tons named *Water Witch*, which had left the port of Bristol for Waterford on the seventeenth of the month, became disabled in a storm off the Wexford coast. Losing its way in a dense fog, the ship found itself on rocks off the coastline of the parish of Kilmore. At daybreak, 'in one of the worst hurricanes ever witnessed', two small boats set off from the shore, and succeeded in saving some of the crew and passengers. A public subscription was raised in recognition of the men's bravery.[49] This was not an isolated incident and throughout the years, there were different men at various times prepared to risk their lives to save others. Medals for gallantry and bravery were awarded to these heroic men.[50]

THE QUAY AT KILMORE

For years the fishermen fishing off Crossfarnogue felt frustrated by the fact that their efforts were being hindered by lack of a quay for their boats. In 1836 it was estimated that an expenditure of £3,000 would greatly improve matters, but as there were no local quarries, nothing was done.[51] Finally, given that no government help was forthcoming and in keeping with their reputation for self-help and industry, the fishermen of the parish decided in August 1843 to work on the pier themselves. Again, helped by friends and neighbours, and by money raised in both Wexford town and Waterford city, the masters of the various vessels succeeded in raising £224 in cash. When the work finally started, other fisherman provided free labour, estimated at £38 and local farmers gave the free use of 310 horses. Their labour was estimated to be worth 2s. 6d. each.[52] A memorial forwarded to the Office of Public Works dated December 1844 listed the names of the masters (and the names of their respective boats) who had been involved in initiating the work on the pier.

---

48 Alexander Nimmo, *New piloting directions for St George's Channel and the coast of Ireland* (Dublin, 1832), pp 140–1. **49** *Wexford Independent*, 21 December 1833. **50** 'A story of heroic tragedy at sea', in *KPJ* (1978–9), pp 2–3. **51** *First report ... state of Irish fisheries*, 1837, xxii, p. 176. **52** NAI, OPW8 210/1 doc. 1, memorial 18 December 1844, John Rowe et al. to OPW.

Table 3 Masters and their boats in August 1843

Nicholas Fardy	*Recovery*	John Cousins	*Betsey*
William Cleary	*Lark*	Peter Barry	*Chance*
John McCabe	*Sailwell*	John Wickham	*Mary 2*
Nicholas Rochford	*Hare*	Thomas Walsh	*Nacaday*
James Rochford	*Elisa*	Patrick Clooney	*Fanny*
John Wickham	*Vulcan*	John Harpur	*Fox*
James Walsh	*Pig*	Richard Walsh	*Isabella*
Nicholas Clooney	*Dove*	Patrick Hughes	*Minerva*
Thomas Murphy	*Jane*	John Dake	*John*
John Cousins	*Mary 1*	Richard Rashford	*Brothers*
Nicholas Blake	*Padro*	John Parle [Saltus]	*Rose*
Matthew Devereux	*Aganippe*	John Walsh	*Francis*
Thomas Flaherty	*May-flower*	Matthew Hanton	*Peggy*

Given the ethnic mix of the population in this part of county Wexford, it may be noted that five of the above surnames were of Irish, five of English, five of Anglo-Norman and two of Welsh origin.[53] Seven of the masters' names appear in Griffith's valuation as being householders in Crossfarnogue, with land-holdings ranging from three statute acres to a small garden. Six other surnames appear in Nemestown with smaller holdings ranging from just over one statute acre to a house with no garden. Several of the remaining surnames are listed in neighbouring townlands in the parish. The names given to their boats are also of interest in that none of them are saints' names, while a number appear to be family, animal, historical or fanciful names. Three – *Vulcan*, *Aganippe* and *Minerva* – are named after figures in Greek and Roman mythology.[54] The small harbour at Crossfarnogue, situated as it was at an angle on the southeast coast was always very much exposed to Atlantic weather and during the winter of 1843–4 a large vessel lost its moorings and succeeded in carrying away a portion of the pier which the fishermen had worked on a few months previously. The vessel subsequently lay in a wrecked condition blocking the entrance.[55]

In the spring of 1844 the fishermen discovered that a £50,000 fishery fund had been set up by the government in order to provide grants towards the construction of piers and harbours and that any money collected locally would be met by triple that amount. A committee was formed in December 1844 with Andrew Furlong of Newtown nominated secretary. A memorial signed by 89 locals 'who were nearly all fishermen' as well as 18 local gentry, was forwarded to the board of the Office of Public Works. They were informed that there were

53 MacLysaght, *The surnames of Ireland.* **54** Geddes and Grosset, *Classical mythology* (2nd ed., Scotland, 1997), pp 318, 418, 475. **55** NAI, OPW8 210/1, doc. 2, undated letter John Rowe et al. to OPW.

44 first-class and 33 second-class boats employing 176 men, fishing in the parish, with over 1,000 dependents. The fishermen's collective income was estimated at between £1,000 and £1,500 per annum. The argument was that with improved facilities, they could work out of better boats, gain access to the Nymph Bank and other deep waters, and increase their income threefold.[56] While the type of boats employed by the fishermen in the 1840s compared to the 1830s, appear to be of a better class and show an increase in number from 73 to 77, the number of men employed in the industry during that same period dropped from 384 to 176. However, it is possible that they were many other men fishing out of smaller boats who do not appear in the official records.

The board's engineer, William Fraser, drew up plans and it was agreed that a sum of £2,000 would be spent on improving facilities at Crossfarnogue.[57] The first sum of £30 was lodged to the credit of the commissioners and in due course a grant of £90 was received in return.[58] During the course of the work, certified accounts were forwarded to the commissioners every two, three or four weeks, where appropriate. The following is an example of one account. Dated 21 October 1845, it reads, 'I send accounts of men and horses for this three weeks ending 4, 11 and 18 October. There are 614 men and 50 horses – total amount £37 15s. 11d.'[59] The work on the pier provided an alternative source of employment for the men in the parish and would have been a welcome addition to the local economy. Crossfarnogue, Nemestown and the neighbouring townlands must have been a hive of activity with men and horses, all requiring food and shelter. In June 1845, a second engineer, Barry Gibbons, had visited the site at Crossfarnogue and expressed reservations as to the suitability of the material being used in its construction.[60] Previously, when working on the pier, the fishermen had always used materials that were close to hand. When it was recognised that the taking of large stones from the western side of the pier and from Forlorn Point further exposed the pier wall to Atlantic storms and to silting from Ballyteigue Burrow, an inland quarry was opened nearby. With the approach of the winter, the work on the pier was suspended, while the quarrying of stones continued. However, as had happened so often in the past, part of the pier was twice carried away by severe storms during the winter months. In December 1845 it was declared unsafe.[61]

When work recommenced the following spring, the people of southeast Wexford were unaware of the impending disaster that was facing the whole country. In September 1845, the *Dublin Evening Post* had reported that the potato blight, which had previously been reported in England, was now in Ireland.[62] By

56 Ibid., doc. 1, memorial 18 December 1844. **57** Ibid., doc. 6, letter 10 July 1845, Fraser to OPW. **58** Ibid., doc. 12, letter 25 July 1845, OPW to Furlong. **59** Ibid., doc. 13, letter 21 October 1845, Furlong to OPW. **60** Ibid., doc. 48, letter 4 December 1846, Gibbons to OPW. **61** Ibid., doc. 19, 10 December 1845, Furlong to OPW; OPW8 210/2 doc. 24, letter 20 April 1846, Morgan to OPW. **62** *Dublin Evening Post*, 9 September 1845.

the spring of 1846, the impact of the Famine was beginning to be felt in the parish of Kilmore. With only £18 in hand, the pier committee were unable to raise further funding. In a second memorial, dated 15 April 1846, signed by twenty fishermen, the commissioners were informed that while they had gladly availed of the engineer's plans, the size of the project was much larger than they had originally envisaged. Furthermore, unless government aid was forthcoming, the pier would never be finished. They were also aware that, because of the distress caused by the potato famine, parliament had allotted a sum of £50,000 to encourage and promote the deep-sea fisheries as a source of employment and food.[63] Andrew Furlong informed the commissioners that the people in the area were in want and badly needed employment. If they could not provide work, the men would have to seek it elsewhere. In the meantime, 'an extraordinary effort' was made in the autumn of 1846 to raise £70. In response, the committee received £210, but were informed at the same time that the funds for piers and harbours had been depleted. As no further assistance was forthcoming, the Board recommended that in order to prevent further storm damage, they should do their best to finish off the work already completed 'in a round and sloping form.'[64]

The fishermen had no choice but to comply. However, on 20 November 1846, seven days after their work was completed, disaster struck again. During a severe gale, a 500-ton ship laden with copper on its way from Valparaiso to Liverpool had sought shelter at the pier. A combination of high winds and high tides succeeded in wrenching the ship from its post, taking part of the pier wall with it and exposing it to further damage. The accident caused a breach 60 feet long, 54 feet wide and 9 feet deep in the pier and upwards of 10 feet of the parapet wall had been destroyed. Several stones were left lying level with the beach.[65]

The engineer Barry Gibbons felt vindicated. According to his report on the accident, the fishermen had laboured 'under an extraordinary misconception ... fancying because the old pier, which is a rude structure has stood for many years, that a somewhat similar construction and material would answer for an extension seaward.' Although he recognised that the fishermen both needed and deserved assistance, he could not recommend that more money be spent using similar material, as it would be a mere question of time before another storm washed the structure away again.[66] However, Andrew Furlong persisted in his efforts to acquire further funding. At a time 'of unprecedented want' when the people in the district were 'in a most deplorable state', it had cost £40 to secure the pier temporarily. The situation was, that up to 31 December 1846, over

63 NAI, OPW8 210/2 doc. 24, memorial 15 April 1846, fishermen and other inhabitants of Kilmore parish to OPW; *Appendix to sixteenth report commissioners of public works Ireland, 1847–8,* HC [983], xxxvii, pp 28–9. **64** NAI, OPW8 210/2 docs 36, 39, 44, letters 26 September 1846, 20 October 1846, 23 November 1846, Furlong to OPW. **65** NAI, OPW8 210/2 doc. 44, letter 23 November 1846, Furlong to OPW. **66** Ibid., doc. 48, letter 4 December 1846, Gibbons to OPW.

£1,000 had been spent and the work remained unfinished. He continued to write to the commissioners forwarding 'many applications on the part of these poor men', but often not even receiving a reply.[67]

Fortunately, during this period, work was available elsewhere in the neighbouring townland of Ballyteigue. In 1843, the proprietors of the Lough had submitted a memorial to the Office of Public Works regarding the embankment and draining of the district. Until then, no work on such a scale had ever been undertaken in Ireland. Over 3,000 statute acres were to be reclaimed and the estimated cost of the project was put at £15,650.[68] During the summer of 1848 there was an average of 600 men daily employed on the site.[69] While there were occasional set backs because of bad weather and flooding, much of the work was completed by 1855.[70]

In August 1847 Furlong's persistence with regard to the continuation of the work on the pier had finally paid off. James Farrell, admiralty engineer and county surveyor for Wexford, visited Crossfarnogue and in liaison with the engineer Barry Gibbons, drew up new plans and estimates.[71] In the meantime, the earl of Courtown and Wexford MP, H.K. Morgan of Johnstown Castle, Wexford, lobbied the authorities for 'public relief for the support of the destitute poor' in the parish of Kilmore.[72] Finally, in July 1848, the Admiralty, Harbour and Railway Department in London, advised the Board of Works in Dublin that the project could proceed.[73] The total estimated costs of construction and approach road amounted to £6,000, with £4,000 to be supplied by way of grant and £2,000 by way of loan. The grand jury was made responsible to strike a rate or 'cess' on the inhabitants of all the townlands in the parish of Kilmore to repay the loan.[74]

Work commenced on 24 March 1849. This was the first major reconstruction of the original pier. A stonemason named Patrick Maher was put in charge. On this occasion stones were sourced outside the locality. Machinery was purchased in Wexford and transferred to Fethard-on-Sea where quarrying of suitable material took place.[75] The stones were then transferred to Crossfarnogue by boat. Work depended very much on the weather and when it was fine, boats were kept going day and night.[76] Two years later, the renovations were complete and the parish of Kilmore had:

67 NAI, OPW8 210/3 doc. 62, letter 27 February 1847, Furlong to OPW. **68** *Second annual report commissioners for promoting drainage of land in Ireland and improvement of navigation,* 1844, HC [559], xxx, pp 2–3; John Power, 'A lake that stretched to Bridgetown' in *KPJ* (1975–76), pp 24–5. **69** *Appendix to seventeenth report ... public works Ireland,* 1849, HC [1098], xxiii, pp. 251–2. **70** *Appendix to twenty-second report ... public works Ireland,* 1854, HC [1820], xx, pp 138–9; *Appendix to twenty-third report ... public works Ireland,* 1854–5, HC [1929], xvi, pp 144–5. **71** NAI, OPW8 210/3 doc. 66, letter 26 August 1847, Bruen to OPW. **72** Ibid., doc. 68, letter 20 October 1847, Morgan to OPW. **73** Ibid., doc. 70, letter 22 July 1848, Admiralty, Harbour and Railway Department to OPW. **74** Ibid., doc. 71, declaration OPW Fisheries, 9 Victoria, c. 3, & 10 and 11 Victoria, C. 75. Pier and approach at Kilmore in the County of Wexford, 5 August 1848. **75** Ibid., doc. 75, letter 24 March 1848, Maher to OPW. **76** NAI, OPW8 210/4 doc.

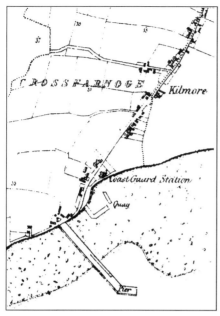

Figure 4 New extension to pier at
Crossfarnogue in 1851

A substantial stone pier, nearly 800 feet in length, and extending into seven
feet of water at low-water springs. Owing to favourable circumstances we
were enabled to extend this pier considerably beyond what was designed,
and it is already found to be so important, not only for the use of the fisheries, but for the more general purposes of a safety harbour, that a much
greater extension is loudly called for. Such an extension would no doubt
be of great value to the coasting and general trade, from the want of such
shelter on this dangerous coast, and the board is anxious to afford every
assistance in its power to so useful a project; but it requires greater expenditure than the present acts enable them to recommend[77] (Figure 4).

While the value of having a further extension to the pier was recognised and
the fishermen of the parish now had far better facilities than they had had previously, in the post-Famine period the fishing industry was in a state of depres-
sion.[78] As there was no local curing establishment in the immediate area and as
transport was expensive, it was very difficult for the fishermen to dispose of their
catch. A small proportion of what could not be used for personal consumption
was used either as manure, given to pigs or just thrown along the shore by the
fishermen and their wives.[79]

89, letter 16 June 1849, Maher to Gibbons.   **77** *Appendix to twentieth report … public works
Ireland,* 1852–3, HC [1569], xli, pp 47–48.   **78** *Appendix to nineteenth report … public works
Ireland,* 1851, HC [1414], xxv, p. 161.   **79** *Report commissioners of fisheries Ireland,* 1853, HC1854,
[1819], xx, pp. 21–7.

As a result of the recession there was also a reduction in the number of boats and men employed in the industry. In 1864, there were about 50 boats (a few weighing 20 tons) and cobles (small flat-bottomed boats with lugsails on a raking mast) and between 100 and 140 men and boys working off Crossfarnogue pier. At a government inquiry held in Wexford that same year, the Revd M. Vicary reported that 'the fishermen of Kilmore are excellent honest men, but they know nothing of that magnificent net [pilchard net] which is used on the coast of Cornwall. They are fishing now in the same way as their ancestors did 600 years ago.'[80] Occasionally, when pilchards and mackerel broke upon the shore, the fishermen surrounded them with a small seine (a large fishing net made to hang vertically in the water by weights at the lower edge and floats at the top) but generally they were still fishing with hand-lines as opposed to long-lines, which the fishermen were considered too 'primitive' to use.[81]

The commissioners found it difficult to analyse why the fishing industry had declined in the area. In his evidence the Revd Vicary stated that since the estuary at Ballyteige had been reclaimed from the sea, bait was scarce and had to be acquired in Wexford. He thought that the situation might improve if a time limit in which the trawlers could operate was implemented. If small lobsters were returned to the water, if the oyster beds, which were 'mines of wealth', could be developed and if the pier at Crossfarnogue was finished, it would encourage the fishermen to use larger boats. He concluded by saying that larger boats would give the fishermen increased access to this 'magnificent locality for the feeding of fish.'[82] Throughout the century, whenever there was a shortage of fish, it was not unusual to blame the large trawlers for depletion of stocks. Mr Vicary reported that he 'saw a man who stated that he had seen the decks covered to the extent of six inches, with ... spawn.'[83] When fish were scarce, it was tempting for the fishermen to lift smaller crabs and lobsters. With regard to oysters, while they were harvested from seas elsewhere along the Wexford coast, the fishermen of the parish of Kilmore had never fished for them, although occasionally they came up on their hooks.[84] Throughout the inquiry, while it was recognised that the seas around southeast Wexford were important where the fishing industry was concerned, after all the effort and expense, what the fishermen actually had at Crossfarnogue was a little tidal harbour, dry at half tide, offering insufficient shelter even for the smaller boats.[85]

TOURISM, EDUCATION AND RELIGION

However, in spite of these drawbacks where the fishing industry was concerned, the harbour area, which had by then become known as 'The Quay', had devel-

---

80 *Minutes of evidence royal commission to inquire into sea fisheries of UK*, 1866, HC [3596–1], xviii, pp 875–6. **81** Ibid. **82** Ibid. **83** Ibid. **84** Ibid. **85** *Report inspectors of Irish fisheries*, 1885,

oped a tourism industry. *Bassett's guide and directory, Wexford,* published in 1885
stated that 'The Quay, as it is proudly referred to by the residents' could offer
visitors a hotel, comfortably furnished 'lodges', and interesting scenery. In addition to the harbour area, tourist attractions included Ballyteigue Bay, with its
miles of sand dunes, and historic Ballyteigue Castle. There was also St Patrick's
Bridge, the narrow outcrop of rocks stretching to the Saltee Islands and upon
which, at low tide, adventurous individuals could walk out a mile or so from
the shore. But the greatest attraction of all was the Saltee Islands, which were
popular with picnic parties. When visitors became stranded in bad weather, the
tenants of the Great Saltee, Patrick and John Parle fed the travellers and provided them with plenty of clean straw in a barn where they could rest overnight.
The Little Saltee, which was a favourite haunt for sea birds, attracted enthusiastic bird watchers.

In addition to providing employment for farmers and fisherman, the Quay
now had a post office and provided work for those involved in trades and in business. Members of the community included four bakers and flour dealers, two boot
makers, two carpenters, four coal merchants, two dressmakers, one grocer, two
grocer and spirit dealers, two post-car owners, three smiths, a draper, a tailor and
a miller who lived in Chapel. Of the 17 boat owners listed in the directory (a
reduction of nine since 1843), five were involved either in business, trade or farming in the immediate area. Other members of the community included two
national schoolteachers, Fanny and Kate Walsh. The nearest barracks of the Royal
Irish Constabulary was located some miles away in Bridgetown.[86]

Prior to the establishment of the national school system in 1831, there were
several schools in the parish of Kilmore. The majority, having evolved from the
old hedge schools, consisted of mud-walled thatched cabins. The quality of the
teaching depended on the educational qualifications of the masters and mistresses,
many of whom were barely literate themselves. Thomas Egan, a member of the
Established Church, was in charge of one of the two schools in Mulrankin. He
was paid £30 per annum. There were 48 pupils in this school, six of whom were
Protestants. Five other children of the Protestant faith attended school elsewhere
in the parish. While the Roman Catholic schools in Mulrankin, Kilmore Upper,
Kilturk and Tomhaggart consisted of small mud-walled, thatched cabins; the
Mulrankin school was built with stone and brick, had a slated roof and was lime-
washed. The nearest school to Crossfarnogue and Nemestown, which was run
by Michael Harpur, was in Chapel. One hundred pupils who collectively paid
£11 per annum for their tuition attended this school.[87]

Over the years, while many of the schools that had been in existence in the
early part of the nineteenth century, did not survive, others gradually applied to

HC 1886 [C.4809], xv, p. 14. **86** *Bassett's guide and directory, Wexford* (Dublin, 1885), pp 167,
180–3. **87** *Appendix to second report royal commission on Irish education (parochial abstracts), 1826–7,*
HC [12], xii, pp 808–13.

become integrated into the national school system. As no national school had been established in the Quay, the children attended other schools in the area. The infant boys attended the nearby boys' national school in Chapel. However, it was felt that as there was only one master in attendance, the younger boys were not being given adequate instruction. All the girls on the other hand, both infant and older, had to walk about two miles to their school in Kilturk and when weather was bad, attendance there was poor.[88] In the early 1900s the parish priest of Kilmore, Father Mark O'Gorman, informed the Department of Education that existing arrangements regarding schooling throughout the parish were unsatisfactory.[89]

The Sisters of St John of God had been invited to Kilmore Upper by Father O'Gorman in 1898 and in addition to teaching had also became involved in training girls in domestic work and lace-making. The nuns were highly thought of and considered to be very successful in their teaching methods.[90] Following consultations with the Department, the Sisters were put in charge of Chapel and Kilmore Upper boys' schools which became schools for older girls and infants of both sexes and Kilturk girls' school became a boys' school. Chapel was one and three-quarter miles from Kilmore Upper and the sisters could be seen travelling to and fro every day in their pony and cart. The broad result of the changes meant that the infant boys of the district were taught separately from the older boys and the infant girls lived comparatively close to their schools. In the words of District Inspector James Dickie, the long walks to school among the senior pupils now fell to the boys instead of the girls, and this was 'a very desirable thing.'[91]

Up to 1875, while the material and educational needs of the community at the Quay were being met from various sources within their own locality, something was lacking. In order to fulfil their religious duties, the Catholic inhabitants had to walk three miles to the chapel at Kilmore Upper on a road 'which in winter is kept in almost constant slop by the droppings of seaweed which is carted along it.'[92] In 1871, the tenants 'at the Quay of Kilmore' had written to the landlord, Henry Bruen, requesting a site for a chapel near the Quay. They also informed him, that 'the Quay people are at great disadvantage in letting their homes to bathers in summer, who are much kept away by the inconvenience of having so far to go on Sundays to Chapel.' Their argument was, that not only would a chapel in the area of the Quay be more convenient, it would also make the place more attractive and be good for business. The visitors, who

88 NAI, ED9/22715, letter 2 December 1911, District Inspector J. Dickie to Secretary, Department of Education. **89** NAI, ED9/22715, letter 13 November 1911, Revd M. O'Gorman, to Secretary, Department of Education. **90** John Scally, *To speed on angels' wings – the story of the sisters of St John of God* (Dublin, 1995), p. 55. **91** NAI, ED9/22715, letter 2 December 1911, Dickie to Secretary, Department of Education. **92** Maritime Museum, Kilmore Quay, copy letter 12 December 1871, Tenants at the Quay of Kilmore to Henry Bruen.

Figure 5 An early picture of St Peter's Church at Kilmore Quay. Note the absence of a
church bell which was not fitted until 1902. (Courtesy of Editor, *Kilmore Parish Journal*.)

had previously stayed in the 'trim white cottages' in the upper village, would in
future be able to stay in the Quay.[93] The chapel was built on a rocky site on a
hill overlooking Ballyteigue Bay. With the consent of the occupier, Johnny
Power, a lease of 999 years at a nominal rent was given to the then parish priest
of Kilmore, Archdeacon Meyler. The new chapel, appropriately dedicated to St
Peter the fisherman, was opened for worship in 1875[94] (Figure 5). The Catholic
community at the Quay were now in a position to have most of their needs satisfied within their own immediate area. Members of the Church of Ireland community attended services at Ballyhealy, three miles away.[95]

FURTHER DEVELOPMENT

While maintenance on the pier at Kilmore Quay was ongoing, by the mid 1880s
it was recognised that in order to reach its potential, further major work was
needed. Following a successful application the sum of £6,375 was made available from the Irish Church Fund to carry out works on the harbour by way of

93 Ibid. **94** *The People*, 23 October 1875. **95** *Bassett's Guide*, p. 182.

Figure 6 Showing two of the boats which were built in 1897 as a result of the storm. The one in the forefront is f.v. 'Saltee' for John Walsh, the one behind it is f.v. 'Lady Maurice' for Richard Rochford. (Courtesy of Editor, *Kilmore Parish Journal*.)

a grant and a further £2,125 by way of loan.[96] Throughout 1886–9 as work on the pier progressed, the men continued fishing. However, the weather off the coast during 1886 was the worst for fifty years and the industry was still in a state of decline. When fish were available, it was the middlemen here, as elsewhere, who took the profit. A fish caught in Kilmore Quay was sold to a middleman for 3*d*. who in turn sold it in Wexford town for 2*s*. In order to avoid waste the fishermen resorted to salting cod for their own use.[97]

On the 14 October 1896 the *Wexford Independent* reported that the worst storm in twenty-five years had swept over the south of Ireland for three to four days, causing considerable damage. The area around Kilmore Quay appeared to have received the brunt of the gales. When the storm subsided, the centre portion of the pier and storm wall had been almost completely washed away and almost 200 tons of stone were scattered over the pier. A large portion of the corner of the concrete breakwater was also badly damaged. Many ships broke from their moorings and those that were neither lost nor sunk were washed up either in Nemestown, on St Patrick's Bridge or on the nearby road. In addition to the fishermen now being out of work, many homes were severely damaged. In order to relieve distress in the area a committee was formed to make an appeal to the public in order to raise funds to repair existing boats and to purchase new ones[98] (Figure 6).

96 *Report inspectors ... Irish fisheries,* 1885, HC 1886, [C.4809], xv, p. 10.   **97** *Report inspectors ... Irish fisheries,* 1886, HC 1887 [C.5035], xxi, pp 13–14.   **98** *Wexford Independent,* 14 October

For some years after the storm damage of 1896, the pier at Kilmore Quay was in a poor state of repair and this is reflected in the number of boats returned in the 'Crossfarnogue Port' shipping return for 1901[99] (Table 4).

Table 4 'Crossfarnogue Port' Shipping Return 1901.

Type	Name	Captain/owner	Men
Fishing boat	–	Nicholas White	3
Fishing boat	–	Richard Rochford	3
Pleasure boat	–	James White	2
Pleasure boat	–	Thomas Gruar?	2
Fishing boat	*Hare*	Richard Rochford	3
Fishing boat	–	James Kehoe	3
Fishing boat	–	John Kehoe	3
Fishing boat	*Eliza and John*	Patrick Parle	3

Only six boats and eighteen men were then officially employed in the fishing industry and of the eight boats recorded, only one, the *Eliza and John,* was listed with its registration number (121) and tonnage (2.5). The records also show that a vessel named *Hare* was still owned by a member of the Rochford family who had appeared on the 1843 list and that a member of the Parle family was also still involved in the fishing industry. Unfortunately, the names of the other boats were not listed. In the 1830s when Thomas Devereux of Nemestown was lamenting the fact that there was insufficient shelter for boats at the pier at Crossfarnogue, there were then 73 boats of varying size and 384 men fishing in the parish of Kilmore. Now seventy years later, there were only four boats and 12 men from the parish employed in the industry.

However, in spite of their difficulties, the fishermen were not ready to give up their plans to improve the pier and lobbied their local member of parliament for support. Following representations made in Westminster in July 1900 by Sir Thomas Esmonde and his subsequent meeting with Mr Horace Plunkett, vice-president of the Department of Agriculture in Dublin, in August 1901, the pier was examined and declared unfit for the purpose for which it was constructed.[1] At this stage, in keeping with changes brought about by the Local Government (Ireland) Act of 1898, responsibility for the pier and harbour had passed to Wexford County Council. At a meeting held at their offices in Wexford on 19 April 1902, after much debate it was agreed that the Council would pay £500 towards the cost of repairs of the pier at Kilmore Quay and that a further £500 would be provided by the Department of Agriculture.[2]

1896. **99** *Census,* 1901. **1** NAI, OPW5 7663/11, ref. 9661/00, report 7 March 1901; *The People,* 10 May 1902. **2** *The People,* 10 May 1902.

Figure 7 The oldest cottage in Nemestown now thatched with reeds and owned by the Molloy family. (Courtesy of Editor, *Kilmore Parish Journal.*)

KILMORE QUAY IN 1901

Throughout the late nineteenth and early twentieth centuries, parts of southeast Wexford and Kilmore Quay in particular were admired for their neat white-washed cottages (Figure 7) Many of these no longer exist, but in 1901, of the 25 houses returned for Kilmore Quay in the census of that year, seven (28 per cent) were substantially built with durable materials. These included two public houses, one owned by Nicholas White and the second by Ellen Monaghan. The remaining 18 (72 per cent) were mud-walled, thatched-roofed dwellings. The offices or outhouses consisted of ten stables, six pig houses, five barns, four sheds, three each of coach houses, fowl houses and potato houses and one boiling house. These buildings indicate that much of the population still had a dependence on agriculture. Of the 52 members of the community who were gainfully employed, the majority, 37 per cent worked in agriculture. Another 20 per cent were employed in domestic service, 13 per cent in the fishing industry, 12 per cent as general labourers and 8 per cent as clerks. Of the remaining 10 per cent of the working population, there was one shopkeeper, one baker, one dressmaker, one grocer and one postmistress.

Of the 12 households returned for the townland of Crossfarnogue in 1901, in addition to those employed in agriculture, domestic service and fishing, there was also one sailor. As can be seen from Table 2 the majority of the population living in the area at the time were returned for Nemestown. In addition to those employed in the usual areas, there were three dressmakers, two carpenters, one grocer/draper, one grocer's assistant, one post messenger and a road contractor.

In keeping with the area's maritime tradition, Nemestown was also home to four boatmen, three coast guards, and one 'Active Chief Officer', all working with Her Majesty's Coast Guard. And finally, there was the harbour master, Edward Flaherty.[3] The services mentioned above compare very favourably with those listed in *Bassett's guide* of 1885.

Repairs and maintenance continued on the pier and the harbour at Kilmore Quay throughout the twentieth century. However, after some improvements in the 1970s, and after years of local pressure (commencing with the formation of a fishermen's co-operative in 1955), support from the European Regional Development Fund, the then Department of the Marine and Wexford County Council, a new harbour, part of the ongoing development of the fishing industry was officially opened in May 1997 at a cost of £3.5 million.[4] This development, the biggest undertaking since the main harbour was first built in the 1840s and described as 'a dream fulfilled', took place *circa* 200 years after the men of the parish of Kilmore had first moored their boats at the small pier at Crossfarnogue in the shelter of Forlorn Point. In 2002, in addition to 25 small trawlers which fish mostly for crabs and lobsters and eight passenger-carrying angling boats, the main fleet at Kilmore Quay consists of 15 large beam trawlers, 12 small beam trawlers and six conventional trawlers, which use traditional nets. A newly constructed marina can accommodate 60 assorted yachts and pleasure boats and over the last two seasons (summer 2001 and 2002) up to 1,000 craft have visited the Quay, with 10 per cent coming from continental Europe and the rest coming from England and Northern Ireland.[5]

CONCLUSION

In 1807 Robert Fraser in his *Statistical Survey*, had recommended that there could 'hardly be any greater permanent improvement made on this part of the [Bruen] estate, than to erect a sufficient harbour at this place [Crossfarnogue], and to lay out a village on a liberal plan.'[6] Clusters of dwellings around a creek do not necessarily form the nucleus of a village. However, where Kilmore Quay was concerned, a combination of geographic and external forces determined that a village would develop at Crossfarnogue and Nemestown during the nineteenth century at a faster rate than it might otherwise have done under more normal circumstances. Humans' basic needs revolve around food and shelter and the landscape in which people live determines their lifestyle. Throughout the nineteenth century the majority of the population of the parish of Kilmore depended on the land for their livelihood and those who fished represented only a small

3 *Census*, 1901.   4 *Wexford People*, 4 June 1997.   5 Conversation with Edward Barrett, harbour master, Kilmore Quay, Co. Wexford, 24 October 2002.   6 Fraser, *Statistical survey*, p. 23.

Figure 8 Sculpture by Ciarán O'Brien,
Mulrankin of grieving figures at
Crossfarnogue, overlooking Forlorn Point.
(Photograph Rita Edwards.)

section of the community. For them, the sea not only provided an alternative food source, but also provided additional family income. During the Famine years, the want of sufficient food, the harbour works and the Ballyteigue drainage scheme encouraged some families to migrate towards the coast, where the population in the townlands of Crossfarnogue and Nemestown reached its peak at 497 in 1861. With regard to emigration, where southeast Wexford was concerned, many travelled to America and Canada, where they hoped for a better life for themselves and their families. Newfoundland (*Talamh an Éisc*, land of fish) is mentioned in many songs traditionally associated with county Wexford.[7]

While it appears that plans for a village, as recommended by Fraser in 1807 were never drawn up, the village that became known as Kilmore Quay, developed organically on the townlands of Crossfarnogue and Nemestown northeast of a small fishing pier lying in the shelter of Forlorn Point. The village is unusual insofar as its location was derived from the existence of a pier. Other villages grew up around a chapel, a crossroads or a bridge, but Kilmore Quay, situated on a peninsula with a consequent limited hinterland, owes its very origin to the pier. The account of the development of the pier is in essence, the story of the evolution of the village. Kilmore Quay continues to prosper and in 1996 its population stood at 406.[8]

Traditionally, fishing has been a male occupation. But, while the men fished what did the women do besides looking after their families? History has shown that they were involved in cottage crafts and industries, caring for animals, gardening and working on the land. All these subsidiary activities also contributed substantially to the family income. Fishing, however, is a dangerous occupation and those who make their living from the sea in Kilmore Quay today require the same perseverance and determination that was portrayed by their ancestors. At the same time, the fishing community does not live in isolation and what-

7 Ó Muirithe and Nuttall, *Folklore of county Wexford*, pp 152, 149–50. **8** *Census*, 1996.

ever affects them affects the community as a whole. In times of worry and tragedy people come together to support and comfort each other. In June 2001 the Kilmore Quay Millennium Committee, proud of its maritime tradition, commissioned a memorial trail and garden in honour of all those who have lost their lives at sea. A plinth contains the names of many who have died and the names of many others who bravely gave their lives in rescue and attempted rescues. The central feature of the garden is a stone sculpture of two grieving figures, one male and the other female, looking out to sea over Forlorn Point and supporting each other. The trail, while having a distinctly nautical character, encompasses 'the universal experience of loss and the journey to recovery.' An inscription reads, 'Remembering the past and living the present, we now look to the future with hope'[9] (Figure 8).

9 Father Jim Cogley, 'Millennium memorial project', in *KPJ* (1999–2000), pp 49–50.

Cloone, county Leitrim: a monastery village, 1798–1801

BRÍD HESLIN

Today the village of Cloone in south Leitrim is compact, neat and attractive. As one travels north through the village, a stone wall on the right-hand side separates a field, locally called the camp field, from the street.[1] This field-name appears on Ordnance Survey maps of the area and begs the question 'who camped there?' The answer is found in the historical episode for which Cloone is famous – the arrival and departure of the French insurgents in 1798 *en route* to Ballinamuck, county Longford, and to final defeat. But the story of Cloone cannot be written by reference to national history only, it involves uncovering 'the often secret life of small people who live among small things'[2] and can be done only partially and with the aid of surviving sources.

A topographical map of Leitrim shows Cloone located on a low hill[3] and as the names of some of the surrounding townlands – Drumdarkan, Drumharkan, Drummeen, Drumhallagh, Drumlaggagh, Drumbore and Drumshanbo – indicate, high ground is never far away. As *drum,* meaning a ridge and *cluain,* meaning a meadow are some of the more common toponyms associated with ecclesiastical sites, they alert the local historian to the possible presence of a monastery in the locality in the past. The traveller to the village will notice a small amount of natural woodland south-west of Cloone, while nearer the village, the northern end of a small esker left by the retreating ice thousands of years ago, tapers to the road and gives Esker townland its name.

A landscape tells the story of the relationship between time, space and human habitation. In this study the focus is on the human habitation aspect of the village during the nineteenth century – 1798 to 1901. But even a nineteenth-century study requires a contextual reference to Cloone's famous abbey, founded in 570, and to its saintly founder, Cruimhther (or Priest) Fhraoch, whose name, anglicised to Criffer Ree, lives on in the name of a holy well near the village.[4] Bishop McNamee referred to a status which Cloone still enjoyed when he wrote in 1954 but which has since been lost,

The author acknowledges the assistance of Leitrim County Library staff in providing sources for this essay. **1** Local folklore holds that the wall was built during the Great Famine of the late 1840s. **2** Patrick J. Corish, *The Catholic community in the seventeenth and eighteenth centuries* (Dublin, 1981), p. 2. **3** Lewis's *Atlas,* County Leitrim, 1837 (not paginated). **4** James J. McNamee, *History of the diocese of Ardagh* (Dublin, 1954), p. 592. Many cures were attributed to the water from this well.

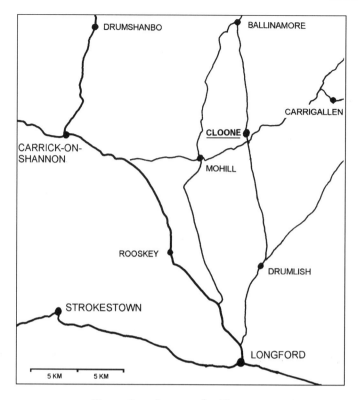

Figure 1 Location map for Cloone.

It is still Cluain-Conmaicne to the postal authorities, the name by which it was long distinguished as one of the six most celebrated *Cluains* in Ireland – Cluain-Mac-Nois, Cluain Iorard (Clonard), Cluain Uamha (Cloyne), Cluain Fearta (Clonfert), Cluain Eois (Clones) and Cluain-Conmaicne, each of them the site of a famous abbey, associated with the memory of a saintly founder in the golden age of Irish monasticism.[5]

It is argued that the element *cluain* predates ecclesiastical settlements and so indicates that the early Christian churches were attracted to areas which already had settled communities.[6] Therefore it is possible that Cloone was a settled community before St Fraoch established a monastery there, one which may not have survived the Norman invasion nor have been transformed into an Augustinian monastery, as was the nearby abbey of Mohill.[7] In 1994 the most tangible evidence of the monastery was discovered as workmen repaired the wall of St James's Church of Ireland building. And a fragment of an Irish high cross of a hitherto unknown type was discovered, as were other related pieces in the same style, in the grounds of the former Catholic church of St Mary.[8] The base of this cross, now referred to as the Leitrim High Cross, rests in Cloone cemetery. The fragments from St James's bear the outline of figures thought to represent St Fraoch and St Patrick and are now to be seen beside the entrance gates to the cemetery in the village.

The Down Survey map of Cloone parish, from *c.*1659, shows two churches in Cloone. It is possible that after the Reformation a Protestant church was built incorporating part of the walls of the monastery, but Lewis writing in 1837, noted that those parts were entirely removed with the building of a new Protestant church in 1821 – 'a plain edifice built in early English style'.[9] There was also a Catholic chapel in the village in 1837; it was extended and rededicated in 1886.[10] The building of the chapel resulted from the relaxation of the penal laws and the modernising thrust of the Catholic Church in the period 1770 to 1840 when the population of Ireland increased rapidly and a network of Catholic parishes with their suite of features – church, graveyard and some land to support the clergy – was established.[11] Placenames in the surrounding countryside, as per the first edition Ordnance Survey map, point to land ownership by the church locally. Cloone's Grange, to the south of Cloone townland, indicates association with a monastery and local folklore associates this one with the local monastery of Criffer Ree. The Glebe of Drumharkan, also bordering Cloone townland to the south, points to a church association in former times. Consisting of land farmed (or leased out) by the clergy, the Glebe may have been created by parishioners donating small portions of land which in time amounted to 323 acres and generated tithes for the incumbent of the Established Church, who was without a habitable glebe-house there in 1837.[12]

CLOONE VILLAGE – ITS LOCATION AND PEOPLE

Cloone is shown on the Down Survey map as a townland of 274 acres plantation measure or approximately 444 statute acres, with 'Thomas Loyd Eng: prot' [English Protestant] as proprietor.[13] The village lies near the centre of the town-

McNamee, *History of Ardagh*, p. 592. **8** Christine Grant, 'New Leitrim High Cross' in *Archaeology Ireland*, viii, no. 4, 1994, p. 17. **9** Lewis, *Dictionary*, i, p. 379. **10** *Leitrim Advertiser*, 18 November 1886, p. 3, c. 3–5. **11** Kevin Whelan, 'The Catholic parish, the Catholic chapel and village development in Ireland' in *Irish Geography*, 16, 1983, pp 1–15. **12** Lewis, *Dictionary*, i, p. 379. A new glebe house was built in 1877. **13** The Ordnance Survey recorded 392 acres in the townland in 1836, indicating that fifty acres may have been included in a bordering townland since the 1650s.

land and of the parish of the same name and occupied thirteen statute acres in
the 1800s. There were 279 people living in 59 houses recorded in the village in
1821, the earliest date for which data is available and the largest recorded number
of inhabitants and houses in any published census to date.[14] John O'Donovan,
placenames expert with the Ordnance Survey, was short on compliments when
he passed through Cloone in 1836: he stated, 'this is but a poor miserable village, a road from Mohill to Ballinamore passes through it'.[15] Both hinterland and
village were given a better report by Lewis the following year: he stated that
limestone was quarried for agricultural and other purposes, while the nine fairs
held annually in the village were well attended and were among the principal
in the county for cattle.[16] The first edition Ordnance Survey map (1836) shows
a Catholic and a Protestant church located in the village, along with a police
barracks, two schools and a number of private and public residences located along
a single linear street.

The Census of 1841 lists 35 inhabited houses in the village. These were occupied by 38 families. Two were 'first-class' houses – with stone walls and slated
roof. The eight 'second-class', stone-wall, houses on the street had from five to
nine rooms while the majority – 22 – were of third-class standard, i.e., mud-walled
with two to four rooms and with windows. The remaining three houses were
mud-walled and consisted of one room with a window.[17] Cloone, therefore, in
the Famine decade, was largely a village of small mud houses, probably with
thatched roofs. By the late 1840s there was also a courthouse in which the petty
sessions were held every second Wednesday.[18] When Griffith's Valuation was carried out in Leitrim in 1856 there were 24 occupied houses as well as a range of
public houses, including one shop, which had not existed during the Famine.[19]
By 1901 the number of occupied houses had decreased to 20 and the occupants
numbered 79, a decrease of 39 houses and 200 people over the previous 80 years.
For most of the study period the population trend was downward.

THE MISSING CHAINS, THE LANDLORD'S WELL AND THE LOCAL
SHOEMAKER

While church history may guarantee Cloone a place in the annals, the incident
which earned the village a place in history in more recent times occurred at the
close of the eighteenth century and within the context of a desperate attempt to

14 *Census of Ireland*, HC 1822 (36), xiv, 737 et seq.   15 NAI, Ordnance Survey Name Books,
Co. Leitrim, i, no. 83.   16 Lewis, *Dictionary*, i, p. 379.   17 *Report of the Commissioners appointed
to take the census of Ireland for the year 1841,* [504], HC 1843, xxiv, 1.   18 Thom's *Irish Almanac
and Official Directory* (Dublin,1848), p. 490.   19 NAI, Relief Commission Papers. Various letters from the Secretary of the Cloone Relief Committee to the Central Relief Committee in
Dublin Castle in 1846/47 complained of the lack of a shop in which provisions could be sold.

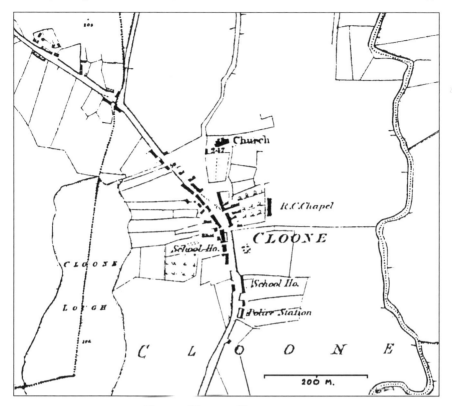

Figure 2 Cloone village, 1836.[20]

follow the lead of France which promised help to those who wanted 'liberty, equality, and fraternity' – the '98 Rebellion.

The involvement of Cloone and its people in this rebellion has been recorded both in history and in folklore. The French, *en route* from Killala to Dublin, arrived in Cloone on the evening of 7 September 1798. They were invited to establish their headquarters in the house of William West 'the wealthiest resident of the locality'.[21] Such an unusual billet for the invading army has been explained as follows: the locals complained to Humbert, the French commander-in-chief, that West was a bad landlord. This led Humbert to consider demolishing West's house, but he was stopped from doing so by the local priests, Father Redehan and Friar Dunne. In gratitude for having his property spared West entertained the French officers and the Catholic clergy in his home in the centre of the village. The army rank and file were 'lavishly entertained by the local residents' in what became known as the 'camp field', where they later

20 *OS County Leitrim, 6″ sheet no. 33,* 1836. 21 Richard Hayes, *The last invasion of Ireland* (Dublin, 1937), p. 108. 22 Ibid.

bivouacked.[22] The food offered included 'half a dozen bullocks – grilled on the iron gates, which had been removed … from the entrance to the Protestant church, while the people came hurrying with bread and potatoes for the hungry men'.[23] Then unfolds the story for which Cloone is most famous – the strange case of the disappearance of the chains and the cannon. There are many versions of this story but they all contain a similar kernel. The wagons carrying the ammunition from Killala were put in West's yard while the French rested after their exhausting journey. The chains were removed from the wagons and placed in safekeeping. The stories of their location vary greatly. Some say that they were put in a well in the landlord's yard, or under the stairs in his house, or under hay in one of his sheds. When the time came to leave Cloone the following morning the chains could not be found, resulting in the soldiers having to push the carts. This exhausting task led them to throw the cannon into Keeldra lake, south of the village so that the approaching English, under General Lake, could not find them. The defeat at Ballinamuck earned West the blame for having the chains taken from their hiding place by a local workman of his – sometimes called Neary, sometimes called Keegan – who became the villain of the tale. The cannon were never found in spite of the many stories they generated and of various attempts to recover them.[24] The entire episode has recently been analysed as a psychological invention. Guy Beiner, who researched the folk-history of 1798 states that 'Souvenirs' or relics as 'objects of memory' are not necessarily concrete items, but may be 'imaginary' or 'remembered' objects surviving vividly in social memory and serving as a focal point to which historical traditions are related.[25]

Beiner sees the narrative of the chains and the cannon as an example of this – a means of shifting the blame for the defeat at Ballinamuck to the story of the stolen chains and an identifiable villain. The story of the defeat could then be remembered without blaming the Irish or the French. Cloone, however, does not hold the monopoly on the tale of the missing chains and cannon: a similar tale is told in relation to Swinford, county Mayo, where the French also spent some time *en route* to Ballinamuck.[26]

Folklore in the south Leitrim and north Longford area still holds that two men were killed attempting to recover the chains from the well in West's yard.[27] However, a newspaper account in 1887 may suggest a basis for this folklore. Three men were repairing a pump in the priest's (formerly West's) yard when one of them, the local shoemaker, John O'Donnell, fell into the well and was killed.[28] It is possible that in folk memory his death is confused with that of men who were supposed to have been killed looking for the missing chains.

23 Ibid., pp 108–9. **24** Attempts to recover the cannon from Keeldra Lake in the late 1990s failed. **25** Guy Beiner, 'To speak of '98: The Social Memory and Vernacular Historiography of Bliain na bhFrancach – the Year of the French' (unpublished thesis) (Dublin, 2001), pp 517–48. **26** Ibid., p. 535. **27** Ibid., p. 533. **28** *Leitrim Advertiser*, 23 June 1887, p.3, c.1.

After its one night of fame and the departure of the French the village disappeared from the national scene and daily life returned to its unobserved state, leaving little on record until the education of the local children was first documented in the early 1820s.

SCHOOLS AND SCHOLARS IN THE CLOONE AREA

In 1824, after the Catholic hierarchy had complained of proselytising by education societies in publicly-funded schools, the Irish Education Inquiry was set up to investigate educational provision throughout the country. The resulting reports clarify where the schools were located, who the teachers were, the quality of school buildings and the number of children in attendance. See Table 1.[29]

Table 1 School provision in Cloone area, 1826.

Parish	Townland	Name of master/ mistress	Religion of teacher	Free or pay	No. of pupils
Cloone	Roculline[30]	John Smyth	Catholic	Free	86 (12 F, 74 M)
	Streamstown	Eliz. Elliott	Protestant	Pay	15
	Cloone	Bernard Hammel	Catholic	Pay	13 (10 F, 3 M)
	Cloone (Latin School)	Owen McMahon	Catholic	Not stated	7
	Cloone (English School)	Patk. Mitchell	Catholic	Pay	60 (13 F, 47 M)

The data in Table 1 indicates that the Cloone area was well served with schools, albeit catering for limited numbers of students, predominantly male. Roculline school, a thatched, clay, rented building, had a Catholic master, John Smyth, earning an income of £7 1s. per annum. He was sponsored by the London Hibernian Society, established in 1804 to diffuse religious knowledge in Ireland, which was reputed to be '… one of the most aggressive of the proselytising bodies'.[31] In nearby Streamstown, Elizabeth Elliott conducted in her own cottage, a school under the aegis of the London Female Hibernian Society and was due 3s. 4d. per quarter from each of her fifteen pupils, making her potentially the highest-paid teacher in the area. Bernard Hammel's school in Cloone was independent; he had no fixed schoolhouse; his income was £2 3s. 4d. Seven pupils, perhaps aspirants to the priesthood, attended a Latin school in Owen McMahon's house. Patrick Mitchell who conducted an English-speaking school in his own thatched, clay house earned £5 from 60 pupils.

29 *Appendix 22 to second report of the commissioners of Irish education inquiry*, HC 1826, xii, 1, pp 1246–47. **30** Spelled 'Racullen' on OS maps. **31** Donald Atkenson, *The Irish educational eexperiment* (London, 1970), p. 82.

The version of the scriptures authorized by the Established Church was read in Smyth's and Elliott's schools but not in the others, even though three of Hammel's pupils were Protestant. It could be construed either that Smyth's school was a proselytising organ of the London Hibernian Society or that Smyth, a Catholic, may have stated that the scripture was read so as not to alienate his sponsors. Alternatively, given that twelve of his pupils were Protestant they may have read the scripture under the tutelage of the local Protestant clergyman. Interestingly, the two schools patronized by the non-Catholic associations generated most income for the teachers. Information on schools in each parish was again collected by the Commissioners of Public Instruction in 1835. Their report showed 26 hedge-schools and five day-schools in the parish of Cloone, together with Sunday schools for religious instruction at Streamstown and at Aughavas. None of the teachers listed in the Inquiry eight years previously were named as teaching in hedge or day schools in the mid-1830s. Data in Table 2 shows the breakdown of pupils by school type.[32]

Table 2 Schools and school attendance in Cloone parish, 1835.

No of schools	Total no. of pupils	No. of pupils in hedge schools	No. of pupils in day schools
31 (26 hedge, 5 day)	1992	1482 (28% female)	510 (37% female)
2 (Sunday schools)	87 (48% female)	not applicable	not applicable

Almost 10 per cent of the total population attended school at this time. The low percentage of female pupils is indicative of the status of females in this peasant society and of the perceived benefits of education for males. However, by the early 1850s, the gender balance in Cloone school, by then under the Scheme of National Instruction, had improved – 40 out of its 93 pupils were female. The teacher's salary was then £10 plus premiums of £12 3s. 4d.[33] All pupils were Catholic and the patron was the Revd C. O'Flynn. The average daily attendance was 40 although over twice that number were enrolled. This disparity may be indicative of the poverty of families, who may not have had the capacity to clothe and provide school requisites for their children as the Famine receded. Child labour may also have prevented school attendance, at least during the spring planting and autumn harvesting seasons. By 1860 there were 97 pupils enrolled with an average attendance remaining around 40. Only five pupils had progressed to Book Four (the highest grade on the curriculum) with 36 studying Book Two and 35 studying Book One, explained perhaps by the low aver-

32 *Second Report of the Commissioners on the state of religious and other public instruction in Ireland,* HC 1835, xxxiv, 1, pp 89a–90a. **33** *Appendix G to Eighteenth Report of Commissioners of National Education in Ireland, 1852–53,* HC xliii, 1, p. 353.

age age of the pupils – 9.7 years. The teacher's salary was £11 5s. 0d. Ten years later Master P.McGowan was paid £24 per annum to teach some of the 64 pupils then attending daily, while the assistant master, P. Healy, was paid a quarter of that amount.[34] The Cloone school finally closed in 1903 when it was decided 'That Cloone mixed NV be struck off the roll of national schools from 28/2/02, after which it has been superseded by the new vested schools Cloone male and female'.[35] The latter building still stands at the northern end of the village. It served as the village's national school until 1963. The lease for it was granted by Guy Lloyd of Croghan House, county Roscommon, possibly the landlord mentioned later in Griffith's Valuation of Cloone.

The inquiry by the Commissioners of Public Instruction in 1835 also collected data on the population and on church attendance. The population of Cloone parish was recorded as 20,279 including 942 Protestants. Church attendance on Sunday and holidays was also recorded. It could be construed that the priests of the parish would not have been very familiar with their flock as only 18 per cent were recorded as attending church on Sundays and holidays. At 16 per cent, the Protestant church had a slightly lower attendance rate than the Catholic church;[36] this rate did not change greatly among the Catholic community until the reforming thrust of the post-Famine church increased Mass attendance countrywide. By the 1880s, attendance at Mass at least during the annual or bi-annual mission, had increased dramatically in Cloone; an item in the local paper in June 1881 noted that ' thousands approached the holy sacraments (between June 4th and 25th) and between 6,000 and 7,000 – 56 per cent-66 percent of the Catholic population of Cloone parish – were present at the closing sermon (by priests of the Passionist order) on Sunday night'.[37]

THE FAMINE DECADE: LETTERS FROM THE GLEBE TO THE CASTLE

With 42 per cent of the population of Cloone village and the entire population of the surrounding townland engaged in agriculture in 1841, the community of 171 persons was very vulnerable to a potato crop failure, a disaster which occurred five years later. The short-term effects of the Great Famine on the population of Cloone village and townland and on Leitrim county generally are shown in Table 3.[38]

These figures, together with contemporary correspondence, give a flavour of the destitution resulting from the loss of the potato crop, particularly in 1847. Writing to the Relief Commissioners in Dublin Castle in September 1846, the Revd Hogg, Protestant clergyman of Cloone Glebe, acting as secretary and treasurer to the Cloone Relief Association, described the parish as being ten miles

---

34 NAI, ED4/236. **35** NAI, ED2/127/48. **36** *First Report of Commissioners on the state of religious and other public instruction in Ireland*, HC 1835, xxxiii, 1, pp 54a–55a. **37** *Leitrim Advertiser*, 26 June 1881, p. 2, c. 7. **38** *Census of Ireland*, 1841 and 1851.

Table 3 Population and number of houses in Cloone village and townland,
1841 and 1851.

Area	Population			Number of houses		
	1841	1851	% decline	1841	1851	% decline
Cloone village	171	123	28	35	25	27
Cloone townland	99	56	43	18	12	33
County Leitrim	155,297	111,915	28	25,896	18,922	19

in circumference but without 'one bread shop or place in which provisions (were) sold'.[39] He urged the establishment of a depot in the parish for the sale of Indian meal and biscuit. To encourage this project he offered

> ... a store house ... and the use of the Cloone Loan Office ... and as there is a large station of police on the spot and a military barrack quite at hand, every facility will be afforded.[40]

This latter offer illustrates the desperate condition of the people from the loss of a second year's potato crop and the threat that this posed to public security. Undeterred by the lack of a favourable answer from the Castle, the Revd Hogg wrote again in December 1846 complaining that the Relief Commissioners had not sanctioned the establishment of a depot in the parish of 23,000 people who still lacked a bread shop. Hogg then informed the Commissioners that with the assistance of the local gentry he had established the Cloone Relief Association for the sale of provisions at cost price to the poor. The members of this association were all members of the Mohill Relief Committee and included George West, JP, Cloone, the Catholic clergy for the parish and the Revd Hogg. The association, established in October 1846, had distributed seventy-nine tons of Indian meal purchased with funds raised from the Cloone Loan Fund by December of that year. The Revd Hogg sought additional funds and permission to purchase provisions from the Government Supply Stores in Longford. Hogg acknowledged the receipt of £60 'which would help alleviate the appalling and unparalleled distress of the district'. In March 1847 he wrote to the Irish Relief Association for funds stating that Cloone was 'one of the most destitute parishes in Ireland, we have a population of 23,000 with only three families of comparative respectability'.[41] By December 1847 Hogg again wrote to the Irish Relief Association stating that '1500 quarts (of soup ... are) gratuitously distributed weekly to 400 people ... it is calculated that 4000 (quarts) will have to be

---

39 NAI, RLFC3/16/26 (5958).   **40** Ibid. The Loan Fund Office was located in the Glebe, possibly in the Revd Hogg's house.   **41** RIA, IRA Papers, 24 Q 29.

distributed weekly to prevent thousands from perishing of starvation'.[42] But beg-
ging letters were insufficient to save the destitute. The long term effects of the
Famine may be gleaned from the continuing decline in population, as indicated
in Table 4.

Table 4 Population of Cloone village and townland, 1841–1901.

Census year	Population of Cloone village	Population of Cloone townland
1841	171	99
1851	123	56
1861	135	61
1871	132	48
1881	112	51
1891	97	44
1901	79	32

The huge decrease in population in Cloone village and townland between 1841
and 1851 – 28 per cent and 44 per cent respectively – demonstrates the vulnerability of the population when the blight struck in 1846 and 1847. Contrary to
what might be expected the largest decrease in the number of families in the village in the intercensal period – 44 per cent – was among those involved with
manufacturing and trades. Those involved in the direction of labour showed the
second highest decrease – 29 per cent – while those involved in agriculture
decreased by 19 per cent. Those families chiefly depending on their own labour
showed the lowest decrease – 12.5 per cent. This is partly explained by the fact
that their numbers increased greatly in the intercensal period rather than that
they were the greatest survivors during the Famine. It is also possible that those
without a permanent tie to the area such as land, departed to the New World
while families who could not afford the fare remained behind.

Folk memory in south Leitrim held stories of distress and deprivation during
the Famine. One account from the immediate Cloone area, contradicts the popular stereotype of the cruel landlord with an abundance of food in his barns
allowing his tenants to die of hunger:

> The time of the famine there was a man living in Cloone Grange called
> Captain White. This man was very wealthy and he had a lot of oatmeal. He
> thought the oatmeal would not last long enough. He started to make it into
> stirabout[43] and the people of the Glebe and Esker came every morning with
> a gallon or bucket for some of the stirabout. Anyone who did a day's work
> for Captain White he gave them half a stone of meal in payment.[44]

42 NAI, RLFC3/2/16/26 (8109). **43** Colloquial term for oatmeal porridge. **44** IFCS., Vol

However, such acts of generosity were not sufficient to save the population of Cloone which was very dependant on the potato. By the time Griffith's valuers arrived in 1856 Cloone and the surrounding area was recovering slightly but temporarily from the massive decrease in population caused by the potato blight in the 1840s.

WHAT THE VALUERS SAW

The Primary Valuation of Ireland was carried out between 1848 and 1864 with the aim of providing a uniform valuation of all property. It was based on the productive capacity of land and the potential rent of buildings. The valuation was carried out in the barony of Mohill in 1856 and continues to provide the most comprehensive and extant survey of people and property for the 1800s. In the Valuation of Tenements 24 occupiers are recorded in Cloone village holding plots varying in area from one rood to nearly two acres.[45] Guy Lloyd was the main stakeholder in both village and townland.[46] There were only two houses of notable value in the village. One was leased by Francis Quinn from Lloyd and valued at £10, while the second was held by Michael Rogan and was valued at £15 – perhaps the house where William West entertained the French officers in 1798. Attached to the house and offices, an acre of land and an orchard were valued at £4. West was also in possession of the courthouse and garden and the two fair-greens in the village. He was entitled to collect the tolls and customs on fair days, evidently a lucrative source of income as they attracted a valuation of £20 in 1856. The Protestant church and yard, on an elevated one-acre site at the northern end of the village, were valued at £22 10s. The Catholic church and yard, for which no area is given, occupied a very different position from that of the Protestant church in Cloone – off the main street and behind a row of private dwelling houses. According to Whelan, such an inferior location is indicative of the attitude of landlords to Catholicism; 'Where the landlord was hostile, the chapel was consigned to the outer fringes of the estate, or to very marginal back street locations in the town.'[47] In addition to West and Lloyd there were three other 'immediate lessors' in Cloone village – Charles Pope, Francis Quinn and Mary Crowther. Their 'house and garden' properties, valued at £2 15s., £2 and 10s. respectively, were occupied by Patrick Rogan, James Connell and Bridget Dekens.

In the townland of Cloone, Guy Lloyd was lessor of land and buildings, valued in total at £217 15s., all of which were tenanted in 1856. George West

---

222, pp 333–4. (Collected from Josephine Heeran.)   **45** Griffith, *Valuation*, Co. Leitrim, parish of Cloone, townland of Cloone.   **46** *Return of owners of land of one acre and upwards in the several counties, counties of cities and counties of towns in Ireland*, HC 1876, lxxx, 61, p. 305. Lloyd is listed as owning 1,262 acres in Leitrim. His address at this time was Croghan, county Roscommon.   **47** Whelan, *The Catholic parish*, p. 5.

appears here as occupier of the largest farm in the townland – 133 acres valued at £58. At the other extreme Mary Ganly occupied 3 roods 10 perches of the herd's (Patrick Hart's) land. If the church building had an inferior position in the village the priest's house did not follow suit – the Revd Charles Flynn occupied house, offices and land in Cloone townland valued at £11. The house and offices, while not highly valued at £4, were nevertheless the highest valued buildings in the townland, while the land – 14 acres, surrounded by West's farm – was valued at £7. Francis Quinn and Charles Pope, minor lessors in the village, may have been residents in the townland at this stage; they are named there as occupiers of houses, offices and land valued at £29 15s. and £18 respectively. There is no indication of subdivision within families in the townland, as evidenced by farms of similar size held by persons of the same surname. This would indicate a successful anti-subdivision stance by local landlords.

The statistics in Table 5 allow a comparison to be made of buildings which existed in 1856 in the village and in the surrounding townland, based on valuation category.[48]

Table 5 Number and percentage of buildings by valuation range in Cloone village and townland in 1856.

Valuation of buildings	Number in Cloone village	Percentage	Number in Cloone townland	Percentage
5s.–£5 19s 11d.	20	83	13	100
£6–£15	4	17	0	0
Total	24	100	13	100

There were no buildings in the higher valuation category (£6 and over) in the rural area of Cloone, while only 17 per cent of the buildings in the village were in this category. At the lower end of the valuation range, 92 per cent of the townland buildings were valued at £1 or less while only 42 per cent of the village buildings were valued at this rate. Therefore, it would seem that the buildings in the townland were of lesser quality than those in the village.

Looking at the housing stock in Cloone in the mid-1850s it is possible to surmise on the reasons why outsiders might visit the village at that time. Those in need of solace might visit their church or clergy. Both Catholics and Protestants came to bury their dead. The farming community came to buy or sell stock or farmyard produce or have their horses shod by the blacksmith James Ryan. His may have been a cosy place for the local men to ceilidhe; some of them may also have read the weekly paper there, to an attentive audience.[49]

---

48 'Buildings' included private dwellings and farm-related buildings. 49 Folklore records this

Some people came to Cloone by official invitation: the Petty sessions were held there every second Wednesday and justice was done according to the standards of the day.

The wide variation in property extent and valuation in the Cloone area, as in many other areas at that time, may have been a cause of friction between various parties. David Fitzpatrick, writing on the causes of rural unrest in nineteenth-century Ireland stated: 'Occupiers of land, despite their common interest in restricting the power of landlords, always threatened to divide into hostile groups according to their share in the inegalitarian distribution of landholdings.'[50] Specifically mentioning Cloone, Fitzpatrick believed that conflict within strata was probably more pervasive than conflict between strata and that jobs, houses, and poteen stills, as well as farms, were sources of competition. The reported outrages within the barony of Mohill have been analysed for 1847 and broadly corroborate Fitzpatrick's statement.[51] The outrage papers for the civil parish of Cloone for the year 1840 have also been analysed and show a wide range of unlawful activities.

Table 6 Type of outrages and occurrence in civil parish of Cloone, 1840.

Type of outrage	Frequency	Type of outrage	Frequency
House burned/damaged	4	Cattle stolen	2
Illegal oath sworn	4	Survey maps burned	1
Money stolen	3	Oatmeal stolen	1
Threatening notice posted	3	Loy irons stolen[52]	1
Attack on person who took farm of evicted tenant	3	Oats burned	1
Animals killed	2		

While the total number of outrages recorded is not large, there may have been other incidents which were not reported for fear of reprisals. Some of the outrages had a significance beyond the obvious material destruction: burning a house was a definite signal to the occupants that they were not wanted in the area. The reasons for such action varied: renting of land from which a tenant had been evicted occurred in the parish on three occasions in 1840. Such action was greatly frowned upon and was interpreted as siding with the landlord against the evicted tenant. A variety of other causes are noted and indicate the complex relation-

practice having taken place in forges in Leitrim in the nineteenth century.   **50** David Fitzpatrick, 'Class, family and rural unrest in nineteenth-century Ireland' in P.J. Drudy (ed.), *Ireland: land, politics, and people* (Cambridge, 1982), p. 41.   **51** Brigid Heslin, 'A study of tenants on three townlands on Lord Leitrim's estate, 1842–1860' (unpublished thesis) p. 72.   **52** A loy was a farm implement used to dig; it consisted of a wooden handle and iron base.

ships between land, tenant and peers at that time. Illegal oaths were administered in situations as variable as compelling a man to make a boundary with his
neighbour to preventing a person from working for Government officials or
landlords. Malicious killing or maiming of animals imposed great hardship on
small tenant farmers and were reported on three occasions in 1840. The less
romantic side of marriage is evidenced in one of the outrage reports: a father-
in-law reported that his son-in-law had stolen a cow in lieu of money which
was promised but never given as his wife's dowry. Anticipating outrages lent
some drama to Cloone life. A report in the local paper of races held in Cloone
on St Patrick's Day 1873 stated that 'forty men of the RIC were on the spot to
preserve the peace whose appearance was the most attractive spectacle of the
day but their services were not required as there were no disturbances'.[53]

But the outrages in Cloone were not without their humorous side. In a report
of the petty sessions in Cloone in November 1884, the local constable in evidence said that on a particular day he heard the beating of a drum near the police
barracks at twelve o'clock mid-day and saw a number of people who refused to
stop drumming but continued past him, while refusing to give the drummer's
name. On the return journey there were between four and six hundred people
in the group who hooted while passing the barracks and stopped at a point above
the village. They looked in the direction of Captain White's place and cheered,
presumably registering their displeasure with him as landlord – a gesture which
the constable felt was calculated to cause terror to her Majesty's subjects.[54] On
being cross-examined, the constable said he would have no objection if the
marchers went in tens or twelves but they were in military array and told the
constable that they were on their way to dig potatoes. The case against the
'potato-diggers' was dismissed.[55]

CLOONE GRAVEYARD – 'ONE OF THE MOST HEALTHY PARTS OF IRELAND'

A very different disturbance arose in Cloone in the 1880s when the condition of
the graveyard occupied much time of the board of guardians, as well as many
column inches in the *Leitrim Advertiser*. The graveyard in Cloone is listed along
with the Protestant church in Griffith's Valuation; together they comprised one
acre. Its use as a graveyard for both Catholic and Protestant families predates the
study period as the dating on headstones there testifies. It was described as being
'a disgraceful place' in August 1888. The gate and portion of the boundary wall
were broken down and pigs and other animals had free access to it.[56] At a meet-

53 *Leitrim Advertiser*, 20 March 1873, p. 2, c. 4. **54** Captain White resided in the Grange,
near Cloone village. **55** *Leitrim Advertiser*, 21 November 1884 p. 2, c. 5. **56** Ibid., 30 August
1888, p.3, c. 3.

ing of the board of guardians in May 1889, notice was directed to be served on the church wardens because of their neglect of the graveyard.[57] On 1 June a deputation from Cloone and Drumreilly, including Messrs Harte, Reynolds, Bohan, Blessing, Nicholl, Feeney, Heslin and Michell, was received by the board. They came to protest at the closing of the graveyard. One of the board, Mr M. Reynolds, said that there were many people in America who would wish to be 'buried in the same ground with their relatives, and they will sacrifice a great deal rather than be separated from their forefathers at time of death'. This statement reflects the forced circumstances in which people left their native area to seek their fortune in foreign lands and wished to return, if only to be buried there.

The inquiry was held in Mohill Workhouse on 2 July 1889 in respect of a representation that the 'Cloone Burial Ground was overcrowded ... and should be closed ... for the protection of public health and public decency and to prevent a violation of the respect due to the remains of deceased persons'.[58] Dr R.J. Dobson, the medical officer for the Mohill District, stated that he believed that there was sufficient room for the burial of 'the people of Cloone having rights there' especially since the population had 'considerably decreased'. Many other witnesses agreed that proper management was the key to eliminating the overcrowding problem. One witness, Patrick Mulholland from Annaghmacoolleen, sanitary officer for Mohill Union (in which Cloone graveyard is located), a position which would have influenced his perception of the problem, stated that he considered the graveyard and its surroundings to be 'in a very sanitary condition'. At a later stage in the hearing he added that 'the graveyard is one of the most healthy parts of Ireland'.[59]

At the board of guardians' meeting of July 1889, it was stated that 'the Board, having carefully considered this matter and having regard to the evidence of the Medical Officer of Health as well as the other witnesses, they do not think it necessary at present to take any further action in the matter'.[60] What was potentially a very divisive issue seems to have been resolved to the satisfaction of all concerned.

The graveyard was again the focus of attention in 1894 when a monument to the memory of the Revd James Keegan, a native of Racullen, near the village of Cloone, was erected there. The monument was in the shape of a Celtic cross '15 ft high surmounted on a base of brown granite (with) two centre blocks of Italian marble'.[61] An inscription in Irish on the headstone reads: *Guidhe ar anam an Athair Seamus Mac Aodagan a fuair bás in aois a chúig bliana triochad. Ba saoi ba file é, ba cara dílis é. Beannacht Dé lena anam.*[62] Father Keegan's place in history transcends the local area in which he grew up. As an active Gaelic speaker, poet

---

57 Ibid., 2 May 1889, p. 2, c. 5.   **58** Ibid., 4 July 1889, p. 2, c. 1.   **59** Ibid., 4 July 1889, p. 2, c. 4.   **60** Ibid., 1 August 1889, p. 2, c. 7.   **61** Ibid., 10 November 1894, p. 2, c. 2.   **62** Translation: 'Pray for the soul of Father James Keegan who died aged 38 years. He was a wise man, a poet, a true friend. God rest his soul'

and translator from the Irish, he ministered for most of his life in the parish of
St Malachy, diocese of St Louis in the United States, and the monument on his
grave in Cloone was donated by his former parishioners in St Malachy's. A pro-
lific writer of poetry, Father Keegan followed the trend of many other emigrants
in choosing themes from Ireland for his ballads. He was also a Gaelic scholar of
note and worked tirelessly for the Gaelic language revival movement. While not
a native Irish speaker he became proficient in the language and collected much
folklore from the Cloone area while still a clerical student in St Patrick's College,
Carlow. This pursuit brought him into contact with the young Douglas Hyde,
who was also a folklorist and Gaelic revivalist and a regular visitor to his relatives in Mohill. A translator of Old- and Middle-Irish texts to English, Father
Keegan was offered the chair of Irish in Washington University but died before
his inauguration.[63]

Within Cloone graveyard also lies the immortal remains of Bishop Flynn,
one of the penal period bishops who was ordained in 1682 and was a priest of
Cloone parish in 1714 when 'he was named at the Carrick-on-Shannon sessions
that year as exercising his functions without having taken the Oath of Abjuration
as required by law'.[64] He died in 1730 and was interred in Cloone. His tomb,
with a defaced inscription was found inside the gate of the old cemetery in
Cloone in the 1950s.[65] Some of the local folklore regarding the defacing of the
tombstone of Bishop Flynn came to light during the 1889 inquiry in respect of
overcrowding in the graveyard. The Revd Cloak, rector, had suggested that the
graveyard should be closed. In reply, J.J. Quinn stated that 'strangers' (referring
to Mr Cloak) should keep silent on the matter 'lest what befell old Atty Deakons,
who attempted to deface the inscription on Dr OFlynn's tombstone, befall him.
He cut off his fingers.'[66] McNamee states that certain locals, who may have
resented the practice of laying the coffins of Catholics on Bishop Flynn's grave
for a brief period as they were being taken into the graveyard for burial, may
have attempted to deface the inscription on his gravestone.[67] Quinn's statement
seems to attribute the defacing to Atty Deakons, a churchwarden in Cloone in
the 1850s.

Priests and bishops were not the only natives whose remains were brought
back to be interred in the 'clay of their forefathers'.[68] The headstone inscriptions
in Cloone graveyard reflect the wanderlust, the spirit of adventure and the sheer
necessity of emigration, particularly in the 1840s and 1850s. Two headstones in
particular bear witness to the pioneering spirit of the locals. In 1892, Francis
Mollaghan of Keonbrook, Carrick-on-Shannon (originally from Cloone parish)
was interred in Cloone graveyard.[69] He had lived and worked in Lowell,

63 Seamus Heslin, 'Fr Keegan of Cloone' in the *Leitrim Guardian*, 2000, p. 20. **64** McNamee,
History of Ardagh, p. 384. **65** Ibid. **66** *Leitrim Advertiser*, 6 June 1889, p. 3, c. 1. **67**
McNamee, *History of Ardagh*, p. 385. **68** *Leitrim Advertiser*, 4 July 1889, p.2, c. 1. **69** Ibid.,
17 November 1892, p. 2 c. 2.

Massachusetts, where, thanks to the Industrial Revolution Irish people, including many from Leitrim, were employed in the mills and canal works there.
Mollaghan returned to Leitrim where he bought property and farmed until his
death. Also interred in Cloone graveyard were the remains of John Brown, a
native of Cloonee, parish of Cloone, where he left as a young man to seek his
fortune in Australia. He eventually settled in British Guiana, South America,
where he was fortunate to buy some land 'rich in gold'. He visited his family
and friends in Leitrim on many occasions and entertained them with stories of
foreign parts. On one such trip he became ill and died. He was buried in Cloone
in November 1901.[70] Finally, a plaque on the graveyard wall to the memory of
Michael and Mary Creegan of Drumkeeran, parish of Cloone (both of whom
were born in the 1860s) 'and their thirteen children laid to rest in Ireland and
America' reminds today's reader of the part played by Cloone families in the
Irish diaspora.

The people who opted for burial in Cloone were either unaware of, or undeterred by, the pronouncement made on Cloone graveyard in the Book of
Fenagh. McNamee, referring to it, stated that 'there is promised to those who
bury in Fenagh an assurance of eternal happiness, when if they dare to bury in
Cloone they are promised – well, the other thing'.[71]

SPLITTING THE DIFFERENCE IN CLOONE

Fairs were of great social, economic and cultural importance in the nineteenth
century drawing people together from different social and geographic backgrounds and allowing the influences of the wider world to be introduced into
the local culture.[72] By the 1850s Cloone was renowned for the nine cattle fairs
which were held annually on the following dates: 12 February, 5 April, 26 May,
13 June, 10 July, 26 August, 29 September, 2 November and 20 December.
There is evidence of an annual fair in Cloone on 26 May from the early 1600s.
It appears that this fair was the only one held in accordance with patent which
gave permission for one fair to be held in Cloone, 'on the feast of Saint Brandon
being May 16th and on the next day'.[73] The difference between the date of the
patent and the date on which the fair was actually held by the 1800s may be
accounted for by the introduction of the Gregorian calendar which added ten
days to the original date.[74] It is possible that all the fairs were held on the feast

70 Ibid., 28 November 1901, p. 2, c. 6. **71** J.J. McNamee, 'Lecture on the history of Ardagh'
in *Ardagh and Clonmacnoise Antiquarian Society Journal*, ii, no.7, 1940, p. 7. **72** Denis A. Cronin,
Karina Holton, Jim Gilligan (eds), *Irish fairs and markets* (Dublin, 2000), p.13. **73** *Report of the
Commissioners appointed to inquire into the state of fairs and markets in Ireland*, HC 1852–53, xli,
79, p. 90. **74** With the introduction of the Gregorian calendar, the difference in dates between
the old and new styles was ten days in respect of the years between 1582 and 1700.

day of local or revered saints; the last fair of the year was held on the feast of Criffer Ree (20 December) while the 2 November fair was held 'between old and new Hallowe'en' when the feast of St Martin was celebrated with ritual in many homes in the parish.[75]

Fairs, because of their capacity to draw people of varying political and religious differences from long distances were often 'fractious affairs ... [where] old rivalries were renewed and faction fighting was often a characteristic ...'[76] Cloone was no exception. The fairs were often referred to in the Outrage Papers for county Leitrim, mainly in the context of requests for reinforcements of constabulary for a particular fair to deal with the predictable encounters between the various factions. On at least one occasion the military was directed, by order from the Quarter-Master-General's Office in Dublin Castle, to keep the peace in Cloone at the fair of 26 May, 1845, as follows:

> I have the honour to inform you that a company of the 88 Regiment en route to Boyle has been directed to proceed from Carrigallen to Cloone on Monday the 26 inst so as to arrive there at 10 oclock am to offer the necessary aid to the civil power if required and to proceed on their route when their services are dispensed with. *E Lucas, Castle.*[77]

The above communication was directed to Mr Veevers, resident magistrate for Leitrim, who had already received information of a likely riot at Cloone on this occasion.[78] Unfortunately, no information is to hand on what, if anything, happened in Cloone at that particular fair.

Sometimes friction could result from something as insignificant in modern terms as the size of the 'luck-penny' given with an animal which had been sold. Agreeing the price of the animal often involved the assistance of a self-appointed 'neutral' third party and much hand-slapping and splitting the difference between the price the seller wanted and the buyer was willing to give. If the luck penny was not up to the buyer's expectations the deal might not be finalised and bad feelings would result on both sides. Derogatory comments on the animals being offered for sale or a faulty animal having been 'put over' on a buyer at a previous fair were the stuff

Encyclopaedia Britannica, (1959 edition), iv, p. 571. **75** IFC, vol. 680, pp 352–354, Peadar Mac Giolla Choinnigh ó John Garvey, Drumlachan, Cluain, 1939. The ritual included the killing of a fowl or drake and the sprinkling of its blood in four corners of the kitchen or on the door jambs of the house or out-offices in silence before midnight. This was done on any night between old and new Hallowe'en nights, i.e., 1 November and 11 November, the latter date was the feast of St Martin. The difference between the old and new Hallowe'en nights may be accounted for by the introduction of the Gregorian calendar. **76** Paul Connell, 'Slaughtered like wild beasts: Massacre at Castlepollard Fair', in *Irish fairs and markets* (Dublin, 2001), p. 144. **77** NAI, Outrage Papers, Co. Leitrim, 16/10877. **78** NAI, Outrage Papers, 16/32289.

of planned fights. Towards evening, supporters of both buyer and seller would have organised strategy, manpower, and a grove of ash-plants in a bid to settle their grievances.[79] A fight lent legitimacy to the fair, 'there were places which considered themselves disgraced if evening came without a blow struck'.[80]

The wider world of land ownership and politics would also cause friction. On at least one occasion – 26 May 1886 – the fair was boycotted. This resulted from the local farmers being incensed by a series of land deals which involved George West, from Drumdarkan. West held the right to collect tolls and customs at the fairs in Cloone which were held on a half-acre site in the village. In an attempt to gain revenge on West the farmers gathered on an alternative 'green' by the lake-side in Kiltyfea, a neighbouring townland, thereby depriving West of the tolls and saving themselves some expense.[81]

Going home from a fair was a journey which needed careful planning. An item in the outrage papers details an incident involving the attack and robbery at Racullen, near Cloone, of John Noble from Carrigallen as he made his way home after the February fair in 1840. The state of Noble's purse may have been known to his attackers. The constabulary from Streamstown, beside Racullen, attempted to apprehend the robbers and were helped in their efforts by a man whom they found stealing a gate. He supplied the names of two men whom he believed to be responsible for the attack.[82]

The fairs attracted crowds to the village which resulted in the purchase of goods and materials and were therefore important days in the shopkeepers' calendar. This is indicated in a notice which appeared in the local paper in June 1882. A newly built two-storey licensed premises on the main street was offered for sale or letting along with three acres of superior land. Reference was made in the notice of sale to the nine fairs which were held annually in the village, 'which is surrounded by a district numerously populated by a well-doing class of industrious farmers'.[83] It could be inferred from this statement that the customers of the licensed premises were drawn, or anticipated, from this category. By the beginning of the twentieth century there were adequate public houses in Cloone to quench a fair-day thirst, as the census return for 1901 shows.

A VILLAGE OF NAILERS, TAILORS, DRESSMAKERS ... AND PART-TIME FARMERS

In 1901 Cloone village had 21 families comprising of 79 people living in 20 houses.[84] As the figures in Table 7 show, self-employment was the most common

---

79 Ash-plants or sticks were used in the area for driving cattle and also for self-defence. **80** Kevin Danaher, 'The fair day' in *Irish Country People* (Cork, 1966), p. 93. **81** *Leitrim Advertiser*, 27 May, 1886, p. 2, c.3. **82** NAI, Outrage Papers, Co. Leitrim, 1840, 16/3702. **83** *Leitrim Advertiser*, 22 June, 1882, p. 2, c. 6. **84** The average number of persons per house was 3.8;

means of earning a living for heads of households as the twentieth century commenced.

Table 7 Occupations in Cloone village, 1901.

Occupation	Number	Occupation	Number
Farmer	3	Tailor[85]	2
Farmer and publican	2	Grocer/publican	2
Farmer and blacksmith[86]	3	Nailer[87]	2
Farmer and shopkeeper	1	Police officers	2
Dressmaker[88]	3	Post master	1
Domestic servant	2	Priest	1
Carpenter	1	Shopkeeper	1

The importance of farming in the locality is borne out by the number of persons in the village engaged in it, i.e., seven out of a total of 21 heads of households. Three were full-time farmers and four combined farming with other occupations. The craft workers – tailors, dressmakers, nailers, blacksmiths and a carpenter – provided services which were required by the general population of the locality. The tailors, Patrick Brady and his son John, produced made-to-measure clothes for men and boys, while the dressmakers, Mary Curran and her sister, Maggie, and Maggie Heslin, provided a similar service for females. The nailer, Patrick McGreal, and his son John made nails of various descriptions for the local populace including the carpenter, Patrick Gannon. James Ryan and his two sons were blacksmiths who, in addition to shoeing the horses of the locality, made and repaired farm implements and machinery as well as the basic item of kitchen equipment, the crane.[89] Four households (18 per cent of total) were headed by a female without spouse, two of whom were widowed with children and two were single. Four of the remaining households were headed by a male without a spouse and, similarly to the female heads of households, two were widowed with children and two were single. The socio-economic condition of the two groups contrasted sharply. The male group appear as persons of substance (publicans/farmers and a craftsman) while the females, with skills that were not highly valued (dressmakers and servants) could be construed as living in relative poverty. Two women entered 'domestic servant' as their occupation. They were also heads of households – one was a widow and the other a spinster. Entering 'servant' in the occupation column does not necessarily mean that they

the national figure, as per the 1901 Census, was 5.2.   **85** Father and son tailored together.
86 Father and two sons included.   **87** Father and son included.   **88** This included two heads of household plus sister of one head of household.   **89** This equipment was used to suspend pots etc. over an open fire.

went out to work in another household but rather that they perceived themselves in this capacity in their own homes. It indicates the lack of status which such women had in Ireland at that time. Mary E. Daly, writing on this issue, states that 'women increasingly opted for unpaid domestic service in the family home instead of paid service for strangers'.[90]

The total population of Cloone village was Catholic in 1901 and was ministered to by the parish priest, the Revd Felix Doherty from county Cavan, who occupied the house in the village which was occupied by William West in 1798. His household included his niece, Winifred Jones and a cook and domestic servant called Margaret McGovern both of whom were also from county Cavan. The peace was kept in Cloone at that time by four men of the Royal Irish Constabulary all of whom were Catholics who had originated outside of county Leitrim. The sergeant, James Coughlan and his wife Lizzy were from county Mayo while one constable came from Donegal and two from Roscommon. The only other public servant resident in the village at this time was John Greany, an 84-year-old postmaster originally from county Galway. He had indicated in the census returns that he could speak both Irish and English. Mary Ann Gannon, the 60-year-old Leitrim-born wife of carpenter Patrick indicated likewise. With only two Irish speaking adults in the village at that time, the dominance of English as the everyday language of Cloone and the extent to which the wider world of commerce and communications had extended to this seemingly remote area is evident.

The standard of housing, as assessed by the census enumerators, was not very high. Only one of the twenty houses in Cloone was of first-class standard. It was occupied by Peter Kiernan, a 34-year-old grocer and spirit merchant whose brother Patrick, classified as a farm servant, also lived there. There were 14 second-class houses and five third-class dwellings. Eleven of the houses had roofs of slate, iron or tiles, while the remaining nine private dwellings were thatched. There were no mud houses in Cloone in 1901 but a quarter of the houses in the surrounding townland were mud-walled. The number of houses relating to farm activities indicate the extent to which Cloone was a farming village at this time and also demonstrates the loose demarcation there was between village and rural area. With 14 piggeries, 13 cow-houses, 10 fowl-houses, five stables and a forge, there were only slightly less farm-related out-offices per domestic dwelling in the village than in the townland, where six of the seven families were engaged in agriculture only.

Non-domestic buildings included the police station, the Catholic and Protestant churches, four public houses, two shops of unspecified type and one grocery shop which may have been part of a public house. The scarcity of grocery shops indicates the extent to which self-sufficiency, particularly in the home,

---

90 Mary E. Daly, *Women and work in Ireland* (Dublin, 1997), p. 32.

was the dominant way of life in the village and surrounding area. The proliferation of public houses in the village since the mid-1850s bears evidence of an unsuccessful temperance movement which was promoted in Ireland from the late 1840s by both Catholic and Protestant groups. Later, the Catholic Church was divided on the temperance issue, favouring moderation rather than total abstinence. This approach may have been tempered by the popularity of 'whiskey shops' in the parish of Cloone from early in the study period: Father McKiernan, parish priest of Cloone and a witness to the Poor Inquiry of 1836, suggested that there were 400 of them in the parish at that time.[91] In the absence of a butcher, baker, saddler or professional person, the business stock in 1901 puts Cloone in the lower order of central places at that time. Such needs would be met in the nearby towns of Mohill or Ballinamore.

When the General Valuation was carried out in 1856 there were 24 families in Cloone village. A comparison of family names which were present then with those of 1901 shows only five names common to both dates indicating a very low level of persistence. Immigration consisted mainly of officials of church and state entering the community. The spouses of all of the Leitrim-born heads-of-households were also from Leitrim. Excluding the police, the parish priest, his niece, his cook and the post-master, the only person listed as having been born outside of county Leitrim was William Mulrennan from county Roscommon, a shop-assistant with Michael Brady, farmer and publican in the village, and owner of the historic camp-field.[92]

At the dawn of the twentieth century the English-speaking, Catholic village of Cloone was a relatively closed community with the majority of its population originating in county Leitrim. The village apparently remained unattractive to outsiders, yet with few central place functions, it survived against the odds. From the exciting days of '98 through the fearful days of the Famine and its aftermath, the village decreasing in population from 1861 onwards, maintained its identity and carried the history and mythology of Criffer Ree's chosen place into the twentieth century.

---

91 *Appendix E to first report of Royal Commission on conditions of poorer classes in Ireland HC 1836,* xxxii, 1, p. 102. **92** RD, 1898–79–234. The camp field of *c.*10 acres, and a licensed house was sold by W. West, Dublin, to John Brady of Keeldra, Cloone, for £200 in 1898.

Carbury, county Kildare, 1744–1911

KARINA HOLTON

LOCATION

Carbury is a small, rural village located in the northwestern corner of county Kildare. The village is a little more than three miles from Edenderry in county Offaly and about seven from Enfield in county Meath. Today the village consists of a scattering of about a dozen houses, a Protestant church, a pub, a garage, a small Garda station, a ruined castle and a demesne house – Newberry Hall. Carbury is also the name of the barony, the civil parish, the Catholic parish and the townland in which the village is located. The barony comprises some 46,000 acres and is the largest in Kildare. In the early part of the twentieth century Carbury was also the most thinly populated barony in Kildare with a ratio of almost fourteen acres per person.[1] The townland of Carbury covers 4,796 acres. Carbury hill dominates the village of Carbury and it is skirted by the bog of Knockirr which lies to the north and northeast. It is in this area of bogland that the Boyne river has its source. To the southeast of the village lies the demesne of Newberry Hall. The demesne and its owners throughout the years have had a profound influence on the village of Carbury and it is not possible to study the village without including the demesne.

The early history of Carbury will be outlined briefly, but the objective of this study is to document the story of the village from the middle of the eighteenth century through to the early twentieth century. A number of elements combine to make the village of Carbury unique and worthy of study. These include evidence of settlement in the area for more than 2,000 years, the influence of the castle and its inhabitants, the construction and habitation of Newberry Hall in the mid-eighteenth century, and the relationship between the different social groups and religious communities associated with the village.

EARLY HISTORY

The early history of Carbury has been well documented.[2] The area is celebrated in sagas and legend. Sir William Wilde, the noted antiquarian, declared in 1850

---

1 Gustavus E. Hamilton, 'The names of baronies and parishes in county Kildare', in *Journal of the Kildare Archaeological Society*, iv (1915–17), p. 241. 2 See Matthew Devitt, 'Carbury and the Berminghams' country', in *Journal of the Kildare Archaeological Society*, ii (1896), pp 85–111;

that there is 'no locality so celebrated as the barony and hill of Carbury'.[3] Archaeological excavations in the 1930s of an extensive burial ground on Carbury hill yielded evidence of occupation dating to the late Bronze Age.[4]

Carbury Hill was originally called *Sidh Neachtain*. By the fifth century, Cairbre, son of Niall of the Nine Hostages, ruled the area and from that time onwards the area has been known as *Cairbre na gCiardha* or Carbury of the O'Kearys. It is believed that the O'Kearys were descendants of Niall of the Nine Hostages. Carbury appears regularly in the annals from the ninth to the twelfth century. Following the arrival of the Anglo-Normans in 1169, the O'Kearys were dispossessed and the lands of Carbury were given to Meiler Fitz Henry, who in turn, granted them to Sir Robert de Bermingham. The Bermingham family built the original castle on the hill and continued to hold the lands of Carbury until the early sixteenth century when the property reverted to the crown as there was no heir. In 1538 Henry Colley was granted a 21-year lease on the site of the castle of Carbury in return for military services.[5] This lease was renewed and Colley was eventually given the grant of the manor in 1569.[6]

While the definition of a town in the sixteenth century was very different from our modern concept, there is mention of a 'town' at Carbury in the state papers of the period. This reference implies that there was a substantial settlement at Carbury at this time. Many of the documents from this period refer to the town as Castlecarbury. In January 1574, Henry Colley stated that the O'Connors and their allies had threatened that they would burn his town at Castlecarbury. In June of that same year Colley wrote that Castlecarbury had been burned 'to the castle gate'.[7] In a petition submitted by Henry Colley to the privy council the following year, the town of Castlecarbury is mentioned again. This petition included a request by Colley to have the advowson of the vicarage of Carbury. In return, Henry Colley agreed to find a schoolmaster and to establish a free school at his own expense for 'the greater glory of God and [the] education of young children'.[8] He also undertook to find a vicar who could instruct the people in both tongues, implying that both English and Irish were spoken in the area at that time. Mary Ann Lyons, in her study *Church and society in Kildare,* suggests that the majority of tenants in the area at this time were of Gaelic origin.[9]

Walter Fitzgerald, 'Two Colley inscriptions in the Castle Carbury churchyard', in *Journal of the Kildare Archaeological Society,* viii (1917), pp 368–87; M. Comerford, *Collections relating to the diocese of Kildare and Leighlin* (Dublin, 1883), ii, pp. 88–97.   **3** Sir William Wilde, *The beauties of the Boyne and its tributary, the Blackwater* (Dublin, 1850).   **4** G.F. Wilmot, 'Three burial sites at Carbury, Co. Kildare', in *JRSAI* 68 (1938), pp 130–42.   **5** *Report of the Deputy Keeper of the Public Records of Ireland,* 7–22 (Dublin, 1875–90), Fiants Henry VIII, no. 442.   **6** Walter Fitzgerald, 'Two Colley inscriptions in the Castle Carbury churchyard', in *Journal of the Kildare Archaeological Society,* viii (1917), p. 375.   **7** Mary O'Dowd (ed.), *Calendar of state papers, Ireland, Tudor period, 1571–1575* (Dublin, 2000), nos. 812, 1016.   **8** Ibid., no. 1351.   **9** Mary-Ann Lyons, *Church and society in county Kildare, c.1470–1547* (Dublin, 2000), p. 35.

It is likely that the Carbury area had been covered in woodland until this period. William J. Smyth states that the final clearance of woodland and waste-land was the most significant environmental change wrought in the late sixteenth and early seventeenth centuries in Ireland.[10] In 1538 Lord Grey wrote to Henry VIII stating:

> Pleaseth your Grace to be advertised that since my last letter sent unto your Grace, I have cut three passes in the county of Kildare adjoining to the borders of Offaly, two in Bermingham's country [Carbury], whereof some of the said passes be a mile in length cut, and so broad cut that four or five carts one by another may easily pass ...[11]

Radiocarbon-dated pollen analysis from Carbury bog clearly showed dramatic reductions in tree pollen percentages, which strongly correlates with these wood-land clearances during the Tudor period.[12] Following these clearances, a further one-eighth of the land in Ireland became available for cultivation. Much of this newly cleared land was used for arable cultivation and for grazing. The Civil Survey of 1654 states that the land in Carbury was suitable for all sorts of grain growing.[13]

A suggestion was made in 1614 that the barony should be planted with English families in order to 'civilise' it. The area would have been an ideal place to colonise, as it was on the main road from Dublin to Philipstown (Daingean) and on the edge of the Pale. However, the suggestion was eventually rejected by the lord deputy as he feared it would so discontent the inhabitants that some mischief would occur.[14]

Considerable damage was done to the castle and the village during the 1641 uprising. In her deposition, Dame Anne Colley, widow, listed the goods and chattels that were taken from her. Three of her servants, John Magwyne, Darby Dolaing and William Dunn were killed in the attack and the castle was burned.[15] Following the rising of 1641, Sir William Petty was contracted to carry out a survey of all the forfeited lands in the country according to their natural, artificial and civil bounds. Protestant lands were not to be measured or subdivided. The lands of Carbury were not surveyed and the subsequent maps of the Down

10 William J. Smyth, 'Ireland a colony' in Terry Barry (ed.), *A history of settlement in Ireland* (London, 2000), p. 164.   11 Quoted in Revd Matthew Devitt, 'Carbury and the Bermingham's country' in *Journal of the Kildare Archaeological Society*, ii (1896), p. 107. 12 B. van Geel, and A. Middeldorp, 'Vegetational history of Carbury bog (Co. Kildare, Ireland) during the last 850 years and a test of the temperature indicator value of 2H/1H measure-ments of peat samples in relation to historical sources and meteorological data' in *New Phytologist* 109 (1988), 377–92.   13 R.C. Simington (ed.), *Civil Survey, Kildare*, viii (1952). 14 'Chichester letter book' in *Analecta Hibernica* viii (1938), p. 173.   15 TCD, MS 813, 1641 Depositions, Kildare, 1404.

Survey show no detail in the Carbury area, implying that the lands were in Protestant hands. The Civil Survey of 1654 shows that the manor, town and lands of Carbury were in the possession of Dudley Colley, a Protestant.[16] William Huston was rector of the parish of Carbury and Kilreany at this time.[17]

The 1660 poll-tax summary gives the first evidence of population numbers for Castlecarbury. Using Gurrin's multiplier of three in an attempt to convert the poll-tax figures to population estimates, it would appear that the population of the village was over 300 persons.[18] Of these, 40 were English, comprising almost one-third of the English population of the whole barony of Carbury. The Irish population of the village made up only 6 per cent of the Irish population of the barony, indicating a largely rural populace.[19]

In 1662 Sir Thomas Vyner, his brother Robert and Sir Daniel Bellingham, goldsmiths to the king, made a petition for the forfeited lands of Carbury, and the adjacent barony of Ikeathy and Oughteranny. The petition included another proposal to plant these lands with loyal English subjects.[20] As had happened previously in 1614, the petition was rejected.

CARBURY IN THE EIGHTEENTH CENTURY

The Colley family continued to hold the lands of Carbury into the eighteenth century. They lived in the castle which had undergone many improvements and additions over the years. The family had built a mortuary chapel near the castle in 1705. This chapel was adjacent to the original parish church. Before this, members of the Colley family had been buried in 'the parish church of Carbury, in the sepulchre and monument of [their] ancestors'.[21] By the 1740s, sisters Elizabeth and Mary Colley were the last remaining members of the Colley family. They were the joint owners of the Colley estate, some seven or eight thousand acres that stretched from Derrinturn to Clonard Bridge. They commissioned a Mr Byrn to carry out a survey of the estate in 1744. The report, now preserved in the National Library of Ireland, gives us a veritable snapshot of the village in 1744. The surveyor describes Carbury Hill as 'the most beautiful hill in Ireland'. The land is so fertile 'that it would bear onions and leeks … It is a delightful and pleasant place for gentlemen and ladies to take the airs.'[22] The lands around the mansion house contained orchards, gardens and meadows but lay wasted and neglected. The castle or demesne house needed to be renovated and another

16 *Civil Survey*, Kildare, p. 178. **17** RCBL, MS N.2.24, Inquisition Kildare, 1657. **18** Brian Gurrin, *Pre-census sources for Irish demography* (Dublin, 2002), p. 75. **19** Seamus Pender (ed.) *Census 1659* (Dublin, 1939), Kildare, barony of Carbury. **20** Robert Pentland Mahaffy (ed.), *Calendar of state papers, 1660–62* (Dublin, 1905), p. 601. **21** Will of Sir Henry Colley 1637, quoted in Fitzgerald, 'Two Colley inscriptions', p. 379. **22** NLI, MS 9212, Map of the Colley estates, Co. Kildare 1744.

Figure 1 Carbury Castle (photographed by K. Holton, 2003).

storey added. The surrounding low land needed to be drained to make it fit for cows or cattle. According to the map which accompanies Byrn's survey, the village itself consisted of at least four substantial houses and some smaller cabins. Settlement was concentrated on the east of the village. Taylor's map of Kildare from 1752 also depicts about half a dozen houses along the road to the east of the village towards Enfield. According to the survey all were thatched. The roofs and thatch were in need of repair. There was also a brew house, a chair house, a barn, a stable and a malt house all in need of repair.

Byrn suggested that the village could be considerably improved by the introduction of some kind of manufacturing, as it was sited on a great thoroughfare to and from Dublin. There was also a good weekly market in the village and two large fairs were held in the year – on 26 May and on 2 October.[23] Taylor's map of 1752 depicts a widened street to the east of the village which was possibly the fair green. Byrn also suggested that dealers and tradesmen should be encouraged to live in the village, as it was then under-populated. This population decline is notable considering that the poll-tax returns suggested that there might have been in excess of 300 inhabitants in the village in 1660.

Apart from the castle on the hill, the other building that would have dominated the skyline of early eighteenth-century Carbury was the Protestant church. This church was situated alongside the road that led across the hill and quite close to the castle. All that remains of this structure today is the belfry. In the

23 *The traveller's new guide through Ireland* (London, 1819), pp 123–4.

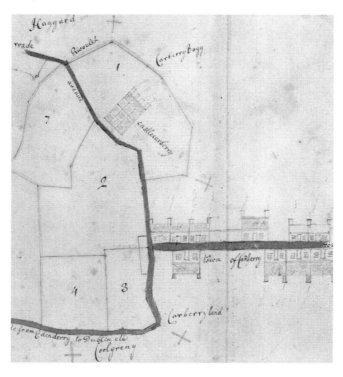

Figure 2 Extract from Byrn's map of Carbury, 1744, showing the village.[24] (Courtesy National Library of Ireland)

early years of the eighteenth century this church was in possession of a substantial collection of silver altar vessels. These included a silver communion cup, a silver patten and flagon and a silver collection plate. All these items were accredited to various Dublin silversmiths and dated 1715.[25]

The report on the state of popery in 1731 declared that the parish of Carbury had six mass houses, more than any other parish in the diocese. There was a generous ratio of clergy to people with three officiating priests as well as several friars who visited from adjacent parishes. These visiting priests and friars said Mass privately for families and stayed with those families for the duration of their visit while continuing to instruct them in their religion. This would seem to suggest that there were comfortable Catholic families in the area at that time who could afford to provide accommodation and maintenance for the Catholic clergy. One of these itinerant friars, a Franciscan named Johnson, died in Carbury parish in 1824.[26] There were also five Catholic schools in the parish in the early eigh-

24 NLI, MS9212.   **25** Con Costello, 'Exhibition of silver' in *Journal of the Kildare Archaeological Society*, xviii (part iii), (1996–7), p. 431.   **26** Thomas McGrath, *Religious renewal and reform in the pastoral ministry of Bishop James Doyle of Kildare and Leighlin, 1786–1834* (Dublin, 1999), p.

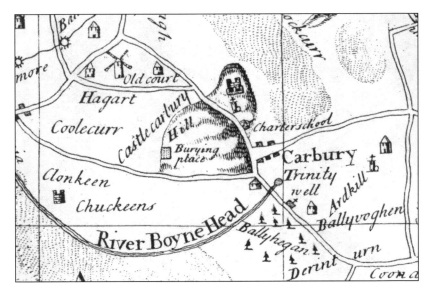

Figure 3 Extract from Noble and Keenan's map of Kildare 1752,
depicting Carbury village.

teenth century where the children of 'popish parents' were 'carefully educated.'[27]
These five schools comprised almost one-fifth of all the Catholic schools in the
diocese of Kildare at that time. The numbers of schools and mass houses in the
parish suggests quite a large population of Catholics. It is also indicative of the
scale and status of ecclesiastical organisation at this period given that the Catholic
Church was still an illegal entity in 1731.

In 1747 Mary Colley from Castlecarbury married Arthur Pomeroy from
Cork. It is likely that they initially settled on Kildare Street in Dublin where
they purchased a property in November 1753 for £1,800.[28] A society diarist of
the period, Mary Granville, referred to her meeting with Mrs Pomeroy and Miss
Colley, her sister, at a reception for the viceroy. She wrote: 'The two best dressed
women there were Mrs Pomeroy and Miss Colley, her sister.' Later that year
the Pomeroys dined at the Delany residence at Delville. Mrs Delany wrote:
'Yesterday Mr and Mrs Pomeroy dined here. I don't like the latter at all; she is
a dry stick of a thing, never commends anything and shows great conceit of her
own understanding … He is sensible, gentle and good-humoured.'[29] Arthur
Pomeroy was later elevated to the title of Viscount Harberton. Eventually the

27 'Report on the state of popery in Ireland 1731' in *Archivium Hibernicum,* iv (1915),
p. 157. **28** Dick Robinson, 'The Pomeroy family in Carbury', in James Robinson, *The
Robinsons of North Kildare* (Dublin, 1997), pp 274–7. **29** *The autobiography and correspondence
of Mary Granville, Mrs Delany, with interesting reminiscences of King George the third and Queen
Charlotte* (London, 1862), pp 52, 89, 118.

Figure 4 Extract from Taylor's Map of Kildare, 1783 depicting Carbury village

Pomeroys had a new home built for themselves in Carbury. Newberry Hall was constructed around 1760 It is a Palladian-style house of red brick with stone facings, and its design is attributed to the architect, Nathaniel Clements.

The 1760s were characterised by a surge in the creation of estate villages throughout Ireland. It was during these years and possibly as a direct result of the construction of Newberry that the village of Carbury increased in size. Taylor's map of 1783 shows almost a dozen houses in the village.[30] It depicts a flour mill on the eastern approach to the village and a new Church of Ireland place of worship had also been built. In 1771 Joshua Glover and his wife, Elizabeth Colley, had granted two roods of land situated on the eastern side of the hill of Carbury to George Tyrrell and William Cave, the churchwardens, as a site for this new church and church yard which was erected for the use of the parishioners of the parish.[31] Taylor's 1783 map depicts this church as well as the older ruined church on the hill.

It was about this time that Carbury castle began to fall into disrepair. Records show that Elizabeth Colley, who had married Joshua Glover sometime before 1770, was living in the castle in 1774. Yet, Taylor and Skinner's map of 1777

30 Alex Taylor, A map of the county of Kildare by Lieut. Alex Taylor of His Majesty's 81st Reg't, 1783. **31** RD 281/490/187638. William (Billy) Cave also served as agent to Lord Harberton.

shows the castle as a ruin.[32] Therefore it would seem fairly certain that the castle was deserted sometime in the mid 1770s when the Glovers moved to Hampton in the county of Middlesex in England. Tradition states that they had the roof removed from the castle. A sketch of the castle dating from 1799 shows it in much the same ruined state as it is today.

CARBURY CHARTER SCHOOL

In 1733/4 a charter was granted to the Incorporated Society for Promoting English Protestant Working Schools in Ireland. This charter empowered the society to receive gifts of money or property for the purpose of establishing and supporting its schools. The society also retained the right to appoint school-masters and mistresses. It was envisaged that the Incorporated Society's schools would instruct children in 'husbandry, housewifery, trades and manufactures so that [the children] would be brought up, not only in virtue, but also in labour and industry'.[33] Castlecarbury charter school was established in 1748 by the Colley family. The two Colley sisters, Mary and Elizabeth, had granted two acres rent-free on a renewable lease along with twenty acres on which low rents were to be paid. The school also received £100 from the will of Thomas Dallzell and another bequest of £20.[34] It was the third school set up under the charter of 1733 and was built to accommodate forty girls. The particular objective of the Castlecarbury school was to instruct the

> children of Roman Catholics and other poor natives of Ireland in English, writing and arithmetic, in husbandry and housewifery or in trades, man-ufactures or other manual occupations, in scriptures and in principles of Protestant Established religion.[35]

It is not clear what motivated the Colley sisters to establish such a school in their locality. However, there was a general feeling at this time that the Catholic masses were disaffected and posed a very real threat to Protestants. Rebellion was seen as endemic among the Catholic Irish, and at one of the first meetings of the Incorporated Society it was stated that it was obvious to every Protestant ... 'what blood and treasure their many Rebellions and publick Massacres have cost England, especially in the year 1641, when by their unparalleled Massacres in cold blood they had almost extirpated the very name of Protestant in Ireland.'[36]

32 George Taylor and Andrew Skinner, *Map of the roads of Ireland, surveyed 1777* (Dublin, 1778). **33** Kenneth Milne, *The Irish charter schools, 1730–1830* (Dublin, 1997), p. 25. **34** A family called Dalyell lived in Ticknevin in Carbury parish until the end of the nineteenth century. **35** *Evidence taken before Her Majesty's commissioners of inquiry into the state of endowed schools in Ireland* (Dublin, 1857), pp 132–3. **36** Quoted in Michael Quane, 'Castledermot charter school' in

Figure 5 Cartographer's impressions of Castlecarbury Charter school – Noble and Keenan 1752 and Taylor 1783.

It is possible that the memory of Dame Anne Colley's experiences in 1641 in Castlecarbury had not been forgotten in the family and that, as a result, the Colley sisters felt obliged to become involved with the Incorporated Society. The Society at this time also emphasised in glowing terms the advantages that would accrue to its benefactors:

> But when gentlemen shall consider that the only aim of the Society is to promote the protestant religion and interest, and to train up the rising generation in a habit of virtue, labour and industry … [M]ere prudence must instruct every protestant who has a stake in his country, to encourage a scheme that bids fair to secure his personal property against a common enemy …[37]

As with other charter schools, the 22 acres of land at Castlecarbury school would have been divided into about ten acres for grazing three or four cows to support the school, six acres devoted to corn, an acre or two of flax and the rest to potatoes and the kitchen garden.[38] No images of the Castlecarbury charter school are known to exist. However, an examination of contemporary maps reveals the engravers' impressions of the school at that period. These same maps depict Newberry Hall quite accurately, so it is possible to assume that their depictions of the charter school as a substantial, single-storey building are quite accurate.

During its years in Castlecarbury, the charter school provided apprentices to weavers in Dublin and supplied servants to farmers throughout the local area. A new nursery was established in York Street, Dublin in 1772 and the master of the Castlecarbury school was directed to send girls there to await apprenticeship.[39] In that same year, on the recommendation of the local committee, the Society awarded a premium to the Jacksons, master and mistress of Castlecarbury, in consideration of their extraordinary care of the children and of the school. By the end of the 1770s the school had some fifty children enrolled.[40]

Journal of the Kildare Archaeological Society xiii (1961–3), p. 470. **37** Quoted in Milne, *Irish charter schools*, p. 40. **38** Milne, *Irish charter schools,* p. 31. **39** Ibid., p. 166. **40** *Samuel Watson's*

During the early years of their existence, establishment clergy and politicians continually praised the work of the charter schools and none of the annual reports issued by the Society contained any material which would reflect adversely on themselves. However, in 1784 the philanthropist, John Howard, after visiting some of the charter schools, declared that 'the state of most of the schools I visited was so deplorable as to disgrace Protestantism, and to encourage Popery in Ireland rather than the contrary'.[41]

By November 1786 there were 18 girls and 14 boys at the Castlecarbury school. In that same month Sir Jeremiah Fitzpatrick, the inspector-general of prisons, carried out an inspection of the school. It was found that the pupils of the school were in a shocking state of neglect. It was reported that many of the children were without basic clothing; that those who were clothed were ragged and dirty; that the children were suffering greatly from the cold; that the beds were dirty and inadequately covered and many were wet and sodden and that the glass was broken in the windows. Fitzpatrick was scathing in his condemnation of many masters and mistresses of charter schools. In Carbury he noted that the master and his family occupied the greater part of the house which was comfortable and well furnished. It was recorded that John Jackson was 'a very improper person to be continued master of the school and it was moved that he should be dismissed'.[42] Subsequently, twelve 'sickly and almost naked boys' were sent from Carbury to Longford charter school. Interestingly, the local committee had made no criticisms of the Jacksons despite the fact that committee meetings were conducted in the parlour of the school and the members would have had ample opportunity to view the condition of the children for themselves.

On 3 January 1787, Mrs Sabina Lennon of Athlone, widow of Lieutenant William Lennon, was offered the position of mistress of Castlecarbury charter school. She was to be allowed to appoint two persons of her choosing and the board was willing to transfer the gardens and lands belonging to the school to her possession. However, she resigned her appointment at the end of the first month and Stephen Sparks, son of James Sparks, master of the Athlone school, was recommended for the position.[43]

Cows were purchased to supply the children with milk and the local committee agreed to carry out necessary repairs to the school. Life seems to have settled down in the school by June of 1787 when catechisms, twelve copies of the Book of Common Prayer, abridged versions of the Bible and spelling books were purchased. Clothing was provided for eighteen girls.[44] In August of that year, however, Lord Harberton and the other members of the committee, again seemingly unaware of the conditions in the school, expressed their surprise at complaints of lack of food from the children of the school.[45] Although Lord

Gentleman's and Citizen's Almanack (Dublin, 1778), p. 81.   **41** Quoted in Michael Quane, 'Castledermot charter school', p. 470.   **42** TCD, MS 5239, 20 December 1786.   **43** Ibid., 31 January 1787.   **44** Ibid., 13 June 1787.   **45** Ibid., 8 August 1787.

Harberton sat on the charter school committee, it would appear that the family were absentee landlords during these years.

New school furniture was purchased in October and a group of twenty-one girls arrived from the charter school at Santry. Two girls were apprenticed locally to the Lummox (Lomax) family as servants. The following month the Revd William Lambert was obliged to provide proof that a Mr George Kelly, who wished to take one of the girls as an apprentice, was a Protestant.[46] In January of the following year, Stephen Sparks and his wife were awarded a premium of £4 for the good care of the children.[47] Mary Reilly, one of the pupils of the school, was apprenticed to a Mr Platt of Weaver's Square, Dublin, in April, as a woollen weaver and to work on a Spinning Jenny. Later that summer, clothing was ordered for forty children and extra books were to be sent to the school. It was also reported that additional buildings would be necessary to house the school. In 1789 Sparks received an £8 premium for the good care of the children.[48] The school continued to provide apprentices both to the immediate area and to Dublin. In 1793 the local committee was informed that a farmer holding less than twenty acres was not entitled to receive an apprentice from the charter school.[49] By 1794 some 159 girls had been apprenticed by the Castlecarbury Charter school.[50]

CARBURY IN 1798

It is generally accepted that conflict broke out in the barony of Carbury some time prior to the rebellion of 1798. Castlecarbury charter school was to feature prominently in that conflict. As early as August 1792 John Pomeroy, son of Lord Harberton, was informing his father that the 'peoples' minds were very uneasy' and that the Catholics of the country were agitating their claims and oppressions in an impudent and barefaced manner.[51] Richard Musgrave states that Carbury was disturbed as early as 1795 when the houses of Protestants were plundered of arms and Protestants themselves were murdered in broad daylight.[52] In May of 1797 John Pomeroy, sensitive to the mood of the period, declared that if a civil war should break out, the family would lose its property. He also referred to the 'rebellious dispositions that now prevail among the idle and lower classes of people' in the countryside.[53] A letter dated May 1797 from Mr Alex Ker, a landowner close to Carbury village, claimed that he lived in a state of blockade and told how 'hundreds of men for this week past have gone about the coun-

46 Ibid., 28 November 1787. **47** Ibid., 16 January 1788. **48** Ibid., 24 January 1789. **49** TCD, MS 5227, 3 July 1793. **50** *Samuel Watson's Gentleman's and Citizen's Almanack* (Dublin, 1794), p. 81. **51** PRONI, Harberton Papers, T2954/4/24. **52** Sir Richard Musgrave, *Memoirs of the different rebellions in Ireland* (Dublin, 1801), p. 266. **53** PRONI, Harberton Papers, T2954/8/13.

try under the pretence of selling potatoes and have carried white flags, singing republican songs.'[54] Sir Fenton Aylmer wrote of ' murders, assassinations and robbery.' The whole barony, he wrote, 'will become the scene of depredation and without doubt soon, unless measures and that immediately are taken to suppress it.'[55] The committee of fifteen of the charter school also stated that 'disturbances broke out in Carbury some time previous to the rebellion. It was proclaimed to be in a state of disturbance early in 1797 – near a year before any of the rest of the county was proclaimed.'[56] It was also stated that ' no good subject is safe in his house at night; robberies, burglaries and murders are frequently committed insomuch that the gentlemen of the country were compelled to apply to the Government for a military force.'[57]

Matters came to a head on the night of Saturday, 6 May 1797. Stephen Sparks, the master of the charter school, declared that between seven and eight o'clock that evening groups of men had begun to gather on Carbury Hill. By ten that night, they had formed themselves into fifteen companies and were exercising and carrying out manoeuvres. Later that same night the charter school was attacked 'by a numerous armed mob ... which was driven off by the spirited conduct of a few yeomen ...'[58] Sparkes stated in his evidence that he believed there were almost 300 men involved in the attack. Most of them were armed with guns, he declared. There were eight in the charter school house that night including Sparks' own son. They fired back at the attackers. Eventually the assailants left the scene vowing to return to send him and his family to hell. Almost immediately, however, Sparks saw a party coming across the hill towards the house. Thinking it was the attackers returning, he fired on them. When he heard the words 'Wicklow friends' he stopped firing, recognising the Wicklow Militia who were quartered in Edenderry. Damage to the school from the night's attack was estimated at £15.[59]

Later that night the Wicklow Militia arrested a man called William Kennedy, a local brogue maker from nearby Kishavanna. Kennedy gave no answer when Sparks asked him what had induced him to attack the school. He was tried in August in Athy and was found guilty of the attack. Despite the protestations of many local gentlemen and some grand jurors, the lack of evidence against him, and a plea to the lord lieutenant, Kennedy was executed. Brownrigg, the marquis of Downshire's agent in Edenderry, wrote to Edward Cooke at Dublin Castle on 27 August 1797 stating that a popish mania had recently begun to spread among the lower classes in the area. He also stated that the conviction of Kennedy was the main topic of conversation on the street in Edenderry in August 1797 and that many spoke favourably of him as being an honest man.[60]

---

54 NAI, Rebellion Papers, 620/30/36. **55** Ibid., 620/30/38. **56** TCD, MS 5228, 6 April 1803. **57** *Freeman's Journal*, 14 October 1797. **58** Ibid. **59** *The Press*, 24 August 1791. **60** NAI, Rebellion Papers 620/32/77.

The Insurrection Act, which had been passed in 1796, had authorised an assembly of justices of the peace to petition the lord lieutenant to have a troubled area 'proclaimed.' Two days after the attack on the charter school, Carbury barony was proclaimed on 8 May 1797, effectively placing it under martial law. The assault on the charter school, combined with the other attacks in the area highlighted the vulnerability of the loyalist community. It also served to reveal the strength of sympathy and support for the United Irishmen's cause. Following the attack on the charter school, Stephen Sparks became the focus of hatred because of his vigorous defence of the school and because of the fact that the school, as a Protestant institution, symbolised all that was hated by the insurgents. There were also demands for revenge to be exacted for the execution of Kennedy.[61] The *Union Star,* an anti-government publication that specialised in unmasking informers, carried the following notice on 29 November 1797:

> The Star offers to public justice the following detestable traitors as spies and perjured informers … Stephen Sparks; master of the charter school, Castlecarbury and Michael Sparks, his brother, and Gilbert Walshe, his brother-in-law.[62]

The Incorporated Society had granted Sparks the sum of ten guineas as a reward for his good conduct during the attack on the school. He was also offered the opportunity to move to a school nearer to Dublin. Sparks declined the offer, as there was no suitable person in the area to whom the care of the forty-four girls at the school could be entrusted. The following month Sparks found a petition posted on the door of Carbury Church which he believed had been placed there ' to encourage the feeling of disaffection carried on in the lower order of people in this county'.[63]

It was now necessary to place the school under the protection of the military for fear of further attacks. After the events of May 1797, a party of Fencibles had defended the school. This party was withdrawn one year later on 24 May 1798. Six nights later, on 30 May, the school was attacked again and set on fire. Various reports stated that there were between 800 and 2,000 men involved in this attack.[64] It is likely that in the reports of the two attacks on Carbury the numbers of attackers were greatly exaggerated by loyalist commentators. Returns

61 The incident was commemorated in poems and songs of the period: '… and home we then returned, Sparks's house we burned,/ In recompense for Kennedy that died there on a tree' and 'It was on Carbury hill, Our precious blood they spilled,/ When Kennedy our hero, they hung him', quoted in R.R. Madden, *Literary remains of the United Irishmen of 1798* (Dublin, 1887), pp 31–5; 170–3. **62** Milne, *Irish charter schools*, p. 220. **63** NAI, Rebellion Papers, 620/31/103. **64** *An impartial narrative of the most important engagements which took place between his majesty's forces and the rebels during the Irish rebellion, 1798* (Dublin, 1799), p.7. Liam Chambers in *Rebellion in Kildare, 1790–1803* (Dublin, 1998), states that the group was almost 2,000 strong.

of numbers of United Irishmen in Kildare county in early 1798 vary from between 10,000 to 13,000 members. However, Carbury had only 384 members at that time. This low number can probably be attributed to the proclamation of the area in 1797 which would have greatly affected the organisation there.[65]

According to Musgrave, the day before the attack, the parish priest had told some of the children of the charter school and an old woman who accompanied them, that they would not be molested and need not worry unduly about what was going to happen.[66] This implies that the parish priest was aware in advance of the plan to attack the school. Whether or not this is a true reading of the attack is impossible to say.

Immediately following the assault, the Revd Charles Palmer went to the school and made arrangements to have the children accommodated locally. He wrote at once to the Incorporated Society informing them of the situation.[67] He was thanked for his generosity and requested to dispose of the children according to his own discretion. If it was possible to convey them to Dublin then he should do so. If, however, the journey proved too difficult, the master of the Maynooth school was asked to accommodate them. A further grant of £50 was paid to Stephen Sparks on 4 July 1798 and a certificate of good and loyal conduct was awarded to him in November of that year to enable him to apply for compensation being offered to suffering loyalists.

Later, the school building was put at the disposal of the Barrack Board for the reception of troops. The building had been badly damaged and in February 1800 a letter written by direction of Lord Tyrawley, barrack master general, stated that the troops quartered at Castlecarbury were in a wretched state for want of accommodation. It was further stated that there were two out-offices at the charter house which could be made sufficient for accommodation and that the barrack master general was prepared to repair these offices at the expense of the barrack board if the commissioners would allow him permission to do so.[68] In September 1801, the society's carpenter was instructed to inspect and find the best way of preventing further dilapidation of the building.[69] In April 1806, following an order of the general board of the Incorporated Society, the lands and endowments of the school were returned to the representatives of the original donors.[70]

Musgrave claims that several houses of Protestants in the vicinity of the charter school were burned during the summer of 1798. Claims submitted for damages suffered in 1798 included those of John Jackson, a farmer, of Castlecarbury village, who claimed £89 2s. 6d. for the loss of cattle and hay; Laurence Nary of the village who claimed for a house and furniture worth £4 11s., and Arthur Smith for a house. Stephen Sparks submitted a claim for furniture and clothing.[71]

65 Chambers, *Rebellion in Kildare*, p. 57. **66** Musgrave, *Memoirs of the different rebellions in Ireland*, p. 267. **67** TCD, MS 5227, 1 June 1798. **68** Ibid., 19 February 1800. **69** Ibid., 2 September 1801. **70** *Evidence taken before her majesty's commissioners of inquiry into the state of endowed schools in Ireland* (Dublin, 1857), pp. 132–3. **71** NLI, PC 12,467, List of persons who

Newberry Hall also suffered damage. On 11 July the house had been taken over by a party of Wexford men whose force had fallen back from a six-hour battle at Clonard. They raided the larders and cellars of the house, as well as other houses in the neighbourhood. Sheep were captured and killed to provide food for the men.[72] According to some reports, up to 1,000 men were camped on Carbury Hill. The following day, two dairymaids, Mary and Esther Grattan, the only Protestants in the employ of Viscount Harberton, were murdered and their bodies dumped in the pond on the grounds. Again, the attack seems to have been sectarian. Witnesses stated that they heard it said that the two Protestant women had been 'put out of the way'. There was also a suggestion that there was clear mutual dislike between the two women and the rebels who were coming and going from the house. Five men were later found guilty of their murders and four of them were hanged at the scene of the crime.[73] A fifth man escaped from jail in Dublin dressed as a woman. It is interesting that neither Tyrawley, the Barrack Master General, nor Brian Ford, clerk to Lord Harberton, mention the murder of the two dairymaids in their correspondence with him.

Tyrawley wrote to the second Lord Harberton in June 1799 giving a comprehensive picture of the state of Newberry at that time. Apparently the first Lord Harberton had not invested a great deal of money or energy in the estate for a considerable time and this neglect, combined with the damage done to the house in 1798 meant that the place was in a sorry state. The house and offices were in poor repair. New sashes would be required in the windows and painting and whitewashing throughout. The doors on the ground floor had been destroyed and the roof was leaking. All the external doors and gates were decayed. The hot houses in the gardens were in need of major reconstruction work. In his correspondence Tyrawley offered to take over the care of the estate and the repair of the house and out-offices.

Tyrawley also suggested that Lord Harberton not renew leases for the seventy or eighty acres close to the house and that they should instead be incorporated into the demesne as the estate at that time was 'not sufficient for the supply of a gentleman's table who lives as he ought to do.'[74] He mentioned too that the previous Lord Harberton, Arthur Pomeroy, had been surrounded by a 'most infamous pack of rebels and cut throats' and that until some of them were hanged, Newberry would not afford a safe residence to anyone.[75]

The available sources for this period shed little light on the views of the local people during these years. However, it is likely that the effects of the Insurrection Act, followed by the events in the village in 1797–8 and the execution of William Kennedy, culminating in the murder of the dairymaids on Newberry estate and

have suffered losses in their property in the county of Kildare, 1799. **72** Peter O'Shaughnessy (ed.), *Rebellion in Wicklow – General Joseph Holt's personal account of 1798* (Dublin, 1998), p. 49. **73** NAI, Rebellion Papers, 620/5/58/17. See also Patrick C. Power, *The courts martial of 1798–9* (Kilkenny, 1997), pp. 65–7. **74** PRONI, Harberton Papers, T2954/6/2. **75** Ibid.

the subsequent execution of the four men found guilty of the crime, left the villagers traumatised and distressed. While the Kildare countryside was generally in a state of lawlessness and disorder during the autumn and winter of 1798, the available evidence would seem to suggest that Carbury village remained relatively peaceful during this period.[76] Five years later, during the events of July 1803, many of the villages in Kildare which had been involved in the struggle in 1798, were active again. Carbury was not represented in Emmet's rising and remained peaceful. However, this would not remain the case.

THE EARLY NINETEENTH CENTURY

At the dawn of the nineteenth century, Charles Lindsay, bishop of Kildare, made his visitation to the parish. The Revd Charles Palmer had been vicar since 1796. The curate's assistant at that time was Nicholas Lockwood.[77] In 1752, Elizabeth Colley and her sister, Mary Pomeroy, had reserved for themselves the right to nominate and appoint vicars to the church at Carbury.[78] William Angier was the schoolmaster and was supported by the vicar.[79] He also acted as the vicar's catechist. He had been in the village since before 1797 when he was a member of the select vestry of the church. Angier died in 1806, aged 77. He had lived in a house owned by James Ford, the owner of the public house in the village.[80] Ford was also the owner of other dwelling houses and tenements in the village. Father Patrick Murphy had been parish priest until his death in March 1794.[81]

The bishop visited again in August 1808. The Protestant schoolmaster at this time was William Richmond. The church owned a house and two acres of ground. Elizabeth and Joshua Glover had granted the land to the church in 1771.[82] The house had been built at the charge of Mr Palmer, on land donated by the Revd John Pomeroy, then fourth Lord Harberton.[83] The church building was in excellent repair.[84] In 1813, John Pomeroy gave the lands that had formerly housed the charter school to the Church of Ireland as glebe lands.[85] This grant was further confirmed by his son, Henry, Lord Harberton, in a deed of February 1824, whereby the lands and the buildings of the former charter school were granted for life to the Revd Charles Palmer for a yearly rent of £37 13s. 9d.[86]

A Catholic mass house had been built in Derrinturn (one and a half miles away) in the early 1730s. It stood near the present Roman Catholic church, but

76 Chambers, *Rebellion in Kildare*, p.102.   **77** John C. Erck, *An ecclesiastical register* (Dublin, 1830), p. 102.   **78** RD, 155/342/10494.   **79** Raymond Refaussé, 'The visitation note book of Charles Lindsay, Bishop of Kildare, 1804–1808' in *Journal of the Kildare Archaeological Society*, xvii (1991), p. 132.   **80** RD, 654/50/449300. Also Carbury Parish burial records.   **81** Comerford, *Collections*, ii, p. 97.   **82** RD 281/490/187638.   **83** Ibid., p. 146. Arthur Pomeroy was raised to the peerage as Lord Harberton in 1787 and in 1791 he was advanced to the title of Viscount Harberton.   **84** *Papers relating to the Established Church in Ireland* (Dublin, 1807), p. 78.   **85** PRONI, Harberton Papers, T2954/8/33.   **86** RD 798/441/539176.

on the opposite side of the road.[87] The new church was built in 1809 on land donated by the Murphy family.[88] According to Catholic church records there were fifty or sixty 'devout persons' who received the Eucharist monthly by 1820[89]. Father Maurice Kearney had been appointed parish priest of Carbury in 1816.[90] He continued to minister there until he was transferred in 1820.

A Catholic school had been established in Carbury village by May 1824. Patrick Moore, who was about 50 years old, was the schoolmaster and had established the school himself. He may have been born in Thomastown as he attended school there. He had trained in Newtown and Balyna schools in the 'New System of Education'. He taught reading, writing and arithmetic. The schoolroom at Carbury was built of lime and stone and had a thatched roof. Four Protestant Testaments had been given to the school by the Protestant minister. The curriculum included reading, spelling, geography, arithmetic and religious instruction.[91] The establishment of schools that were independent of the Kildare Place Society was strongly supported by Bishop Doyle of Kildare and Leighlin. In 1826 he published a pastoral on the education question in which he offered a system of education funded by Catholic parishioners. Each parish should build a spacious schoolhouse. These schools were to be open to pupils of all denominations with religious instruction as the basis for education. As soon as these schools were ready to receive children, Catholic clergy were instructed to 'suffer no child of our communion to remain in any school wherein the rules of the Kildare-street Society or of any other anti-Catholic society, are observed'.[92] In early 1827 the parish priest of Carbury, Edward Earle, wrote to Bishop Doyle stating that he expected to have his schools ready by the following spring in accordance with the bishop's plan.[93] A substantial schoolhouse had been opened in Derrinturn in July 1815. The parish priest had appointed the teacher, James Canavan. The school building included a dwelling house for the teacher. It is likely that it was this school which was improved by Father Earle in 1827 and subsequent education reports refer only to the Derrinturn school throughout the middle and end of the nineteenth century.[94] In June 1838, Father Earle made a further application for this school at Derrinturn. Its projected enrolment would be 160 males and 40 females. The application was supported by both Protestant and Catholic men of the community.[95]

In his correspondence with the bishop, Father Earle also noted that some moral and well-disposed persons throughout the parish taught catechism in the chapels on Sundays and holydays. He estimated the numbers who attended these

87 Comerford, *Collections*, p. 93.   **88** John Duffy, *The churches of Kildare and Leighlin 2000 AD* (Strasbourg, 2001), p. 106.   **89** Thomas McGrath, *Politics, interdenominational relations and education in the public ministry of Bishop James Doyle of Kildare and Leighlin, 1786–1834* (Dublin, 1999), p. 140.   **90** McGrath, *Religious renewal and reform*, p. 85.   **91** Martin Brenan, *Schools of Kildare and Leighlin, AD 1775–1835* (Dublin, 1935), p. 204.   **92** McGrath, *Politics*, p. 200.   **93** Ibid., pp 199, 201.   **94** Brenan, *Schools of Kildare and Leighlin*, p. 203.   **95** NAI, ED 1/43, no. 39.

classes as being over 300 at morning sessions, 120 at evening sessions and some 180 at various locations throughout the parish. He also stated that no efforts were made in either the Catholic or Protestant schools to encourage children to change religions.[96] Yet, in February 1827 he informed the bishop: ' I have the children of two or three Protestants learning the Catholic doctrine privately, and now and then stealing themselves to Mass.'[97]

The countryside continued to be disturbed during the first decades of the nineteenth century. Rents and prices had risen sharply leaving smaller tenants and the poor in considerable distress. The army battalion stationed in the village in 1814 was increased to twenty rank-and-file soldiers with two senior officers.[98] In 1816 James Brownrigg, Lord Downshire's agent in Edenderry, wrote that 'the labouring classes are here in great distress this moment, nearly starving in the midst of plenty, they are beginning to grow turbulent ...'[99] The bad harvests of 1816 and 1817 added to the distress. In March 1817 an armed mob robbed and plundered four carts that were on their way through Carbury village to Dublin with sacks of flour. The car men were held prisoner with a guard of four armed men in a house opposite the gate of Newberry demesne. Brownrigg spent the night searching houses in the village.[1] He subsequently advised Downshire that the remedy to the poverty in the area would be the provision of employment. Later that month he reported that he had several men employed in potato plant-ing and in turf cutting. However, he was still fearful of a potentially explosive situation when he reported that

> nothing can be worse than the disposition of the lower orders, particu-
> larly in the Co. Kildare, from everything I hear they are fully as wickedly
> inclined as in the year 1798 ... and I fear the Government are not suffi-
> ciently aware of the danger that hangs over the lives and properties of the
> peaceable and well disposed in this country.[2]

Car men had discontinued using the road that led through the village because of the danger of attack. In April the gentlemen and farmers of the barony of Carbury held a meeting where it was agreed that all respectable persons living near the high road through Carbury village would be sworn in as special con-stables to protect traffic using the road. Following this action, cars began to use the road again and there were no further reports of assaults.[3] Other houses in the area were attacked later that year, however, and in one case the owner and his wife were flogged with sally rods.[4]

In 1821 there were further disturbances in the area. The following year two houses near the village were burned.[5] Two years later Edward Earle, the parish

96 McGrath, *Politics*, p. 206. 97 Ibid., p. 140. 98 NAI, SOC/1562/12. 99 PRONI, *Letters of a great Irish landlord: A selection from the estate correspondence of the third marquess of Downshire, 1809–45* (Belfast, 1974), no. 55. 1 Ibid., no.56. 2 Ibid., no. 58. 3 Ibid., no. 59. 4 NAI, SOC/2368/75. 5 NAI, SOC/2368/47.

priest, reported that the people in the parish were poor and their children naked. He went on to state that:

> They are proud … and distressed, laborious and industrious to excess; their endurance is great, but their fortitude and public spirit is greater; they neither murmur or complain, though often reduced to nearly the last extremity for the necessaries of poor human nature.[6]

By the 1830s tensions were running high. In November 1835 a farmer had been arrested at the market in Edenderry for non-payment of tithes. This action alarmed many of the people in the area. On Sunday 29 November, the marquis of Downshire's agent, Thomas Murray, wrote that there was 'great abuse and threats held out against all concerned in the arresting of those who will not pay their tithes in the barony of Carbury.'[7] A few days later trouble erupted in Carbury village. On the morning of Saturday 5 December, Isaac Bagley, a Protestant youth from the village, had been sent by the rector with a message to a local Catholic farmer and had met with a hostile reception there. He fled the farm and sought refuge in the house of a local Protestant family. On hearing shots, Bagley's father assumed he had been murdered and at once the police set out from the station leaving one newly-qualified policeman on duty there. Almost immediately 200 people descended on the police barracks armed with sticks and fork handles and sounding horns. After some time the crowd dispersed. The barrack guard, being new to the area, was not able to recognise any of the party.[8] Bagley was questioned that afternoon at the station but he refused to give a statement at that time.

Obviously there were still underlying tensions in the community and when given the opportunity, these tensions rose quickly to the surface. In nearby Johnstownbridge, ricks of hay and wheat were set on fire and one man, asleep in a loft, was accidentally burned to death.[9] In February of 1836 sheep belonging to William Murphy from Carbury village were killed and the wool taken away.[10] The properties of others who had paid their tithes were damaged and in May 1836 a notice was pinned to the pier of Johnstownbridge chapel gates calling for a meeting to petition parliament for the abolition of tithes.[11]

During these years the population of the village of Carbury continued to increase. Returns for the 1821 Census show that there were 32 inhabited houses in the village. Thirty-three families lived in these houses and the population of the village was 188 persons. Less than one-third were employed, with 20 people being employed in agriculture and 22 in trades. There were 44 children attending the village school.[12] By 1837 the population had reduced slightly to 159

6 Brenan, *Schools of Kildare and Leighlin*, p. 207. **7** *Letters of a great Irish landlord*, no. 46. **8** NAI, Outrage Papers, Kildare 1835. **9** Ibid., 1835. **10** Ibid., 1836. **11** Ibid., 1836. **12** *Abstract of*

inhabitants. There were 27 dwellings and a constabulary police station. The new Protestant church had been built. Lewis reported that the parochial school had 40 boys and 20 girls and was supported by subscriptions. There were also two pay schools with 60 boys and 30 girls.[13]

Griffith's Valuation gives the names of all the occupiers of land in the village in 1853 and a description of each tenement as well as the acreage and the valuation of both land and buildings. When the information from Griffith is compared with parish records for Carbury, it becomes apparent that by 1853, almost 75 per cent of the rateable holdings in the village were in Protestant hands. There were 15 houses in the village and five on the demesne. Of the various surnames recorded in Byrn's survey of 1744, not one is to be found in Griffith's Valuation. It appears that immigration was a regular feature of the life of Carbury village with families settling in the village to carry out specific roles, particularly in association with Newberry Hall, and moving on once those roles had been discontinued or were no longer viable. In contrast however, surnames of people living in the hinterland of Carbury village have survived, in some cases for at least three centuries.

Griffith's Valuation shows that the village had a corn mill at this time, which was operated by William Murphy. This mill was valued at £70, indicating that it was one of the largest mills in the area.[14] William Murphy held some 102 acres around the village. Ellen McCann held the fair green and received the tolls of the fairs. She received 6*d.* per head on all animals sold there. A sketch map from the 1930s depicts the site of the former tollgate in the village on the road towards the castle, just beyond the Protestant church. It would appear that there was no longer a weekly market in Carbury by the mid-nineteenth century. However, the two annual fairs continued to be held on 26 May and 2 October although there were no patents for the fairs.[15] The guardians of the Edenderry poor law union had established a dispensary in the village. It is impossible to glean information on the occupations of the people from Griffith's Valuation. However, Thomas Mooney who lived on the demesne had a forge and there was also a flax mill on the demesne which at that time was vacant.

Nineteen acres of the demesne land were covered with water. Eleven of the houses in the village are listed as having gardens attached. As can be seen from Table 1 the majority of the holdings were between zero and five acres in size, each comprising for the most part a house and garden.[16]

answers and returns for county Kildare, 1821, HC 1824 (463), xxii, p. 28.   **13** Samuel Lewis, *A topographical dictionary of Ireland* (London, 1837), i, p. 252.   **14** The corn mill in Garrisker was valued at £13; Clonkeen at £36 and Dunfierth at £20.   **15** *Royal commission on fairs and markets, 1852–3; Report of the commissioners appointed to inquire into the state of fairs and markets in Ireland*, HC 1852–3 (1674), xli, p. 79.   **16** Griffith, *Valuation*, county Kildare, barony of Carbury.

Table 1 Size of holdings in Carbury village and demesne (Griffith, *Valuation*)

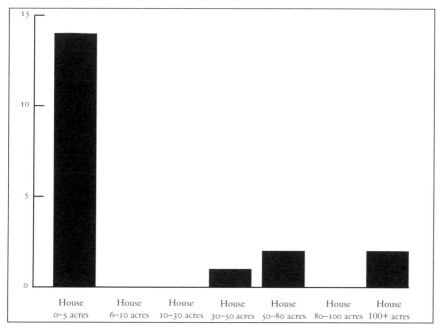

House 0–5 acres	House 6–10 acres	House 10–30 acres	House 30–50 acres	House 50–80 acres	House 80–100 acres	House 100+ acres

Father Michael Flanagan, parish priest, gave evidence on Carbury to the Poor Inquiry of the 1830s.[17] He stated that the houses in the area were generally built of clay, while those near the bog were built with sods and sticks. These houses had no furniture. Some cabins had bedsteads and bedding which was supplied by the charity of individuals.[18] Generally labourers were employed by the same employer for the entire year. Women were seldom employed unless by the few resident proprietors during planting or digging of potatoes and were paid half of the men's wage. Many of the labourers had the grass and hay for two cows, an acre of oat land and half an acre of potato land. They also reared poultry, calves and lambs. The low price of domestic produce such as butter, pork, eggs and poultry added to the distress of the poor. The report stated that the condition of the poor in the area was much worse than it had been during the war, particularly for those who were employed part-time.[19] Many were surviving by obtaining credit from shopkeepers at rates of about 25 per cent per annum. The typical diet of the people consisted of potatoes in winter and spring with salted herring on special occasions. Father Flanagan had known of women who walked a mile to purchase one herring which would be divided among their large families. Milk could be procured at dairies or at farmhouses. Oatmeal was purchased to make stirabout

17 *Selection of parochial examinations relative to the destitute classes in Ireland* (Dublin, 1835), p. 36. **18** Ibid. **19** Ibid.

for breakfast. During these years there was a significant number of abandoned infants in the area, possibly as a direct result of the distress of the people. These children, when found alive, were usually supported by the Church of Ireland and given such names as Henry Carberry, John Field and Eleanor Newberry.[20]

The village of Carbury was administered by the Edenderry poor law union following the 1838 act which extended the English poor law system to Ireland. Each union consisted of a market town and the district surrounding and depending on it. The workhouse was the keystone of each union. Edenderry workhouse was completed in January 1842. The members of the poor law guardians felt however, that the building work was defective and initially refused to take possession of the workhouse. Edward Wolstenholme, who had taken a lease on Newberry Hall sometime in the 1830s, was the chairman of the Edenderry board.[21]

Census returns from 1841 show that the number of houses in Carbury had fallen to twenty-one with a population of 128 persons.[22] The acreage of land planted with potatoes began to decline steadily through the mid-1840s. However, in the whole of county Kildare only 8 per cent of arable land was planted with potatoes. In fact, compared to all Irish counties, Kildare had the smallest area of arable land devoted to potato production.[23] In Carbury, 73 acres had been planted in 1844 and this had fallen to 62 acres by 1846.[24] In the neighbouring area of Ardkill the total acreage under potatoes had fallen from a total of 106 acres in 1844 to 62 acres in 1846. In 1846 one-third of the potato crop was lost in the area and one-sixth of the labourers were unemployed. In March of that year it was predicted that a great scarcity of food would prevail on the Carbury estate and in the neighbourhood within the following few months. Thomas Trench, George Colley's agent, had been instructed to secure employment for all persons on his properties who were not able to get to the poorhouse and to provide 'wholesome food at such a price as would place it within their reach'.[25] In that same month Viscount Harberton applied for funding to purchase Indian corn to feed some 2,500 on the Carbury estate.[26]

A poor relief committee was established in January 1847 and was chaired by Edward Wolstenholme of Newberry. The Church of Ireland minister, Francis Hewson, and the parish priest, James Phelan, were joint secretaries, while James Murphy of Derrinturn acted as treasurer. In their correspondence over the next few months they stated that the poor of the area were in a 'fearful state of poverty and destitution'.[27] In late February the duke of Leinster wrote a letter of approval

20 RCBL, Carbury parish – Baptism Register.   **21** Edenderry Union, HC 1843 (607) xlvi, p. 382.   **22** *Census Returns 1881.*   **23** Frank Taaffe, ' Athy and the Great Famine' in *Lest we forget – Kildare and the Great Famine* (Naas, 1996), p.57.   **24** Constabulary Returns for Carbury in *The Famine in county Kildare,* iii, Kildare County Council.   **25** NAI, RLFC2/Z565021, Relief Commission Papers, March 1846. It would appear that John Pomeroy's son, George, reverted to the surname Colley. Some subsequent family members were known as Pomeroy-Colley.   **26** NAI, RLFC3/1, Relief Commission Papers, 30 March 1846.   **27** *The Famine in*

Table 2 Population of Carbury village, 1821–1911, based on Census returns.

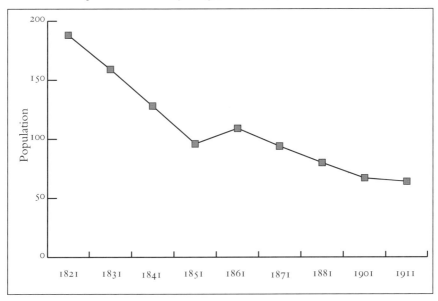

for the committee which was forwarded with the committee's own correspondence to the commissary general in Dublin.[28]

Conditions during the winter and spring of 1847 were very difficult in the area. Snows and rain meant that the men who had been employed in drainage schemes on the rivers were no longer able to work. This catastrophe meant that even more families became dependent on the relief committee. The committee distributed meal both free of charge and at reduced prices to the poor. Landowners in the area contributed the considerable sum of £102 towards the relief fund. Of this amount about 75 per cent was contributed by the Church of Ireland community.

By 1851 the population of the village had decreased again. There were now 20 houses with a population of 96 persons. The decline continued throughout the second half of the nineteenth century. By 1861 the number of houses had been reduced to 18 but there was a slight rise in the number of people in the village to 109. However, by 1871, the population had fallen again and by 1881 there were 80 people in the village, almost exactly 50 per cent less than at the end of the 1830s when Samuel Lewis had reported a population of 159 persons. This population decline in Carbury is much higher than the overall percentage decline for county Kildare. Between 1841 and 1881 the population of the county decreased by 38 per cent.[29] The continued decline in the population of Carbury

county Kildare: Relief Commission, ii, Kildare County Council, p. 36.   **28** NAI, RLFC3/2/13, Relief Commission Papers.   **29** Thomas Nelson, *The land war in county Kildare* (Maynooth,

village is almost certainly attributable to the absence of a Catholic church in the village. Throughout the nineteenth century the nearby chapel village of Derrinturn began to attract services to itself including the Catholic school, shops and public houses.

COMMUNICATIONS

Communications between Carbury and the outside world improved immensely towards the end of the nineteenth century. By 1871 the village had its own post office. Richard McCann was postmaster and letters arrived and were dispatched twice daily from Carbury. Christopher Dunne ran a public house in the village and was also involved in a coach-building business. William Waters was the surgeon in the dispensary. During these years Frederick Pilkington was resident in Newberry Hall. The Revd Henry Johnson was the Church of Ireland clergyman and Father Henry Dunne was parish priest.[30]

A railway station had been opened in Carbury when the Midland and Great Western Railway Company laid a branch line from Enfield to Edenderry. The extension had been proposed in November 1864 at a meeting in Edenderry courthouse. Miss Nesbitt, a local landowner, was keen to exhibit her prize cattle at the Royal Dublin Society in Ballsbridge and, as the cattle lost condition while being walked to Ballsbridge, she felt it would be much more advantageous to have them sent by rail. Therefore she became one of the sponsors of the branch line, donating £10,000 in gold and three miles of her land for tracks. A tender of £20,500 was accepted, and work commenced in late 1875. The first train passed through Carbury station on Tuesday, 10 April 1877. The main traffic on the branch line was livestock. At a shareholders' meeting the following September, it was reported that a train of 44 loaded cattle wagons had travelled on the line the previous day. Large numbers of cattle were loaded in wagons at Carbury station for the Dublin markets.[31] On Tuesdays up to 60 wagons were loaded. Merchants in Edenderry also used the trains. Furniture manufacturers, Ailesbury's in Edenderry, sent a load of chairs daily to Dublin.[32] Indeed, so successful was this railway line during these years that a proposal was made in 1898 to extend it as far as Limerick. However, the plan was never developed further.[33]

The first stationmaster in Carbury was James Marr, a Protestant. He was succeeded by John Buchanan, a native of Drumkeerin, county Leitrim in 1900. Buchanan had travelled widely with the railway company, having been previously stationed in Achill, county Mayo, and in Mallow, county Cork.[34] By 1911,

1985), p. 10. **30** *Slater's Directory of towns in Leinster* (Dublin, 1871), p. 409. **31** Ernie Shepherd, *Midland Great Western Railway of Ireland* (Leicester, 1994), p. 32. **32** Offaly county library, Edenderry. Notes collected by Seamus Rafferty, manuscript copy. **33** Shepherd, *Midland Great Western Railway of Ireland*, p. 32. **34** *1901 Census*

Figure 6 Carbury railway station *c.*1931 (courtesy National Library of Ireland).

John Clinton from Westmeath had become the first Catholic stationmaster. Clinton had also travelled widely, having lived in Mayo, Roscommon and Galway. By this time the station had become sufficiently busy that a railway foreman and a porter were also employed there. Trains went through the station four times each day. Two left Edenderry for Dublin and there were two from Dublin daily. Passengers travelling to Carbury or Edenderry had to use the last few carriages which were taken off the train at Enfield and brought to Edenderry by a smaller engine.[35]

The arrival of the railway was probably an important factor in the establishment of an annual sports day in Carbury, which began in 1881. Over the next few years the sports developed into a great event with large contingents of visitors arriving by rail. There were amusements and the elite of the neighbourhood danced to the popular string band of the Gasparro Brothers. In 1885, one year after the establishment of the Gaelic Athletic Association, the Carbury sports day included football played under the rules of the Association.[36] From 1885 the numbers attending the sports day began to decline, when the Midland and Great Western Railway Company refused to continue to run an evening return train as far as Enfield.[37]

35 Notes, Seamus Rafferty, Edenderry Library. **36** Con Costello, *A most delightful station: the British Army on the Curragh of Kildare, Ireland, 1855–1922* (Dublin, 1996), p. 187. **37** *Leinster Leader,* 8 August 1885.

THE LATE NINETEENTH CENTURY

During the years of the Land war the people became politically aware both through their membership of national organisations and through the influences of their local newspapers. In October 1882, Parnell, seizing the opportunity arising from the proscription of the Land League, launched his own political organisation, the National League. Its primary objective was the promotion of political affairs. Agrarian issues were of secondary importance. County Kildare differed from many other parts of the country at this time in that economic survival was not as much of a struggle for its population as it was in other counties. There were no mass evictions of tenantry and there were few reported incidents of agrarian crime compared to other counties.[38]

A branch of the National League was set up in Carbury parish on 18 November 1884. Priests were encouraged to become actively involved and the initial meeting of the branch was held in the parochial house attended by some eleven local men, including D. Fury, parish priest, J. McCrea, CC, and Christopher Dunne, the publican. Clerical participation was important to the League to ensure that no radical groups could gain control of local branches. It was agreed at the first meeting to approach the gentlemen of the adjacent Balyna parish to join in the formation of a baronial branch of the National League.[39] In January 1885, fifty members were enrolled in the League after a meeting at Kilshanroe. The establishment and growing strength of the National League in Carbury left the members of the Protestant community in the area feeling vulnerable. Father McCrea recorded in the minutes of the July meeting that he sincerely regretted the fact that his Protestant neighbours could entertain the 'absurd and false idea that the National League was sectarian.' He went on to state that among themselves in the Carbury branch they had 'Protestants who had read the history of Ireland aright and were above such narrow minded prejudices'.[40]

The National League managed to secure rent reductions on the local estates without recourse to violence. In December 1885 Lord Harberton had voluntarily offered a 20 per cent reduction on all holdings on his property.[41] By February of 1886 the chairman was able to report to the branch that through the actions of the League, rentals in the district had been reduced by £3,000 without a single eviction.[42] In 1886 the labourers of the village had applied to the board of guardians for cottages to be built. However, the chairman reported at the National League meeting on 8 May that the magistrate had stated that no cottages were required in Carbury except one for his own workman. This decision was widely condemned.[43] There was further disquiet when the labourers of the village applied for housing from the Edenderry union, and a pump was

38 Thomas Nelson, *Land war in Kildare*, p. 17. **39** *Leinster Leader*, 22 Nov 1884. **40** Ibid., 18 July 1885. **41** Ibid., 12 December 1885. **42** Ibid., 13 February 1886. **43** Ibid., 8 May 1886.

installed in the village instead at the insistence of 'a landed proprietor to accommodate the police – his tenants'.[44]

The members of the Carbury National League also kept themselves acquainted with the plight of tenants in other parts of the country. Sympathies were expressed for the tenants of the Luggacurren and Clongorey estates who were evicted and funds were established for both groups. Strongly worded editorials in the local newspapers rallied the support of people throughout the area. A police report stated that 'In Kildare ... the chief trouble comes from the influences of [the] mischievous nationalist paper the *Leinster Leader* ... By the aid of these pernicious prints, boycotting and intimidation has been carried on by local branches of the National League.'[45]

The sudden death of the parish priest, Father Fury, at the age of fifty-five, in January 1890 was a great shock to the area and a huge blow to the local branch of the National League. He had been parish priest for ten years and was described in his obituary as a 'true type of the *sagart aroon* and a sterling Nationalist'.[46] The severe weather during that winter had greatly damaged his health. His possessions were auctioned at the parochial house the following month.[47] Following his death attendances at National League meetings began to decline. Attendance numbers had already been reduced when the united branches of Balyna and Carbury had split in January 1887 with Balyna setting up their own branch of the League.[48]

Petty sessions, established early in the nineteenth century, were held in the courthouse in the village. In the 1880s they were held bi-monthly before three prominent landowners of the district – Charles Palmer, Francis Metcalf and Garrett Tyrrell. The local Catholic curate was present on occasions. The cases that were heard concerned many issues important to landowners in the area such as the setting of illegal traps, possession of illegal firearms and labourers suing employers for wages. Cases of domestic violence were also heard.[49] Justice was not always seen to be done at the petty sessions, however. In February 1885, following a prolonged case in which a defendant was obliged to pay excessive costs, the local newspaper, taking up the defendant's case, reported that the magistrates of Carbury who, 'under the shade of Carbury castle were supposed to administer the law, without fear, favour or affection' were 'singularly unanimous in their magnanimity' towards their own friends – Messrs Colley and Pilkington![50]

Fairs continued to be held twice yearly in May and October. The October fair in Carbury was known as the Apple Fair. Fiddlers, fifers and pipers came to the village to entertain. Licensed beer tents were erected with boards outside for dancing. Booths were constructed and there was much 'carrying on'.[51] Hundreds of people attended the day's entertainment.

44 Ibid., 25 January 1887. **45** NAI, Crime Branch Special, DICS Reports, Box 4 – Midland Division. **46** *Leinster Leader*, 25 January 1890. **47** Ibid., 25 January 1890; 15 February 1890. **48** Ibid., 22 January 1887. **49** Ibid., 24 January 1885; 7 February 1885. **50** Ibid., 7 February 1885; 21 February 1885. **51** Kildare County Library, ITA topographical and general survey,

Trinity Well on the grounds of Newberry Hall boasted the most popular and well-attended pattern in county Kildare. On Trinity Sunday each year locals gathered at the well and the rosary was recited. Afterwards people drank the water from the well as a cure for all ills. Tradition dictated that the parish priest should be the first to drink the water. After the religious ceremony was over, a 'promenade' was held. Everyone was dressed in his or her best clothes and young couples seen together were expected to marry within three months. Attempts to organise football matches in conjunction with the pattern were not initially successful as it was felt that they interfered with the essential element of walking around in the promenade. In later years, athletic competitions and football matches were held nearby at the crossroads. Hawkers attended the sports selling their wares and booths were erected along the roadway outside the entrance gates to Newberry Hall. Later in the evening there was dancing outside the RIC barracks. It is claimed that the door of Dunne's public house in the village was taken off the hinges for the step dancers to dance on. A local piper called Myles O'Gorman supplied music.[52]

The memory of the events of 1798 had not been forgotten in the area. During the centenary year, on the night of 23 May 1898, the hill was ablaze with bonfires 'and the utmost enthusiasm was manifested by the concourse of people assisting at the demonstration'.[53] Later that summer a crowd of some 3,500 attended another memorial gathering on Carbury Hill that was organised by the Edenderry '98 Club.[54]

THE EARLY TWENTIETH CENTURY

By the end of the nineteenth century the Protestant proportion of the population in Carbury had begun to decrease. The 1901 Census shows that there were 16 households in the village with a population of 67 people. The households ranged in size from two persons (five households) to seven persons (one household) with an average of four people per household. Five of the households were headed by a female. Some 42 per cent of the village's population were members of the Church of Ireland. Most of the important positions in the village were still occupied by Protestants. The school in the village was operated by schoolteacher, Julia Goodbody, who had been born in London. There were two shops; one, which was part of the public house, was run by Christopher Dunne, a Catholic, while the other was run by Elizabeth Bell, a Protestant. Daniel Halpin was the civil bill officer. The majority of the Protestant population of the village were employed on the Newberry estate. The gamekeeper on the estate was

county Kildare, Carbury parish.   **52** Quoted in P. Jackson, 'The holy wells of Kildare' in *Journal of the Kildare Archaeological Society*, xvi, p. 138.   **53** *Leinster Leader*, 28 May 1898.   **54** Mario Corrigan, *All that delirium of the brave – Kildare in 1798* (Naas, 1997), p. 97.

James Gray from Scotland, who lived with his family in Newberry Lodge. Many of the labourers on the estate had been born outside the area. John White was born in England and John Dagg, the shepherd, was from Tipperary. The clergyman, Canon Henry Johnson, had been born in Queen's county, while his wife, Mary Dorothea, came from Portrush in county Antrim. They employed a nurse, a maid, a cook and a general servant. There were five men stationed at the RIC barracks in the village – four Catholics and one Protestant. The post office was well established in the village by this time and employed a postmistress, a telegraph messenger and two postmen. The literacy rate among the village population was 85 per cent, which was extremely high. This high rate bears testimony to the success of the national school system in the area.

Canon Johnson resigned in 1903 having served in the parish for thirty-five years. He was replaced by Canon Charles W. Follis, an ex-British Army chaplain, from Kerry. A new Church of Ireland school was established in Carbury on 14 September 1903. It was located on the road from the village to the old churchyard and its first patron was Canon C.W. Follis. In his application he stated that the Church of Ireland population of the village at that time was twenty-seven persons. The school was a one-roomed, stone building with a slated roof and was in good repair at that time. Lord Harberton had funded the construction and the Hon. E. Pomeroy of Malvern Wells, England, owned the site. Alexander White, the first teacher there had been trained in the Church of Ireland training college, and this was his first position. The initial enrolment of the school consisted of a total of thirty-one pupils, all belonging to the 'Irish Church'.[55]

Vestry meetings at the church were attended by all the prominent Protestants in the parish. In 1901 the vestry expressed their sympathy with the royal family on the death of Queen Victoria and congratulated her son, Edward VII, on his accession to the throne.[56] The death of Sir William Pilkington in 1906 dealt a severe blow to the vestry. He had handled all the financial affairs of the parish.

Throughout the nineteenth century the Colley/Pomeroy family had continued to have an interest in Carbury. In 1904 under the terms of the 1903 Land Act, Arthur Colley sold the lands of his Carbury estate to the Land Commission. William Waters, the medical doctor at the dispensary in the village and Patrick Murphy, one of the principal landholders in the village were among the trustees of the sale.[57] At a meeting of the parish vestry in that same year, it was agreed that the operation of the Land Purchase Act would cause great financial loss to the parish and it was decided to make every effort to ensure that the parish finances were sound and secure.[58]

The 1911 Census shows that there were fourteen households in the village with a population of 64 persons. The number of police stationed at the RIC

55 NAI, ED 9, 17148 Carbury. **56** Carbury Parish vestry book in the possession of Sam Holt. **57** RD, 1904/53/285. **58** Carbury Parish vestry book.

barracks had been reduced somewhat and there were now only three men there. Sergeant Leonard was in charge and had two constables. The inclusion in the 1911 Census of a column showing the number of years married and the number of children born, makes it possible to discover that the average age of marriage for men in the village was 28.7 years while the average age for women was 26.1. The proportion of Protestants had decreased slightly to 31 per cent. This decrease was reflected in the fact that the RIC men, the railway staff, coachman, and post office staff were all Catholic by 1911. The Protestant-owned shop was no longer operating. Thomas Dunne and his wife, Mary, had taken over the running of the public house from his father. William Clarke was the petty sessions clerk while Dr William E. Waters was still stationed at the dispensary.[59] The Goodbody sisters, who were now in their seventies, continued to live in the village and a Miss Toombs is also listed as the teacher of the school there.[60]

By 1931, the railway company had suggested suspending the service to Edenderry. A delegation of businessmen from the town met with the traffic manager of the company and the suspension was averted. However, the writing was on the wall for the branch line. The company stated that the line had been a total financial loss to them but agreed to continue the service at that time. Bus travel had now become the preferred option for the people of the area. Perhaps this was due to the length of time the train took to make the journey to Dublin. A train that left Edenderry at 1.15 p.m. took four hours to make the 37-mile journey to Amiens Street![61] Passenger transport on the Edenderry branch line ceased on 1 June 1931. It continued to remain open for the transport of goods until 1 January 1935.[62] By the 1950s the main traffic on the railway line comprised special trains to football matches at Croke Park or outings of the Pioneer Total Abstinence Association to rallies in Dublin.[63] In June 1958, an excursion train was organised to Croke Park when Offaly were playing Louth in the Leinster final. The train took two hours to reach Enfield as the line began to subside in Knockirr bog.[64] The service eventually ceased on the branch line on 1 April 1963 and the tracks from Nesbitt junction to Edenderry were removed.

CONCLUSIONS

Documentary and archaeological evidence shows that there has been some form of settlement in Carbury village and its hinterland for the past three thousand

---

59 William E. Waters is buried in the churchyard at Carbury. His tombstone states that he served as medical officer for some 48 years until his death in November 1934, aged 69 years. 60 *Porter's Post Office Guide and Directory of the counties of Kildare and Carlow* (Dublin, 1910), p. 7. 61 *Leinster Leader*, 16 January 1992. 62 Stephen Johnson, *Johnson's gazetteer of the railways of Ireland* (Leicester, 1997), p.88. 63 *Leinster Leader*, 23 May 1959. 64 Notes, Seamus Rafferty, Edenderry Library.

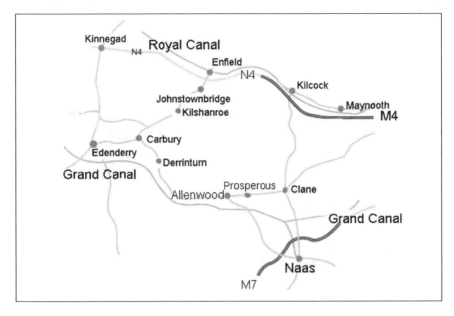

Figure 7 Map of Carbury area – not to scale

years. By the mid-eighteenth century, the village lay in a state of neglect, its potential apparent but unexploited. The building of Newberry Hall brought renewed life to the village with the centre of influence shifting from the castle to the Hall. It is especially interesting that the Colley family maintained an interest in the Carbury area from the mid-sixteenth century to the early twentieth century. This may explain the generally good relations that existed between landlord and tenants on the estate, even during the years of the Land War.

Much of contemporary life was reflected in Carbury village. The community experienced the ebb and flow of conflict and cooperation over the years. Events occurring on a national scale, such as the construction and operation of the charter schools, the events of 1798, the distress of the early nineteenth century, the Famine, the land war and the late nineteenth century resurgence of nationalism, were all mirrored on a small scale within the village of Carbury.

The physical fabric of the modern village of Carbury retains significant traces of this long and distinguished past. The layout of the village, the topography of the local area, the ruined castle on the hill, the imposing structure of the Church of Ireland nestled into the hillside, the once-magnificent Newberry Hall – all are a legacy of the contributions of the past generations who lived and died there.

Carbury village has been an open community for many generations, a community where immigration was a regular feature of life. Census returns give one indication of the origins of the village's inhabitants. An examination of surname

Figure 8 Carbury village with RIC barracks on right, *c.*1901

survival from the mid-eighteenth century to the early twentieth century provides further evidence that this community was a transitory one, with families
settling in the village in various roles, particularly as workers on the estate, and
moving on once those roles had been discontinued or were no longer viable.
This is in strong contrast to families who lived outside the village, some of whom
have been represented in the area for hundreds of years and whose descendants
continue to live there today.

The growth and development of Carbury village seems to have been haphazard from its very establishment. The original settlement developed sponta-
neously around the castle with people who worked at the castle settling nearby.
Suggestions for colonisation in the seventeenth century and for improvements
in the survey of 1744 were never acted upon. After Newberry Hall was built,
the population of the village showed an increase with the majority of the village's inhabitants being employed on the demesne. Yet, no great efforts were
ever made to improve or extend the village. This is probably due, in part, to
the fact that the Harbertons were absentee landlords for almost the whole of
the nineteenth century. As a consequence of the absenteeism and the lack of
patronage, the village's expansion seems to have been unplanned and unstruc-
tured. With the exception of the construction of the railway, the impetus for
its growth does not seem to have come from its hinterland, but rather from
within the village itself when the need arose. Development of the village was

Figure 9 Carbury village, 2003

always constrained physically and economically by the presence of bogland to its north and northeast. The village also suffered due to its location – some three miles from Edenderry and six from Johnstownbridge. Perhaps the proximity of both of these was too great to allow Carbury village to prosper as a separate entity.

The fact that the Catholic church and school were located in Derrinturn has probably been the greatest contributory factor to the lack of growth of Carbury. In the late twentieth century Carbury village began to be superseded by the growth and development of Derrinturn. This village has gradually attracted other functions to itself such as a school, parish hall, parochial houses, post office, medical centre, shops and other services and is currently experiencing the growth associated with urban settings in the Dublin hinterland of the twenty-first century.

The story of Carbury village is one of change and adaptation. Yet, it retains today the vestiges of its past history, its people and its structures. The advent of the twenty-first century has made little impact on this village. A comparison of photographs taken in the village in 1901 and in 2001 show little change in the physical fabric. (See Figures 8 and 9.) Yet, Carbury has been the location of human settlement for over three thousand years and is likely to remain so for many more years to come.

Acknowledgements:
A special word of thanks to the following for their help and advice in compiling this article: Mario Corrigan, Kildare County Library, Newbridge; Seamus Cullen, Baltracey, Donadea; Sam Holt, Coolvacoose House, Carbury and Noel Whelan (RIP), Offaly County Library, Edenderry

Portlaw, county Waterford, 1870–1901:
the decline of an industrial village

TOM HUNT

INTRODUCTION

Portlaw, county Waterford, is located in the civil parish of Clonegam, in the barony of Upperthird, approximately eleven miles from Waterford city and five miles from Carrick-on-Suir. One of the defining characteristics of the village is its industrial tradition. In the nineteenth century the most successful Irish attempt at establishing a cotton industry was centred on the village. Subsequently, in a fifty-year renaissance period stretching from the mid-1930s to the mid-1980s Portlaw was the leading centre of the Irish leather industry. Uniquely, in a south of Ireland context, industrial employment catering for both males and females was a characteristic feature of the village.

The river Clodiagh, a tributary of the river Suir, flows through the village with the confluence of these rivers located about one mile away. The Suir formed one of the most important transport arteries for the village during the nineteenth century as raw cotton was imported from Liverpool via Waterford and upriver on the Suir to Portlaw. The processed cotton was in turn transported back down the Suir to Waterford city from where it was exported to markets worldwide.

H.P.R. Finberg has suggested that the task of the local historian should be to 're-enact in his own mind and to portray for his readers the origin, growth, decline and fall of a local community'.[1] An attempt has already been made to examine the origin, growth and characteristics of the community and industrial village of Portlaw.[2] This essay examines some aspects of decline in the village following the collapse of the Malcomson multi-national business empire in 1876.

Portlaw was a purpose-built industrial village developed to house the workers for the cotton plant that began operation in 1825. The enterprise was the inspiration of David Malcomson, a Clonmel-based member of the Society of Friends who extended and diversified his business empire in the early 1820s to embrace cotton manufacturing. Portlaw, which offered the potential of water-power by means of the river Clodiagh, and the advantage of river transport by means of the river Suir, was chosen as the centre for this enterprise. Over the next fifteen years, the new enterprise was successful and expanded considerably

---

1 H.P.R. Finberg, *The local historian and his theme* (Leicester, 1952). **2** Tom Hunt, *Portlaw, county Waterford 1825–76: portrait of an industrial village and its cotton industry* (Dublin, 2000).

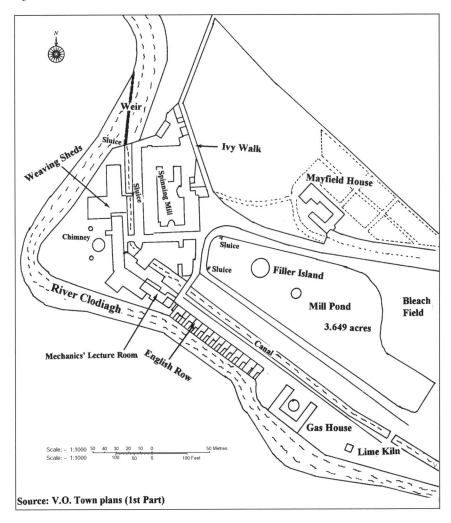

Figure 1 Factory complex and residential areas within factory compound, 1850.

so that by 1840 the plant was a fully integrated operation that embraced the three distinct cotton manufacturing activities of spinning, weaving and finishing including dyeing and bleaching. A range of ancillary activities designed to make the complex as self-sufficient as possible, supported the primary enterprises and allowed the basic manufacturing activities to continue without interruption (Figure 1). This sector of the enterprise formed an impressive industrial complex in its own right. It included

> A large foundry and workshops in which every implement and appliance required in the mill was especially manufactured. Everything in the way

> of machinery and fitting, from the huge 20ft. iron mill wheel to the tiny
> wooden bobbin is produced here for the establishment, and such is the
> wear and tear of a huge mill like this that the whole series of workshops
> and their staffs of mechanics are kept in full employment.[3]

The industrial infrastructure also included the canal linking the factory to the tidal
reaches of the Clodiagh, the large millpond, the bleach fields and the gas works.

David Malcomson retired from the business in 1838 and the management of
the enterprise was placed in the hands of his seven sons who traded as Malcomson
Brothers. Of the brothers, Joseph, until his sudden death in 1858 and William,
who was in charge when the company became bankrupt, made the most significant impact on company enterprise.[4] Due to the absence of company records
it is difficult to evaluate the input of the other brothers to company development. Robert maintained his involvement to the end and was a partner when
the business became bankrupt in 1876. Both John and Thomas retired from the
business on 31 October 1847. Two other brothers died before the enterprise
collapsed – Joshua in October 1858 and David junior in July 1867.[5] The death
of the latter precipitated a crisis in the company as his widow, Mrs Nannie
Malcomson, began legal moves shortly after his death to remove her son's share
of the business from the company.

In parallel with the expansion at Portlaw, the Malcomson commercial empire
also expanded and diversified, so that by 1870, the firm of Malcomson Brothers
formed a multi-national, multi-faceted business empire of extraordinary magni-
tude. The empire embraced a disparate range of economic activities. Initially
this included flour milling at Clonmel and Pouldrew (county Waterford) but
was expanded to include salmon exporting from Limerick, oil processing in
Scotland, marine insurance from London, shipbuilding in Waterford, linen spinning and weaving in Belfast and Carrick-on-Suir, a brick-making plant in
Chester, cotton manufacturing in Manchester, coal-mining interests in Germany
and an international merchant marine. The brothers also possessed an impressive portfolio of railway company shares with William Malcomson acting as
chairman of the Waterford and Limerick Rail Company throughout the 1860s.

An analysis of the Custom House registers of shipping reveals the scale of the
merchant marine section of the business. This analysis reveals that various combinations of Malcomson brothers were the registered owners of at least 108 different ships at Waterford port between 1844 and 1877. All but three of these
registrations were made in the twenty-five year period between 1844 and 1869.
The ships traded between London, Liverpool and other ports of the United
Kingdom as well as with Bordeaux, Rotterdam, Amsterdam, St Petersburg, the
River Plate and various other South and North American ports.[6] The most active

3 *Waterford Mail,* 14 January 1870. **4** Hunt, *Portlaw,* p. 69. **5** NAI, 975/14/7, Malcomson
family papers.

period of expansion of this shipping empire occurred between 1859 and 1866, during the period when William Malcomson was the chief partner, when forty-one ships were registered.[7] Bill Irish in his outstanding work on the history of shipbuilding in Waterford has established the importance of the Malcomson owned Neptune yard to the history of Irish shipbuilding.[8] The earliest reference to the Neptune shipyard dates to 1840.[9] In 1846 the first iron-hulled screw pro-pelled ship, the 146-foot-long S.S. *Neptune* was launched. Although, essentially the Neptune yard built ships for Malcomsons' fleet only, the requirements of the firm were such that all types of vessels were built as they advanced from moderate sized vessels to the largest transatlantic liners, four of which exceeded 300 feet in length.[10] Several of the ships constructed involved innovations and technological advances that were at the forefront of iron steamer development. These included the introduction of watertight compartments, the use of a coat-ing of Portland cement on the inside hull to prevent rusting and the introduc-tion of iron decks in the early 1860s. The installation of a lifting mechanism to raise the propeller clear of water was fitted to the S.S. *Avoca* in 1861 and this allowed the sails to take full advantage of the wind without experiencing under-water drag. The following year an innovative steering mechanism was fitted to the S.S. *Cella* and allowed a vessel to be steered from mid-ships or aft.[11] Thirty-one different vessels had been launched from the Neptune yard by 1870.[12]

In 1870, Mrs Nannie Malcomson, widow of David Malcomson junior, and testamentary guardian of her son Joseph, 'a minor', applied to the court of chancery to have her son's share of the family business, amounting to almost £200,000, withdrawn. Material prepared for the court of appeal in chancery provides important financial detail on the state of company finances at the time and indicates the relative importance of the component parts of the Malcomson commercial enterprise.[13] In May 1870 the net annual profit from the entire range of business activities was calculated at £86,500 with almost 60 per cent of the total derived from the company's shipping interests. The company's investment in railway shares returned dividends of £14,000, the Prussian mines profits were valued at £6,000 while the Lax Weir Shannon fishery exports contributed £1,000 of the total. The remainder of the profits were derived from the family's textile business. Profits from Belfast and other northern Ireland interests were valued at £10,000 while the Portlaw mixed textile plant returned profits of £6,000, less than 7 per cent of the total company profits. Company assets were

6 *Munster Express*, 18 January 1892. **7** NAI, *Register of ships, 1845–55, revenue I, Waterford: Register of ships, 1855–77, revenue II, Waterford*. **8** Bill Irish, *Shipbuilding in Waterford, 1820–1882: a historical, technical and pictorial study* (Bray 2001), p. 225. **9** The *Waterford Newsletter* dated 31 October 1840 lists a consignment of 358 bars of iron and ninety–seven boilerplates for the Neptune foundry. **10** Ibid., pp 228–9. **11** Ibid., p. 228. **12** Ibid., p. 260. **13** NAI, 975/14/6, The petition of appeal of Robert Malcomson, William Malcomson, George Pim Malcomson and Frederick Malcomson,

Table 1 Age and gender balance of workforce of Malcomson textile workers in Waterford region in 1870.

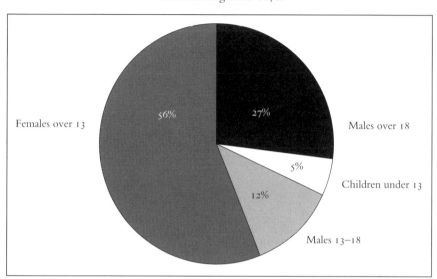

also valued at the time. Total assets amounted to £1,472,950 with liabilities assessed at £830,230. The building and machinery at Portlaw were valued at £100,000; the workers' houses at £14,000 and lands held at Portlaw by William, Frederick and George Pim Malcomson were valued at £5,000. Although the Portlaw enterprise was the most visible element of the Malcomson business empire and the symbolic representation of its stature and power, the total Portlaw assets represented less than 8 per cent of the total.

Malcomson enterprises employed in excess of 2,300 workers, both male and female, in the Waterford region in 1870. In Portlaw alone 1,445 were employed, a linen spinning and weaving plant in Carrick-on-Suir employed 620, a linen weaving operation in Clonmel employed 194.[14] Also at the Neptune shipbuilding yard in Waterford 72 males (including 10 males aged between 13 and 18 were employed.[15] The age and gender balance of the 1870 textile workers is illustrated in Table 1.

RESTRUCTURING THE URBAN ENVIRONMENT

The original Portlaw village was developed between 1825 and 1850 with the core Malcomson development consisting of two parallel streets, Mulgrave Street

14 *Returns of the number of manufacturing establishments in which the hours of work are regulated by any Act of Parliament in each county of the United Kingdom*, p. 71, HC 1871 (440) lxii, 105. **15** Ibid., p. 80.

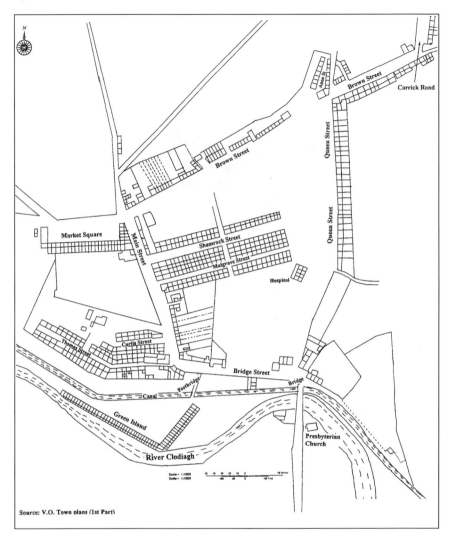

Figure 2 The original Portlaw village development, *c.*1850.

and Shamrock Street, forming the village centre (Figure 3). This core area of
the town was an orderly and pre-planned development. Constructed at right
angles to Main Street, Shamrock and Mulgrave Streets were rectilinear and parallel to each other, whilst the form of Market Square suggests the concern of
the planners to create a civic space with an urban character. A second
Malcomson development, Green Island, also exhibits the characteristics of a
planned development and the desire to provide a pleasant living environment
for some factory employees. It was an L-shaped development of fifty-seven
houses located between the canal and the river Clodiagh with frontage facing

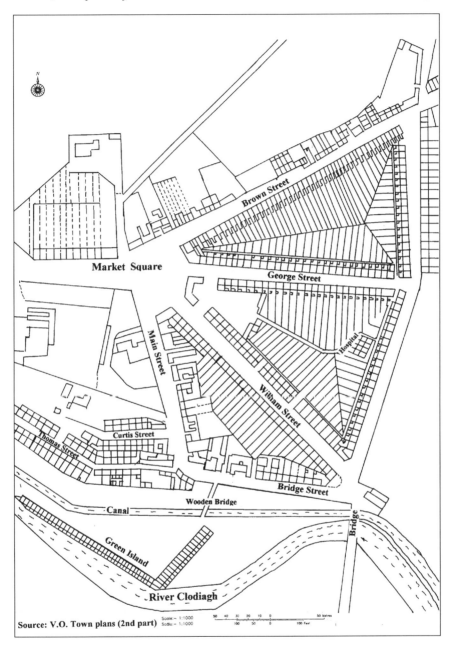

Figure 3 Portlaw, *c.*1870, with its unitary planned central core.

a green area of almost four acres.[16] Queen Street formed the eastern boundary
of the village. Brown Street, Curtis Street and Thomas Street were property
developments by individuals who invested capital in housing and took advantage of the business opportunity presented by the Malcomson intervention in
Portlaw.[17] This development attracted positive comment from several English
travellers who visited the village in the 1840s. The comment made by factory
inspector, James Stewart, in his report of 1842 was typical of the type of reaction of visitors at the time. As an experienced observer of working and living
conditions throughout the United Kingdom his comments are particularly valuable. He believed that

> Portlaw in Ireland afforded far better and more comfortable accommo-
> dation than, so far as I have observed, is to be found for any other of the
> working population in any other parts of Scotland and Ireland.[18]

Despite the favourable response of contemporary visitors, the quality of housing
failed to meet the exacting standards required by the Malcomson family. In 1861,
factory doctor, James Martin, contemptuously dismissed the eulogised village as
but 'a wigwam of mud walls and thatched roofs, uncomfortable, un-cleanly and
unwholesome'.[19] Starting in the late 1850s the core element of the village was radically transformed. The parallel streets were destroyed and replaced by an original and formal design plan unique to Portlaw (Figure 3). The village was laid out
on a 'polyvium' plan, an urban planning technique that had not been previously
attempted in Ireland. The polyvium plan created triangular blocks with the apex
of each triangle meeting at an open square. This square in turn was linked to the
factory gates by a wide street that replaced the previous Market Square. George's
Street formed the central east-west axis of the new layout.

The revolutionary intervention began with the construction of a terrace of
50 two-storey houses on the south side of Brown Street, work that was completed in 1859. By August 1861 the factory proprietors had

> Taken down nearly all the old houses and erected good roomy comfort-
> able houses to the number of about 120, and are continuing to work at the
> erection of at least as many more, with large windows, provision for the
> separation of the sexes, and other appliances for comfort and decency.[20]

Much of the development was completed by 1867 when the 63 houses of
William Street and the 55 houses of George's Street were completed and fully
occupied.[21] Other property developers in the village were inspired by the

16 Hunt, *Portlaw*, p. 17.   **17** Hunt, *Portlaw* pp 16–20.   **18** *Returns of the inspectors of factories*,
July–Dec. 1842, p.18, HC 1843 [429], xxvii, 289.   **19** *Waterford Mail*, 30 August 1861.   **20**
Ibid.   **21** Hunt, *Portlaw*, pp 24–6.

Malcomson intervention. Thomas Medlycott for instance constructed 10 small slated cottages on the northern edge of the original Market Square.[22]

The quality of the Malcomson housing developed at this time was far superior to the original and is reflected in the assessed valuation. The new single-storey houses were valued at £3 each, double the valuation of the old Shamrock and Mulgrave Street houses while the Brown Street two-storey houses were valued at £5.[23] This re-constructed village contained houses of three basic internal design types. George's Street, William Street, Queen's Street and Bridge Street contained single-storey, three-bay, four-roomed houses. The entrance was directly into the front room with three rooms opening off this room, one to the front and two to the rear divided by a hallway.[24] The south side of Brown Street contained two house types. The first was a two-bay, narrow frontage, two-storey house. The ground floor contained a hall with a room to the front and a room to the rear opening off it. The second type of house in this street was a two-storey, two-bay, wide frontage house with three rooms on the ground floor, two to the front and one at the back as well as two bedrooms on the first floor.[25] The generous floor to ceiling height of eleven feet in the new houses reflected a concern to encourage a healthy living environment that would provide fresh air and daylight. Each dwelling had a fireplace and chimney, a small kitchen range, an oven and side tank with a tap that supplied hot water. Privies were provided to the rear with a dry closet.[26]

A variety of motives inspired this re-development. The need to deal with the serious overcrowding in the village was a priority.[27] William Malcomson was the chief partner of the firm when much of this radical intervention took place. As a Quaker, he was motivated by a strong belief that employers had a moral responsibility to provide a proper living environment for their employees. In doing this he believed 'they were only doing their duty to their neighbour, their country, and their God'.[28] This altruism would also have practical advantages as 'the more they identified the labourer with the locality in which he was the more they identified him with the success and interests of the farm or estate on which he worked'[29] Macniece has concluded from his study of Ulster industrial villages that the practice of house building by industrial entrepreneurs in the later decades of nineteenth century in Ulster was a response 'to the regional difference in the economics of house-building rather than in excessive dreams of paternalism'.[30] As the

22 Ibid.   **23** Ibid., p. 26.   **24** Majella Walsh, 'Portlaw, a model industrial village', 2 vols. (unpublished MSc thesis in urban and building conservation, UCD, 1985), p. 93.   **25** Ibid., pp 94–5.   **26** Over the past three years work has been carried out on the preparation of a conservation plan for Portlaw co-sponsored by the Heritage Council, Waterford County Council and the Department of the Environment. I wish to acknowledge the advice and expertise of the architect to the project, Garry Miley, Limerick, in explaining the architectural and urban planning significance of Portlaw.   **27** Hunt, *Portlaw*, pp 21–4.   **28** *Waterford Mail*, 31 October 1862.   **29** Ibid.   **30** D.S. Macniece, 'Industrial villages of Ulster, 1800–1900'

nineteenth century progressed, rising building costs in England reduced the attractiveness of the provision of workers housing as an investment. The economics of building were much more attractive to Ulster industrialists who continued to provide workers' housing to the end of the nineteenth century, and were more attractive still in Waterford where the reported building costs of the Portlaw houses were considerably lower than Macniece's Ulster estimates. The single-storey dwellings in Portlaw cost £40 to construct with the total Malcomson investment in housing estimated at £10,000 in 1871.[31] In Portlaw the use of the mass-produced, prefabricated, curved, trellised, softwood frame roof trusses was a key design feature in the reduced development costs. The framework was designed to provide substantial overhanging eaves at the front and back of the houses. This framework was then covered with several layers of tarred calico, the tar a by-product of the gas manufacturing plant located within the factory complex on the banks of the river Clodiagh (Figure 1). Both frames and covering material were manufactured at the factory and this allowed a 50 per cent reduction in the cost of roofing the Portlaw houses compared to using conventional slate roofs.[32] The curved roofs also provided the Portlaw houses with their most distinctive architectural feature, a design that had no precedent in vernacular architecture. The austere outward appearance of the houses, with the use of a bargeboard the only decorative feature of significance, belied an internal sophistication of plan that was rooted in concerns for utility, hygiene and the supply of fresh air. A system of regular inspection carried out by factory personnel ensured standards of cleanliness and maintenance were maintained.[33]

At least one contemporary visitor was surprised by the planned nature of the development and found it difficult to mentally adjust to its distinguishing features. David Wark found the village to be 'peculiar in appearance', and that

> Its houses do not present that picturesque variety of form and colour and size found elsewhere. There is a monotonous sameness about its streets … Seen from a distance the rows of houses seem like huge caravans, for they are of uniform and small elevation, while the roofs are slightly rounded, with little stove-pipe chimneys standing above them at regular intervals, giving an effect that causes first amazement and then amusement at the first time.[34]

Possession of a new house encouraged a lifestyle change amongst some of the occupants. Although a small minority still showed a tendency 'to grovel in their old filthy ways', the majority according to Dr Martin seemed to compete with each other in their efforts towards neatness and tidiness. Almost every house dis-

in *Plantation to Partition*, P. Roebuck (ed.) (Belfast, 1981), pp. 188–9. **31** *Waterford Mail*, 5 December 1862, 5 Oct. 1871. **32** Hunt, *Portlaw*, p. 26. **33** *Waterford Mail*, 30 August 1861. **34** *Missionary Herald*, 1 March 1900.

Table 2 Population structure of Portlaw in 1871.

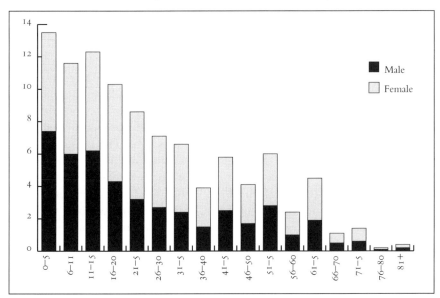

played 'its neat muslin curtain' while 'handsome fuschia, geranium or musk, neatly trained', was to be seen in every window.[35]

THE COMMUNITY OF 1871

An examination of material contained in the 1871 census report allows the characteristics of the community at that time to be identified.

The village contained 581 houses in 1871 only one of which was un-inhabited. The houses were inhabited by 3,774 people, 1,703 males and 2,071 females, described as 'a heterogeneous mass drawn together from all parts of Ireland'.[36] Despite the diversity of origin of the people it was the opinion of the factory surgeon Dr Martin that regular employment and discipline had produced a population that matched the people of any town in Ireland in their 'obedience to the law, honesty, chastity and temperance'.[37] It was a youthful population with 48 per cent under 25 years of age with an imbalanced gender structure. Females comprised 55 per cent of the total population and in the age sectors between 15 and 40 the imbalance was more pronounced with 14 per cent of this group male and 22 per cent female. This imbalance resulted in the Portlaw population in 1871 having large numbers of single females and was itself a direct result of the nature of the employment available, where young females were required in the

35 *Waterford Mail*, 30 August 1861.   36 *Census of Ireland, 1871; Waterford Mail*, 30 August 1861.
37 *Waterford Mail*, 30 August 1861.

weaving sheds, a form of employment that was a female speciality in textile mills.[38] The overall imbalance was less than that displayed by textile industrial villages in the north of Ireland as the presence of the workshops at the Portlaw plant provided opportunities for male employment that was atypical. Approximately 15 per cent of the employees at the mills were skilled male trades-men and labourers.[39] Emigration, at times of downturn in the local economy, is reflected in the uneven nature of the population pyramid (Table 2).

The community was a multi-denominational one, embracing five different religious persuasions. The first reliable source of information on the religious affiliations of the village people is the 1861 census returns. This census included the results of the enquiry into the religious persuasions of the people. Although the 1861 population of 3,852 was 94 per cent Catholic, it also included 126 mem-bers of the Established church, 92 Presbyterians and four members of the Methodist congregation. Outside of the main cities of Munster, only Clonmel and Fermoy had larger Presbyterian populations.[40] The proportion of Catholics in the population remained at 94 percent in 1871 but the number of Protestants increased to 167 with the Presbyterian element of the community reduced to 25 representatives. Twelve members of 'other denominations' as well as four Methodists completed the religious affiliation of the community in 1871. At this time 36 per cent of the population could read and write; another 15 per cent could read only and despite the best efforts of the paternalistic Malcomson family, 49 per cent of the population of the village were still illiterate.[41]

The census returns of 1871 include a detailed breakdown of the labour force of the village and the occupational structure of the community is illustrated in Table 1.[42]

The dominant occupational group was industrial with the single largest occu-pation within this group that of cotton manufacturer, an activity that employed 95 males and 235 females. The numbers employed in this branch of manufac-turing only slightly exceeded those who were described as weavers in mixed fabrics (93 males and 201 females), providing a clear indication that the firm's specialisation in cotton manufacturing was ended. During the 1860s the enter-prise had diversified from primarily cotton manufacture to the manufacture of mixed fabrics. It was this diversification that allowed the business to survive the challenges presented by the outbreak of the civil war in America and to increase the numbers employed in the 1860s. William Malcomson, the managing part-ner of the time was responsible for two crucial interventions that provided effec-

---

38 Tom Hunt, 'The Portlaw cotton plant: work and workers, 1835–1904', in *Decies, journal of the Waterford archaeological & historical society,* (56, 2000), pp 135–46. This article contains a detailed examination of the extent and nature of the employment opportunities available in Portlaw.   39 Ibid., p. 143.   40 *Census of Ireland 1861, pt. iv: Reports and tables relating to the reli-gious professions, education and occupations of the people, vol. ii,* p. 257, [3204–III], HC 1863, lx,1.   41 *Census of Ireland* 1871, p. 973.   42 Ibid., pp. 946–2.

Table 3 Occupational structure of Portlaw population, 1871.

Class	Male		Female	
	Under 20	Over 20	Under 20	Over 20
Professional	2	16	2	7
Domestic	3	26	20	292
Commercial	11	59		12
Agricultural	1	50	1	3
Industrial	147	270	233	288
Indefinite labourer	107	326	84	79
Children/un-stated	629	54	563	484

tive survival strategies.[43] Linen weaving was introduced using yarn procured in Limerick and Belfast and as a result of this

> the firm found that the machinery it employed was not able to manufacture at profit and consequently it displaced it and introduced new machinery in its stead, which with inferior material, produced a large amount of results.[44]

The census-defined industrial category is not inclusive of all factory employees and therefore understates the importance of factory-based employment to the village as 161 females and 160 males are classified as factory labourers ('branch undefined') and are included in the 'indefinite labourer' category. Domestic servants provide the next most important category, forming almost 31 per cent of the female labour force, and many in this category may not have worked outside the family home. Both the professional and commercial categories were important minority occupations and both displayed significant male majorities. In the former category teachers, schoolmasters, students, policemen, army and navy pensioners were represented. The most important commercial gentlemen were commercial clerks (19), followed by 14 general shopkeepers, eight coachmen and, reflecting the mercantile marine element of the Malcomson commercial empire, 'six boatmen on seas'.

THE POST-BANKRUPTCY ECONOMIC EXPERIENCE, 1870–1901

In 1876 the firm of Malcomson Brothers became bankrupt with accumulated liabilities of £349,800. An analysis of the reasons for this collapse is outside the scope of this essay but it was an event that the firm had been battling to prevent since

43 Hunt, *Portlaw*, pp. 64–5. **44** *Munster Express,* 7 October 1865.

the early 1870s.[45] The impact of this collapse was devastating for the village. The factory inspectors' returns provide the quantitative evidence of the implications of the bankruptcy on employment in the village.[46] A total of 1,141 jobs were lost between 1874 and 1878. Male and female employees were affected in almost equal measure, 577 males and 564 females became unemployed. Enumerating the unemployed by the categories used by factory inspectors identifies 142 children, 163 males under eighteen, 496 females over thirteen and 340 adults males who were presented with the problem of finding alternative employment.

Table 4 Employment in Malcomson brothers in 1874 and Mayfield Spinning Company
1878, 1884, 1890 and 1896.

Category	1874	1878	1884	1890	1896
Children (half-timers)	144	2	21	19	2
Males under eighteen	196	33	38	42	8
Females over thirteen	709	213	206	167	65
Males over eighteen	430	90	95	109	26
Total males	701	124	142	165	36
Total females	778	214	218	172	65
Total employees	1479	338	360	337	101

The collapse however did not bring about a total eclipse of the industry in the village. In 1877 William and Joseph Malcomson, sons of William Malcomson, the senior partner in the firm of Malcomson Brothers at the time of bankruptcy, established the Mayfield Spinning Company, 'engaged in the business of cotton spinning similar to that formerly carried on by Malcomson Brothers'.[47]As can be seen from Figure 4 the firm were also engaged in other branches of the industry such as dyeing, bleaching and manufacturing.

This new business continued for another twenty-five years on a small scale in comparison with the former Malcomson Brothers venture. Based on the consistency of the factory inspectors returns, it seems that the firm employed over 330 between 1877 and 1890, a level of employment comparable in scale to the later tannery development but insignificant in comparison to its predecessor. In

45For a brief examination of the reasons for the collapse of the business empire see Hunt, *Portlaw*, pp. 65–6; Cormac Ó Gráda, *Ireland, a new economic history, 1780–1830* (Oxford, 1994), pp. 280–1. For an interpretation heavily influenced by the Malcomson family memoir that places the blame for the collapse squarely on the allegedly poor economic decision making of William Malcomson see Irish, *Waterford shipbuilding*, pp 132–42.   **46** *Return of number of factories authorised to be inspected under the factories and workshops acts*, HC, 1878–79 (324), lxv, 201; 1884–85, (340), lxxi, 1081; 1890, (328), lxvii, 169.   **47** NAI, 975/14/6, Joseph Malcomson with William Malcomson, deed of dissolution of partnership.

Figure 4 Mayfield Spinning Company, Portlaw, county Waterford, 1886.

1887 the brothers also formed the Mayfield Dairy Company for the manufacturing and trading of dairy and creamery products.

The brothers' partnership was dissolved in November 1895 when Joseph Malcomson retired from the business and withdrew his share valued at £1,316. At this stage the industry was offering employment to only 100 persons. In the 1901 census enumerators' forms, 86 (including 11 males) still claimed they were employed in the cotton industry in Portlaw. William continued the business of cotton spinning until 'the last bobbin ceased to revolve on 1904'.[48] The same year the Belfast firm of Messrs W.J. McCoy were reported to have purchased the entire machinery of the plant and were expected to remove the 'greater portion of it to Belfast'.[49]

ESCAPE FROM PORTLAW: MIGRATION AND POPULATION DECLINE

The immediate reaction of almost half the people of Portlaw to the Malcomson bankruptcy was to leave the village. In the five-year period 1876 and 1881, 48 per cent of the village's male population and 52 per cent of the female popula-

48 P. Power, 'The Portlaw cotton factory', in *Waterford and South Eastern Archaeological Society Journal*, 13 (1910), p. 64.   49 *Waterford News*, 16 September 1904.

tion migrated. This migration continued in the succeeding decades so that by
1901 the population had declined to just 29 per cent of the 1871 total. The mon-
umental decline of the village's population is perhaps best indicated by the following stark statistic. The total number of factory-based employees in 1874
exceeded the total village population in 1891; the number of female factory operatives was 50 in excess of the total female population of 1891, and the number
of male factory employees was 35 greater than the total male population of 1891!
The population change of the village for the period of this study is summarised
in Table 5.

Table 5 Population change in the village of Portlaw, 1871–1901.[50]

Year	Male	Female	Total
1871	1,703	2,071	3,774
1881	887	1004	1,891
1891	666	728	1,394
1901	505	596	1101

Tracing the destination of the migrants who departed is a difficult task and,
despite the variety of contemporary Waterford local newspapers, none of them
seem to have reported or commented on the exodus from the village. Waterford
local historian, Matthew Butler, suggested in a local history column in the
Waterford News in 1935 that the operatives migrated to Lancashire. According to
Butler,

> Lancashire offered the only opening where people with the training and
> skill of the Portlaw operatives could find suitable occupation. The fame
> of the goods produced at Portlaw was spread wherever cotton fabrics were
> known, and the skill of those who produced such goods was equally well
> known. Hence, when the workers, or a portion of them, at Portlaw
> became unemployed they offered their services to the cotton mills of
> Lancashire and where they were at once engaged. Here we find another
> example of the generosity of the Malcolmsons [sic]; in every case they
> paid the fare of an employee from Portlaw to whatever point or village
> in Lancashire he decided to go; in June 1876 over 150 workers left Portlaw
> for the English cotton centres in Lancashire and in every case their fare
> was paid by the Malcolmsons [sic] of Portlaw.[51]

The certainty is that Lancashire was the favoured point of destination for some
of the migrants, as a well-established contact network was already in place and

50 *Census of population of Ireland, 1871, 1881, 1891, 1901.*   **51** *Waterford News and Star*, 23 August

had been operative in the 1860s when a number of 'starving' Lancashire operatives were brought to Portlaw on the initiative of William Malcomson because
that area was experiencing the vicissitudes associated with the American Civil
War.[52] In 1861 factory doctor, James Martin, in a presentation to the social sci-
ence congress praised the ability of those who qualified as skilled tradesmen from
the Portlaw workshops and their achievements in Lancashire. They were able
to 'hold the highest places as tradesmen in the most eminent engineering and
machine making establishments'.[53]

THE EXPERIENCE OF THE RELIGIOUS MINORITIES

The presbyterians

The two minority religious communities were particularly disadvantaged by the
collapse of the Malcomson enterprise. The decline of the Presbyterian community within the village was total, with no member of the Presbyterian church
living in the village in 1901 although a small number still lived and worked on
the nearby Curraghmore demesne. The Protestant community was also considerably reduced in numbers decreasing from 167 in 1871 to 35 in 1901. The following information, extracted from the baptism and marriage registers of both
the Protestant and Presbyterian churches, illustrates the changing circumstances
of both church communities over a fifty-five-year period.[54]

The origin of the Presbyterian community in the village was directly related
to the development of the cotton industry, where skilled and semi-skilled individuals and those with management skills from Scotland and Ulster were
recruited. The spiritual needs of this community were catered for with the establishment of a Presbyterian place of worship in Portlaw in the early 1840s. A 999-
year lease was obtained on a plot of land from the marquis of Waterford and
work on the building of a Presbyterian church was completed in 1845.[55] The
first minister of Portlaw was Mr James Cleland, who was ordained on 9 May
1843 by the presbytery of Munster. He resigned in 1854 and emigrated to the
USA. His successor, Mr David Ferguson, was ordained on 31 May 1854, and
served the congregation until his death in February 1887.[56] 'Under his ministry
the congregation attained its greatest prosperity and became large and flourishing.'[57] A visitation to the presbytery held in May 1848 reported that there were

1935.   **52** Hunt, *Portlaw*, p. 64.   **53** *Waterford Mail*, 30 August 1861.   **54** Presbyterian Historical
Society of Ireland (PHSI), Register of marriages, Portlaw 1845–1904, CR 457; Baptismal register, Portlaw CR 454; at RCBL, Registers of parish of Clonegam (Lismore); Register of
marriages, P0646/03; Register of baptisms, P0646/02.   **55** Alexander Stuart Cromie,
Controversy among southern Presbyterians (Belfast, n.d.), p. 172.   **56** PHSI, *A history of congregations in the Presbyterian church in Ireland, 1610–1982* (Belfast, 1982), p. 706.   **57** *Missionary Herald*,
1 March 1900.

Table 6 Marriage and baptism trends in Church of Ireland and Presbyterian
communities in Portlaw, 1845–99.

	Presbyterian Church		Church of Ireland	
	Marriages	Baptisms	Marriages	Baptisms
1845–49	3	17	19	46
1850–54	5	24	25	45
1855–59	4	25	10	22
1860–64	5	22	2	17
1865–69	4	28	9	24
1870–74	3	11	4	32
1875–79	2	7	2	37
1880–84	4	5	4	25
1885–89		3	1	23
1890–94			2	24
1895–99			1	27

30 families and three individuals attached to the congregation. The average attendance at Sunday worship was 65 in the morning and 45 in the afternoon. The
membership remained consistent over the next two decades, as an 1867 visitation reported a membership of 40 families with an average attendance of 55 at
worship.[58] At this time, twice-daily Sunday services were held at 11.30 a.m. and
5.00 p.m and the associated Sabbath school began lessons at 9.00 a.m.[59] In 1848
the Sabbath school had 12 teachers and was attended by 50 students.[60] In 1867
eight teachers taught in the school that had 50 registered pupils.[61]

Members of the community 'were practically all immigrants from Scotland
or the north of Ireland', and as such many failed to establish roots in the district.
[62] It was also felt that many of the members' attachment to the congregation was
'by a very slender thread, having been educated in other sections of the church'.[63]
Analysis of the disjunction certificate book and the communion roll for the district indicates a membership that was extremely mobile with a number of members migrating annually. The disjunction book recorded 15 members leaving in
the 1850s, 25 in the 1860s, 16 in the 1870s, 12 in the 1880s and 11 in the 1890s.[64]
In the early decades the members were replaced, but following the bankruptcy
of 1876 this became less common so that by March 1879 a visitation recorded
only eight families in Portlaw and the once thriving Sabbath school had closed.[65]

58 Cromie, *Controversy*, pp. 172–3. **59** PHSI, Financial report of the Portlaw congregation
for the year 1866. **60** Cromie, *Controversy*, p. 172. **61** PHSI, Superintendent's roll book,
Sabbath school, Portlaw, CR450. **62** *Missionary Herald*, 1 March 1900. **63** PHSI, Session
minute book, CR 461, 17 November 1858. **64** PHSI, Disjunction certificate book, CR460.
65 Cromie, *Controversy*, p. 173.

Although the connection with the textile plant was considerable, there was another source of Presbyterian employment in the district. The Curraghmore demesne of the marquis of Waterford was located on the edge of the village, and this estate also employed many Presbyterians. The place of residence of those receiving communion was recorded in the communion roll for the period 1845–69. Of the 121 individuals listed as receiving communion over the period, 66 per cent had Portlaw addresses and 31 per cent lived at Curraghmore. There, they were mainly employed in a range of farm-related occupations, such as land stewards, gardeners, blacksmiths, shepherds, ploughmen, foresters, gatehouse keepers and servants. The Portlaw resident communicants were employed as policemen, teachers, factory 'over-lookers', factory managers, flax instructors, in skilled trades and as servants.[66] A similar occupational structure is revealed by an analysis of the register of marriages. This register, which records the occupations of bride and groom and their fathers, reveals a similar concentration of skilled occupations, with a greater concentration of factory-related skills, such as dyers, roller-coverers, mill-wrights, spinning and weaving over-lookers and factory managers, represented. In the 1860s, two of the stipend payers, Mr Barker and Mr Brabazon, acted as factory manager and chief accountant respectively and with a number of the spinning and weaving 'over-lookers' also employed, members of the Presbyterian community possessed considerable influence in factory management. This was the cause of occasional tension with members of the Church of Ireland. The session meeting of 18 February 1856 discussed the most advisable mode of dealing with 'a calumny propagated by the Episcopal curate to the effect that a number of those attending the Presbyterian church only did so, through undue influence being brought to bear on them, in connection with their employment in the factory'.[67] Unfortunately the follow up is not recorded.

The collapse of the firm ended Presbyterianism in Portlaw although some members of the congregation continued to find employment in Curraghmore (the Curraghmore demesne census return forms of 1901 record eleven Presbyterians in the demesne). The visitation of September 1885 recorded seven families in Portlaw and by October 1893 only two families were resident there. The congregation was then united with the congregation of Waterford and on 6 November 1888 the Revd John Hall, minister of Waterford, was installed as minister of Portlaw. He conducted weekly services, alternatively in Portlaw and Carrick-on-Suir. On his resignation the Revd David Wark was installed as minister of Waterford. Regular service was ended in Portlaw in the early 1890s. The service was replaced by a monthly evening meeting at Portlaw and Carrick-on-Suir. It was held at premises offered by the Society of Friends and attracted an average attendance of fifteen.[68] In Portlaw this evening meeting gradually declined

66 PHSI, Communion roll book, Portlaw, CR 455.   **67** PHSI. Session minute book, CR 461, 18 February 1856.   **68** Cromie, *Controversy*, pp173–4.

and was finally discontinued. The church became 'seriously dilapidated and almost ruinous'.[69] The influx of several Presbyterians to Carrick-on-Suir in association with industrial development, the arrival of some new Presbyterian families to the Portlaw district (Curraghmore estate), combined with the pressure on David Wark to fulfil his obligations to these rural congregations resulted in the appointment, on his recommendation, of a licentiate, the Revd R.H. Gilmour, to work once again in the Portlaw district. As the church was too dilapidated to use, William Malcomson granted the use of the lecture hall for the meetings. Mr Gilmour initially attracted an attendance of between 40 and 50 to his services, the majority from Carrick-on-Suir. The success of the services encouraged an attempt to restore and repair the church. In the summer of 1899 an appeal for finance launched throughout the United Kingdom was so successful that the building, 'after being closed for about twelve years' was reopened for public worship on 19 November 1899. At the turn of the century service was again held at the Portlaw church for Presbyterians in the district. Although none were from the village itself, David Wark had cause for satisfaction:

> A number of non-church going people had been influenced and brought into church connection. Many who were becoming careless have been roused, spiritual life in the district has been quickened and a church that was twelve months previously nothing 'other than disgraceful is now a credit to us and an ornament to the village'.[70]

The Church of Ireland

> So small is the number of Protestants in some parishes that the clergyman might almost begin the service as Dr Swift once did, by addressing his clerk instead of his audience.[71]

The observation of Wakefield on the Church of Ireland strength in county Waterford is applicable to most of the parishes in the diocese of Lismore, but the parish of Clonegam is one of the five exceptions, where the Protestant population recorded in a diocesan survey, carried out in 1836, exceeded 5 per cent of the total population recorded in the 1841 census. Only the parishes of Lismore (494), Tallow (352) and Dungarvan (335) exceeded the Clonegam (245) total recorded in this survey.[72] In 1861 the parish of Clonegam had a Church of Ireland population of 224 with over half of these resident in Portlaw.[73] Until 1850 Protestants worshipped at a church located at Clonegam, within the Curraghmore

69 *Missionary Herald*, 1 March 1901. **70** Ibid. **71** S. Wakefield, *An account of Ireland: statistical and political* (London, 1812), ii, p. 633. **72** M.B. Kiely and W. Nolan, 'Politics, land and rural conflict in county Waterford, *c*.1830–1845', in William Nolan and Thomas P. Power (eds), *Waterford, history & society: interdisciplinary essays on the history of an Irish county* (Dublin, 1992), p. 466. **73** *Census of Ireland* 1861, p. 359.

demesne, two miles uphill from Portlaw and built in 1741 by Viscount Tyrone (Sir Marcus Beresford). The influx of Protestants, attracted by the cotton factory, changed the epicentre of the group and a new church was built at Portlaw and dedicated under the name of the Holy Trinity in June 1852.[74]

The occupational structure of the Protestant community of the district may be explored using the marriage register for the parish.[75] This register offers a representative cross-section of the members. Wider ranges of economic activities were represented at both the lower and upper tiers of the economic pyramid, than was found in the Presbyterian community. The occupation of labourer was the most common one recorded followed by farmers, whilst the most common female occupation was that of servant maid, followed by that of weaver in the cotton mill. A wide range of skilled trades were represented, both factory and estate-related. The Church of Ireland community also gained two high profile members of the Malcomson family as members during the late 1860s. Following the baptism of a number of Malcomson children, two adult members were baptised, David on 30 March 1867 and Frederick on 22 February 1869.[76] George Pim Malcomson, although not baptised in Portlaw, was also an active member of the Protestant community in the 1880s and 1890s.

In 1871 important administrative changes were made to parish organisation in the diocese. The Clonegam union was re-constituted to embrace a number of parishes. Clonegam and Feonagh were united in 1867 and the unification of these areas with Guilcagh, Newcastle, Mothel, Rathgormack and with Coolfin townland, were sanctioned by the diocesan synod of 1871 and became operative as their incumbents died.[77] These changes were related to the changed circumstances, following the disestablishment of the Church of Ireland and the passing of the Irish Church Act of 1869, which came into force on 1 January 1871. The Malcomson bankruptcy was the second blow the Protestant church members received within a short period. The latter event happened as the members were beginning to adjust to the former. The only source material available that allows an examination of the impact of the events on the community is the Clonegam vestry minute book, 1876 and 1920.[78] This book records the minutes of the meetings of the select vestry of the parish held between 1876 and 1920. The select vestry, composed of the rate-paying Protestants of each parish, was in essence the governing body of the parish and was responsible for the management of the church buildings, education and the recruitment and payment of parish officers.[79] The Clonegam book's chief records are concerned with the building, furnishing and maintenance of

74 R.B. MacCarthy, 'The diocese of Lismore, 1801–1868' (unpublished MA thesis, UCC, 1965), pp 81–2. **75** RCBL, Marriage register, P.O646/03 (like the Presbyterian register it also listed the occupations of both parents of the bride and groom). **76** RCBL, Register of baptisms in the parish of Clonegam, P.O646/03, p. 18. **77** W.H. Rennison, *Succession lists of the diocese of Waterford and Lismore* (Waterford, 1920). **78** RCBL, Clonegam vestry minute book, 1876–1920. P.0646/05. **79** Raymond Refaussé, *Church of Ireland records* (Dublin, 2000),

churches, schools, glebe houses and the presentation of the monthly parish accounts. The monthly parochial account passed for payment on 13 January 1876 for instance featured expenditure of £20 4s. 2d. and included expenditure on fuel for the school and church, expenditure on the cleaning of both premises, printing and advertising costs and the most expensive item, the monthly salary of the parochial teacher which amounted to £7 3s. 4d.[80] This account material for the period shows a Protestant community under constant pressure to meet the financial demands placed upon it. A retrenchment measure introduced in May 1883 featured the dismissal of the schoolmaster and his replacement by a married couple and their daughters 'as schoolmaster and mistress, clerk and organists at a salary of £60 per year (paid monthly) with house, and in addition to be allowed £2 per year for washing out of school rooms after each court day, paid half yearly'.[81] Finally, in April 1889, the select vestry decided to take advantage of the financial aid offered by the state supported system and applied to affiliate the parochial school to the national board system.[82] The financial obligations presented by the diocesan assessment fund proved to be equally problematic.

The decline of both communities impacted on the cultural and intellectual life of the village. Members of both communities, supported by Malcomson patronage, were active and enthusiastic promoters of the virtues of rational recreation. A variety of intellectually challenging and entertaining activities were promoted through the medium of the Mayfield Literary Society (or the Mayfield Library and Scientific Society as it was known in 1871). Esoteric debates, lectures, musical evenings, literary reading sessions and the more mundane spelling competitions were organised as well as physical recreation by means of the Mayfield cricket club.[83] The supporters of these initiatives, from both religious communities, viewed leisure as a preventive measure against immorality and delinquency among young people, and offered rational, wholesome and uplifting activities as an antidote.[84] Dr Martin referred to these 'elevated pleasures' as alternatives to 'wasting the hours at the corners of the streets, indulging filthy jests and hateful slang', or spending time 'within the sphere of the brutalizing influence of strong drink'.[85] The Malcomson Brothers firm provided both financial and physical support. At the 1871 annual soiree the brothers were thanked, for providing without charge, a reading room, a lecture hall, gaslight, coal, attendants as well as 'a supply of the daily newspapers and periodicals'.[86] The library in 1871 was reported to hold '780 volumes, exclusive of £2 worth of new works' recently ordered.[87] These interventions ceased following the collapse of the Malcomson business empire and the resultant decline in the numbers of the two religious communities that were the activities main supporters.

p. 16. **80** RCBL, Minute book, 13 January 1876. **81** RCBL, Minute book, 29 May 1893. **82** RCBL, Minute book, 6 April 1889. **83** Hunt, *Portlaw*, pp 40–3. **84** Catriona M. Parratt, *'More than mere amusement': working-class women's leisure in England, 1750–1914* (Boston, 2001), p. 147. **85** *Waterford Mail*, 22 April 1863. **86** *Waterford Mail*, 25 August 1871. **87** Ibid.

EDUCATIONAL ADJUSTMENTS.

The provision of schools was one of the chief social institutions encouraged by nineteenth century paternalistic employers. Malcomsons' intervention was responsible for the development within Portlaw of a set of educational institutions that were unparalleled within the county. Provision for education was made from the beginning but the Malcomson contribution was increased substantially in the late 1850s. In excess of £2,000 was invested in the construction of an imposing school building and within this impressive complex separate male, female, evening and infant schools, known as the Mayfield schools, were organised, each affiliated to the national board of education from 1855 onwards. Affiliation to the national board brought considerable state funding to the schools but despite this a Malcomson estimate in 1868, suggested that their annual contribution to education at Portlaw amounted to at least £200 annually. Following the bankruptcy of 1876 the Malcomson family continued to provide for the education of the young people of Portlaw but with some re-adjustments arising from the changed economic circumstances. Evening classes were abandoned and numbers attending the Mayfield schools declined, a trend that reflected the changed demographic circumstances and the reduced social control of the paternalistic Malcomson family. In August 1883, numbers attending the schools had declined to 74 male, 64 female and 56 infants.

The parish priest of the district, Thomas Hearn, availed of the opportunity presented by the decline in the Malcomson-promoted secular system to introduce and promote a different model of education in the village. He recruited a community of Mercy sisters from Cahir, county Tipperary. He rented three houses on the new road north of Brown Street from Thomas Medlycott and converted seven of the eight apartments of these houses to schoolrooms. The new school catered for females and infant boys and was established on 30 July 1883. The Catholic-promoted school proved an immediate success and when visited by the inspector, M. Moloney, on 29 August 1883, 124 males and 143 females were present. They benefited from the teaching of nuns, who were according to the inspector 'possessed of considerable experience and aptitude in teaching'.[88] The school manager, Father Hearn, expected the school to attract an average attendance of over 200, but the Presbyterian minister, the Revd Ferguson, objected to the affiliation of the new school to the national board as he believed it would 'subvert' the Mayfield female and infant school.[89] Despite this objection, the inspector recommended affiliation to the commissioners, as he was particularly impressed with the potential this school offered for social improvement in the village. He believed that the large numbers of children, who 'had been habitually idling through the village or worse mischievously occu-

---

88 NAI, ED. 1/88/49. **89** Ibid.

pied, had been attracted within its walls and in addition to these the school is attended by nearly all the pupils who frequented Mayfield female and infant school'. Despite the 'almost certain extinction of these schools', approval of the new school, he believed, would 'promote harmony in the locality and will ultimately prove of great public benefit to the poorer classes of the community in Portlaw and its vicinity'.[90] The inspector's considerations were proved correct on both counts. Large numbers of students were attracted to the school with an average attendance of 230 reported in November 1889.[91] His fears for the future of the Mayfield female schools also proved prophetic. The decline in average attendance at the female and infants school, resulting from the competition of the convent school, is illustrated in Table 7.

Table 7 Average quarterly attendance in 1883–4 for Mayfield female and infants school.[92]

Quarterly period	Infants school	Female school
31 March 1883	46	61
30 June 1883	60	73
30 Sept. 1883	41	52
31 Dec. 1883	19	19
31 March 1884	18	14

The decline in average attendance had serious consequences for the Malcomson managed female schools, as an average attendance in excess of 30 for two successive quarters, was essential for the retention of state support. Management responded by amalgamating the schools but the decline continued, with attendance at the combined schools averaging 21 and 17 for the June and September 1884 quarters respectively.[93] Finally, in October 1884, William Malcomson junior informed his district inspector that it had been decided to close the Mayfield female school as there did not 'seem to be a prospect of the numbers getting up'. The school was struck off the roll of national schools and all grants to it cancelled from 6 October 1884 'from which date it ceased operation'.[94] Competition and the availability of a church-promoted system, that provided an alternative education curriculum, ended a system that since 1855 had provided female education in Portlaw.[95]

The convent school received an additional financial boost in February 1884, when the deceased parish priest, Father J. McGrath, bequeathed a sum of '£90 a year for ever to the community of nuns who shall conduct schools in Portlaw'.[96] The school management placed a heavy emphasis on religious education with

90 Ibid.   **91** NAI, ED. 9/6066.   **92** NAI, ED. 9/2601.   **93** Ibid.   **94** Ibid.   **95** NAI, ED. 2/183/ *folio 91*.   **96** Ibid.

thrice daily religious classes organised from 9.05 to 10.00 a.m, from 12.00 to 12.30 p.m and from 3.00 to 3.10 p.m. Secular instruction was given between 10.00 and 12.00 a.m. and from 12.30 to 3.00 p.m. In 1886 the basic curriculum was extended when permission was granted to introduce the teaching of geography, French, music and drawing. An element of vocational education was also introduced at the same time when training in the use of cotton manufacturing machinery was permitted. In 1893 this industrial training was reported to be proceeding satisfactorily.[97] As the 1890s concluded, the commissioners encouraged the management of the Portlaw convent school to improve 'the present unsatisfactory accommodation' and they began to exert pressure on management to construct a new school premises. Finally, plans were approved in February 1902 and £628 was awarded in grant aid towards expenditure of £942 for the construction of a school large enough to accommodate 300 pupils and the sum of £62 6s. 8d. to enclose the area. An evening school was also established under the management of Father Hearn in July 1883 which catered almost totally for young girls that worked in the cotton factory. Classes were taught each evening from 6 to 8 p.m. from Monday to Friday with reading, writing, spelling and arithmetic lessons organised for the first four evenings and religious instruction given on the Friday.[98] The experiment was relatively short lived as the school ceased to operate from 31 October 1888.[99]

The Malcomson-managed system continued to provide education for the boys of Portlaw once they had progressed beyond the infant stage. Church and factory personnel co-operated in 1886 to establish an evening school for the young male adults and teenagers of the village. The application of William Malcomson junior for affiliation to the national board was supported by the letter of the Catholic curate, J. Keating, who believed from his 'intimate knowledge' of the boys that 'the reckless habits contracted by many of them are to be attributed to the want of an elementary education'. This exclusively secular school, designed to serve the basic literacy requirements of the mill hands and agricultural labourers, was established in September 1886 with 77 pupils enrolled and was approved for acceptance by the inspector S.E. Stronge in November 1886.[1]

Throughout the period of this study, male education was provided by the Malcomson-managed Mayfield boys school. The history of this school is revealed by the information recorded in the pages of the registers maintained by the national commissioners and three main areas of concern were recorded in the documents. Firstly the school struggled to maintain the numbers that would justify the hiring of an assistant teacher. The regulations required that an average attendance in excess of 70 for two successive quarters was essential for the payment of an assistant's salary by the commissioners. Under the changed economic circumstances of Portlaw, the school frequently found this a difficult target.

97 NAI, ED. 2/184/*folio* 39. **98** NAI, ED.1/88/49. **99** NAI, ED. 2/184/ *folio* 39. **1** NAI, ED. 9/3937.

Secondly, there were the usual reprimands admonished by the inspectors for failure to deal with routine administrative matters and, more seriously, concern was
expressed at failure to maintain reasonable discipline or adequate teaching standards. Some examples illustrate the nature of these complaints. The principal
was cautioned in January 1887 to be more careful in keeping accounts as the
inspector found the rolls unmarked when he visited the school on Christmas
Eve. The same individual was severely reprimanded in May 1895 for 'his cruel
treatment' of one of the pupils who was kept kneeling continuously for two days
instead of bringing the boy's improper behaviour to the attention of the manager. The principal was also fined the sum of 5s. for a delay in forwarding an
arithmetic text book to the student, despite having received the money for the
book. Finally, reflecting the changed economic circumstances of the village and
of the Malcomson family in particular, there was frequent reference to the decay
in the physical fabric of the school building with attention regularly drawn to
the need for repairs to be carried out.[2]

The Protestant community also eventually converted to the virtues of the
state regulated and funded system. In August 1889, the Protestant rector, the
Revd Flemyng, applied to the commissioners for permission to affiliate a school
to the national board. This application was motivated by financial pressure, as
an examination of the select vestry minute book for the period reveals a church
community under considerable pressure to fulfil its financial commitments. The
provision of a teacher's salary for the parochial school was one of the chief
demands made annually on the parochial fund.[3] For much of the history of the
National Board of Education, the Church of Ireland had nothing to do with the
national system of education, treating it as Akenson memorably suggested, 'as a
product of the devil rather than a convenient source of government funds'.[4] The
initial application was refused as the proposed venue for the school was already
used as the venue for the petty sessions court once a month. The Catholic parish
priest vigorously opposed this application, and articulated his objections in a
series of letters to the administrators of the national board. In a letter, dated 29
August 1889, he questioned the need for an additional national school in a village in which the 'population had dwindled by half', and where two schools
already existed 'within a stones throw of each other'. He claimed the demand
for the new school was inspired by 'nothing but the sectarian spirit of a half
dozen bigots,' a development that he believed would prove to be 'a very trou-
blesome child of sectarianism'. In addition, he argued, that 'petty tyranny' would
compel the children of the employees of the Curraghmore estate to attend the
school thus encouraging 'religious troubles and strife in Portlaw'. A few days

2 NAI, ED. 2/183/ folio 90.   3 RCBL, select vestry minute book, Clonegam parish
1876–1920.   4 Donald Harman Akenson, The Church of Ireland, 1800–1855 (London, 1971),
p. 202.

later on 2 September he pointed out to the commissioners that Protestants, Presbyterians and Catholics attended the Mayfield boys' national school that was under Protestant management without any complaint from parents or pupils. On this occasion, he alleged that a personal vendetta lay behind the move to establish the new school. The plan had its 'origin in a falling out between a Protestant malcontent lady and the Protestant teacher'. The lady and her friends now attempted 'to move church and state to dislodge the teacher and his family and try to establish a new and unnecessary school in order to assert and uphold her dignity'. Finally, on 4 February 1890, Father Hearn repeated his objections, this time expressing concern for the future of the Mayfield boys school, where 'the first unfortunate result of the establishment of this un-necessary school is the withdrawal of the salary of the assistant teacher in the present school. The good gentleman is probably ruined'. The second result he believed would be 'attempts to proselytise Catholic children'. These arguments were rejected by the inspector, S.E. Strong, who pointed out that one of the reasons for the low average attendance in the Mayfield national school was due to the failure of the Father Hearn – managed Portlaw convent school to remove from their rolls boys over eight years, following their examinations and to transfer them to Mayfield school.[5] In December 1889 the school application was accepted by the board of the commissioners and was granted a £44 salary with results fees to the teacher, Mr W.H. Clelland and a £4 grant of free stock.[6] This school, with the usual administrative admonishments from the inspectorate, provided satisfactory education for the Protestant community of Clonegam parish.

The provision of education survived the collapse of the Malcomson commercial empire and if anything a more inclusive educational system developed, albeit promoted on a denominational basis. During the peak of the Malcomson commercial era the factory-promoted educational system attracted less 'than half the children between the ages of three and thirteen'.[7] The more inclusive postbankruptcy system was helped in 1892 by the introduction of a modified form of compulsory attendance for children between the ages of six and fourteen.[8] New power brokers emerged, namely the Catholic parish priest and the Protestant rector, who managed education at the local level and organised the infrastructure to maximise for their denominations, the available state funds.

THE VILLAGE COMMUNITY IN 1901

On the night of 31 March 1901, the 255 householders in the village of Portlaw completed their census forms.[9] The householders were required to furnish

5 NAI, ED. 9/6066. **6** NAI, ED. 2/184/ *folio 97*. **7** *Waterford Mail*, 30 August 1861. **8** Maeve Mulryan-Moloney, *Nineteenth-century elementary education in the archdiocese of Tuam* (Dublin, 2001), p. 52. **9** NAI, Census – Waterford 4, DED Portlaw 11c/1–11c/11.

Table 8 Population structure of Portlaw, 1901.

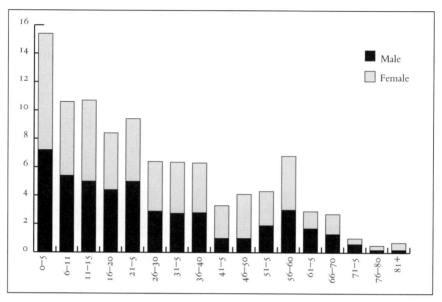

detailed information on their background and economic circumstances including their age, religion, occupational status, places of birth, relationship between household members, type of house, the number and type of outbuildings, ability to read and write and their fluency in the Irish language. The individual census forms provide a mass of socio-economic data and provide the basis for the reconstruction of the geography and community of the village in 1901.

The population in 1901 remained an essentially young one with 26 per cent under 15 years of age and 52 per cent aged less than 30. The normally non-economically productive sector of the population (those under 15 and over 65) accounted for 42 per cent of the total, compared to 44 per cent in 1871. This was a high dependency ratio and would have placed considerable economic pressure on the economically active sectors of the community, a pressure that the economically viable community of 1871 would have been much more capable of managing. The proportion of males and females remained unchanged from 1871, the village's population being still 54 per cent female. The position of the gender imbalance within the overall age structure of the population had shifted considerably and this reflected the extent to which migration was a male phenomenon. In 1901 12 per cent of the female population was aged between 41 and 60, while the corresponding male figure was 7 per cent. The cultural diversity of 1871 was no more with only 35 Protestants now resident in the village. Levels of literacy amongst those over 16 years of age had shown significant improvement since 1871. Illiteracy was reduced from 49 per cent to 23 per cent. Just 8 per cent could read only, compared to 15 per cent in 1871, and 53 per cent were fully literate, an increase of 13 per cent on the 1871 situation. The improved levels of literacy present one of the few positive aspects of post-Malcomson bankruptcy Portlaw.

Analysis of the census forms also allows a detailed re-construction of the socio-economic structure of the village population. The type of work carried out by the people of the village can be summarised in nine different categories. Table 9 records the main occupational categories identified by the people on the completed census forms.

Table 9 Occupations of the inhabitants of Portlaw in 1901.

Occupation	Male	Female
Labourer	186	21
Unspecified	11	129
Domestic servants	4	54
Skilled labourer	56	21
Shopkeeper/Publican/Assistant	27	24
Housekeeper	1	54
Professional	4	4
Cotton worker	11	75
Other	10	6
Total	310	388

Based on the above analysis 62 per cent of the male population of the village and 53 per cent of the female population were in employment. Excluded from the calculation are those who were described as either scholars, unemployed children below the age of 16 or pensioners. Also excluded are those who were described as housekeepers and those who left the occupational category blank in their census form. The majority of the village dwellers fell into five occupational groups. Unskilled workers, including farm labourers, dominated the male grouping with 60 per cent of the village's male labour force in this category. Although we have no indication of the exact nature of this employment, it is reasonable to suggest, given the nature of the economic difficulties experienced by the village, that much of this employment was of a casual nature. Thomas Dooley, in a study dealing with Waterford city, identifies four characteristics that distinguished members of this class from the rest of society. Firstly, their earnings were minimal and they made no financial contribution to the state. Secondly they formed a pool of unemployed or under-employed labour and lived precariously close to pauperism. Thirdly, a great many of the class were illiterate or semi-literate. Finally placement in the labouring sector was a life sentence as any movement into the skilled category of labour was as difficult as moving between the working and upper classes.[10] Forty-seven per cent of the female labour force of the village did not work outside the family home. This was the group of 129 females listed in the unspecified category above, who left the category 'rank, occupation or profession' in the census return blank and the 54 who categorised themselves as a house-keeper. Despite the setbacks endured by the cotton industry from 1875, the industry was still the most important single source of non-domestic employment for women. Seventy-five females ranging in age from 14 to 60 continued to work at the Mayfield spinning company. The majority of these women worked as spinners in the mill. Domestic service represented the next most important source of female employment with almost one in five employed females represented in this category. The economic stagnation of the village is clearly expressed in the small number employed in service and retail activities as well as in the minimal number of professional people living within the village. The change since 1871 in the labour force structure was considerable. Regular factory based employment, offering opportunities to both skilled, semi-skilled and unskilled males and females, had been replaced by a system of uncertain casual labour.

The census returns of 1901 also allow an analysis of the household structure. The type of household represented in Portlaw is analysed in Table 10.

Table 10 Household type in Portlaw in 1901.

Household type	Number	Percentage
Person alone	30	12
Brother/sister alone	7	3
Married couple alone	15	6
Married couple & children	86	34
Widow & children	30	12
Widow, children & boarder	19	8
Widower & children	6	2
Widow, children & grandchildren	8	3
Married couple, children & grandparent/s	6	2
Married couple, children & boarder	25	10
Lone parent & child(ren)	5	1
Unrelated people	4	1
Other	11	5

Kinship was the principal means by which individuals came together to live. Most people formed households through marriage, resulting in households com-

10 Thomas P. Dooley, *Irishmen or English soldiers? The times and world of a southern Catholic Irishman (1876–1916) enlisting in the British army during the First World War* (Liverpool, 1995), pp. 11–12.

posed of a simple nuclear family unit composed of married couples with or without children and widows or widowers with children.[11]

The majority of households (34 per cent) were headed by a married couple who lived with their children, as might be expected from a population structure exhibiting such a high proportion of young people. An additional 10 per cent of families also included a boarder in the household. A widow residing with one or more of her children represented the second highest ranked category of household. In addition, a variety of other widow-headed household combinations were present in Portlaw, with a widow living with some of her children and at least one boarder the most popular option. One quarter of the total households of Portlaw were headed by a widow and formed one of the most economically disadvantaged groups in the village. Widowhood, at the turn of the century, was a common experience marking the transition of many women to later life-cycle stages.[12] The average age of a Portlaw widow was 57. Only females living alone were likely to have been more economically disadvantaged. These widows would have found it difficult to make ends meet after the death of the principal wage earner and the difficulty would have been exacerbated in Portlaw with the reduced importance of the traditional outlet for female employment. Children were the principal supporters of widow-headed households. In Portlaw, only nine widow-headed households did not include unmarried sons or daughters who remained at home to support a widowed parent. The most popular additional income boosting strategy adapted by the widows of Portlaw was to include a boarder in the household.

Ninety-one households in Portlaw had a female head of household. Of these, 68 per cent of female heads of households were widows, 15 per cent were single and 16 per cent were listed as married but not living with their husbands. All of these faced financial difficulties due to asymmetrical wage scales, women in general earning about half the wages of men.[13]

THE SOCIAL GEOGRAPHY OF THE STREETS, 1901

The village in 1901 consisted of eleven streets and the extent of habitation and the distribution of the population within these streets are illustrated in Table 11.

Brown Street was the pre-eminent street of the village. William Malcomson was the landlord of the 50 distinctive two-storey houses that formed the south side of the street. The landlord of the north side of this street was John Medlycott who controlled the remaining 40 houses. It was a street of second-class houses (as defined by the 1901 census) but also contained five houses that were classified as first-class, three of which were used as business premises. The street was

---

11 Marilyn Cohen, *Linen, family and community in Tullylish, county Down, 1690–1914* (Dublin, 1997), p. 193. **12** Ibid., p. 201. **13** Ibid.

Table 11 Distribution of population and inhabited and uninhabited houses in
Portlaw, 1901.

Street	Male	Female	Total	Inhabited houses	Uninhabited houses
Brown Street	151	181	332	75	16
William Street	79	94	173	39	25
George's Street	37	33	70	11	44
Carrick road	62	58	120	29	0
Queen Street	60	81	141	34	13
Main Street	37	29	66	17	3
Thomas Street	30	48	78	19	1
Factory avenue	16	23	39	11	0
Curtis lane	18	23	41	11	2
Haugh's lane	13	13	26	7	1
The Square	4	5	9	2	4
	507	588	1095	255	109

the prime street for retail activities offering the choice of four public houses, four
general shops, a grocery and hardware store, a green grocers shop as well as a
saddler's workshop to the shoppers of Portlaw. These activities were predominantly located on the north side and tended to cluster towards the Market Square
end of the street. Although 19 of the 91 houses were uninhabited, 30 per cent
of the population of the village lived in this street. It was a heterogeneous population that displayed a diversity of origin and a social stratification atypical of
the village. If a form of social segregation existed in Portlaw it was centred on
Brown Street where many of the residents belonged to the apex of the village's
economic pyramid. An analysis of the head of household returns for the street
reveals that 31 per cent of the heads were returned as general labourers, but 21
per cent were skilled labourers and another 18 per cent self-employed engaged
in a commercial retail activity. The advantages of a civil service employment
were enjoyed by 7 per cent of the household heads, whilst another 7 per cent
shared the relative luxury of having retired to a civil service pension. The
employments listed included a telegraph and dispatch clerk, a number of RIC
personnel, school teachers, an accountant, a surgically trained nurse and a variety of people engaged in skilled trades such as victuallers, saddlers, dressmakers,
carpenters and painters. Thirty-nine of the residents were born outside the county
with 13 different places of birth represented. Nineteen were natives of the bordering county of Tipperary with one Canadian-born and one American-born
resident in the street. The street also displayed a religious mix that was unusual
with 23 Protestants resident there.[14]

14 NAI, Census – Waterford 4, DED Portlaw 11c/2.

Figure 5: The Square, Portlaw with George's Street evident in the centre and Brown Street in the left centre.

William Street, Georges Street and Queen's Street were essentially streets of third-class houses.[15] Although classified as third-class, the small four-roomed, single-storey Malcomson houses offered good quality accommodation to the residents. The economic difficulties of the industrial village are reflected in the number of uninhabited houses in these streets. Thirteen of Queens Street's 47 houses were empty, and 25 of the 64 William Street houses were uninhabited. George's Street was virtually abandoned with only 11 of the 55 houses occupied. Despite the availability of accommodation in the streets, these areas contained some notable examples of overcrowding. Number 4 William Street was home to 12 persons headed by a 34-year-old general labourer who lived with his 30-year-old wife and their eight children ranging in age from thirteen years to eight months. Also resident in the house was the head of the household's brother and sister. This rate of occupancy was matched by the residents of number 16, where a 57-year-old house-painter and his 50-year-old wife lived with ten children, ranging in age between 24 and 4 years of age. A radical intervention was made to the streetscape of north William Street in 1895 when seven houses were converted to alms houses for the use of retired employees of the Curraghmore estate – an intervention carried out 'in memory of John Henry, fifth marquis of Waterford by his loving wife and mother, A.D. 1896'.[16] The change in the material used in re-constructing the roofs of these houses was suf-

15 NAI, Census – Waterford 4, DED Portlaw, 11c/4, 11c/5, 11c/6. **16** Inscription on wall plaque in William Street.

ficient to elevate them to the status of second-class houses for census classification purposes.

The once thriving Market Square was reduced in status and in 1901 offered only two commercial premises and four uninhabited houses (Figure 8).[17] Ellen Harney, assisted by her two sons and a domestic servant, was the proprietor of Harney's hotel, grocery and spirit store, whilst Wheddon F. Harvey and his family managed the village's post office. The family were also the only members of the Society of Friends resident in the village.

Extending from the Square leading to the cotton mill was the appropriately named Factory Avenue, a small terrace of eleven second-class houses, the property of Thomas Medlycott.[18] Six of these households were headed by widows, the most economically vulnerable section of the community.

Curtis Lane and Thomas Street, the property of Thomas Curtis, were located between the core of the village and the cotton mill[19]. These were the oldest inhabited houses in Portlaw, constructed in the 1830s to cater for the accommodation demands of the growing labour force of the village's industry. Although classified as third-class (Curtis Lane, 100 per cent and Thomas Street 80 per cent) and second-class houses, the quality of accommodation offered by these houses was significantly inferior to that available in the similarly classified Malcomson houses. House valuation provides a more reliable guide to the quality of a house and the valuator's assessment of these houses confirms their inferior quality compared to the houses of William Street and George's Street. They attracted a valuation of £2 each, whilst the majority of those of Thomas Street-Curtis Lane were valued at £1 in the 1890s.[20] There was a particular concentration of unskilled labourers in these two streets; 14 of the 19 of Thomas Street and five of the 11 in Curtis Lane were classified as general labourers or farm servants. In addition, unemployed widows headed five of the households.[21] Main Street was a street of 20 houses of mixed quality, three of which were uninhabited.[22] The three first-class houses were in use as business premises and there were four second-class houses and 13 third-class houses. The majority of these were located in an extension of Main Street most likely the present-day Bridge Street. Finally Carrick Road formed an extension of Brown Street, linking Portlaw with the main road between Carrick-on-Suir and Waterford city.[23] Twenty-six of the 29 houses of this street were classified as second-class.

Uninhabited houses provide a reliable indicator of economic decline and evidence of whole family migration. However, to concentrate on uninhabited houses as the only physical evidence of economic stagnation is to underestimate the scale of decay. In 1901, 24 per cent of the housing stock of Portlaw was unin-

17 NAI, Census – Waterford 4, DED Portlaw, 11c/4.   18 NAI, Census – Waterford, DED Portlaw, 11c/11.   19 Ibid., 11c/10, 11c/6.   20 VO, Valuation lists, No. 8, county Waterford, district of Carrick-on-Suir, ED Portlaw 1868–1909.   21 Hunt, Portlaw, p. 19.   22 NAI, Census – Waterford 4, DED Portlaw 11c/1.   23 NAI, Census – Waterford 4, DED Portlaw 11c/3.

habited but in addition there were approximately 120 houses in varying stages of dereliction that went unrecorded by the census enumerators.[24] The chief area of concentration of these derelict houses in 1901 was in the Malcomson owned area of Green Island where 55 houses were abandoned. The eastern side of Queen's Street was also a zone of dereliction with thirty houses in varying states of collapse, while in the Thomas Street-Curtis Lane area a similar number were in ruins.[25] Visitors now perceived in a negative fashion, the village that had been eulogised by several English travellers in the 1840s. David Wark, the Presbyterian minister from Waterford city, who visited the village in 1900, found a 'general air of decay' pervading throughout the village. It was a village of

> long rows of houses, with windows boarded up, and stuck over with a patchwork of advertisements in various stages of decay, or with gaping holes where the glass has been broken away, while off the outsides the plaster has fallen in great patches giving the walls the appearance of having been attacked by some devastating skin disease.[26]

CONCLUSION

Specialised industrial villages such as Portlaw represented the ultimate in potentially vulnerable socio-economic entities. Portlaw, dependent on a singular and somewhat exotic economic activity and enmeshed in the web of international global economy market forces, that were themselves 'governed by complex and often uncontrollable forces of finance, raw materials and geo-political upheaval,' was particularly vulnerable.[27] Inevitably, the almost total collapse of the textile industry sent the village of Portlaw into immediate decline. Continuous economic migration characterised the village after 1876. Uninhabited houses, partly deserted streets, economic stagnation and decay, reflected in the physical disintegration of the village and in the zones of dereliction, characterised the once showpiece village. In 1900 it was far removed from its representation as a model village, eulogised by a variety of English travel writers in the 1830s and 1840s.

24 The 'new village' of 1871 contained 588 houses, 120 more than the village of 1901 so it is safe to assume that a similar number of houses were lying derelict at the end of the century. **25** VO, Valuation lists, No. 8, county Waterford, district of Carrick-on-Suir, ED Portlaw 1868–1909. **26** *Missionary Herald*, 1 March 1900. **27** James Walvin, *The Quakers-money and morals* (London, 1997), p. 193.

Kilmainham, county Dublin, 1536–1610:
the decline of a manorial village

EITHNE MASSEY

This examination of the village of Kilmainham as it existed in the sixteenth century constitutes an exploration of a world that is well and truly lost. The community, which had as its physical and spiritual focus the priory of the Knights Hospitallers, no longer exists; if Kilmainham can still be described as a village, it is an urban one, an inner suburb of Dublin. It is a community, which has suffered the ravages of both long-term neglect and, most recently, unsympathetic development. Like all of modern Dublin and indeed most of Ireland, it is currently undergoing a rapid transformation in terms of the physical environment as well as cultural and economic change.

The second half of the sixteenth century was a time of major disruption in the life of the inhabitants of Kilmainham, although in this case the change in the social and economic power-base was brought about by religious reform. During the period of the Reformation the village lost the priory of the Knights Hospitallers, which for centuries had been the focus of its economic and social life. Yet the dissolution provides a unique source of detailed information on the structure of the village community. Land use and ownership, buildings and family names are recorded in the accounts, which were put together for the government at the time of the dissolution of the Hospitaller house. Through the *Extents of Irish monastic possessions* as collated by the Revd Newport White, and the other records of the time, this essay attempts both to re-create that world as it existed and to examine, as far as possible, the impact the major changes of the late sixteenth century had on the community. The sources have their limitations and in some cases they raise more questions than they answer. How was it, for example, that the villagers are described as being poverty-stricken when the Hospitaller house was one of the richest in Dublin? And while the Hospitaller order was hardly in the vanguard of either charitable works or religious fervour, they left a legacy to the community that survived long after the order was dissolved. How did it happen that local people remained so attached to their church that its site continued to be a place of popular worship for centuries after the building was destroyed?

The *Extents of Irish monastic possessions* consists of the survey and valuation of religious lands confiscated by Henry VIII. After the prior surrendered his lands to the crown in November 1540, royal officials were assigned to record the Hospitallers' lands at Kilmainham. These officials were dependent on a jury of local individuals of good standing, 'true and lawful men' in order to compile this

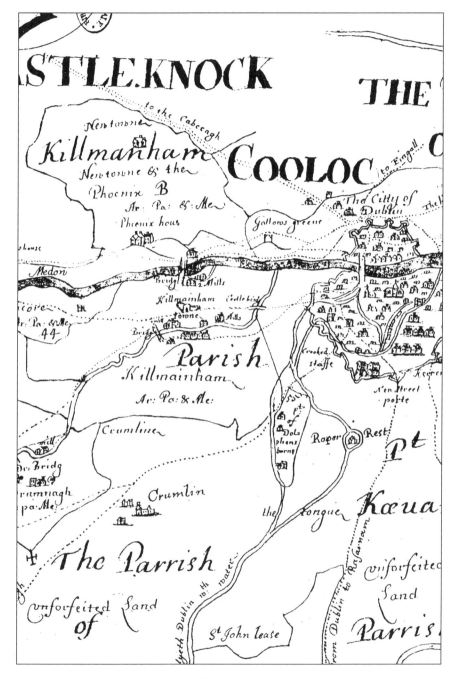

Figure 1 Kilmainham 1654 – drawn by Girdler for the Down Survey. Source TCD
Map Library.

record. The jury who worked on the Hospitallers' possessions was a large one, consisting of 22 men, three of them described as 'of Kilmainham' and holding land in the district; others were from surrounding districts such as Crumlin, Lucan, Newcastle and St Michan's; while a small number came from outside the Dublin area.[1] They produced a detailed account of the Hospitaller house and the surrounding district. The fact that there appear to have been guidelines laid down for the calculation of valuations – for example, arable land in county Dublin is generally estimated at a value of 1s. an acre – makes comparisons possible with other areas of Dublin and gives some sense of Kilmainham in the context of a wider society.

This wider society was undergoing major changes during the years from 1535 to 1610, the time span of this essay. Historians have seen this era as marking the birth of modern Ireland. During this period the status of Ireland changed from that of lordship to kingdom, there were on-going and successful attacks on the Pale by the surrounding Gaelic population and, perhaps most dramatically, the monasteries were closed and the character of the church transformed. The village of Kilmainham was significantly influenced by all of these factors.

Kilmainham is located less than a mile and a half from Dublin city, which in the sixteenth century consisted of the walled area around the cathedrals of the Holy Trinity (Christchurch) and St Patrick. The house was sufficiently near Dublin to experience constant comings and goings between the village and the town and it was on the major western route to the city, so the inhabitants would have been very aware of the people entering and leaving Dublin, whether they were merchants, soldiers or agents of the king. Nevertheless, the village was never considered near enough to the city to constitute a suburb, but had a specific local identity. This identity was mainly related to the presence of the priory of the Knights Hospitallers of St John of Jerusalem, who owned all the land in the vicinity and as early as the fourteenth century described the village as 'our vill of Kilmainham'.[2] The settlement had grown up during the years of Hospitaller power, and in the sixteenth century still bore the marks of a manorial village. However, settlement had existed in the area prior to the arrival of the Hospitallers – the village derives its name from St Maigneann, a seventh century saint who established some form of monastic settlement there. Settlement continued through the Viking period; the Kilmainham/Islandbridge area holds some of the richest Viking gravesites in Europe outside Scandinavia, and it has been argued that the Islandbridge site is the location of the original longphort, the pre-urban river camp of the early Scandinavian settlers.[3] By the time of the arrival of the Knights Hospitallers the

1 B. Newport White (ed.), *Extents of Irish monastic possessions, 1540–41* (Dublin, 1943), pp 80–1. **2** Charles Mc Neill (ed.), *Registrum de Kilmainham, 1326–39* (Dublin, 1932) p. 95. **3** John Bradley, 'The topographical development of Scandinavian Dublin' in F.H.A. Aalen and Kevin Whelan (eds), *Dublin city and county: prehistory to the present* (Dublin, 1992), p. 44.

community already had a history stretching back centuries and the settlement incorporated an established burial ground, sacred places and an ancient stone marking one of its boundaries.[4]

The Hospitallers were introduced into Ireland in the late twelfth century as part of the colonising force of the Norman invasion. The order was granted large tracts of lands stretching from Bow Bridge as far as Ballyfermot and enclosing much of what is now the Phoenix Park. The order was primarily military in its nature and through their long sojourn in Ireland Hospitaller knights acted as agents of the English crown and the Anglo-Irish colony. The order held high posts in the administration of Ireland and performed the duties of soldiers, bankers, jailers, diplomats and bureaucrats. They were never a noticeably devout order, living the life of soldiers rather than monks. Kilmainham became their chief house, an immensely wealthy and complex social organisation with an important strategic role in the defence of the colony. The priory at Kilmainham was in a perfect defensive position, both topographically from its aspect on high ground between two river valleys and in terms of its location on the southwestern reaches of the city facing towards the mountains. It effectively constituted a barracks of highly-trained soldiers who could be called upon by their order to take part in the Hospitallers' campaigns in Mediterranean Europe but who also formed a defence force for the colony during periods of threat from the native Irish. In addition, it was a centre of administration and government on a par with Dublin Castle, and it remained almost equal in importance to the Castle up until the latter half of the sixteenth century.[5]

In addition to their military and political activities, the Hospitallers increased the importance of the priory by developing it as a kind of long-term lodging house, where in exchange for money or services people of wealth and importance could live in the priory with the guarantee of being looked after in their later years. This granting of corrodies (commitments on the part of the order to provide board and lodging for life in exchange for favours done or money given) acted as a kind of early life assurance system and reached its height during the early fourteenth century under Prior Roger Outlaw. The presence of such individuals – rich, high-maintenance guests – meant that there was a requirement for a large number of servants, many at a senior level and some even entitled to corrodies in their own right.[6] It is likely that the original settlement of Kilmainham developed into a village partly as a response to this need for the services of horseboys and valets, bakers and brewers, smiths and millers and dairy workers. By the sixteenth century the corrody system had fallen into decline, as had the fortunes of the Hospitaller order in both national and international terms. There were very few active knights *in situ* by this time, and much of the land in the

4 Colum Kenny, *Kilmainham, the history of a settlement older than Dublin* (Dublin, 1995), pp 26–7. 5 See pages 13–18 below. 6 Eithne Massey, *Prior Roger Outlaw of Kilmainham* (Dublin, 2000), p. 15.

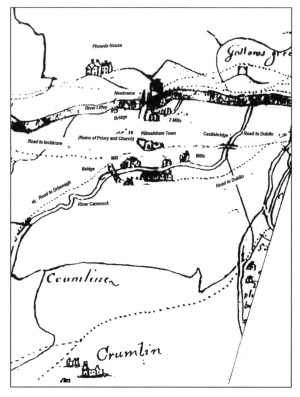

Figure 2 The priory in 1654 – drawn by Girdler for the Down Survey.
Source: TCD Map Library.

Kilmainham area had been leased out. The priory itself had begun to suffer from neglect, but the village remained, with its focus still firmly placed on the priory.

THE VILLAGE

The village lay on the banks of the Camac river, bordering the road, which led from the southwest to Dublin, situated no more than a thirty-minute walk to the east. Directly to the west of the village, there was the wood of Inscore; to the south and south-west the manor of Cromblyn and the Gylden Bridge; to the north, across the Liffey, a large wood (the Grete Wood mentioned in the *Extents,* which was connected with Salcock's Wood) – out of which anything, including wolves and the hostile Irish, had been known to appear. To the south and west there was also the threat of attack from the Irish of the mountains, a threat that became more immediate towards the end of the sixteenth century. The area as a whole was heavily wooded, hilly and inarguably rural.

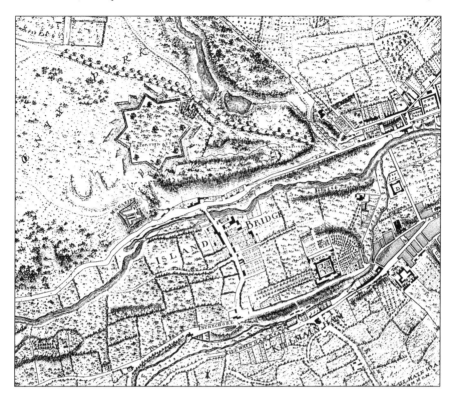

Figure 3 Kilmainham: John Roque's map of 1756

The *Extents of Irish monastic possessions* give a picture of the physical layout of the village as it existed in 1540. While the priory straddled the gravel ridge between the Liffey and the Camac rivers, from the contemporary descriptions and later maps it is clear that the village lay both to the north and south of the Camac, although the main part was south of the river. (See Maps 2 and 3.)

On the north bank of this small river the ground rises steeply and at the crest of the ridge lay the highway, which led eastwards to Dublin. The outer, fortified walls of the Hospitaller priory bordered this road in a similar way to the manner in which the walls of the Royal Hospital extend along the present Kilmainham Lane. What is described as the 'Great Southern Gate' (there were also gates to the north, west and east) opened onto the road, giving the building the aspect of a fortress.[7] This outer enclosure was a very large one, with the northern walls bordering the Liffey and incorporating a drawbridge. This physical layout – with the priory, either sheltering or towering over the inhabitants of the village, depending on one's interpretation – must have had implications

7 Myles Ronan, *The Reformation in Dublin, 1536–58* (London, 1926), appendix xi, p. 497.

for the way the villagers viewed their Hospitaller lords. In order to pay their
rent, attend at court or go to mass, the villagers had to make the journey up from
the village street to the fortress. The power of the Hospitallers – their ascendancy in the community – was reflected in the physical action of crossing the
bridge and climbing the steep bank towards the high stone walls of the manor.
With its four towers, its great hall, numerous buildings and gardens and its adjoining church, the complex dominated the village and formed its own enclosed
world separate from it. From the evidence of the Down Survey map – the earliest one available – it is likely that the main bridge across the Camac was located
in the same place as the present small bridge at Kearn's Place. This bridge leads
to Rowserstown Lane and this lane and the path that leads via steps back to
Kilmainham Lane formed the half-circle of one of the village streets. There was
also a green, held by the villagers as common land for grazing, located between
the mill and the bridge. Fields, orchards and gardens were interspersed between
the houses of the village.

The land was a mixture of pasture, arable, meadow, underwood and scrub,
in some cases quite marshy from the flooding of the rivers. The *Extents* mentions bogland to the north of the Liffey and there seems to have been large numbers of trees grown, including willows, which grow well on damp ground. When
the nave of Christchurch collapsed in 1562 wattles were purchased from the
keeper of Kilmainham for its repair.[8] Timber was a carefully husbanded resource;
in 1589, one of the conditions given in the lease of a mill and lands was that no
timber was to be cut except for building and repairs, and two trees were to be
planted for every one cut.[9]

Because the *Extents* list numerous messuages and gardens without giving their
size, it is not possible to gauge the total acreage of the area. However, in terms of
what can be examined, the proportion of pasture land as compared with arable
land appears to be a ratio of 7:3. This is in keeping with the normal pattern for
the Dublin area during the late medieval period.[10] Most of the arable lands lay in
the immediate vicinity of the village itself or within the outer walls of the priory.
Within this outer wall lay 260 acres, including three small gardens and an orchard
as well as numerous buildings such as barns, a malt-house, granaries and stables.
There was one very large barn, which acted as a major grain store; this is the 'great
barn', which was burnt down by Thomas Fitzgerald (Silken Thomas) when he
broke the truce of 1534 in a direct attack on Prior John Rawson, who stood firmly
loyal to the crown.[11] Some of the holdings have names connected with their
owners, past or present, such as Sangwenslands and Quaytrott's Park (both the

8 Raymond Gillespie (ed.), *The proctor's accounts of Peter Lewis, 1564–65* (Dublin, 1996), pp 27,
36. The cart of Kilmainham was also frequently used during the rebuilding of Christ Church.
9 Margaret C. Griffith (ed.), *Calendar of inquisitions* (Dublin, 1991), p. 445.   **10** Anngret Simms,
'Core and Periphery' in W.J. Smith, Kevin Whelan (eds), *Common ground: essays of the historical geography of Ireland* (Cork, 1988), p. 35.   **11** White, *Monastic extents*, p. 81.

Sanguins and Quaytrotts are listed as tenants in the *Extents*). Some names are descriptive and easily deciphered, such as Hyghfeld, Woodfeld, Castelhouse and the Millemeade (meadow of the mill). Others are more open to question – for example, while Walsshmanslands would seem to indicate Welsh connections and 'the Stryffe more' a Gaelic link (possibly from *An Srath Mór*, low-lying land along a river), names such as 'the Droges' are harder to interpret. Some of the names are also impossible to decipher with confidence from the documents; one site, identified with the present day Bully's Acre, has been read as both 'Bayleyard' and 'Pereyard'. A boundary marker, the 'langstone' (long stone) mentioned in the records still exists today in the form of the decorated shaft in Bully's Acre. This dates at least from the Viking period and it may have originally been a cross associated with the early monastic settlement. It may also be the 'procession meere' (boundary marker) mentioned in the records in 1599 and may have marked one of the boundaries of the priory lands.[12] The stone bridge over the Liffey was another important boundary marker and was also significant in terms of military defence, for beyond it lay Salcock's wood, out of which the warlike O'Tooles came in 1535, on their way to attack the city.[13] A further sortie at this bridge in 1536 left 40 dead, and a further 100 soldiers made ill by the torrential rain after wading through the flooded river.[14] The bridge itself had been neglected at the time of the priory closure, when it was described as dilapidated and in very bad repair.[15] In 1575 John Holman was paid £20 to repair it.[16]

The river Liffey was extremely important in terms of the village economy. It acted as a significant means of transportation: coal was transported from Dublin to Kilmainham by water in the time of Lord Deputy Fitwilliam in 1591.[17] The rights to fishing were owned by the Hospitallers and they were the first group recorded as having built a salmon weir there – thus, according to John De Courcy Ireland, being the first to make the Liffey freshwater and non-tidal above this point.[18] The salmon-pools were valued very highly at £261 13s. 4d. There was also an important mill on the Liffey, and two other mills on the Camac – a flour mill and a fulling-mill for cloth. The importance of the mills is demonstrated by the fact that no other buildings in the village are described by function. During the fourteenth century the priory had within its walls a forge, breweries, and dairies but none of these are mentioned in the *Extents*. However, the level of detail in the material presented in the *Extents* varies, so it may be that these buildings were simply not individually specified.

12 Morrin, James (ed.), *Calendar of the patent and close rolls of chancery in Ireland, 1599* (Dublin 1862), ii, p. 514. **13** Walter Harris, *History of the city of Dublin* (London 1766), p. 295. **14** J.S. Brewer and William Bullen (eds), *Calendar of Carew manuscripts, 1515–1574* (London 1867), p. 63. **15** White, *Monastic extents*, p. 82. **16** C.L. Kingsford (ed.), *De L'Isle and Dudley manuscripts, 1557–1602* (London 1934), ii, p. 31. **17** 'The Fitzwilliam manuscripts at Milton, England' in *Analecta Hibernia*, iv (1932), p. 307. **18** John de Courcy Ireland, *The Liffey in Dublin* (Dublin 1996), p. 206.

In terms of the economic and social structure of the village, the records are less useful. At the time of the dissolution there were 18 houses or messuages listed in the village with 38 different individuals listed as landholders. Some of these held the land jointly with another person. No information is available on those who did not hold land and thus we know nothing about those at the bottom of the economic ladder. In some cases the owner or tenant's social position is mentioned such as gentleman, widow or alderman. The tradesmen mentioned are two bakers – Martin Kelly and William Kerne – both, interestingly enough with Gaelic names in a list, which has a largely non-Gaelic bias. (Kearns' Place still exists and is located at the site of the original village, but it is not possible to ascertain whether the name comes from this period.) Other local street names, such as Lady Lane, and Cut-throat Lane – arguably a variation on the local name Quoytrott – may also date from this time. Walter Dohite (White?), a tailor, is listed as a former owner of lands granted by the prior to Agnes Perpoyn in 1538.[19] There were social obligations associated with some leases – for example, Nicholas Quoytrott was obliged to keep the village ditch mended as part of his contract for rent of a stone house with a garden and a small close.[20] The village appears to have possessed its own mechanism for local law enforcement – William Matthew and John Dunne are described as serjeants of the vill of Kilmainham.[21]

In addition to a money rent, the tenants at Kilmainham were obliged to pay an assize on the beer produced and miscellaneous dues were also paid to the manor court amounting to 53s. 4d. Part of these were known as the 'Merry Gallons' or Mary Gallons.[22] There are various interpretations of what these dues were, ranging from a tithe of beer brewed or a tub of butter, to the produce of a particular ridge of corn.[23] These dues were granted to Robert Napper in 1599.[24] They may have included an element of labour, but the Hospitallers seem to have operated a local economy, which was primarily based on money rather than service. This contrasts with establishments such as the nunnery of Grace Dieu in north Dublin, which required service from its cottager tenants in the form of four days' labour for the autumn sowing, one day haymaking, one day weeding and one day cleaning the millpond.[25] Again, unlike some other orders, the Hospitallers never seem to have engaged directly in either charitable or educational care of the community, and even services attached to their lands, such as the leperhouse in Chapelizod, had ceased to function by the 1540s.

It can be assumed that the farming system in Kilmainham followed the normal pattern of agriculture at the time. Cropland was farmed on the basic three-strip openfield system that had survived from the Middle Ages with fields used for winter corn, spring corn or left fallow to recover their nutrients. There were

19 Griffith, *Inquisitions*, p. 89.   **20** White, *Monastic extents* p. 85.   **21** White, *Monastic extents*, p. 119.   **22** *Cal. pat. close roll*, ii, p. 514.   **23** Sylvester Malone, 'What were the 'Merry Gallons?' in *JRSAI*, xii (1902), p. 194.   **24** *Cal. pat. close roll*, ii, p. 514.   **25** White, *Monastic extents*, p. 73.

fields in the village, which were farmed communally and referred to as the common green and some twenty acres of pasture within the manor, which were also held communally by the tenants of the village. The holdings, from the numerous references to gardens attached to houses, would have been widely spaced along the village street. From the evidence of other manors and descriptions of diet, we know that pulse crops of beans, peas and vetches were grown. Winter corn consisted of wheat or rye, spring corn of barley or oats. Barley was an important crop as it could be used for brewing and as an animal feed. The villagers would also have grown pulses. From the *Extents*, the picture of land ownership in the village that emerges is of small landholders engaged in mixed farming, sometimes in different parts of the village. Agnes Perpoyn, for example, held numerous separate plots of land and tenements – some adjoining the city liberties and some in the direction of Crumlin. Farming was carried out on a small scale. Of the acreages listed, none, with the exception of the Hospitallers' own land and the lands held by St Anne's Guild, exceeded fifty acres and most are much smaller. Like similar villages in England tradesmen also farmed on a small scale. This was the case with James Whyte, the organist in the village church, who held three and three quarter acres in the village fields. There is evidence of cattle and sheep being held on the Kilmainham lands, and pigs and poultry would also have been kept by the tenants to supplement their diet. A 'colvyrhouse' (from the Latin *columba*) or pigeonhouse is mentioned in a lease from St Anne's guild to William and Marion Helyn in 1513.[26] Fishing rights were a jealousy guarded prerogative but poaching salmon from the Liffey was no doubt as regular an activity in the sixteenth century as it was in later times.

The village was thus a mixture of small, individual landholders, tradesmen such as millers and bakers, larger landholders and land held by corporations, such as the powerful Dublin Guild of St Anne and the messuage and lands held by the canons of St Patrick's cathedral. At the time of the closure of the monasteries, the villagers are described as suffering from 'extreme poverty' and this was not just a formulaic lament, as it is not used to describe the tenants of any other religious order in the Dublin area. It indicates clearly that the dissolution was not a primary cause of economic hardship among the villagers. However, after 1540, the priory tenants' land belonged to the crown, to be granted or sold at royal will. The old structure whereby the Hospitallers' ownership had lasted for literally hundreds of years was replaced by change and some confusion as regards land ownership. The seventeenth century saw a major legal battle over rights to the farms originally held by St Anne's guild. The guild had held eighty acres of mixed arable and pasture in Kilmainham, divided between the great and the small farms. It kept its interest in the lands there at least until 1621, when it granted the smaller farm to Edward Janes.[27] After this point confusion set in and

---

26 Henry F. Berry, 'History of the religious guild of S. Anne, in S. Audeon's church, Dublin,' in *RIA Proc.*, xxv (1904), p. 91.   **27** Ibid., p. 93.

litigation continued for many years.[28] In addition, the late seventeenth century saw a large number of land transfers[29] and there seems to have been conflict over rights to the common green – an inquiry was set up in 1596 to examine this.[30]

All those listed in the *Extents* as holding land in the Kilmainham area did not necessarily live in or near the village. Some landholders mentioned, especially the larger ones, may have had little or no connection with the community. But from the tenants listed it is possible to examine the social make-up in some very basic ways. Of the 38 individuals listed in the *Extents* as tenants of the village and its immediate surroundings, 33 are men and only five are women. Of these women most are either joint tenants with a man or with another woman. Agnes Perpoyn, a widow, held some land in her own right as well as being co-tenant with Catherine Rawson for other farms. She had been resident in Kilmainham for a long period; it is recorded that in 1521 some of her lands were transferred to the guild of St Anne.[31]

The vast majority of the surnames listed as tenants are of Norman or English origin, as indeed are the first names. Lachlan Oquoyne (Lochlann Ó Cuinn) is the most 'Gaelic' name in the group and seems to have been a reasonably prosperous small tenant with lands valued at 8s. John Oqouyne is also listed in the *Extents* and he is more than likely the same John Oqouyne who was a member of the jury who valued the lands. 'Dwyn' is probably a variation on Dunne. Kelly and Kerne, the bakers already mentioned are of Gaelic origin. Many of the names listed in the tenantry list, such as Barnewall, Quoytrott and Ussher, are resonant of the great families of the Dublin patriciate, as described by Colm Lennon his book *The lords of Dublin in the age of Reformation*.[32] Many of these families intermarried or were connected to each other in other ways, and there is evidence of such intermarriage in the village of Kilmainham. The Barnewalls were connected by marriage with the Taylors, an important and lasting family connection in the Kilmainham district. All of the prominent families listed in the Kilmainham *Extents* had strong leanings towards the old Catholic faith.

Some of the wills of the villagers have been recorded, and through them it is possible to follow through stages of the family histories of the Kilmainham population. The Thondyr family, for example, held land in the area between the late fifteenth and late sixteenth centuries. We also know that Martin Kelly, the baker who had on lease burgages and pasture in 1541, had three sons and two daughters by his first marriage. He later married Janet Sanguin, daughter of William, and thus inherited rights to the mills at Kilmainham. Their daughter, Ellinor, married Thomas Halman of Kilmainham and the mills were left to

28 NLI, MS 11,314, Domville papers, Sir Richard Parsons vs Sir W. Domvile.   **29** NLI, DOD 430, Bellew Papers, Special List no. 66.   **30** PRONI, T.779, Interrogatories concerning the common green of Kilmainham; answers of deponents, May 1597; NLI, Microfilm pos. 363.   **31** Ibid., p. 91.   **32** Colm Lennon, *The lords of Dublin in the age of reformation* (Dublin, 1989), *passim*.

Halman's son John.[33] By the time of the '1659 census', however, no Halmans, Sanguins or Kellys are listed – indeed, the only name common to the *Extents* and to the census is that of Taylor. While by 1659 the population had increased rather than declined in the village, the family names are new ones.

Although detailed evidence is sparse, descriptions of the area in the late sixteenth and early seventeenth century in the state papers stress the decay of the manor and the *Extents* note the poverty of the inhabitants.[34] This situation on the outskirts of Dublin contrasts with the villages and towns of comparable size in England, where during this period household inventories demonstrate a significant increase in wealth.[35] But it is difficult to place the economic situation of the villagers in the context of either decline or improvement in terms of Ireland during the adjacent periods. There is no comparable material for either pre-1540 or for the seventeenth century. The village in 1654 is described as having two double mills and a single mill, and a street of good habitable houses, an arched stone bridge across the Liffey, and the ruins of a large castle. Four hundred and ninety-two acres were reckoned as profitable.[36] In 1659 the poll tax lists 130 taxpayers living in Kilmainham – 60 English and 70 Irish. If this is multiplied by the commonly accepted figure of three, this would bring the population to around 390 people. The surrounding districts also had a slightly greater proportion of Irish rather than English inhabitants.[37]

THE PRIORY

The Rawson name is one, which had disappeared from the village by 1649, although both Catherine and Richard Rawson are listed as tenants in 1540. Catherine was engaged in a joint tenantry with Agnes Perpoyn; and Agnes' heir, Alison Wallington (Patrick Ballyngton is listed as her husband in the *Extents*) eventually gave over her interest in these plots to Catherine Rawson and Catherine's husband Roland White.[38] This indicates some kind of family relationship between the two women. Myles Ronan states that Catherine was the natural daughter of Prior John Rawson, and, although it has not been possible to source the origin of this claim, the possibility that Rawson set up his natural daughter in the village casts an interesting light on the less orthodox social contacts between villagers and priory.[39] Richard Rawson, who is described as Rawson's nephew, held a valuable lease on the fulling-mill. There is still a mill on the Camac, located on a lane coming up from the river towards where the

33 Griffith, *Inquisitions*, pp 391–3.   **34** White, *Monastic extents*, p. 81.   **35** M.M. Havendin, *Household and farm inventories near and in Oxford* (London, 1965), p. 32.   **36** R.C. Simmington (ed.), *Civil Survey of Co. Dublin, 1654* (Dublin, 1945), vii, p. 292.   **37** Seamus Pender (ed.), *A census of Ireland c.1659* (Dublin, 1939), p. 379.   **38** Griffith, *Inquisitions,* p. 374.   **39** Ronan, *Reformation in Dublin*, p. 214.

main gate of the priory was. This lane has the unusual name of Rowserstown
Lane, and it is possible that 'Rowser' is a variation of Rawson. There is also a
'Rouerstowne land' marked on the Down Survey barony map; it lay between
Ballyfermot and Palmerstown on what was also Hospitaller land. The settlement
of lands on relatives (whatever their exact connection) on the part of the aged
John Rawson was not unusual and must have increased the close identification
of the village with the priory. Like many religious orders, in the lead-up to the
dissolution, the Hospitallers alienated lands from the order and gave long leases
(some of over ninety years) at ridiculously low rents not just in Kilmainham but
on other Hospitaller lands.[40] The last Hospitallers may, of course, have charged
huge entry fines to the leaseholders. This is one explanation for the huge variation in the valuation of some plots. Forty acres at Hyghfeld, for example, was
valued at 17s. 3d. and six acres of arable land within the manor were rented by
Robert Barnewall for just 6d. This indicates an element of exchanging favours
both on the part of the prior and possibly the jury. Rawson also paid out numerous 'life interests' for 'good counsel' and 'good service'.[41] He may have felt jus-
tified in setting up a situation where the king could not profit enormously at the
expense of the community, and as his priory was the last of the Pale houses to
be dissolved, he had ample time to plan his campaign in advance of the take-
over. He appears to have had almost complete control of the riches of the order
as very few Hospitallers remained in Ireland by this time. The order had suffered major losses in the Mediterranean during the second half of the sixteenth
century and was no longer the major multi-national power it had once been.
The attempted reversal of the fortunes of the Hospitaller order in Ireland during
the reign of Mary, when the brothers returned to the priory under Prior Oswald
Massingberd in 1557, lasted no longer than her short reign.[42]

Rawson himself did not choose to stay in the Kilmainham area, but was given
the Hospitaller lands at Clontarf, with a sizeable pension of 500 marks and an
annuity of £10 per annum from the Kilmainham farm. Prior Rawson was
English by birth and had served the Hospitallers with honour in Rhodes and
Malta. He had been a presence in Kilmainham for many years, having been first
made prior of the order in Ireland in 1511 at the age of 40. During his career in
Ireland he had served almost continuously on the Dublin Council, which administered the king's will in Ireland and his loyalty to his king was never in doubt.
This loyalty had been amply demonstrated during the revolt of Silken Thomas
in 1534, when Kilmainham was the site of the arrest of Fitzgerald's uncles. After
a great feast in the priory they were manacled and taken to the prison in Dublin
Castle.[43] Kindness to Rawson, in his feeble old age, was one of the reasons the
Hospitaller house was left so long undisturbed by the king.[44] St Leger talks of

40 Brendan Bradshaw, *The dissolution of the religious orders in Ireland under Henry VIII* (Cambridge,
1974), pp 28–9. 41 Griffith, *Inquisitions*, p. 90. 42 Ronan, *Reformation in Dublin*, p. 435. 43
L. Miller & E. Power (eds), *Holinshed's Irish Chronicle* (New York, 1979), p. 283. 44 Bradshaw,

the prior's honesty and long experience being missed in Council and there is an affectionate tone in the Council's letters to the king which deal with him. Even his old opponent, Archbishop Browne, was a signatory to a request to Henry VIII for a pension for Rawson. In 1542:

> (the signatories) interceded for payment to the Lord of Clontarffe of £173 11s 4d, due to him on his account when Lord Treasurer here, because without it he is unable to live as he has done. He is bedridden and very sick, and his debts to the King amount to more than the above sum.[45]

Despite his infirmity, Rawson had managed a style of hospitality much admired by his companions in council. For many years the house acted as a diplomatic centre where feasts were held and the great and the good, both foreign and local, were entertained. St Leger described him thus:

> And forasmoche as … the said Lorde Kilmaynam hathe, for the longe tyme of his aboode here, ben the person, whiche, next to Your Magesties Deputie, hath always kept the best house, and Englishes sorte, and at al tymes when straungers of other countreys hath repared thither, fested and intertayned theym to Your Hieghnes honour.[46]

In the years immediately following the dissolution, as residence of the lord deputy, the priory continued this tradition of hospitality. Influential persons still stayed there, as in 1556 when the earl of Sussex 'nobly feasted him at Kilmainham'.[47] The deputies took refuge in rural Kilmainham most often during the summer months, when the castle could become particularly 'noisome', and there were even some improvements made to the building. In 1591, during the time of Deputy Fitzwilliam, who from the evidence of his accounts obviously knew how to enjoy life, the chamber in Kilmainham was rehung and a bowling green was laid at the manor.[48]

In addition to being a centre of hospitality, however, the priory was also a court, a fortress and a barracks. In the fourteenth century it had held a prison – the 'dismal house of little ease'[49] – and this is one local tradition that continued through the centuries, as did the siting of a court of law in the district. Inquisitions continued to be held here throughout the sixteenth century and one of Rawson's grants was that of the office of sub-seneschal (a minor official) of the courts of Kilmainham to Thomas Bermyngham.[50] Gaelic lords came to lay depositions and parley with the English at the manor and it remained the starting point of

Dissolution of the religious orders, p. 89. **45** *Letters and papers, foreign and domestic of the reign of Henry VIII* (London, 1900), xvii, p. 652. **46** *State papers of Henry VIII* (London, 1834), iii, p. 238. **47** *Calendar of Carew manuscripts, 1515–1574*, p. 258. **48** 'The Fitzwilliam manuscripts at Milton', p. 309. **49** Mc Neill, *Registrum*, p. 26. **50** Griffith, *Inquisitions*, p. 90.

many an expedition against those same lords. The priory functioned as the barracks of the deputy's standing army and a centre for stabling the army's horses.
There is little documentation whereby the economic and social implications of
having a military force in place in the priory can be studied, but while both the
Hospitallers and the deputy brought the security of a standing army to a community, which lay exposed to the mountains, there were possible negative as
well as positive effects on life in the community. Apart from the drain on local
resources and the social implications of a large number of soldiers wandering the
streets of the village, the presence of the deputy and a strong military force made
the villagers a target of attack from the Irish. In 1574 a robbery on the manor
was committed by Gabhall Raghnall of the O'Byrnes and his 'mountain men'[51]
and in 1575 it is recorded that 'Kildare devised that Rory Oge with 500 kerne
should go suddenly to Kilmainham and fetch away the lord deputy's wife and
children.'[52] Colm Lennon notes that the safe hinterland around towns was shrink-
ing at this period, so the threat of attack was increasing rather than decreasing
during the final years of the sixteenth century.[53] One such attack came from the
mountains in January 1598, when 'the mountain rebels yesternight burnt all the
town of Kilmainham, and part of Crumlin, so it is apparent that the Pale is the
only mark they now shoot at'.[54]

   However, the military importance of Kilmainham was set to decline with
the shift in the priory's role. During the last years of the century it changed from
being the main house of an important military and religious force to that of 'a
house of pleasure outside Dublin' − a venue very much subsidiary to Dublin
Castle.[55] Already in need of repair in 1541, by Elizabeth's reign the queen was
writing to Sidney requesting details as to the expense involved in restoring it as
she 'would be loth to have it decayed if any reasonable charges might mayn-
tayne it.'[56] The charges were obviously too much for restoration to be undertaken, as by 1588 the priory had fallen into decay; 'the fort by which the whole
was surrounded presenting a complete wreck'.[57] The request for money for
restoration work to prepare the place for Deputy Essex met with disapproval
from the treasurer, who described it as a 'superfluous charge'. Deputy Arthur
Chichester spent years looking for funds to repair the priory, describing the place
as 'the only house in the Kingdom meet for the deputy to reside in' and 'a goodly
vast building, but like to be utterly ruined and blown down by next winter'.[58]
He pleaded in 1604:

51 Mary O' Dowd (ed.), *Calendar of State Papers of Ireland in the Tudor period, 1571–1575* (Dublin,
2000), p. 618. **52** *Calendar of state papers, 1574–85* (London 1867), p. 52. **53** Colm Lennon,
Sixteenth century Ireland (Dublin, 1994), p. 32. **54** *Calendar of state papers, 1598–99* (London,
1867), p. 461. **55** C.L. Falkiner, 'The Phoenix Park, its origin and early history, with some
notices of its royal and viceregal residences' in *R.I.A. Proc.*, xxvi, (1900–2), p. 469. **56**
O'Dowd, *Calendar of state papers of Ireland in the Tudor period*, p. 130. **57** Falkiner, 'The Phoenix
Park', p. 468. **58** Ibid., p. 469.

The abbey at Kilmainham is most ruinous, and yet the repairing thereof very chargeable to His Majesty. There is but 50 acres of land adjoining to it that yeildeth any profit to the Deputy, and 200 acres that he holds upon the north side of the river in common that yeilds no profit at all; and for the House, no Deputy hath used it since Sir William Fitzwilliam's time, but only as a garner to serve their grain; which may be laid up in the King's storehouse in Dublin far more commodiously.[59]

The house was being used more and more as a store for Dublin Castle, not just for grain, but also for livestock, as an account of 1600 notes, when a herd of milch cows was captured from the Irish and Sir Oliver Lambert promised that '40 of the likliest to be beef will be sent to Kilmainham'.[60]

Chichester eventually gave up in his efforts to acquire funds for the restoration of the priory, in 1610 he observed that it was in such decay that it would be as cheap to build a new house as to repair the old one. He advised that it be destroyed, leaving only the stables and garner standing.[61]

During the last years of the sixteenth century a series of keepers were appointed to look after the demesne, but they did not live in the castle. The *Calendar of patent and close rolls for 1597* reads:

> Appointment of Andrew Greene to the office of Keeper of the House of Kilmainham, Keeper of the Garner, and of the woods and demesne lands; To hold during good behaviour, with a fee of 12*d*. a day. Her Majesty also grants him the mansion house over the south gate of Kilmainham, with the garden and orchard on the east side of the gate, and the grazing of ten kine, two horses, and forty sheep, on the demesne lands of the house.[62]

Andrew Greene was probably related to Paul Greene, a servant of Lord Sidney and a previous keeper of Kilmainham. Fitzwilliam, who took over from Sidney, complained in 1572 that Sidney had let a third part of Kilmainham to 'his man' Paul Greene, indicating that the provision of leases on special terms to friends did not cease with the exit of Rawson.[63] Paul Greene surrendered the keeper's post to his son-in-law Thomas Chambers in 1592 and it was obviously passed from Thomas to Andrew.[64] The last keeper of Kilmainham, Beverley Newcomen, resigned in 1617. By the time of the Down Survey in 1649 all that was left of the priory were the ruins of the church. A villager born in 1530 would

59 *Calendar of state papers of Ireland, 1603–6* (London, 1872), p.195. **60** *Calendar of state papers of Ireland, 1600* (London 1903), p. 336. **61** *Calendar of state papers of Ireland, 1608–1610* (London, 1874), p. 423. **62** *Calendar of patent and close rolls* (Dublin, 1862), ii, p. 425. **63** O'Dowd, *Calendar of state papers of Ireland in the Tudor period*, p. 129. **64** De Burca, Eamonn (ed.), *The Irish fiants of the Tudor sovereigns* (Dublin, 1994), ii, nos. 5790, 5795 pp 206–7.

have been aware of the departure of the Hospitaller lords from the village and during his lifetime would have seen the church and the once great house fall into decay. By the middle of the seventeenth century there would have been few traces to remind his grandchildren of the Hospitaller presence apart from the ruins of a church and a yearly festival celebrating their patron, St John. The focus for communal activity was disintegrating and a window on a wider society had been closed. Reflecting the decay of the house, the bridge, mills and weirs of the Kilmainham area were described as being badly in need of repair as early as the 1570s. The decay of the house inevitably affected the prosperity of the dependent village, in terms of both loss of patronage and the decline of a market for goods and labour.

THE CHURCH

If the community of Kilmainham had looked towards the priory as their physical stronghold against attack, the local church provided their defence against the terrors of death and hell. The church stood beside the priory, probably on or slightly to the east of the area now known as Bully's Acre. This site became notorious in later years for its use as a burial place by the poor of Dublin who could not afford to pay for a grave. It was also adjacent to the well of St John, which became a significant place of pilgrimage and the site of many disreputable midsummer fairs.[65] The physical history of the church building is in itself instructive of the change in the religious lives of the people. Unless the churches attached to religious houses were in use as parish churches the *Extents* describes them as already having been destroyed or recommends that this is done. If left intact they often suffered the indignity of being used as stores for munitions or cattlesheds. At Kilmainham:

> The church annexed to the site is the parish church, and is at present too large. Part of it, namely the chapel on the south, can be thrown down without loss, and this ought to be done, as the parishioners owing to their extreme poverty are unable to maintain the church, and what would remain is sufficient to them.[66]

This suggestion gives an indication of the size and importance of the original church as built by the Hospitallers and indeed it would be unlikely that such a powerful and rich house, with so many important visitors, would not have had a large and probably quite lavishly decorated church. Surviving Hospitaller churches at Kilteel in Dublin and at Hospital in Limerick give evidence of fine

---

65 Kenny, *Kilmainham*, chapters 6 and 7.   **66** White, *Monastic extents*, p. 81.

Figure 4 Hospitaller Church at Hospital, Limerick

carving. In common with other churches of the period the church would have held the great rood-screen that separated laity from clergy, statues, candles, the baptismal font, the piscina, highly decorated walls and tiled floors.[67] Like Hospital, there may well have been elaborate carvings to mark the tombs of dead knights, but all that remains of the church in Kilmainham are fragments of a tiled floor found in the twentieth century. Surprisingly, the goods recorded from the church

67 H.A. Jefferies, *Priests and prelates of Armagh in the age of reformations, 1518–1558* (Dublin 1997), p. 23.

at the time of the dissolution came to a relatively low value of 26*s*., as compared
to 36*s*. from the chapel of St Begneta and the parish church of Donabroke, and
£5 15*s*. 6*d*. from the Priory of Holy Trinity.[68] This leads one to suspect that
there may have been a rather energetic spring-cleaning of the treasures of the
church before the government officers arrived on the scene. The removal of
wealth might not have been done for purely monetary reasons. Eamonn Duffy
cites numerous examples of religious treasures such as chalices and bells being
hidden by local people for safe-keeping at the time of the dissolution.[69] In some
of the monasteries, the *Extents* list the bell as being the property of the parishioners, while in others it is noted that there is still a bell or bells in place, which
can be included in the valuation of the king's profit. There is no bell mentioned
in the Kilmainham listing. A bell, now known as the Kilmainham Bell and dating
from sometime between the ninth and the twelfth century was found buried
deeply in soil when cuttings were made for the railway line in 1844.[70] Although
this bell is quite small, it is unlikely that it would have been thrown away care-
lessly, as it is made of bronze and therefore of some value, so it may have been
buried for safe-keeping.

The images and relics were replaced by the creed, the Lord's Prayer and Ten
Commandments 'in gilded frames' and after 1541, the church was left to the
upkeep of the parish.[71] The income of parishes in Tudor Ireland consisted of what
could be obtained from great tithes, which consisted of offerings in corn, hay or
wood ; small tithes, which consisted of fish and shrubwood and personal tithes,
which were usually collected in the form of a small yearly cash payment. The
priest would also have the use of the glebe and manse – a house and its surrounding
land, and whatever income would be provided in offerings for services such as
christenings and burials.[72] The priest's income was thus highly dependent on the
wealth and size of his parish. While the tithes of the rectory of Kilmainham were
valued at £7 6*s*. 8*d*.[73] it appears that the Kilmainham parish did not have the wealth
or the will to continue to support a priest, for as early as 1546 Archbishop Browne
had amalgamated it with the parish of St Catherine and St James, nearer the city
– 'in consequence of the tenuity and proximity of the parishes.'[74] This rationali-
sation of poor and underpopulated parishes removed the official religious focus
from the community: even today the Kilmainham area is neither a separate Church
of Ireland nor a Catholic parish. By 1572 St John's, the main church of the
Hospitallers, was roofless and the subsidiary chapel of St Mary's was being used as

68 Ronan, *The Reformation in Dublin*, p.145. See also Bradshaw, *The dissolution of the religious
orders*, pp 105–6.   **69** Eamon Duffy, *The stripping of the altars* (London, 1992), pp 490–1.   **70**
E. Perceval Wright, 'On the bell of Kilmainham', in *JRSAI* xxx–xxxi, (1900–1901), pp 40–43.
71 Walter Harris, *History of the city of Dublin* (London, 1766), p. 304. **72** James Maguire, 'The
sources of clerical income in the Tudor diocese of Dublin, 1530–1600' in *Archivum Hibernicum*
xlvi, (1991–2), pp 139–60.   **73** White, *Monastic extents*, p. 86.   **74** Maguire, 'The sources of
clerical income', p. 152.

a stable and had its steeple broken down.[75] Most of the church had been dismantled by 1612, but there seems to have been a continuing respect for the building.
By the time of the construction of the Royal Hospital the only building that had
left any trace behind it was the church. The rest of the priory buildings had no
doubt been cannibalised by local builders for useful blocks of stone. Stones from
the church, however, were still present and were used by the builders in the construction of the chapel that forms part of the Royal Hospital complex.[76]

Thus a major focus of community life was removed from the area and in addition, a connecting point with the wider world disappeared, for it is clear from the
records that the church of Kilmainham had been a place of worship not just for
the local community but for the important persons of Dublin. The main evidence
for this lies in the references to sermons held in the late 1530s in Kilmainham. The
most significant of these is the part Kilmainham played in the controversy between
Archbishops George Browne of Dublin and Edward Staples of Meath. This is not
the place to examine the rivalry between the two prelates in detail, but it seems
clear that by the mid-1530s George Browne (who initially seems to have been a
somewhat sluggish reformer but made up for this in later years) was locked in conflict with Bishop Edward Staples. Browne had come into conflict with the bishop
of Meath over the extent of his reforming zeal, and in particular on his advice on
prayer, *The form of the beads*. The two bishops made the rounds of the important
churches of Dublin, taking turns to preach against one another and counter each
other's arguments. Firstly, Staples denounced Browne in St Audoen's. Browne
then made a counter-attack on Staples in Christchurch and matters came to a head
at Easter 1538, on Palm Sunday at Kilmainham, when Prior Rawson gave Staples
the opportunity to reply to Browne's most recent attack. Browne himself was present at the sermon, and described the attack as 'viperous'. He notes that Staples
had chosen his venue carefully: the Hospitallers' church was exempt from the
jurisdiction of the archbishop of Dublin. He describes Rawson as the 'pecuniose'
prior of Kilmainham and there was obviously no love lost between the two men.
'Pecuniouse' basically means rich or moneyed, but it also has implications of
avarice. The controversy became so heated that there was an official inquiry into
the event. But in terms of the village of Kilmainham its significance lies in the fact
that the village church is shown to be a venue where the powerful in the land
came to undertake their religious obligations on such important feasts as that of
Palm Sunday, which began the great liturgical cycle of Easter week. Palm Sunday
was no doubt chosen deliberately to guarantee maximum numbers and exposure
for Staples' attack.

What is also interesting is the archbishop's reference to the nature of the ceremony at the church: Browne's letter of complaint contains references to 'pardons' and 'stations.'

---

75 Falkiner, 'The Phoenix Park', p. 468. **76** Kenny, *Kilmainham,* p. 43.

He (Staples) hath not onlie, sithens that tyme, by penne as you know his wonte full well rayled and raged ayenste me, calling me heritike and begger, with other rabulouse revilings, as I have written unto my Lorde, which I am ashamed to rehearse; but also on Palme Sunday, at after none, in Kilmaynam, where the stations, and also pardons, ben now as bremely usid as ever they were …[77]

The most likely meaning for the word 'pardons' here is indulgences, as there is a further reference to the texts of the indulgence hanging in the church in Kilmainham 'according to that day of station before time used there for the maintenance of the Bishop of Rome's authority'.[78] A station has several possible meanings in ecclesiastical terms, but all are connected with the idea of a religious activity held at a particular place on a particular holy day. The clergy and people at the Kilmainham church, therefore, under Rawson, were still in April 1538 engaging in ways that were falling into disrepute with officialdom; in this case traditional ceremonies associated with the beginning of Holy Week.[79] Palm Sunday was one of the high points of the religious year, the day upon which the ceremony of the blessing of the palms was held. Eamonn Duffy describes the ceremony in *The stripping of the altars:*

> The parish mass began as usual with the blessing and sprinkling of holy water. Immediately that had been done the story of Christ's entry into Jerusalem and greeting by the crowds with palms was read from St John's Gospel. The priest then blessed flowers and green branches, which were called palms but were usually yew, box or willow. The palms were distributed and clergy and people processed out of the church, led by a painted wooden cross without a figure. The procession moved to a large cross erected in the churchyard, normally on the north side of the building at its east end, the choir singing a series of anthems recapitulating the biblical story of Palm Sunday.[80]

A shrine was erected and the community engaged in a ceremonial procession around the church, carrying the host, singing hymns and scattering flowers and branches. The ritual ended back in the church and finished with the mass, at which three clerks sang the entire Passion story from St Matthew's Gospel. In some cases the 'palms' were burnt and the ashes used in the Ash Wednesday ritual. Duffy also notes:

77 *State papers of Henry VIII* (London, 1834), iii, p. 65. **78** Ibid., p. 66. **79** Some historians have suggested that the reference is to a pattern associated with St John's Well, but there is no traditional association of Palm Sunday/Easter with John the Baptist, whose feastday is 24 June. It is however likely that the traditional procession around the church on Palm Sunday included a ceremonial visit to the local holy well. **80** Duffy, *The stripping of the altars*, p. 23.

It was widely believed that crosses made during the reading of the passion narrative had apotropic powers, and many people brought sticks and string to the church on Palm Sunday to make up into crosses, a dimension of popular participation in the ritual, which became a particular target of reformed criticism.[81]

The Kilmainham area was, as already noted, a district known for its production of willow. It may be that the populace of Dublin traditionally travelled to this rural, riverside setting to gather green branches and celebrate the first feast of spring. The drama of the liturgy, the visual beauty of the relics brought from the church and the flowers and branches strewn before them, the music of the choir, all would have provided a focus for communal bonding; an entertainment in itself and an exposure to aesthetic experience for the people of the village. The sermons preached would also have linked the community at Kilmainham to the wider world of political activity and religious fervour. All of these important aspects of community life disappeared with the closure and rapid decay of the church. It could be argued that those villagers who attended services in the new parish of St Catherine and St James still had access to the wider world. However, there is a huge gap, psychologically, between a villager making the journey to a church outside his own milieu and seeing persons from the great world there and important persons from the great world coming into his own village to worship at his local church. An additional small, sad loss to the community was that of its communal music. The *Extents* record a pension to be paid to James Whyte, organist, for his service in the choir at the Hospitallers' Church, so it is clear that music had played an important role in the liturgy there.[82]

Given the preponderance of Catholic recusant families in the Dublin area (those families who refused to attend the reformed services), it is interesting to speculate as to what might have begun to happen at a popular level. While the wealthy families were in a position to hold Masses in their houses this was not the case with the poor, who had to find other modes of expressing any loyalty they had to the old ways. By the end of the seventeenth century St John's Well, located to the west of the burial ground, which is now known as Bully's Acre, had come into prominence as a place of religious devotion and of midsummer celebration. Is it possible that there was a displacement of popular worship and religious feeling from the church to the well, which lay so close to the site of the old church and was further hallowed by the number of burials, both recent and very ancient, in its precinct? The first record of a named well in the Kilmainham area is in a lease of 1589, which mentions Kilbraine's Well.[83] This

81 Ibid., p. 26. **82** White, *Monastic extents*, p. 84. **83** Griffith, *Inquisitions*, p. 445. This name (church of Brian?) may indicate that the well was in some way linked to a religious building or site associated with Brian Boru. In local tradition, the 'langstone', originally sited near the well, marked the place where Brian was buried after his death at the battle of Clontarf. It is

may be the well now known as St John's well, which had become an established focus for quasi-religious activity by the eighteenth century. The tradition of attendance at holy wells goes back many centuries in Ireland and there are references to the devotional practices at various wells around Dublin.[84] Raymond Gillespie has noted that the popularity of such gatherings in Ireland in general was such that by the middle of the seventeenth-century synodal decrees tried to control attendance at these holy wells.[85] No conclusive proof of this displacement of religious devotion is possible, and there are few sources available on the survival of Catholic practice among the poor in the locality of Dublin, but a location outside the walls of Dublin seems a likely centre for this kind of unofficial religious activity. While easily accessible, Kilmainham was no longer a focus for political attention and the neglected priory buildings would have provided physical shelter as well as a religious context in which to celebrate the ceremonies of the old religion. The celebration, however, would have differed from those of previous times in that those in power would be unlikely to attend and the participants' identification with the *status quo* no longer existed. Despite this loss of respectability, celebrations at St John's well continued until well into the nineteenth century.[86]

In addition to losing the focus of the actual church building, the way of life and the pattern of the year were in the process of changing for the villagers. The major changes in religious practice only began in the period 1560–1580 – interestingly enough, the period when resistance to change appears to have begun to set in among the Dublin patriciate. The cycle of the great feasts, which had divided the calendar of the year, continued. Christmas and Easter continued to be marked, but over time the lesser feasts celebrating the saints and the veneration of the Virgin (Eamonn Duffy notes that there may have been between forty or fifty of such days celebrated) were no longer marked. As late as 1610, Barnaby Rich complains of the number of "popish holy days" still celebrated in Dublin.[87] There are references to the duty of the butchers of Dublin to light the flame of St John's Eve in the old fashion in 1563 and 1567.[88] The masons at work on Christ Church (despite commands to the contrary) did not show up for duty on Corpus Christi.[89] However, the reformed church had made it very clear by this stage that the paraphernalia of procession and pilgrimage was no longer acceptable.

possible that the connection of the name of the well and the ancient stone to a tradition that reaches back before the Normans indicates that this was a very ancient site of popular worship.   **84** Lennon, *The lords of Dublin in the age of reformation*, p. 149.   **85** Raymond Gillespie, *The sacred in the secular; religious change in Catholic Ireland, 1500–1700* (Vermont, 1993), p. 19.   **86** Kenny, *Kilmainham*, chaps. 6 and 7.   **87** Barnaby Rich, *A new description of Ireland* (London 1610), p. 63.   **88** J.T. Gilbert (ed.), *Calendar of the ancient records of Dublin* (Dublin, 1891), ii, pp 30, 49.   **89** Gillespie, *The proctor's accounts of Peter Lewis,* p. 87.

Figure 5 Photograph of Bully's Acre shaft

CONCLUSION

This portrayal of Kilmainham at the end of the sixteenth century is, because of the nature of the information available, fragmentary, and the sources have remained frustratingly elusive on one central question – what exactly was the impact of the Hospitaller exit on the community? The evidence indicates that the order's final exit was not a primary cause of economic decay, but that the village, both before and after the dissolution was made up of a mixture of very poor and relatively prosperous individuals. But other effects of the dissolution can be explored, in particular the villagers' relationship with the priory and their church, and perhaps most interestingly, the apparent survival of local attachment to a site long considered sacred. As of 2002, no vestige of the Hospitaller foundation survives over ground, and the faint traces of the original village, which may remain – most significantly in the street pattern leading from the bridge at Kearns Place to Kilmainham Lane – is unlikely to withstand current development. Such development is literally 're-forming' the landscape, in terms of digging deep and shifting the street and settlement patterns of the past. This new 'reformation' has its own implications for the shape of the local community, not all of them positive. As for whatever archaeological evidence may still lie under the surface of the land, having quietly survived the religious, political and socio-economic cataclysms of past centuries, in all likelihood it will, like the Hospitaller village, be recorded only at the very moment of its final destruction.

APPENDIX I

List of tenants and land values in Kilmainham

Feature	Main tenant/owner	Location	Description	Size	Value
Messuage		East of Edmund Browne's	Not built upon		20d.
Inscore Wood		Liffey south	Wood; underwood and pasture	16 ac	
Demesne Lands		Liffey – both sides	Pasture and heath	260 ac	
Grete Wood		Liffey north	Wood	41 ac	
Garden					
Bridge		Liffey	Stone, dilapidated		
Melaghe's Meadow		Meadow		1 ½ ac	2s. 6d.
Barnegyll	Barnewall, Robert of Drimnagh (heirs)	In the manor	Arable	6 ac	6d.
Walsshmanslands	Bathe, James	Goldenbridge, crossing Camac	Pasture	30 ac	No rent
Messuage	Bellowe, Nicholas (heirs)				16d.
Village Fields?	Brasyer, Gerald	Village Fields	Arable	6 ac	8s.
Messuage	Browne, Edmund	West of above			6s. 8d.
Garden	Browne, James	Near western gate/ part of village	Garden		2s. 8d.
Newtone	Brymymgham, Nicholas	Unknown			
Messuage and lands	Brymyngham, Amea				12s.
Burgage	Brymyngham, Thomas				2s.
Hyghfeld	Chyllan, Patrick	Hyghfeld near Thomas Wood	Arable	40 ac	17s. 3d.
Village Fields?	Drake, Richard	Village fields?	Arable	5 ac	6s. 8d.
House	Dwyn, John, Dwyn, Alison		House		Annuity
Messuages and lands	Fytszymond, John – heirs of Fytzsymonds, Richard				26s.
Burgages and land	Harbard, Francis		Arable, meadow and broom	15 ac	11s.
Garden	Harford, William	East	Garden		8d.
Watermill	Hospitallers	Liffey	Two pairs of millstones; operating		4li

Weir	Hospitallers	Liffey	Salmon		26li, 13s. 4d.
Demense lands	Hospitallers	Fields surrounding the hospice	Meadow/ arable	260 ac	13li, 22s.
Droges	Hyllock, Thomas		Pasture and underwood	14	13s. 4d.
Burgages (2 1/2)	Kelly, Martin				5s. 4d.
Land	Kelly, Martin	Camac; both sides south of Bowbridge	Pasture	1 1/2 x 3	16s.
Kyngs yards	Kerne, William	Camac; on the west called Sangwenslands	Gardens		8s.
Garden	Lane, Thomas	North part of village street	Garden		12d.
Gardens	Myne, Richard		Two Gardens		20d.
Half-burgage	Myne, Richard (formerly Thomas Inglond's)		Half-burgage		16d.
Village Fields	Newman, Tamesina, heir to William	Village Fields	Tenement and arable	1 1/4 ac	3s. 2d.
Garden	Oqouyne, John (formerly)	Near western gate /part of village	Garden		2s.
Arable	Oqouyne, John (formerly)		Arable	3/4	
Garden	Oqouyne, Lachlan	East of Lachlan's messuage	Garden		12d.
Messuage	Oqouyne, Lachlan	East of garden above	Messuage not built on		12d.
Garden	Oqouyne, Lachlan		Garden		2s.
Messuage	Oqouyne, Lachlan		Messuage		5s.
Kings land	Oquoyne, John	East and south of 2 acres			
Pasture	Oquoyne, John	Village field	Pasture		8s. 9d.
Messuage	Oquoyne, John				6s.
Messuage	Perpoyn, Agnes	Near John Fitzsimond's land	Not built upon		20d.
Messuage	Perpoyn, Agnes		Messuage – waste		10s. 8d. (with grove)
Gyfford's Grove	Perpoyn, Agnes	Between Crumlin and Kilmainham	Small bushy grove of pasture		10s, 8d. (with messuage)
Burgages & tenements	Perpoyn, Agnes (formerly Kelly's)				Rent obliterated
Castelhouse	Perpoyn, Agnes, Rawson, Catherine	Vill	Messuage		10s.
Bayle Yard	Perpoyn, Agnes, Rawson, Catherine	Near Quoytrott's land	Land	3/4 ac	
Arable	Perpoyn, Agnes, Rawson, Catherine	West of vill, adjoining city liberties	Arable	5	
Pasture	Perpoyn, Agnes, Rawson, Catherine	Near park	Pasture	2 ac	
Quoytrot's Park	Quoytrot, Nicholas	West of the vill	Burgage and a half		3s.
Messuage with garden etc	Quoytrot, Nicholas		Messuage with a garden and close		18d.
Quoytrott's Park	Quoytrott	West of 2 acres			
Messuage	Raban, Rory		Messuage		5s.
Fulling-mill	Rawson, Richard	Camac	On rent		60s.
Garden	Rery, James		East Garden		2s.
Village Fields	Rery, James	Village fields	Arable	3 ac	3s. 10d.
Woodfeld	Savage, Richard		Arable and pasture	15	15s.
Tyrrell's Wood	Scurlock, Nicholas	In the ville	Meadow		2s. 6d.
Village Fields	Smyth, William	Village Fields	Arable	8ac	10s. 8d.
Village Fields	St Anne's Guild	Village Fields	Messuage, 1 close, arable	24 (arable)	18s. 5 1/2d.

Village Fields	St Anne's Guild (form. E. Dowdall's)	Village Fields	Arable and pasture	56½ ac	56s. 6d
Messuage and land	St Patrick's		Arable	9½	10s. 7d.
Messuage and land	Talbot, William		Arable	50 ac	26s.
Gardens	Taylor, Brian	Near Lady Anne Byrmyngham's lands	Gardens x 4		10s.
Village Fields?	Taylor, Brian	Village Fields	Arable	¼ ac	4d.
Messuage	Taylor, Brian	West of Thos. Berymgham's land	Messuage/ small garden		18d.
Common Green	Tenants of the vill	In village	3/4 burgage		18d.
Stryffe more	Tenants of the vill	In the manor	Pasture	20 ac	No rent
Dammes	Tenants of the vill in common	In the manor	Pasture	20 ac	No rent
Garden	Toker, Denis	East of Rery's	Garden		12d.
Newtone	Ussher, Orlonton	Near the Grete Wood	Mixed	130?	6li 13s. 4d.
Village Fields	Whyte, James	Village Fields	Land	3 ¾ ac	Annuity
House	Whyte, James	Village	House		Annuity

Source: Extents of Irish monastic possessions

Kilnalag to Williamstown, north county Galway, 1820–50

MAEVE MULRYAN-MOLONEY

INTRODUCTION

Williamstown and Kilnalag are situated in the north-east of county Galway on the high road from Tuam to Roscommon, within eight miles of Dunmore, six miles of Glinsk and eight miles of Castlerea, county Roscommon. The civil parish of Williamstown is coextensive with the ecclesiastical parish of Templetogher – the most northerly county Galway parish in the archdiocese of Tuam. The parish is in the ancient territory of Clann Conmhaigh. In medieval times it was part of the manor of Glinsk or the half-barony of Ballymoe in county Galway. Williamstown was in the barony of Ballymoe for fiscal purposes until the enactment of the Local Government Act of 1898 when the county was divided into urban and rural districts and baronies ceased to exist as administrative areas.

People have inhabited Templetogher's 13,700 statute acres from time immemorial. We are not certain how, or from whence, they came. There are several possibilities. It is probable that the first habitations were on the banks of the river Suck, a tributary of the river Shannon. Then, after a generation, or generations, persons found their way from the Suck to the hinterland of its tributary, the Islands river. They penetrated an area covered with dense forest and bog alongside some of the finest land in Connacht. Abundant water, a fine trout stream, lush grassland, a plentiful supply of turf and firewood, and some quarries of good limestone showed its suitability for a settlement. The early habitations and paths (toghers) are preserved in the placenames Castletogher and Templetogher.

The most plentiful surnames in the parish, according to Richard Griffith's valuation in the mid-nineteenth century were 35 McDermotts, 18 Burkes, and 16 Connollys. There were more than 10 of each of a small number of families – Brennan, Connerton (spelt Connaughton in the tithes), Finigan, Kearns, Kenny, Knight, Lyons, Nee, Reilly, Smyth, Tully and Walsh.[1] The number of McDermotts and Burkes – one Old Irish, the other Norman, is very significant, and may stem from the thirteenth and fourteenth centuries when the fertile lands of the leading Connacht families were granted to the Norman De Burgos.

---

1 NLI, 'An index of surnames of householders in Griffith's primary valuation and tithe applotment books', pp 116–17.

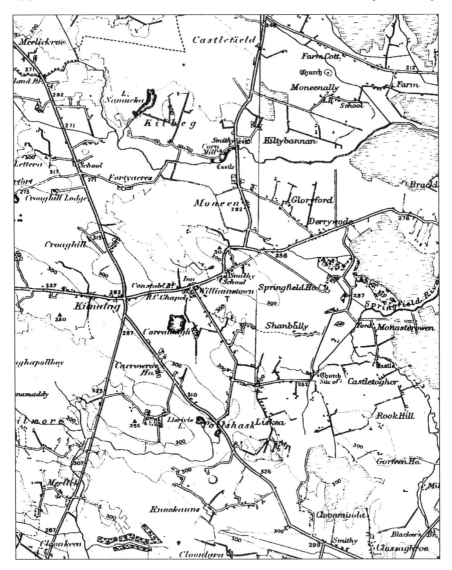

Figure 1 OS Map – Kilnalag and Williamstown area *c*.1840.

The intrusion of the De Burgos onto the O'Conor ancestral ground and their acquisition and retention of lands led to many tribal conflicts. In 1255 the O'Conors and McWilliam Burkes conferred at Tochair Mona Conneda (Templetogher) and agreed to coexist peacefully.[2] The O'Conors anticipated

---

2 Martin Freeman, *The annals of Connacht* (Dublin, 1983), p.113.

that peace would not endure, so to protect their livestock they drove them to Tír Connaill (Donegal). The Normans were intent on overcoming the Gaelic families, so within the next decade, in 1262, McWilliam Burke and his fighting men advanced from Castletogher, crossed the Suck to join other Norman warriors, and then plundered everything O'Conor had left behind in Connacht. A further treaty was brokered between the Burkes and the O'Conors.[3] Battle cries were again heard in Templetogher, in 1316, when in a conflict over the kingship of Connacht, Ruaidhrí O'Conor – 'the most valiant and valorous of the Gaels, the destroyer of marauders and the banisher of foreigners out of Ireland' was killed. Diarmait MacDiarmait, king of Moylurg was also killed.[4]

The names of many of the local townlands and their extent are catalogued in the indenture which is known as the Composition of Connacht.[5] The physical features of the landscape helped to distinguish local areas. Many local placenames pertain to the woods and bogs such as Moneen, Derryvode, Carrownderry and Kilnalag, to the fertile soils of Carrowroe and Ballyroe, and to the waters of Corralough.

In Connacht a townland had a nominal area of 480 acres divided into quarters each containing four cartrons. The quarter (in Gaelic *ceathrú* or carrow) was of uncertain quantity, a measure of value – not of actual acreage. The arable and pasture content was equal to so many quarters of standard land. Immediately northwest of Templetogher parish is Ballinlough parish, which had an influx of people from English-speaking areas, the 'Quarter' as in Castlequarter is established in its placenames. In Templetogher parish Carrowroe, Carrowneany and Carrownderry preserve the Gaelic forms.

The Burkes were held in high esteem by successive British governments. The manor of Glinsk had 1,000 acres in demesne, power to make tenures, power to hold courts leet and baron, a court of pie-powder and the usual tolls. Constables were appointed twice a year by court leet. The loyalty of the Burkes was further rewarded when on 25 January 1618, James 1 granted Ulick Burke of Glinsk, lands in Templetogher parish including Carrowroelisnashamer and Croghall one quarter each, Coillnalogg (Kilnalag) a half quarter, and Leaderry two quarters.[6] That document shows that Kilnalag was a placename for nearly two centuries before a chapel was built there. In the 1585 indenture it is Coill na Logg, probably derived from *coill* meaning forest or wooded place and *logg* possibly referring to the lake nearby at Corralough. Tradition has it that Illannolanamaddogy – the island of Nuala (Burke) of the knives – is in Corralough lake.[7] The land was intensely drained and cultivated, and pathways were widened as stone and gravel roads were laid. Stonewalls throughout the parish, which give character to the landscape, are

3 Ibid. **4** Ibid. **5** Martin Freeman, *The compossicion book of Conought* (Dublin, 1936), p. 83. **6** *Irish patent rolls of James* (Dublin, 1966), p. 348. **7** Olive Alcock, Kathy de hÓra, Paul Gosling, *Archaeological inventory of county Galway* (Dublin, 1999), p. 30.

evidence of that period. The placenames were never anglicised. The Gaelic language was the vernacular in Templetogher parish until the advent of local national schools in the latter half of the nineteenth century.

KILNALAG VILLAGE

By the early nineteenth century a village had developed around Kilnalag crossroads at the centre of Templetogher parish. Larkin's map, published in 1819 at the request of the grand jury of county Galway, shows a church to the east of the crossroads and a row of houses to the west, but no fair green, constabulary barracks or school. Hely Dutton in his *Statistical and agricultural survey of county Galway* expressed some reservations about the accuracy of Larkin's map but it is probable that in this instance Larkin's map is partially correct. Kilnalag markets and fairs were legalised when on 10 April 1806, King George III granted a patent to Henry E. Taaffe, the local landlord, who lived in county Mayo. He was empowered to hold a market every Friday, and fairs on 27 May, 20 June, 24 August and 20 December.[8] Tradition has it that the farmers and traders assembled, not in a fair green, but at Kilnalag crossroads. Graziers from the pasturelands in Leinster attended the May and June fairs to buy sheep and store cattle. In September fat cattle and sheep were sold.[9]

Enterprising people established schools at Kilnalag. In the mid 1820s Charles Finnegan held a school in the chapel for forty boys and twelve girls.[10] Ten years later Thomas Tracy taught reading, writing and arithmetic to sixty-two males and twenty-one females and Patrick Geraghty taught eighteen males and seven females.[11]

A constabulary barracks was established, probably after 1822. In 1787 the lord lieutenant divided counties into police districts, consisting of one or more baronies and appointed a chief constable to each district. The grand juries were authorised to appoint eight sub-constables, all Protestants, to each district. The County Constabulary was established in 1822 when under the Constabulary Act subtle changes were made to the composition of the police force. The lord lieutenant was empowered to appoint a county inspector for each county, with two head constables, sixteen constables and a number of sub-constables for each barony. Religion was not enquired into and this non-denominational force helped to foster confidence in the police. Constables were usually single men who could be transferred at the whim of a superior officer. Promotion was up

8 *Report of commissioners appointed to inquire into the state of fairs and markets in Ireland 1852,* App. HC 1852–3 [167], xli, pp 52, 83–4, 123.   9 Hely Dutton, *Statistical and agricultural survey of the county of Galway* (Dublin, 1824) p. 120.   10 *Second report of the Royal Commission on Irish education,* HC 1826–7 (12), xii, p. 1194.   11 *First report of the commissioners of public instruction in Ireland, province of Tuam, diocese of Tuam, class 1 rectories and vicarages,* 1835, HC 1834 [45], xxxiii, p. 36.

through the ranks. In 1853 only one-fifth of constables were married.[12] A head constable was appointed to divisional headquarters at Dunmore with a sergeant, constables and sub-constables at Kilnalag.

Gradually Kilnalag became a well-developed centre of population with its own church, schools, licensed premises, constabulary barracks, fairs and markets. However by mid-century most of these had ceased to operate, or were duplicated a kilometre to the east, where the village of Williamstown was the emerging centre of commerce and services. The nearest post office was at Dunmore. The story of the decline of Kilnalag village and the growth of Williamstown is, to a great extent, the story of William McDermott.

WILLIAM MCDERMOTT

The surname McDermott was assumed in the eleventh century and its representative maintained a high position in Connacht for 500 years. William McDermott was the descendant of two of the great high-ranking families, McDermott of Moylurg and O'Kelly of Ui Máine, of the eastern part of the province of Connacht. His ancestor, James Kelley, was granted a patent for about a quarter of Templetogher parish in the late seventeenth century.[13] The land continued in the Kelley family for over 100 years until the marriage of Honora Kelly (Kelley) to barrister Owen McDermott, the fourth son of Edward McDermott and his wife Ellen Kelly of Emla, county Roscommon.[14]

Owen and Honora's only son William was born on 4 March 1800.[15] When William reached his teens a suitable bride, seventeen-year-old Anna Eliza Bodkin, was found for him. The landed families of county Galway married within a well-defined circle of equals. Major Thomas Bodkin of Kilclooney (near Milltown in north Galway) and his wife Eliza Smith formerly of Topcroft Hall, Norfolk, England owned 2,700 acres of land[16] and the McDermotts of Springfield owned 2,500 acres. William and Anna began their married life in 1821 at the paternal home. The McDermotts mortgaged their estate for £3,000 to provide for the children of the marriage. Owen, William, John, Thomas, Elizabeth, Anna, Catherine and Victoria were born over the following twenty-three years. Owen McDermott Senior died on 24 May 1825 and William was granted a life interest in the Springfield estate.[17]

In the census recorded in 1821 in the parish of Templetogher, the population was fairly evenly divided between employment in farming and cottage indus-

---

12 Mr and Mrs S.C. Hall, *Handbooks for Ireland* (Dublin, 1853), p. 36.   **13** NLI, Irish Land Commission, Record EC 3344, box 227, Patent in favour of James Kelley, 20 June 1678.   **14** *King's Inns admission papers* (Dublin, 1982), p. 307.   **15** Ibid.   **16** Christy Molloy, 'The Bodkins of Kilclooney' in *Journal of the Galway Family History Society*, iv (Galway, 1997), p. 75.   **17** NAI, MS 5651 (1–2), McDermott papers.

tries, with 1,062 persons in agriculture and 1,043 in trades, manufacturing and handcrafts.[18] Most looked directly or indirectly to the land for their livelihood. The milling of corn was central to the local economy and corn mills were dispersed throughout the parish. In 1822 the Egan family opened a corn mill at Templetogher.[19] The people lived mainly on their garden potatoes, oatmeal and cow's milk. Arable land (corn-acre or conacre) was let for one or two crops of corn or potatoes in lots of from one to five acres. A few farms had up to twenty acres. It was a precarious existence as one harvest – or worse still successive poor harvests – could see deaths outstripping births as disease took its toll. Tenants held their land at the will of the landlord year-on-year as long as rents were paid. With each succeeding generation people moved on to more marginalised land, and each group of families was given a share of bog. As the number of families increased, more and more people depended on the land and bog for sustenance and home comforts. Land partnerships in villages led to strong friendships that were generally strengthened by intermarriage. The main outgoings of tenants were rent and tithes. Occupiers struggled to pay the rent – with rent due in May paid in August and rent due in November paid the following March, but evictions were rare, due to good landlord-tenant relationships.

The people were resourceful. Nearly every family had a spinning wheel, some had a weaver's loom; many people clicked on their knitting needles, turning out garments for the home and export trade. Fleeces of sheep wool were processed locally after shearing time in early summer. Flax was seen as a cash crop. When the linen trade flourished women could support their families decently by spinning flax into yarn and by creating exquisite lace. The yarn and lace, sold to the travelling agents of Dublin or Belfast merchants, yielded the major portion of a family's income.[20] With the advent of the power loom in England, wages were pushed lower and lower, as hand weavers tried to survive against competition from machinery. The fatal blow to the craft workers in linen came when the Linen Board was abolished in 1828. By the mid-1830s there was no demand for their products, so, in 1834 Archbishop John MacHale of Tuam reported that a woman could scarcely earn a penny a day by spinning from morning till night.[21]

Tithes, a tax on the produce of the land, were levied for the support of Protestant ministers from the mid-sixteenth century. The injustice of the system is evident in Templetogher parish where there were no Protestants. In 1822, much to the relief of an impoverished people, the government exempted the produce of potato gardens from tithes. Tithes were then payable on the average

18 *Census of Ireland 1821, County of Galway, Ballymoe half-barony, Templetoher parish*, p. 757 HC 1824 (577) xxii, p. 323.   19 Sarah Agnes Lennon, *Egan's Mill, Templetogher* (Williamstown, 2003), p. 59.   20 W.H. Crawford, *Domestic industry in Ireland* (Dublin, 1972), p. 12.   21 *First report of the commissioners for inquiring into the state of the poorer classes in Ireland*, evidence of Archbishop MacHale, Appendix A, HC 1835 (369), xxxii, p. 121.

price of oats, which was the grain principally grown in county Galway, during the period of seven years prior to assessment. The Catholic parish of Temple-togher is in the deanery of Dunmore. The Protestant church authorities claimed it as a rectory and vicarage forming part of the union of Kiltullagh.[22]

Here is the affidavit of the tithe commissioners.[23]

> We, Bernard Sweeny and Samuel Potter, commissioners duly appointed and sworn, under and by virtue of an act made in the fourth year of George IV (1820–30) entitled an act to provide for the establishment of composition of tithes in Ireland for a limited time to ascertain and fix a true and just composition for all tithes arising, proving and yielding or payable within the three-fourths parish of Templetogher in the county of Galway, do hereby certify that the true and just amount of composi-tion for all tithes whatever within the said three-fourths parish is one hun-dred and twenty pounds sterling by the year, of which sum of £120, one half belongs to Thomas Carter as dean of Tuam and the other half to George Beresford as provost of Tuam.
>
> Given under our hand, 9 June 1826.
>
> B. Sweeny commissioner; Samuel Potter commissioner.

In the time of William IV (1831–7), tithes' commissioner Edward Strickland of Loughglynn House assessed the other quarter of the parish. He certified that on the first day of November 1831 the average price of oats was 12s. 11d. per barrel. Tithes that amounted to £29 13s. 8d. were payable to the rector at Ballinlough.[24] Kilnalag was a day's journey from Tuam and six miles from Ballinlough and the three clergymen would have no reason to visit the totally Catholic parish. Local collectors brought the tithes to the central collection point.

Table 1 Tithe collectors on McDermott's estate.[25]

Townland	Tithe collectors
Ballyroe	James Connell
Carrenderry	John Bligh
Corrolough	Patrick Geraghty, Robert Dowling
Gortduff	Michael Jennings, Thomas McLoughlin, Michael Mulligan

22 *First report of the commissioners of public instruction in Ireland, province of Tuam, diocese of Tuam, class 1 rectories and vicarages*, 1835, HC 1835 [45], xxxiii, p. 800. **23** NAI, Tithes' index, film number 38, 1828. **24** NAI, Tithes' index, film number 38, 1833. **25** NAI, Tithes' index, film number 38, 1828.

Table 2 Tithe payers on Taaffe's estate.[26]

Townland	Tithe payers
Carraroe	Walter Cussane, Michael Timothy, John Tully, Mathew Geraghty, Pat O'Rourke and Widow Kenny.
Kilnalag	Pat McDermott, John Gillfoil, John Smith, Pat Smith, Thomas Flynn, John Tighe, Mrs Dowling, John Kelly, John Kerins, Widow Cunningham, John Timothy, Daniel Kean, John Archbold.

The tithe collector penned the following:

> William Boyd is my name and Ireland is my nation
> Coolfarna is my dwelling place and thrift is my salvation.
> When I am dead --- this little book will tell my name
> When thousands are forgotten.[27]

In the 1821 census, 3697 (1888 males and 1809 females) formed 735 families in 718 houses. A population explosion was on the way. It increased by one third to 4881 (2440 males and 2441 females) in the following ten years. The number of families increased from 735 to 866.[28] One of the most worrying statistics was that 50 per cent of the population was under 20 years of age, with the vast majority of them living and working at home. Families were under severe strain as women were left to cope with children and old people, because a quarter of the fathers of families and many single men left the parish and went to England in spring and in harvest time. The women were devoted to their homes and children, and frequently took a very active part in outdoor work. Some employment was available locally as 66 occupiers employed some of the 404 male agricultural labourers and 111 female servants. Most had never been to school. Parents were slowly becoming more conscious of the need to formally educate their children.

In 1826 William McDermott entered Trinity College as an undergraduate and following graduation in 1830, he continued his legal studies at Gray's Inn in London. All schools were fee-paying schools until the non-denominational national education system was initiated in 1831. In the euphoria of the expectation of government grants it was nearly forgotten that one third of the building costs of the school and a contribution towards the teacher's salary had to come from local funds. All that money had to be paid by smallholders as their priest struggled to raise the parish contribution to get a grant for a national school.

26 Ibid.   **27** Ibid.   **28** *Census of Ireland 1831, County of Galway, Ballymoe half-barony, Templetoher parish, 1831*, HC 1833, xxxix, p. 38.

The total number of scholars in the Kilnalag schools in 1834 was 80 males and 28 females. There was a practical reason for this because the older girls stayed home to care for the younger children while their mothers tended the gardens and animals. Men mainly migrated, so with a limited supply of money for school fees it was deemed right that boys should face the world with some level of literacy. William, by then the father of a young family and practising as a barrister in Dublin, was eager to access education for his family, so he promised a site and £10 towards building a national school. The non-denominational system of education established in Ireland in 1832 went against the ideals of Catholic elementary instruction. Archbishop MacHale's deeply entrenched ideological differences with the Board of Education led to an embargo on the national schools system in Tuam archdiocese from 1839, much to the dismay of parents like William and Anna McDermott.[29] They were privileged to be financially capable of sourcing tuition for their family in Dublin, but many families were not so fortunate. The following literacy tables in the censuses of 1841 and 1851 show the slow gains in reading and writing skills in Templetogher parish prior to the first national school.

Table 3 Templetogher parish, reading and writing, 1841 and 1851.[30]

Year	Read and write		Read only		Neither read nor write	
	Males	Females	Males	Females	Males	Females
1841	307 (14%)	82 (4%)	154 (7%)	85 (4%)	1733 (79%)	1978 (92%)
1851	468 (27%)	164 (9%)	166 (10%)	199 (11%)	1079 (63%)	1517 (80%)

A whole generation was denied a subsidised education until Marlborough-Street-trained John Carabine commenced teaching in a good two-storey former shop and dwelling house in Williamstown village in 1862.[31] The girl's national school opened a generation later.[32]

William McDermott, as a part-time farmer in one of the finest corn districts in county Galway, maintained a passionate interest in the politics and current events in his home parish and county. This interest in local affairs was sharpened by a tragic occurrence at Kilnalag fair on Whit Monday in June 1835. Fair

29 Maeve Mulryan-Moloney, *Eighteenth century elementary education in the archdiocese of Tuam* (Maynooth, 2001) pp 19–20. **30** Irish University Press series of British Parliamentary Papers, *Population 2*, 1841 census Ireland, p. 374; Irish University Press series of British Parliamentary Papers, *Population 14*, 1851 census Ireland, p. 540. **31** NAI, ED 1/35 f. 48. **32** Maeve Mulryan-Moloney, *Recollections of the past* (Williamstown, county Galway, 1999) p. 6.

days were seen as one of the few days in the year when riotous merrymaking was tolerated. This sometimes led to faction fighting after copious amounts of locally brewed alcohol were consumed and old feuds revisited. Taaffe, the local landlord, seems to have turned a blind eye to the behaviour of his tenants. A riot ensued on that Whit Monday in 1835, and tragically, an innocent bystander was killed. It is likely that some of the responsible local people saw the need for a petty sessions court at Kilnalag to deal with misdemeanours arising from the abuse of alcohol. In the absence of action from the remote disinterested Taaffes, McDermott needed to gain control over the lawlessness of his neighbourhood, so he made an application to hold a petty sessions court on his estate.[33] In 1836 the lord lieutenant was mandated to appoint magistrates to reside in such districts as they saw fit. They were to report regularly to the Chief Secretary's Office at Dublin Castle on the state of their districts and they were to attend fairs and petty sessions in their districts. The Irish Constabulary was established in 1836 and in 1867 Queen Victoria granted it the title Royal Irish Constabulary (RIC).

McDermott's application had not yet been approved, when on Whit Monday 15 May 1837, a large crowd assembled at Kilnalag crossroads for the eagerly awaited fair. The magistrate and police from the district headquarters of the constabulary at Dunmore rode in to assist the Kilnalag police. Dunmore military barracks was on stand-by. As the day advanced stones were thrown by opposing factions and several persons were severely wounded. The Dunmore Chief Constable Atkinson ordered Sergeant Hicks, Constables Henry Beaty and Peter Croughan and Sub-Constable John Tighe of Kilnalag barracks to arrest the stone throwers. They marched them to Dunmore where local magistrates Michael Bermingham and W.H. Handcock awaited them. They were returned to Tuam assizes on 24 June. Ten respected local persons whose conduct, as stated in court, was unusual, were each sentenced to six months hard labour at Galway jail. They were each bound to the peace for ten years on the enormous sureties of £10 and £20.[34] Overindulgence at fairs was a countrywide problem. In 1839 the Capuchin priest, Father Theobald Mathew, preached on temperance to huge gatherings of people, but Archbishop MacHale forbade him to preach in Tuam diocese as he wished to foster his own temperance movement.[35]

William McDermott's superior knowledge of the legal system led to the favourable consideration of his application for a petty sessions court. His brother-in-law, John James Bodkin, and Michael Blake Bermingham were the first presiding magistrates in September 1837. Bodkin was the local member of parliament for eighteen years. Members of the Guilfoyle family were petty sessions clerks for the next half a century. The punishment handed down following the fracas at Kilnalag the previous June meant that the court opened on a low key,

33 *Tuam Herald*, 27 September 1837. **34** Ibid., 24 June 1837. **35** NAI, Outrage Papers, 1843, county Galway, 11/25003.

and the only fines imposed were on several pound-keepers who had exacted illegal fees for cattle seized for trespassing.[36]

The establishment of the court on McDermott's land began the degeneration of Kilnalag. Tradition accords other reasons for the decline of Kilnalag, such as a dispute over the election of 1837 when McDermott supported Thomas Martin as MP for county Galway. Another tradition has it that landlord Taaffe refused permission for the slating of Kilnalag chapel. The chapel probably dated from the alleviation of the penal laws in the 1780s so by the 1830s it was in dire need of weatherproofing. In 1834 the average number of persons attending Sunday Mass in Templetogher parish was about 2,500.[37]

WILLIAM'S TOWN

A vision unfolded before William and Anna McDermott – that of a new town, their lasting unique memorial. The local villages, Glenamaddy and Ballinlough, took their names from the topography of the neighbourhood. It was not unusual for landed proprietors in the west of Ireland to permit villages to grow up around their mansions. Mount Bellew, Frenchpark and Castleplunkett are typical examples where family names were preserved for posterity.[38] Williamstown was different. Sometimes a name is given by popular acclamation, but William McDermott proudly called his proposed town Williamstown possibly to commemorate either himself, his son William or the recently deceased King William IV.

William, as a fledgling barrister, worked in Dublin in 1834 when the first railway in Ireland (and the world's first suburban railway) opened from Dublin to Kingstown (Dun Laoghaire). The expansion of the railways to the provinces could open up the west of Ireland within a decade. He planned a substantial development that would be adequate for the commercial and social demands of a railway town. In his submission to Samuel Lewis for Lewis's *Topographical dictionary of Ireland*, published in 1837, he wrote about his comfortable new hotel. In addition the *Tuam Herald* noted that an ample grain store was being built at Williamstown, which buyers could use from one market day to another without any charge. Did McDermott envisage that his grain store and hotel would be added inducements to having a railway line brought through his town? His law colleague and Catholic Association friend Daniel O'Connell played a leading role in the formation of the National Bank, so with the advent of the railway, a bank was likely to follow. It is evident that McDermott compiled his answers to Lewis's questionnaire from what he planned to build rather than from what was actually on the ground. He is quoted in the topographical dictionary –

---

36 *Tuam Herald*, 27 September 1837. **37** *First report of the commissioners of public instruction in Ireland, province of Tuam, diocese of Tuam, class 1 rectories and vicarages, 1835*, HC 1835 [45], xxxiii, p. 801. **38** Sir Bernard Burke, *Dictionary of the landed gentry* (London, 1858), p. 873.

There are chapels at Kilnalag and Williamstown – six acres of land for the use of the parish priest on which a neat dwelling house has been erected – constabulary barracks at Kilnalag and Williamstown – petty sessions weekly at Williamstown.[39]

All this was written prior to 1837, when the first public building – the court-house – was opened on his estate, a kilometre east of Kilnalag crossroads.

McDermott's plans gathered momentum. He proceeded to plan a fair green south of the courthouse. He obviously saw the new *Tuam Herald* as an important medium to publish his ideas. The second edition, 23 September 1837, hailed William McDermott as

> a landed proprietor generously coming forward, offering every encour-agement to promote the interests of his tenants, the occurrence [of which] is unfortunately so rare, that we joyfully hail him as a generous benefac-tor; in this latter character we are glad to see Counsellor McDermott of Springfield. Not alone have his superior talents and strenuous exertions been engaged in advocating these measures of enlightened policy, which the spirit of the age demands, but are also devoted to the improvement of his locality. Williamstown belongs to this genteel man. It will be seen by the advertisements in our paper today, how likely it is that it [will] be soon a town of trade and some importance. He will give to any person who builds in Williamstown, five acres at a moderate rent, and facilities for building.

He advertised a toll-free weekly market for the sale of oats and other grain at Williamstown on Tuesday 26 September 1837. The toll-free market was an unusual idea.[40] In Dunmore the sum of 2*d.* was levied on every pig brought to market; at Ballymoe fair it was 4*d.* The proprietor of every tent, booth and stall at Ballymoe paid 1*s.* in tolls. Charges were made for the use of the weighing scales. Animals and all other farm produce – corn, potatoes, butter, wool fleeces, as well as wool processed and woven into flannel and frieze – were subject to tolls at Dunmore. These were an added imposition on sellers especially at that period when the market for home-produced goods was in decline. The initial toll-free market was a huge success and more than 200 sacks of oats were sold at from 4*s.* 4*d.* to 5*s.* 2*d.* a hundredweight.[41] The other market proprietors took note and by 1843 no tolls were collected at any markets or fairs in Ballymoe, Glenamaddy or Williamstown.[42]

There was obviously a demand for the market so McDermott planned a fair green. During the spring of 1838 a large area in front of the courthouse was

39 Samuel Lewis, *A topographical dictionary of Ireland* (London, 1837), p. 616.   **40** *Tolls and cus-toms, Ireland*, HC 1830 (634), xxvi, p. 80.   **41** *Tuam Herald*, 30 September 1837.   **42** *Tolls and customs from 1840 to 43*, p. 173 HC 1843 (589), l, p. 11.

cleared and gritted as standing areas for donkey-drawn carts of pigs, and a weighing platform was erected beside the main road. On Whit Monday, the lowing of cattle and the bleating of sheep were first heard at daybreak as drovers and livestock neared the village fair green. Stallholders trundled in with carts laden with tents, clothes – new and second hand – delph and kitchenware and farm implements. Publicans at Kilnalag saw their friends pass by, as people hastened to Williamstown to witness the beginning of a new era. For William McDermott it was an epoch-making day as so many persons and animals converged in a peaceful manner. There were no riots, which according to the *Tuam Herald* 'was unusual for that neighbourhood, due to the good management of the patriotic and spirited proprietor'.[43] Williamstown was relatively inaccessible, but by William's initiative in the summer of 1838, a well-horsed Bianconi car from Ballymoe went through the town regularly to meet the mail coach at Dunmore.[44] The mail coach left 11 Tighe Street, Dublin, at 6 a.m. on Mondays, Wednesdays and Fridays and returned the following day. Now livestock and produce buyers would have easy access to future markets and fairs, with overnight accommodation at Williamstown's comfortable lodging houses.

Major Waters and Lieutenant Wynne of the Ordnance Survey Office in the Phoenix Park in Dublin probably travelled in Bianconi's car to Kilnalag and Williamstown in 1838.[45] The two villages were in a transition period. Waters and Wynne surveyed a chapel, a schoolhouse, a constabulary barracks and a pound at Kilnalag crossroads. Williamstown had only a fair green. This explains why the new village was not noted on the first edition of the six-inch-to-one-statute-mile Ordnance Survey map.[46] Did McDermott confer with Waters and Wynne and their team of land measurers? It seems unlikely because, using his highly persuasive powers, McDermott might have had them defer surveying until his new village was built. There is no record of how the publicans and pound keeper at Kilnalag viewed the new enterprise at Williamstown. They were certainly on the map, but subtle changes were on the way.

McDermott splashed out his money for the encouragement of the February 1839 fair and to get the second year of the fair off to a good start. He was certainly a generous man who was keen to encourage good husbandry and to attract good quality buyers by awarding premiums that totalled £10 5s., a sum exceeding the annual salary of £8 paid to national teachers. The prizes generated great interest as farmers and jobbers eyed each other warily as they marked ewes and lambs, cows and heifers and cartloads of fat pigs, sows and bonhams. The poor donkeys did not feature in the prize list even though they probably outnumbered the horses.

43 *Tuam Herald*, 4 June 1838.   **44** Ibid., 5 August 1837.   **45** OS Map No. 6 County Galway, 1833–44.   **46** Ibid.

Table 4 Premiums awarded by William McDermott at Williamstown fair,
February 1839.[47]

Prize awarded for:	To buyer	To seller
Best ten sheep	£1	£1
Best ten lambs	10s.	10s.
Second best ten sheep	15s.	15s.
Best fat cow	15s.	15s.
Best two-year-old heifer	10s.	10s.
Best horse	10s.	10s.
Best fat pig	10s.	10s.
Second best fat pig	7s. 6d.	7s. 6d.
Third best fat pig	5s.	5s.

A loan fund operated in Ballymoe and farmers could borrow to buy a cow and the advance was repaid from the sale of milk.[48] The villages existed side by side and cooperated in the holding of fairs for the next decade. Williamstown fairs were held on the feast of the Epiphany (also called little Christmas), Easter Monday, Whit Monday and 8 September; Kilnalag fairs took place at mid-May, at the end of June and at the end of August.[49]

McDermott enticed entrepreneurs to Williamstown with the offer of five acres of land each at a moderate rent and facilities for building. Several local families had houses erected along the main road in the townlands of Corralough and Ballyroe. By 1840 the development of Williamstown was well under way. McDermott's leases specified a good substantial dwelling house, two storeys high, roofed with slates, 32 feet long by 16 feet broad.

Table 5 Census of Ireland, Templetogher parish, 1841.[50]

Area	Acres	Population		Houses
		Male	Female	
Ballyroe	172	4	4	1
Corralough	529	72	56	22
Kilnalag	214	41	59	22

The loan fund at Ballymoe was possibly dipped into by local entrepreneurs eager to get the seed capital for their enterprises in the new village. One of the earli-

47 *Tuam Herald*, 2 February 1839.   48 *Evidence number 444 of James Kelly of Ballymoe taken before her majesty's commission of inquiry into the state of law and practice in relation to the occupation of land in Ireland, HC 1845, (672), xxxiv, p. 368.*   49 Thom's *Irish almanac and official directory* (Dublin, 1850), p. 486.   50 Irish University Press series of British Parliamentary Papers, *Population 2*, 1841 Census Ireland, p. 374.

Figure 2 Parish church Williamstown, mid-twentieth century.

est publicans was John Guilfoyle. Is it the same Gillfoil family mentioned in the Kilnalag tithes but of whom there is no mention in Richard Griffith's valuation of Kilnalag? It probably is. In the absence of information on pre-1870s public house licences we can only surmise that he foresaw the advantages of moving to a prime site on Williamstown Square. The town was soon a town of trade and importance being the headquarters of the petty sessions for the barony of Ballymoe.[51] In 1841 the population of Williamstown parish was 4976 (2515 males and 2461 females). It had increased very little since the previous census but the number of houses had gone up by 25 per cent. Fifty-six were good quality houses and one, Springfield House, was a superior house. Further analysis of the 1841 census shows that two-thirds of the houses were one-roomed, one-windowed traditional mud cabins; 27 per cent were larger thatched cottages.

The McDermotts had catered for the temporal needs of their tenants. Now they attended to their spiritual welfare. They endowed a site for a church in Templetogher parish to the south of the fair green and promised £50 for materials and building costs.[52] William convened a meeting of parishioners to discuss his plans for the church. The site chosen was historically significant in that it was directly opposite the penal Mass site, known in Gaelic as *Closh an Aifrinn*.

51 *Tuam Herald*, 18 May 1839. **52** Lewis, *Topographical dictionary*, p. 616.

In January 1838 Garett Kelly of Knockanes was delegated to invite tenders for building a new church.[53] Potential contractors were given a month to prepare plans and specifications and to guarantee sufficient surety for the due completion of the work. Masons and plasterers, carpenters and slaters began work on Williamstown's new church. Disaster struck when two weeks after Christmas 1838 a ferocious hurricane swept in from the Atlantic Ocean. To the horror and dismay of the community, striving to protect their own homes from the elements, the seemingly impregnable roof of their church was severely damaged.[54]

Church endowment was a tradition in Anna McDermott's family – the Bodkins – as they built a church on their estate at Kilclooney in 1803, and just around the time that Williamstown church was under construction her brother, John James contributed generously to the new parish church at Milltown. William McDermott was a well-established barrister when, in 1838, in addition to his private practice, he was appointed assistant barrister in county Kerry at a salary of £300 per annum. He held the post for the next twenty years. Travel by coach and then by flyboat on the Grand Canal to Dublin and from there to Kerry was exhausting. The toll which his absences from his delightful home at Springfield had on their home life made William and Anna decide to move their school-age family to Dublin. They acquired a house in the fashionable district of Mountjoy Square.[55]

Springfield was a long eleven-roomed, thatched, two-storey house enclosed by a verdant plantation near a spring. The house was accessed through a long straight avenue from the gate lodge on the Williamstown-Ballymoe road. The road to Castlerea branched off near the gate lodge. In February 1839 an auction of the entire household furniture and farm implements and stock took place. Anna McDermott had certainly furnished her Springfield home according to her station. In the absence of removal vans she would have to furnish again in Mountjoy Square. Sales catalogues described Springfield furniture as mainly new. It included the best mahogany drawing room chairs lined with rich crimson moreen, several mahogany four-poster beds, china, and delph and rich cut glass. Among the farm animals were several remarkably fine milch cows, horses and a well-bred brown stallion, described as a safe and well-bred hunter. Bidders vied for a large quantity of capital oats, some very fine wheat, ploughs, harrows, other agricultural implements, a jaunting car (nearly new) with two sets of capital harness and three carts.[56] The auction and the removal of the family to Dublin must have been met with a certain amount of sadness for the family and tenants.

The McDermotts had laid out the town around the market square. Six houses built to the side of the square shielded the church from the clamour of the market

53 *Tuam Herald*, 24 February 1838.   **54** Ibid., 7 January 1839.   **55** *Thoms Directory*.   **56** *Tuam Herald*, 12 February 1839.

place. A large site on the corner of the square was given to William's friend, John Guilfoyle; on another corner Michael Connell the rate-collector lived. The road west of the square was laid out in one wide street. The shops grew in response to the demands for goods that could not be produced locally – fresh meat, tea, sugar, tobacco, leather and shoes. Williamstown was evolving from a greenfield site when the Great Famine suspended development.

THE GREAT FAMINE

Famine conditions were a constant threat in the populous district of Williamstown. Home-grown potatoes, particularly the lumper, which had a poor taste but yielded a very good crop of white-skinned potatoes, were the main food of the majority of people. The potato blight began in America and spread to Europe and on to Ireland by mid-1845. Farmers looked in amazement and terror as fields of potatoes, which looked healthy and promised an abundant crop, went black overnight as leaves curled and shrivelled as if exposed to a hard night's frost. The imminent desolation so alarmed the officials at Dublin Castle that by the third week of October they had prepared forms for the constabulary in each barracks to assess the local damage. The constabulary at Williamstown barracks discovered that half the potato crop and some of the oats were diseased in Templetogher parish and that there was no prospect of employment.[57] Within a few months panic buying caused the price of corn at Williamstown market to escalate by nearly 100 per cent.[58] Meanwhile, in Galway port, ships were waiting to load corn and sail to Liverpool at the same time as supplies of Indian corn from Mediterranean countries and from America converged on the port.

The government recognised that relief was urgently needed but the rules drafted by its officials for the composition of relief committees were a bureaucratic nightmare, because the members had to be selected from the following: lieutenant or deputy lieutenant of county, magistrates of petty sessions, Board of Works officers, clergymen of all persuasions, poor law guardians, resident magistrates and others as might be selected by the lieutenant. What was a parish such as Templetogher, which had no resident landlord or leader in society to do? The cumbersome process of dealing with the relief commissioners and the Office of Public Works prompted that organisation's officer, J.C. Walker, to inquire if a committee had been established for Williamstown.[59] When the commissioners contacted the county lieutenant for county Galway, the marquess of Clanricarde, he consulted his new ordnance survey map and then disclaimed any accurate knowledge of the remote region of Williamstown.[60] It was not on the

57 NAI, Distress Papers 439, 15 March 1846. **58** NAI, Distress Papers 8650, 20 January 1847. **59** NAI, RLFC3/1/2824. **60** NAI, RLFC3/1/3131.

map. McDermott, living in Mountjoy Square in Dublin, was kept aware of the plight of his tenants. In October 1845 he began a letter-writing campaign to the Mansion House Committee under its chairman, Lord Cloncurry. Despite his onerous workload McDermott became chairman, while the local publican John Guilfoyle immediately applied, as committee secretary, to the relief commissioners for information on procedures.[61]

Williamstown was the petty sessions headquarters for the barony of Ballymoe, so it became the official centre for coordinating famine relief for the portion of the barony situated within Galway county. Vice-lieutenant for county Galway, Sir Joseph Burke (Glinsk), Deputy-Lieutenant Denis H. Kelly of Castle Kelly (Ballygar) and John Ross Mahon (on behalf of local landowner, Lord Fitzgerald) donned their topcoats and tall hats for the miserable bone-crunching journey. Their phaetons and jaunting cars assembled regularly at Williamstown Square while the gentlemen met with ratepayers Roderick Kealy, Thomas Cornwall and John Scanlan under the chairmanship of the Ballymoe justice of the peace, Thomas Nevil Bagot.[62] They discussed proposals for local employment. It quickly emerged that road works were the optimum way of providing for the truly destitute. This opportunity of upgrading existing roads and providing new roads in the locality of the newly built village led Captain Donnellan, Board of Public Works engineer for Ballymoe barony, to study and favourably assess their applications. Over the next few months he recommended schemes on all roads leading to the new village.

Table 6 Captain Donnellan's estimate for road works.[63]

Cut new road to avoid Carrownderry hill	£60
Cut Knockanarra hill to improve the Ballinlough to Williamstown road	£160
Improve the Chequerhill to Williamstown road	£200

Local landlords were successful in having some roads of immediate interest to them sanctioned for improvement or construction. William McDermott got a strategic road past Springfield House from Michael Concannon's at Derryvode to Thomas Egan's corn mill.[64] The road opened up the east side of Templetogher parish. Lord Fitzgerald, through whose estate a road from Kilnalag to Cashel was planned, promised to contribute one-fifth of its cost.[65] That was probably the first local road planned by surveyors and it runs in a straight line between the two crossroads. The proposals were forwarded to J.F. Kempster, the Galway

61 NAI, RLFC3/2/11/09. **62** NAI, W 3594, 23 February 1846. **63** NAI, Distress Papers 5094, 5478. **64** NAI, Distress Papers 798, November 1846. **65** NAI, Distress Papers 439, 6 April 1846.

county surveyor. He was a very pragmatic man and perceived that some people might leave their lands untilled during the spring planting season. He therefore postponed starting the public works.[66] In the meantime Guilfoyle requested some work tickets and books for Williamstown relief committee.

The only employment envisaged was the proposed road works. The role of the relief committee was to raise funds to access the government grant of up to 100 per cent of the amount collected. It issued work tickets to those who had no other funds. These could be exchanged for subsidised Indian meal. It was a slow cumbersome process and many families were in dire distress. Martin Connolly, parish priest, brought the plight of his parishioners to the attention of the Office of Public Works.[67] The new shopkeepers tried to facilitate numerous customers who bought on credit in anticipation of earnings from work. Money generated by the public employment of up to 400 persons brought welcome relief, but such was the distress, that within months their resources were depleted. Archbishop MacHale spoke out strongly in a letter to Lord John Russell, the newly elected prime minister:

> You might as well issue an edict of general starvation as stop the supplies, which the feeble creatures are trying to earn by the sweat of their brows. The pittance doled out this year for their relief would be but a small item in the millions abstracted without any return by absentees whom the Irish legislature would have kept at home to fulfil their duties as well as to enjoy the benefits of property.[68]

Potatoes were the main part of the diet. A hardworking adult male could eat six or seven kilos of potatoes a day, so dysentery became widespread as a result of the change to Indian meal, a new and inadequate source of nutrition. Soon typhus and fever were rampant from the lack of a suitable diet and warm clothing.[69] The nearest medical service at Glenamaddy was not designed to cater for a booming population in a widespread area. The over-worked medical superintendent, Dr Donelan, resigned and was elected to Dunmore dispensary. Secretary Martin McDonnell convened a meeting of Williamstown and Glenamaddy dispensary subscribers at Williamstown at 1 p.m. on 11 November 1846 to discuss the election of a doctor. The subscribers resolved to ease the workload by creating two dispensary districts. The application for a grant from the rates for a separate dispensary district for Williamstown was favourably received and £55 5s. was allocated.[70] The new dispensary committee for Williamstown comprised parish priest Hugh O'Connell (chairman), R.J. Kealy (treasurer), William McDermott, W. Burke, John Guilfoyle, James Kelly, William

66 NAI, Distress Papers 8650, 2 January 1847.   **67** NAI, RLFC3/1/4389.   **68** *Roscommon Journal,* 8 August 1846.   **69** NAI, RLFC3/2/11/06.   **70** *Tuam Herald,* 6 March 1847.

J. Kelly, Thomas G. Kelly, William Lynch (shopkeeper in the village), Martin McDonnell and J. Ronan. They elected William Lynch's brother, James Lynch of Lowberry, a graduate of the Royal College of Surgeons in Ireland, as the medical officer.[71] This was a welcome appointment. The Lynch brothers were kinsmen of McDermott through the marriage of Isabella McDermott and Martin Lynch of Lowberry and Roseberry.[72] A public meeting convened in the week before Christmas 1846 recorded the appreciation by the people of Williamstown of the interest and paternalistic care shown by McDermott through his untiring attention to them at all hours, day and night, so as to alleviate their dire distress.[73] This intense, unrelenting pressure caused McDermott to write 'the eyes of all are turned towards me'.[74]

Local medical services did not begin a moment too soon. Starvation was imminent. Many returned home empty-handed as the cost of meal at the 1846 Williamstown Christmas market escalated to 24*s*. 6*d*. a stone.[75] Snow fell from mid-December and the bitter cold of January 1847 was harrowing, as women and children felt the worst effects of the Famine.[76] McDermott described how he saw 'in the frost and snow, hands of the poor fellows bleeding from using crowbars on the hard ground – to earn the price of one meal a day.'[77] The men, who a few months earlier welcomed the cutting of new lines of roads in the area, were totally disheartened because before the roads were half-built, the funds were depleted. There was an outcry as families were cut off from their land, and animals strayed when fields, divided by the new roads, were left unfenced. Farmers along these routes still own land on both sides of the roads. Extra government money was needed urgently to complete public works. Appeals for further funding fell on deaf ears so food distribution in kind began as soup kitchens were set up. Recipes for soup abounded, as for example a concoction made from twelve pints of water with four pounds of ox cheek, eight ounces of rice and of oatmeal, seasoned with an onion, salt and pepper. Another recipe used twenty pints of water with animal bones, two pints of peas, a large carrot, an onion and some salt and pepper.[78] Denis H. Kelly, deputy-lieutenant for county Galway, rightfully refused the offer of a soup boiler, but requested 'something to put in it and make it boil'.[79] He was dismissive of the government programme of assistance, writing that 'it would look ridiculous to have a troop of dragoons guarding a few hundredweight of biscuits'.[80] The government still maintained that self-sufficiency was the only way out of the desperate situation.

71 Ibid., 7 November 1846.   **72** NAI, MS 5652, McDermott family papers.   **73** *Tuam Herald*, 2 January 1847.   **74** NAI, Distress Papers 8650, 20 January 1847.   **75** Ibid.   **76** *Tuam Herald*, December 1846–January 1847. It recorded the biggest fall of snow in years. It was seven to ten feet deep.   **77** NAI, Distress Papers 8650, 20 January 1847.   **78** *Relief of distress in Ireland, Commissariat, 1847*, HC 1847 [761], li, p. 575.   **79** NAI, RLFC3/2/11/67.   **80** NAI, Distress Papers 6670, 25 October 1846.

Many families had no cash for rent, so landlords looked to the tenants' stack of corn as rent-in-kind. The poor law guardians of Castlerea Union eyed it too. In March 1847 Laurence Reilly and Francis Hurly were granted the contract at £21 17s. to applot Templetogher parish for rates.[81] It was a very tense situation when Thomas Nevil Bagot warned the lord lieutenant that 'anarchy will prevail if nothing [is] done'.[82] In September 1847 the resident magistrate declined to provide police protection for rate collector Michael Connell, as he considered the situation too dangerous.[83] The finances of the union became so desperate that the magistrate was forced to grant police protection in the first two weeks of March 1848.[84] People resolved to overcome their total dependence on the potato, so large quantities of turnip, cabbage, carrot, parsnip and mangle seeds were sown for the first time in the parish, from seeds supplied through Castlerea union.

The fight to provide sustenance for families led to a period of disintegration of the whole fabric of society. Many people who intended to marry postponed their marriages. However, William and Anna McDermott celebrated the marriage of their daughter Anna to Patrick Balfe of South Park, Castlerea on 5 November 1847.[85] William had recovered from a severe fever he contracted while on official duties in county Kerry.[86] Robert Blundell, Protestant rector at Ballinlough, was chairman of Williamstown relief committee in his absence.

In Boyanagh and Templetogher parish there were 21 marriages in 1847 and 63 in 1848, with 70 per cent of them just before Lent and at Easter before the men migrated. There were 122 baptisms recorded in Boyanagh in 1847, but over 200 for each of the years 1848 and 1849.[87] Parents tried to nurture their children, but infant mortality rates were high. The censuses record that the number of children under five years of age fell from 637 in 1841 to 427 in 1851. In an open letter to Lord John Russell, Archbishop MacHale wrote of the scene all around him with depopulated villages and flourishing graveyards, poorhouses springing up as the mansions of the gentry were falling down, Ireland wasted of her perishing people, which the instinct of self-preservation was pouring onto the shores of England. Some townlands in the immediate vicinity of Williamstown village had massive depopulation. It was a heart-breaking period as people emigrated – one per family – without saying goodbye to friends or neighbours, when they got paid for corn. They walked to board sailing ships at Galway, Sligo or Westport for a passage to Canada. About 30 per cent of those arriving at Quebec availed of free travel to New York, Vermont, Connecticut, New Hampshire or Boston. William McDermott's son John settled as far west

81 *Tuam Herald*, 6 March 1847. **82** NAI, Distress Papers 4291, 5 March 1847. **83** *Tuam Herald*, 27 September 1847. **84** *The relief of distress, and state of unions in Ireland*, HC 1847–8 [955], lv, p. 796. **85** *Burke's Irish family records* (London, 1976), p. 55; NAI, MS 5652, McDermott family papers. **86** *Tuam Herald*, 24 July 1847. **87** NLI, P 4211, parish register.

as St Louis Missouri.[88] There are many colonies on the east coast of America that owe their origins to the people who silently left their county Galway homes in the later years of the Great Famine for a better life in America.

McDermott tried valiantly to help his tenants. He told the authorities that his private resources were exhausted and that his own health was suffering from trying to help. He spent an enormous amount of his personal fortune in assisting his people towards a better future. Despite his law practice and his rental income he was declared bankrupt. His estate was sold to his son Owen in the Landed Estate Court on 20 June 1863.[89] William and Anna left Ireland in 1863 and went to live at Boulogne-sur-mer in northern France. Sixty-four-year-old Anna died there on 5 August 1869. Owen's widow Catherine inherited Springfield in 1872. William died on 21 January 1877. The family continued at Springfield until the death of William McDermott's bachelor great-grandson James McDermott, in 1993.

CONCLUSION

Kilnalag was a thriving village when the first Ordnance Survey was made in 1838. The name is still on some maps but little remains of that once busy village. The Taaffe estates, which included the town of Ballyhaunis, were sold in the bankruptcy courts in the 1850s. The Kilnalag to Williamstown road is lined with modern homes, and more houses are planned. Pupils are now bussed in from all over the parish to a central school in Williamstown village because six national schools that were built in the last quarter of the nineteenth century closed after a hundred years. Since then reunions of the national schools have strengthened bonds between past pupils who are scattered worldwide.

Williamstown succeeded Kilnalag as a centre for fairs and markets, but the noises of the marketplace are gone. Egans' corn-mill closed in 1964. A new life awaits it thanks to the leadership of the local Heritage Group. The fine mid-nineteenth century church was razed to the ground to make way for a new garda station. A generous benefactor who had left the parish many years previously funded a modern church dedicated to St Thérèse. Anna McDermott would have been proud in summer 2001, when the St Thérèse reliquary from her beloved France visited St Thérèse's church, Williamstown.

Williamstown did not forget the McDermott family. In 1990 the people of the village greeted many descendants from all over the world of those who were forced by economic necessity to emigrate. They joined in the weeklong celebrations for the 150th anniversary of the founding of the village. Many of the present generation choose to spend some years in other countries, but they go now, mainly to experience alternative cultures and societies.

88 NAI, MS 5652, McDermott family papers.   **89** Ibid.

Figure 3. Williamstown, 2003 (photo: Clare Mulryan).

The local Heritage Group is keen on preserving the past. The national school at Ballyroe has been splendidly restored as a parish centre. The old bog road, which winds north of the village, has a well-signposted nature walk. The centre of the square is now restored as the village green, and people gather here to take a bus on the Sligo-Galway route, or to begin a stroll around the Parish Heritage Trail. Local people and visitors appreciated wool spinning, tin-smithing and blacksmithing together with a photographic exhibition and a display of items from a past age, during Heritage Week 2002. They gathered at demonstrations of the near-defunct skills of butter making, bread making, woodcraft and straw-craft. The familiar melodies of a traditional Barn Dance brought the festivities to a close.

The McDermotts were generous people of brave ideas. Did the Famine of the 1840s leave them devoid of confidants such as Denis O'Conor of Clonalis, who was MP for county Roscommon, and Sir John Burke, former MP for county Galway, who owned part of Templetogher parish? Both MPs died from famine fever. Did the enormous post-Famine financial difficulties, which bur-dened not only themselves but also their wealthy family members – Balfes of Southpark,[90] Bodkins of Kilclooney,[91] and Lynchs of Lowberry[92] – lead them to realistically reappraise the town they had started with such altruism and pride?

90 *Tuam Herald,* 23 February 1850. **91** Ibid., 9 March 1850. **92** Ibid., 14 January 1851.

We can speculate what might have happened had the Great Famine not come in the 1840s. Williamstown might have gone on to become a fine railway town. Yet William and Anna McDermott laid down a foundation that has persisted for one hundred and sixty-five years with only minor changes.

Ballycastle: a village on the north Mayo coast

MEALLA C. NÍ GHIOBÚIN

The village of Ballycastle is situated between two very different landscapes. To the west and south lie the vast expanse of mountain and bogland plains of Erris, which James Hack Tuke described in 1847 as 'a district almost as distinct from Mayo, as Mayo is from the eastern parts of Ireland'.[1] The whole area consists of a large tract of bog with a number of rivers passing through it. By contrast, lowlands lie around the village of Ballycastle and stretch out eastwards towards Downpatrick Head and Killala Bay. The Ballinglen river, which flows into the sea at Bunatrahir bay, forms a natural dividing line between these two contrasting landscapes (Figure 1). The lowlands encircling Bunatrahir bay, about a mile and a half from the village of Ballycastle, known collectively as the Laggan since the seventeenth century, are associated with intensive arable cultivation. The word 'laggan' derives from *lugán* meaning a hollow or level land beside the sea or a river.[2] The largest concentration of the remains of megalithic culture in Ireland is found in the coastal districts of Mayo and Sligo.[3] The density of distribution of court cairns around the Bunatrahir and Killala bays of north Mayo is unequalled in any other county.[4] The more recent discovery of the pre-historic settlements, known as the Céide Fields, located five miles west of Ballycastle village, indicates that this area was inhabited at least 5,000 years ago.[5]

Ballycastle village is linked by roads with the towns of Killala (nine miles) and Ballina (15 miles) to the east, Crossmolina (24 miles) and Castlebar (41 miles) to the south, along with the village of Belderrig (10 miles) and the town of Belmullet (30 miles) to the west. Ballycastle can be seen therefore as a village at an important crossroads connecting the isolated north-west coast of Mayo with other centres of population. (Figure 2).

ORIGINS OF THE VILLAGE

In discussing Ballycastle it is important to distinguish between the district electoral division of Ballycastle with its various townlands, including a townland

---

1 James Hack Tuke, *A visit to Connaught in the autumn of 1847; a letter addressed to the Central Relief Committee of the Society of Friends, Dublin* (London, 1848), p. 18. **2** John Curry, 'Ballycastle: The social geography of a north Mayo parish', unpublished thesis, UCD (1968), p. 3. **3** Seán P. Ó Riordáin, *Antiquities of the Irish countryside* (London, 1964), pp 60–1. **4** OS map, *Discovery series,* number 23, covering part of county Mayo (Dublin, 1994), scale 1:50 000, section showing location of megalithic structures between the Céide Fields and Killala bay. **5** *The Céide Fields, Ballycastle, county Mayo,* booklet of the Céide Fields interpretative centre (no date but *c.*1992), p. 2.

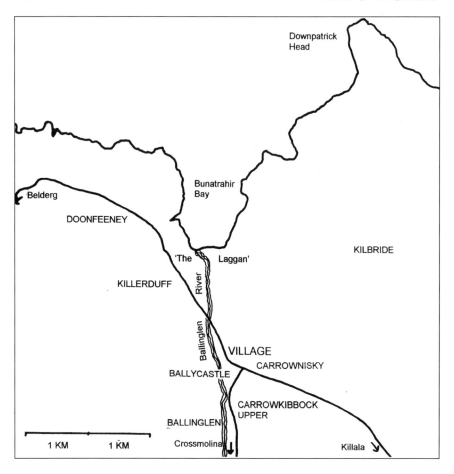

Figure 1. Location map showing Ballycastle in the context of its immediate
surroundings. (See also *Figure 2.*)

called Ballycastle, and the village of Ballycastle itself, for which census returns
were given separately for the first time in 1841.

The village consisted of two streets, Main Street and Pound Street, and was
spread over parts of three townlands, Carrownisky, Carrowkibbock Upper and
Ballycastle. The western part of the village was in the townland of Ballycastle
and occupied an area on both sides of Main Street. Carrownisky lay to the north-
east and Carrowkibbock Upper to the south-east of Main Street (Figure 3).
Pound Street was located in the Carrownisky townland. The three townlands
Ballycastle, Carrowkibbock Upper and Carrownisky, together with the adjacent
townland of Ballinglen, were in the parish of Doonfeeny in the barony of
Tirawley. Doonfeeny townland and village with its church and glebe lay to the
north-west of Ballycastle village.

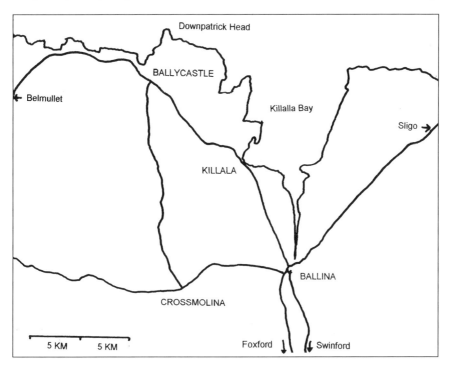

Figure 2. Location map showing Ballycastle in the context of north Mayo.
(See also *Figure 1*).

Nowadays, approaching the village of Ballycastle from the direction of Killala, the road passes through modern housing before descending a steep hill towards the Ballinglen river in the valley below. This is Main Street, and half way down on opposite sides of the street are the Church of Ireland and the Catholic Church. Pound Street is off Main Street at the top of the hill, and is a relatively short street, sometimes referred to as a lane. It is difficult to give a clear picture of the layout of the village back in the 1830s because of the uneven distribution of houses over the three townlands. The Ordnance Survey map of the village (Figure 3), shows the townland boundary between Carrowkibbock Upper and Carrownisky to the south and north of the Main Street, roughly as far as the Catholic chapel (later church), as it descends towards the river.[6]

Among the parishes in the barony of Tirawley were Doonfeeny and Kilbride. In 1198, Donatus, bishop of the newly formed diocese of Killala, laid claim to Killerduff, Doonfeeny and Kilbride churches. Killerduff was likely to have been extinct by 1198, but its name survives as a townland in Doonfeeny which together with Kilbride were the local civil parishes.[7] The Catholic parish of

6 VO, Map of the village of Ballycastle (Dublin, 1850s). 7 Rt Rev E. MacHale PP, VG,

Doonfeeny incorporated the same two parishes, which had remained separate until penal times. From 1835 to 1889 the name was given as 'Doonfeeny and Ballycastle' and it then became the 'parish of Ballycastle'. The area of the modern parish is roughly the area of 'the Laggan'.[8]

It appears that the name of Ballycastle was in use about 1470, but it is not clear whether this was a reference to lands only, or also to a settlement. In 1607, a Pierce Barrett of Ballysakeery was seeking a crown grant of 'the castle and town of Ballycastle and the four quarters of land named Cashel, Carrownisky, Carrowhibbock and Drumagora' as well as claiming that his ancestors once owned Carrowcur, Moyney, Carrownedin and Namahull. The name Drumagora may have been another name for Ballyglass.[9] Ballyglass was a townland west of Ballycastle village.

The Ordnance Survey letters noted that 'Ballycastle, which is in Irish called *Baile an Chaisil*, i.e., the town of the Cashel, or stone fort, would according to the Irish name be anglicised Ballycashel'.[10] The letters also noted that in 'Ballycastle town, within the churchyard and to the north-west of the church, there is pointed out the site of a castle which was, tradition says, erected and occupied by one MacDonnell'.[11] Prior to the end of the sixteenth century, 'MacDonnells were settled at Rathlacka, Ballycastle, Ballinglen, Ballykinletreagh, and Cloonenass. Most of them were of a family called the Clan of Aedh Buidhe.'[12] Rathlacka, presumably Rathlackan in the parish of Kilcummin, lies north-east of Ballycastle village, Ballinglen, in the parish of Doonfeeny to the west, Ballykinletragh, in the parish of Kilfian, to the south-west, and Cloonenass to the south-east of the village.

The founder of the extended Knox family in north Mayo is said to have been William Knox, who came from Lifford and purchased the estate of Castlerea where he built a house in 1680. He was succeeded by his son Francis, and he, in turn, was succeeded by his son Francis, known as 'old Frank'. It was 'old Frank' who appears to have founded the family fortunes, mainly by moving cattle from the area to Dublin. It is believed that, in order that his cattle would arrive in Dublin in good condition, he purchased estates along the way where his cattle

Killala, *The parishes in the diocese of Killala, North Tirawley* (Ballina, 1985), ii, p. 1. **8** Ibid., p. 1. **9** MacHale, *The parishes of Killala*, ii, p. 9. Carrownisky and Carrowkibbock are listed in Griffith, *Valuation* under the parish of Doonfeeny, while Carrowcur, Moyney (Moyny) and Carrownedin (Carrowneden) are listed under the parish of Kilbride, but the other three names are not included under either parish. Ballyglass was one of the townlands in the parish of Doonfeeny. A 'quarter' contained four 'cartrons' and each cartron contained thirty acres. **10** John O'Donovan and others, *Letters containing information relative to the antiquities of the county of Mayo, collected during the progress of the Ordnance Survey in 1838* (typescript Bray, 1926), p. 207, no. 414 (hereafter OS *Letters, Mayo*). **11** OS *Letters, Mayo*, no. 413, p. 207. **12** H.T. Knox, *The history of the county of Mayo to the close of the sixteenth century* (Dublin, 1901; reprint, Castlebar, 1982), p. 295.

could be rested. However, the location of these estates is not known. The Knox family of Castlerea was considered to be the senior branch of the family.[13] Knox and Knox-Gore families had seven seats in the general area of Ballina, as well as Castlerea. They also had estates in counties Kilkenny, Derry and Tipperary.[14] It is clear from the list in Burke's *Irish family records,* that the wider Knox and Knox-Gore families owned a considerable number of properties in the Ballina, Killala and Ballycastle areas of county Mayo. Gore was the family name of the earls of Arran who also owned considerable property in county Mayo.

A memorial in the Registry of Deeds in Dublin, shows that Arthur Knox of county Mayo, obtained some 500 acres of land in the area around 'Ballycashell' from Sir Ralph Gore, Bart., Chancellor of the Exchequer in Ireland, and others, in the year 1720.[15] It is probable that John Knox of Castlerea near Killala, now in ruins was a direct descendant of the Arthur Knox mentioned above.

John Knox of Castlerea, was the son of Arthur Knox (1759–98).[16] He was born on 13 May 1783, succeeded his father in 1798, and died on 31 December 1861.[17] From the evidence contained in Ordnance Survey name books of 1838, the village of Ballycastle was 'founded' by John A. Knox around 1797. Yet, John was only fifteen years of age at that time and therefore, as a minor would not have been qualified to make contracts, sign leases or take any other legal initiatives. Moreover his father was still alive in that year. Therefore, it may be assumed that the establishment of a 'market town' at Ballycastle was already envisaged before the death of Arthur in 1798. The 'founding' of the village may have been an ongoing process and was merely attributed to John at a later date. All other evidence points to the period of intense urban development as being in the 1830s. The apparently conflicting evidence can be resolved on the basis that the first group of houses at Ballycastle were indeed built around 1797, but the development of the village as a centre of administration and trade did not occur for another thirty years.

It should be noted here that the other residence of both Arthur Knox and his son, John, was Woodstock in county Wicklow, and this may have been their principal residence. John married Lady Mary Brabazon in 1808, and was high sheriff for Wicklow in 1809 and for Mayo in 1821. If Arthur and John Knox had their principal residence in Wicklow, then it is more than likely that there was a management structure in place to administer their vast estates in county Mayo. Some idea of the extent of John Knox's estate can be gleaned from the fact that he was the proprietor of twenty-three of the townlands in the parish of Doonfeeny alone, amounting to some 24,000 acres, not including Castlerea or other properties in other parishes. In one of the townlands, Glencolry, he had a cottage which he used occasionally when shooting game.[18]

13 Information provided by the North Mayo Family and Heritage Centre, Eniscoe, Co. Mayo. 14 Burke's *Irish family records* (London, 1976), p. 681. 15 RD, Memorial Gore to Knox, 29–79–16107. 16 Burke's *Irish family records*, p. 656. 17 Ibid., p. 676. 18 John O'Donovan and others, *Ordnance Survey name books for county Mayo* (typescript), iii, p.151 (40). Hereafter

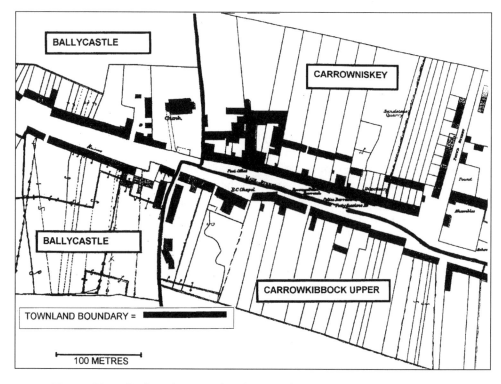

Figure 3. Plan of Ballycastle *c.*1850s based on a Valuation Office map of that period.

    The first cartographic survey of county Mayo was carried out by William
Bald between 1809 and 1817 and his maps were engraved in 1830.[19] The section of Bald's map for the barony of Tirawley shows the village of Ballycashill
(Ballycastle), including – within Ballycastle townland – Ballycashill church and
some 15 other buildings on either side of the road, presumably Main Street. For
Carrownisky townland there were some 17 buildings and Carrowkibbock about
15 buildings. A mill to the east of the Ballinglen river is marked on the map, as
is Doonfeeny church and glebe and about 18 buildings scattered in the surrounding area. The map also shows the road through the Ballinglen valley joining the road coming from the east through the village of Ballycashill (Ballycastle).
The earlier Taylor and Skinner map of Ireland (1778) shows only Ballina, Killala
and Castle Lacken for this north-western part of Mayo.[20] It can be assumed,
therefore, that development in the area of Ballycastle village did not take place
until towards the end of the eighteenth century or in the early three decades of
the new century as shown on Bald's map.

cited as OS, *Names books, Mayo.*   **19** William Bald, *Map of the county of Mayo* (1830). Cartographic
survey carried out 1809–1817; map engraved in Paris, 1830.   **20** George Taylor and Andrew
Skinner, *A new and accurate map of the kingdom of Ireland* (London and Dublin, 1778).

In the early years of the nineteenth century, serious efforts were made to construct a road along the north coast towards Broadhaven bay, in the barony of Erris, linking the village of Ballycastle, in the neighbouring barony of Tirawley, with the village of Belderrig and further west with Glenamoy and Belmullet. One of the two roads proposed by Richard Griffith for county Mayo was a line of road connecting Ballycastle with Broadhaven.[21] It was hoped that this road would provide 'access to the various bays and inlets along the coast, periodically abounding with fish'.[22] It would also open up the area to enable produce to be sent to markets in the east of the county. The reports of engineers Nimmo and Killaly in the 1830s argued that by opening up a road through the vast area of 350 square miles to the west of Ballycastle village, the inhabitants would send their grain to markets rather than use it for illicit distilling.[23] The road beyond Ballycastle was finally opened in the 1830s. It should be remembered that the only other means for the transportation of heavy goods was by sea and these would have been brought from Sligo by steamship, transferred to curraghs and landed at either Bunatrahir bay (near Ballycastle) or Belderig harbour.[24]

DEVELOPMENT OF THE VILLAGE

There is little information available about Ballycastle in the early years of the nineteenth century. However, a description of the village is contained in Samuel Lewis's *Topographical dictionary* of 1837:

> A village in the parish of Dunfeeney, Barony of Tyrawley, county Mayo, fifteen miles north west of Ballina; the population is returned with the parish. This place is situated on the north west coast, and commands a fine view of Downpatrick Head; the beach affords excellent accommodation for sea bathing, and by the outlay of a little capital it might be made a delightful watering place. Several improvements have already been made, many new houses have been built, a market place is in course of erection, and a new line of road is now being constructed through the mountains to Belmullet, which will materially add to the advantages of the place. Petty sessions are held every Wednesday; it is a constabulary and chief revenue-police station and has six fairs in the year and a penny post to Killala.[25]

Some idea of what the village of Ballycastle was like can also be gleaned from one of those who visited it in the early 1840s. Caesar Otway paid two visits to

21 *The fourth report of the commissioners on the bogs of Ireland*, HC 1813–14, vi, appendix 11, p. 182. **22** *Report on progress of public works in western district of Ireland 1829*, 1830, HC 1830, xxvii, p. 299. **23** Return of sums advanced by government for public works in Galway and Mayo, HC 1833, xxxv, p. 575. **24** Curry, Ballycastle, unpublished thesis, UCD (1968), p. 4. **25** Lewis, *Topographical dictionary*, i, p. 128.

the area and left the following descriptions. 'Proceeding from Killala towards Ballycastle, there was nothing that caught my attention worth noticing.'[26] Further on he had this to say:

> Of this village I need not say much; a single street forms it; like most Irish towns near the sea, it has improved and is improving. Small slated houses year after year have been added to it. It lies in the centre of a fertile district called the Laggan, and the vicinity supplies a larger produce of corn than might have been expected; but why this village should have been located as it is on the side of a hill, two miles from the sea shore, away from the river that flows half a mile to the west, is to me unimaginable. I suppose that when the first houses, the chapel and the church were erected, there was no notion that Glasgow or Liverpool would want the corn growing in the Laggan.[27]

He went on to observe:

> The district of the Laggan slopes gradually from a line of secondary mountains, until it touches the sea at Ballycastle [Bunatrahir] and Lacken bays. Between these two, a canal might be cut without much sinking or much intervening lockage; but northward the land rises again gradually to the eminence comprising Downpatrick Head, and forming, as it were, another range of high lands which by the convulsion I have hitherto mentioned, and shall again allude to, is now in a great measure swallowed up by the Atlantic.[28]

No such canal was ever built. Likewise, the suggestion in Lewis's *Topographical dictionary* that the area near Bunatrahir bay could be developed as a 'delightful watering place' was never realised.

To understand the reason for establishing a village, such as Ballycastle, at a particular location, it is necessary to provide information about the surrounding countryside and the possible motivation of the proprietor. According to T. Jones Hughes, the landowner in the mid-eighteenth century was often the supreme arbiter of local life. The landowner 'sought to establish new growth points by way of small villages and towns which would provide basic services in a countryside which hitherto had been remarkably devoid of any form of nucleated settlement'.[29] Cormac Ó Gráda writes that a sign of growing commercialisation in Ireland was the increase in the number of livestock fairs in the country from 700 in the 1660s to 3,000 in the 1770s. By 1845, this number had risen to over

26 Caesar Otway, *Sketches in Erris and Tyrawley* (Dublin, 1845), p. 203.   **27** Ibid., p. 209.   **28** Ibid., pp 212–13.   **29** T. Jones Hughes, 'Society and settlement in nineteenth-century Ireland', in *Irish Geography*, v (1964–8), p. 79.

5,000 fairs spread over 1,000 sites.[30] It is probable that John Knox or his father would have been aware of such developments in other parts of the country and decided to provide a focus for the area in which they had a vested interest. The establishment of the village of Ballycastle, located in the middle of an area far removed for other centres of population, would provide the sort of basic services for the wider community surrounding it.

The writer and playwright, J.M. Synge, who was commissioned by the *Manchester Guardian* to write a series of articles about the congested districts in 1910, had this to say about small towns, using Swinford and Charleston in county Mayo as examples:

> Nearly all the towns of this class are merely trading centres kept up by the country people that live around them, and they usually stand where several main roads come together from large, out-of-the-way districts.[31]

Although there is no record that Synge ever visited Ballycastle, this description can easily be applied to that village, located as it is at a crossroads between isolated agricultural and mountainous districts.

In his *Statistical survey of the county of Mayo,* James MacParlan described the condition of agriculture in the barony of Tirawley at the beginning of the nineteenth century. Broad ridges or lazy-beds, as they were called, were the most common method of planting, although in a very few places the plough and drill were used.[32] The extent of planting was very considerable, especially of potatoes and oats. On the sea coast, barley was grown, all of which was exported to the north, sometimes by sea and sometimes by land. Oats were also exported to Dublin and England. There was a great deal of flax grown in the barony and MacParlan noted that 'the poor take care to raise, beside a sufficiency for their own use, as much as their families can spin into yarn, and large quantities of it, both in yarn and linen, are sold at the market of Ballina and the neighbouring fairs.[33] He mentions that the markets for grain were Ballina and Killala.[34] There was some cultivation of turnips, which was the only green food in the barony.[35] He also said that, 'in general, it [the land] may be called a mixture of good upland and moory pasture, which together with boundless tracts of mountain, serve as excellent nurseries for rearing young cattle, and preparing them for the fattening grounds of Roscommon, Munster and Leinster'.[36] It will be recalled that 'old Frank' Knox appears to have made his fortune by moving cattle from the barony and selling them profitably in the Dublin markets.

The soil in the northern part of Carrowkibbock was of light clay and there was mountain grazing in the southern part. Carrownisky had soil of light moory

---

30 Cormac Ó Gráda, *Ireland: a new economic history, 1780–1939* (Oxford, 1994), p. 41. **31** John M. Synge, *The works of John M. Synge.* (Dublin, 1910), p. 232. **32** James MacParlan, MD, *Statistical survey of the county of Mayo* (Dublin, 1802), p. 24. **33** Ibid., pp 28–9. **34** Ibid., p. 37. **35** Ibid., p. 38. **36** Ibid., p. 40.

clay which produced oats and potatoes. Nearby Ballinglen, on the other hand, had very good land which produced excellent crops.[37] The lowlands encircling Bunatrahir bay, known collectively as 'the Laggan' were associated with intensive arable cultivation.[38]

The agricultural potential of the area around Ballycastle, as shown in MacParlan's survey and in the other sources referred to above, may have motivated John Knox to establish a village in order to serve both the immediate district as well as its vast hinterland. However, one of the main objectives of the 'improving landowner' at the beginning of the nineteenth century was to produce grain and livestock for the lucrative trade with Britain,[39] and Ballycastle may well have served as a transit point for goods en-route to Killala and Ballina. Killala was an important sea port at the beginning of the nineteenth century, at the time more important than Ballina. The local newspaper, the *Ballina Impartial and Tyrawley Advertiser,* regularly noted the arrivals at and departures of vessels from both Killala and Ballina in the 1820s and 1830s. The ruin of a very large two-storey building at the back of what was May's Hotel may still be seen in Ballycastle. This building was most likely used for the storage of oats and wool before they were sent to Killala for export.

In 1836, the Revd Martin Hart PP answered for the Ballycastle area a number of questions put to him by parliamentary commissioners about the condition of the small tenantry in the locality. According to Father Hart there was no public common and no woodland in the district. In the parish of Doonfeeny, there were 3,000 acres of arable and pasture land and 9,000 acres of bog, and in the neighbouring parish of Kilbride, there were 2,640 acres of arable, pasture, waste and bog. He believed that a great portion of the bogs could be reclaimed if given to the very large population of the parishes who were all cottiers and under-tenants of small landholders.[40]

Father Hart also stated that most of the people in the parishes had farms of about five to eight acres, some with only three but others had from 15 to 40 acres. Most of the tenants of such farms held them from the head landlords, and others tenants held them from middlemen. There were very few employed on the government line of road in the parish of Doonfeeny. When labourers were employed, they were paid in cash. When presentments were passed by the grand jury for making or repairing roads, few or scarcely any of the really distressed labourers were employed, but it was the tenants who owed arrears of rent to the landlords who obtained employment.[41]

MacParlan mentioned the growing of flax in the barony of Tirawley in the 1820s.[42] There is also a reference to flax in a newspaper report of 6 August, 1827,

37 OS, *Names books, Mayo.* 38 Curry, 'Ballycastle', p. 3. 39 T. Jones Hughes, 'Landlordism in the Mullet of Mayo', in *Irish Geography,* iv (1959–63), p. 22. 40 *First report of commissioners for inquiring into the condition of the poorer classes in Ireland,* HC 1836, xxxiii, Supplement to appendix F, p. 28. 41 Ibid., p. 28. 42 MacParlan, *Statistical survey,* p. 28.

'on the 29th ult., a storm of thunder and lightening took place at Ballycastle, the most tremendous that has been witnessed for many years'. It seems that this storm came on suddenly and 'the whole was accompanied with rain which fell in cataracts, and also hail of large dimensions which it is said to have proved very hurtful to flax and potatoes'.[43] However, the extent of the flax-growing or where it was grown is unclear. There is no mention of the growing of flax in the submissions from Father Hart and others in 1836. Tom Langan, describing Ballycastle in the 1920s, noted that 'flax was being grown, but not for local use. The impervious sub-soil in the stretch of land known as Páirc Rua in Ballyknock was found suitable for a flax-pond'.[44] Ballyknock is located to the west of Ballycastle village.

The economy of the entire region surrounding the village of Ballycastle was based on farming and the distances from the existing centres of population such as Killala and Ballina must have presented difficulties to those who needed to dispose of surplus produce, to obtain goods or to avail of other services provided by those centres. John Knox probably realised the importance of providing the local farming community with its own trading-place, centrally located in its own district, when he founded the village. Of course, he himself would have benefited from the tolls and customs derived from the fairs and markets to be held there.

The Ordnance Survey name books of 1838 described Ballycastle as 'but an inconsiderable town, situated to the east of the parish [of Doonfeeny] within about a mile of the sea, which bounds the parish on the north'.[45] It consisted of eighty-two stone houses and the market, held every Wednesday, had been established in 1830.[46] This seems at variance with an earlier version which stated that John Knox had 'founded' Ballycastle in 1797.[47] Whichever version is correct, there is no record of a patent being sought or granted for this market.

By 1837 however, the village had grown considerably and could boast of a church and a chapel, a revenue-police barracks, a constabulary barracks, a shambles and pound, numerous houses, shops, schools, a dispensary, post office with a penny post to Killala, a petty sessions court and six fairs a year.[48] Petty session meetings were held on Wednesdays. There was also a coastguard station at Killerduff about two miles away towards the west in the direction of Doonfeeny.[49]

By 1838, the basic layout of the village was complete; the Main Street and Pound Street already existed, but there were few substantial buildings except directly across the Main Street from the Catholic chapel immediately adjoining the Church of Ireland. When the Ordnance Survey was being carried out in

---

43 *Ballina Impartial or Tyrawly Observer,* 6 August, 1827.   **44** Tom Langan, 'Ballycastle seventy years ago' in *North Mayo Historical Journal,* iii (1992–93), no. 1.   **45** OS, *Names books, Mayo,* iii, p. 161 (39).   **46** Ibid.   **47** Ibid., iii, p. 161 (71).   **48** Lewis, *Topographical dictionary,* i, p. 128.   **49** OS, *Name books, Mayo,* iii, p. 151, (39). Griffith, *Valuation, county of Mayo, barony of Tyrawley, union of Killala, parish of Doonfeeny* (Dublin, 1856), Killerduff watch house (coastguard station), p. 7.

Ballycastle in 1838, only some of the buildings fronting the road in Carrowniskey townland had been completed.[50]

There is an old saying in Ballycastle that the village began between the church and the chapel. It is clear from Bald's map (1830), that there was already a church on the northern side of Main Street,[51] and the later Ordnance Survey name books indicate that the church was built in 1827.[52] There may be some confusion about the date when the Catholic chapel was built. The date given by the Ordnance Survey was 1828,[53] but a bell from the original chapel inscribed with the date of 1827 was found when the chapel was being replaced by a new church building on the same site in 1931.[54] The Protestant church was dedicated to St John the Evangelist, and the chapel (later church) to St Bridget.

Detailed information about the village is also given in the Ordnance Survey house books, dated 1842, for the parish of Doonfeeny.[55] A description of property in Ballycastle gives some idea of the state of the village as viewed by the surveyors in the early 1840s.[56] There were then 55 houses, not including the shambles, pound or outhouses. Of these, there were eight shops, including a grocery and a delph shop. There was a coffee house and lodgings, a public house and 50 other houses, of which three were in ruins. In addition, there was the petty sessions court house, the revenue-police barracks, the constabulary barracks, the shambles and pound, the church, vestry and tower. There was no mention of a post office, hotel or chapel in this survey. Twenty-seven houses were exempt, that is their valuation was below £5. In the case of Carrowkibbock Upper, a total of 14 cabins is listed, one of which was in ruins and all exempt, and 29 houses, 26 of which were exempt, and the Catholic chapel with one gallery and no pews.

PROPERTY OWNERS AND LEASE-HOLDERS

The townlands of Ballycastle, Carrowkibbock Upper, Carrownisky and Ballinglen were among the twenty-three townlands owned by John Knox of Castlerea. Ballycastle townland was leased by Knox to Thomas Palmer of Summerhill before 1797.[57] Palmer's lease was later assigned to Patrick Madden, then to Anthony Madden of Ballina[58] who sold it at auction to Daniel Madden of Ballycastle.[59] While the church site was excluded from all transactions subsequent to its leasing to the ecclesiastical authorities in 1770, the site of the village was not referred to and there was no reference to its subdivision among villagers. It is more than likely that any houses in this townland were built by Palmer or

---

50 OS, *6 inch County Mayo, sheet 7*, surveyed 1838.   51 Bald, *Map of county Mayo*.   52 OS, *Name books, Mayo*, iii, p. 161.   53 Ibid.   54 MacHale, *Parishes in the diocese of Killala*, ii, pp 11–12.   55 NAI, OS, House books for the parish of Doonfeeny, 1842.   56 Ibid., pp 5–6.   57 RD, 456–201–191515.   58 RD, 888–53–587533.   59 RD, 1833–14–154.

by one of the Maddens rather than by one of the Knox family. It was noted in the Ordnance Survey name books that Palmer had part of it sublet as town parks to the inhabitants of Ballycastle village and the remainder sublet to tenants by leases of one life at 40s. per acre.[60] It appears that tenants were displaced and given plots in other townlands to accommodate the town parks. Carrowkibbock Upper townland was leased to Major Gardiner of Farmhill, who sublet it to tenants at will, at a yearly rent of £80 for the whole townland.[61] It is likely that the Gardiner family were involved in the early development of this townland. In the case of Carrownisky townland, the property was held from Knox by tenants at will at 15s. per acre.[62] In 1831, however, John Knox leased land in Carrownisky to William Sterne RN, inspecting commander of the Coastguard, Ballycastle, for lives from 11 April 1831 or 31 years from 1 November 1830 at £34 per annum.[63] This lease refers to numbered plots, and townparks, i.e., large garden plots, and to a *proposed* road, all indicating that the development of Carrownisky was only taking place in the 1830s, which ties in with Lewis's description of 1837. Daniel Madden mortgaged his lands to the National Bank in 1837 and this may indicate that he was borrowing £1,000 for development.[64] The south part of nearby Ballinglen was held on a lease of three lives by John Faussett who resided in Ballinglen Cottage. The remainder of the townland was held by tenants at will at a rent of £2.10s. per acre of arable ground.[65] It is interesting to note here that the names of John Knox, Thomas Palmer, Major Gardiner and John Faussett appeared regularly in official lists, including that of the county Mayo grand jury.

Details in respect of the mid-1850s emerge from Griffith's schedules of valuation for the area when compared with the valuation townplan.[66] Most of the important development was in Carrownisky. The shambles, merely a yard with a building or shed, and the pound were operated by Knox himself and these were situated within the former back yard of Ballycastle House. There were three main leaseholders – Daniel Madden, Edward Harte and Bridget May. Madden, who also owned land in Ballycastle townland, housed 'pauper tenants' in hovels as low as 2s. valuation in Pound Street and in a number of poor quality houses fronting on Main Street immediately west of Pound Street, their long gardens and narrow frontages being analogous to layouts of some builders today who aim to squeeze as many houses as possible into a limited area. Further west, Harte had a large holding with a filled-in quarry but sub-leased only the frontages, securing the grand jury, the Board of Guardians and the police as tenants within his own holdings, for the petty session house, the dispensary and the barracks respectively, raising the question of whether he had influence with the author-

60 OS, *Name books, Mayo*, iii, p. 115 (7). **61** Ibid., iii, p. 119 (21). **62** Ibid., iii, p. 119 (23). **63** RD, 1835–19–183. **64** RD, 1837–20–48. **65** OS, *Name books, Mayo*, iii, p. 150 (37). **66** Griffith, *Valuation, parish of Doonfeeny*, pp 5–7, 9–10. VO, Map of the village of Ballycastle (1850s).

ities. Between Harte's property and the church there were a few larger sites with wider frontages leased to individual lessees and these represented the best buildings in the village. Madden who owned the mill outside the town had a large building and stores on this site so it appears to have been the agricultural trading centre of the town. Bridget May had another large premises later listed in part as a hotel. It had a kiln and store so it too was an industrial/commercial property. Carrowkibbock Upper on the opposite side of Main Street had appeared in 1840 as an unplanned development of houses of little significance with the Catholic chapel as the only building of any note. The frontages were wider than for Madden's houses but nevertheless virtually all the houses were valued at under £1 in Griffith's Valuation.[67] Each property was in separate tenancy so no middlemen were involved by that date. Ballycastle townland incorporated the western end of the village on the upper edge of the Ballinglen valley. Here Madden was the main lease holder and, apart from the church, this end of the village consisted of slum property up to at least 1850 – with only one property over £1 valuation.[68]

Griffith's Valuation also provides statistical information about the properties in Ballycastle and their occupiers. A total of 47 entries with descriptions of the various tenements, including the Catholic chapel and a forge, were listed under Carrowkibbock.[69] Under Carrownisky, there were 27 entries in respect of Main Street which included a school house, shambles, dispensary, petty sessions house, barracks, national female school, and a house with a kiln as well as many other houses, gardens and yards.[70] Colonel A. Knox Gore had the shambles and yard and also held the tolls and customs of fairs and markets.[71] In Pound Street there was a house with a store, kiln, offices, garden and yard, the pound, a caretaker's house as well as a number of ruins.[72] Within Ballycastle townland, Main Street had 36 entries relating to the village and there were 35 entries consisting mostly of land in the rural area. The Main Street included the church and graveyard, sundry houses and ruins, as well as the male national school house.[73] Entries for rural Ballycastle included a corn mill, kiln and tuck mill as well as houses, cottages and land.[74] Of all the premises listed in Griffith's Valuation, for the above areas, only six were described as unoccupied.

THE VILLAGERS

Having examined details of housing in Ballycastle, consideration must now be given to the population of the village in so far as it is possible to ascertain this from the records.

67 VO, Map of the village of Ballycastle (1850s). 68 Ibid. 69 Griffith *Valuation, parish of Doonfeeny*, p. 5. 70 Ibid., p. 6. 71 Ibid., p. 6. 72 Ibid., p. 5–6. 73 Ibid., pp 9–10. 74 Ibid., p. 9.

Included in the census of 1831 are the population figures for the years 1821 and 1831 in the parishes of Doonfeeny (incorporating the townland of Ballycastle) and Kilbride, both of which were in the diocese of Killala (Table 1). Figures for individual townlands were not provided.

Table 1 Population of the parishes of Doonfeeny and Kilbride 1821 and 1831.[75]

Parish	1821	1831
Parish of Doonfeeny	3564	4110
Parish of Kilbride	1808	2023

In 1835, the Commissioners of public instruction, gave details of the religious denomination for the total population of the parishes of Doonfeeny and Kilbride, based on the census of 1831. However, again there was no separate enumeration of the population of either the townland or village of Ballycastle given. Both the 1831 figures and those determined by the commissioners are set out in Table 2 below.

Table 2 Religious denominations of population of parishes of Doonfeeny and Kilbride in 1831 and 1834.[76]

Townland	Roman Catholic	Denomination Established Church	Other	Total
Doonfeeny 1831	3,642	468	–	4,110
Doonfeeny 1834	3,909	502	–	4,411
Kilbride 1831	1,985	38	–	2,023
Kilbride 1834	2,130	40	–	2,170

The commissioners' report also gave details of the services held by the different religious denominations. In the case of the Protestant parish, there was one church in Doonfeeny where Divine Service was held on Sundays and holidays. The average attendance at the service was seventy persons which had increased over the previous five years. There was a resident vicar and a glebe house in the benefice.[77] The tithes from this parish amounted to £300, half of which went to the dean and precentor (Union of Killala) and the remainder to the vicar.[78]

Mass was celebrated in the Catholic parish church of Doonfeeny every Sunday and holiday. The average attendance was 1,250 and this had been increas-

75 *Census of Ireland, 1831*. **76** *First report of the commissioners of public instruction, Ireland* HC 1835, xxxiii, province of Tuam, diocese of Killalla, p. 51d, parish of Doonfeeny, pp 54d–55d. **77** Ibid., p. 55d. **78** Lewis, *Topographical dictionary*, i, p. 574.

ing over the previous five years. It is not clear if the attendance figures include both the church in Doonfeeny and the chapel in Ballycastle village which was erected in 1828. There was one resident priest. In the case of Kilbride, the average attendance was 400, which had increased over the previous five years and there was one priest attached to the church.[79]

In Doonfeeny there was a meeting-house of Wesleyan Methodists who were in communion with the Established Church. A meeting was held once a fortnight on weekdays with an average of thirty in attendance and this number had been increasing during the previous five years. There were two preachers who were non-resident.[80]

There were no Presbyterians or other Protestant dissenters returned for either parish.[81] While the statistics make no reference to Presbyterians, it is known that there was a Presbyterian community in Ballinglen which was in the Doonfeeny parish. The Presbyterian community built a church in 1850 on the castle farm, known locally as the Scots farm. This church has only been deserted since 1959.[82] If the Presbyterian numbers were included in those of the Established Church, it would account for the unusually high percentage of Protestants within the population of the parish of Doonfeeny – 13 per cent within the parish against 5 per cent for the diocese of Killala. It is believed locally that the Presbyterians in Ballinglen may have come originally from Scotland. Teachers and farm stewards were brought from Scotland to run the Scots farm, but there is no record of these in the commissioners' report.[83]

There were eight schools in Doonfeeny and one in Kilbride in 1835. None of these schools operated under the new national school system which was introduced in 1831. There were four day-schools and four hedge-schools. Of the four day-schools, two were supported by the London Hibernian Society and the Irish Society. A third school received support from the Baptist Society and Mr Knox and the fourth school received funding from the Baptist Society. The subjects taught in these schools were reading, writing, arithmetic, English grammar, and scripture reading in English and Irish. In the case of the four hedge-schools in Doonfeeny as well as the one in Kilbride, contributions from the children were their main support. The subjects taught in the hedge schools were reading writing, arithmetic and the Catholic catechism daily.[84]

The 1841 census was the first to give details of the population of individual townlands, towns and cities of Ireland. The commissioners for the census of 1841 stated that they had adopted the word 'town' for every assemblage of contiguous houses, instead of town, village and hamlet. They further adopted the number of twenty as the minimum number of houses constituting a town in that sense.[85]

79 *First report of the commissioners of public instruction*, p. 55d.   **80** Ibid., p. 55d.   **81** Ibid., p. 55d.   **82** McHale, *The parishes of Killala*, ii, pp 10–11.   **83** Ibid.   **84** *Second report from the commissioners of public instruction, Ireland*, HC 1835, xxxiv, province of Tuam, diocese of Killala, parishes of Doonfeeny and Kilbride, pp 86d–87d.   **85** *Census of Ireland, 1841*, p. vii.

However, the figures given in 1841 for Ballycastle 'town' appear to include the figures for rural Ballycastle but not rural Carrowkibbock Upper or Carrowniskey.

Table 3 Population of Ballycastle in 1841 and 1851 – *estimated.[86]

Location	Population 1841	Population 1851	Houses 1841	Houses 1851
Village	655*	372	124*	77
Ballycastle	143*	82	24*	15
Carrownisky	164	48	25	8
Carrowkibbock	95	66	18	15
Totals	1057	568	186	115

Table 4 Classes of houses in Ballycastle, urban and rural – census of 1841[87]

	1st class	2nd class	3rd class	4th class	Vacant	Total
Houses	2	20	64	53	9	148
Families	2	21	71	61	–	155

According to the 1851 census, all the fourth-class houses were mud cabins containing only one room. Third-class houses were a better condition of cottage, also built of mud but varying in size with windows and from two to four rooms. Second-class houses were good farm houses, or in the case of a town, a house in a small street, having five to nine rooms and windows. First-class houses were all of a better condition than any of the preceding classes. It is clear therefore from Table 4 that most of the families in the village and townland of Ballycastle were living in poor class cottages. Between the 1841 and 1851 censuses the decrease in the number of fourth-class houses in Ireland was equal to as much as 72 per cent, with the rate of decrease in county Mayo of 75 per cent. There was an increase in the other three classes, the third class still being principally built of mud.[88]

Table 5 shows that the families living in the village were almost equally divided in their occupations between agriculture and various trades. This points to the importance of the location of the village both as a centre for trade and for the support of the farming community in the surrounding areas.

86 In the 1841 census statistics the population of the village is recorded as 798. This appears to include the figure for the entire townland of Ballycastle. Making an adjustment based on the proportionate division of population between Ballycastle village and townland in 1851, an estimated revised figure of 655 for the village in 1841 has been substituted. Similarly, a figure of 124 is used for the number of houses. **87** *Census of Ireland, 1841.* **88** Ibid., p. vii.

Table 5 Families classified according to their pursuits –1841 census.[89]

Employment sector	Number	Employment status	Number
Agriculture	67	Professions etc.	4
Manufacturing	69	Directing labour	65
Other	19	Manual labour	78
		Other	8
Total	155		155

In the 44 years from its foundation, the village of Ballycastle increased its population to a high figure of 655 in 1841. It is clear that the village had prospered and was able to sustain a growing population. However, the census figures for subsequent decades showed a declining population for which famine, migration and emigration were largely responsible. Like many other parts of county Mayo, Ballycastle had its share of suffering during the years of the Great Famine. The census of population returns for the years 1841 and 1851 clearly illustrate what a major impact the Great Famine had on the village.

Table 6 Population of the village of Ballycastle in 1841 and 1851[90]

	Males	Females	Totals
1841	318*	337*	655*
1851	189	183	372

*estimated – see note to Table 3.

These figures represent an overall decrease in the population of the village in the decade of 43 per cent (males 40 per cent and females 46 per cent).

From 1841 onwards, the decline in the population of Ballycastle village can be traced from the census returns. These returns, together with details of housing during the same period, provide a picture of the village during a span of seventy years. Apart from a slight increase in 1861 and 1881, possibly due to persons moving into the village from surrounding areas, the picture is one of a steady decline in the population.

Table 7 shows the percentage changes in the total population of the village in every census year. The overall decline in the population between 1841 and 1911 was 54 per cent. Over the same period, the number of males decreased by 52 per cent and the females by 57 per cent. The higher percentage of females may be attributed to assisted emigration schemes.

89 Ibid.   **90** *Censuses of Ireland, 1841–1851.*

Table 7 Population of the village of Ballycastle, 1841–1911.[91]

Census year	Males	Females	Totals	Percentage change
1841	318*	337*	655*	
1851	189	183	372	−43
1861	204	208	412	+11
1871	175	197	372	−10
1881	182	228	410	+10
1891	151	169	311	−24
1901	145	160	305	−2
1911	153	146	299	−2

*estimated – see note to Table 3.

Table 8 Number of houses in the village of Ballycastle, 1841–1911.[92] *estimated – see note to Table 3

Year	Total houses	Percentage change	Out-offices / Farm steadings
1841	124*	–	–
1851	77	−38	–
1861	91	+18	–
1871	83	−8	57
1881	92	+11	130
1891	69	−25	121
1901	72	+4	116
1911	61	−15	145

*estimated – see note to Table 3.

The overall decrease in the number of houses from 1841 to 1911 was 51 per cent. The list of out-offices included the following – stable, coach house, harness room, cow house, calf house, dairy, piggery, fowl house, boiling room, barn, turf house, potato house, workshop, shed, store, forge and laundry. Others were a meat shop, slaughterhouse, closet and bake house.[93] Tables 7 and 8 show that, while there was a decrease in population, the number of out-offices and farm steadings increased, perhaps pointing to greater prosperity for fewer people.

The workhouse in Ballina first opened its doors in November 1843 to cater for 1,200 persons but its catchment area, which included Killala and Ballycastle, extended as far away as Belmullet.[94] By 1851, the workhouse population of the

91 *Census of Ireland, 1841–1911*.   **92** Ibid.   **93** *Census of Ireland, 1911*.   **94** John O'Connor, *The workhouses of Ireland: the fate of Ireland's poor* (Dublin, 1995), appendix 13, p.259.

country reached its peak and to ease the situation, provision was made for an additional thirty-three workhouses. In 1852, workhouses were opened in Killala and Belmullet to cater for 500 persons each.[95] It is outside the scope of this essay to provide an analysis of the period of the Great Famine in the barony of Tirawley. However, Table 7, showing a decrease of 43 per cent in the population of the village between 1841 and 1851, gives some idea of the impact the Great Famine had on the village. The extent of destitution in the village and surrounding townlands, can be gleaned from the newspapers of the time.[96] An agricultural area which relied to a very great extent on its ability to feed its own population from its own resources was bound to be severely affected in a period of food scarcity, especially from the failure of the potato crop on which so many of the poorer people depended for their very existence, and destitution in the townlands would have had serious consequences for the prosperity of the village and its population. According to local tradition, a soup kitchen was operated by Presbyterian ladies in Ballinglen and Indian meal was distributed from a centre in the village of Ballycastle during the period of the Famine.

Another cause for concern during the 1849–50 period was an outbreak of cholera. It was no respecter of class and affected poor and rich alike. A fever hospital was attached to the Ballina union in order to cope with the crisis during which many people died.[97] In August 1849, James Kirkwood, magistrate and merchant, and the wife of the Revd William Bourke died of cholera in Killala, and Charles Atkinson, coroner, and the wife of Francis Knox, died of the same disease in Ballina.[98]

Emigration throughout the nineteenth century was a feature of life in county Mayo. Father Hart, giving evidence to the commissioners inquiring into the condition of the poorer classes in Ireland (1836), said that from 140 to 170 of the comfortable and labouring classes in his parish had emigrated and he believed that half of the parishioners would have emigrated if they had had the means to leave the country. Those who emigrated, went to America, sometimes with assistance from family or friends.[99] Very often, whole families emigrated at one time. One of the older residents of Ballycastle related that emigrants from the village went to work in the coal-fields of Scranton, Pennsylvania, and that one emigrant who returned to Ballycastle described his occupation in Pennsylvania as a 'stone picker', that is, he had to pick the stones from the belt conveying coal from the mine.[1] After the onset of the Great Famine in 1845, the numbers emigrating from county Mayo increased dramatically. A total of 29,317 persons (14,474 males and 14,843 females) emigrated from the county in the decade 1851–61. The total for the period from 1 May 1851 to 31 March, 1911 was 194,550 (86,692 males and 107,858 females).[2]

95 Ibid., pp 177–8, 259–60.   96 *Ballina Chronicle*, May 1849 – December 1850, for return of destitute persons relieved in the Ballina workhouse from 26 May to 15 September 1849.   97 *Ballina Chronicle*, 20 June–26 August, 1849.   98 Ibid., 23 August, 1849.   99 Ibid.   1 Personal comment from a resident of Ballycastle, August 2001.   2 *Census of Ireland, 1911, Province of*

A report in the *Tyrawley Herald* of 23 April 1846 indicated that

> The number of people emigrating this season to America from the shores of Mayo and Sligo exceeds that of any previous year within our recollection. These emigrants are chiefly from the more comfortable class of farmers, persons from the poorer classes being prevented by poverty from seeking a better livelihood in a foreign country.[3]

This echoes the evidence given by Father Hart a decade earlier when he said that those leaving his parish were of the 'comfortable and labouring classes'.[4]

VILLAGE TRADE

Fairs and markets were major elements of Ballycastle's economy. In 1837 there were six fairs in the year but this number was later increased to eleven a year. According to local comment, fairs were originally held to coincide with feast days, such as 25 March and 29 June, but as time went on, they were held on the nineteenth day of the month. In 1843 Ballycastle was described as a 'fair and market town' but no tolls were charged.[5] Markets were held every Wednesday in Ballycastle village but there was no patent for this, probably because the proprietor did not seek one.[6] It will be recalled that, according to Griffith's Valuation of 1856, Colonel A. Knox-Gore had the shambles and the tolls and customs of the fairs and markets.

Monthly fairs and weekly markets were held on the main street of Ballycastle, and by all accounts these were lively occasions. Fairs were mainly concerned with the buying and selling of cattle but other animals such as sheep and horses were also included. According to Ó Gráda, there was a tendency for fairs 'to specialise by seasons and function. Early spring was the best time for horses, May for grazing cattle and August for beef. While fairs had their origin in the trade for cattle and sheep, they gradually acquired a much wider economic and social function'.[7] At the fairs, among other goods, delph, sweets and apples were also available, while other features included a shooting gallery and someone offering to take out corns.[8]

Connaught, table xli, p. 173. Emigration from the county of Mayo during each year, from 1 May 1851 to 31 March 1911, compiled from the returns of the Register General. **3** *Tyrawley Herald*, 23 April, 1846. **4** *First report of commissioners for inquiring into the condition of the poorer classes in Ireland*, HC 1836, xxxiii, Supplement to appendix F, p. 28. **5** *Return of number of disturbances in Ireland at fairs and markets in collection of tolls and customs*, 1840–3, HC 1843, L, p. 163. **6** *Report of commissioners appointed to inquire into the state of fairs and markets in Ireland*, HC 1852–3, xli; list of market towns in county Mayo. **7** Cormac Ó Gráda, *Ireland: a new economic history, 1750–1939* (Oxford, 1994), p.41. **8** Langan 'Ballycastle seventy years ago', p. 83;

In Ballycastle, lambs, sheep, cattle, pigs and horses were all brought to the market. There were also creels for fish, cod fish and salted mackerel, as well as bonhams, potatoes and seed oats. These were all laid out in front of the shambles at the top of Pound Street. Second-hand clothes were also for sale. Hard bargaining took place on these occasions and very often proceedings were adjourned to the nearest hostelry, such as the room at the back of the pub in May's hotel. The cattle all stood in little groups down the main street and it was in the interest of the proprietor of the hostelry to ensure that the cattle of the appropriate seller and buyer remained outside his premises until the sales were completed. At the beginning of the twentieth century, there were fourteen public houses in the village and it is likely that most sellers and buyers did the rounds of these during market days. According to Robert Polk, who gave a recording of his reminiscences to the Folklore Commission in the 1960s, it was quite hazardous going anywhere along the roads after a market when farm animals were being driven home in the evening and nothing could pass by them.[9] Fairs continued to be held up to the 1970s but the opening of a cattle mart in Ballina signalled the end of the fairs in Ballycastle.

VILLAGE SURNAMES

The Ordnance Survey house books and Griffith's Valuation are the main sources of information about individuals living in Ballycastle in the 1840s and 1850s. In some cases, additional information was supplied by present residents of the village. Among the names which feature prominently in the village is that of Barrett. It appears that the Barretts lived in Milltown in the Ballinglen valley before moving into the village of Ballycastle about the year 1820. The Barretts built a public house, had a sawmills, drapery, hardware and general store. They obtained a licence for the public house about 1827. In the Ordnance Survey house books for Ballycastle village, a John Barrett is listed as head tenant having six acres of land with a house, an office in front which was falling down, another office also in front and an office at the rear. In Griffith's Valuation, the only Barrett is a George Barrett having a garden, house, office and yard, and as immediate lessor of a house at the rear. The tithe applotment book in 1834 names a Pat and a Michael Barrett.[10] In the 1901 census, William Barrett is shown as owning a public house with three stables, two cow houses, a piggery and four stores. He also had a private dwelling with a forge which was occupied by a Michael Clarke. Also in the house books for Ballycastle, Daniel Madden is described as head tenant with a house and a delph shop with a slate roof in Carrownisky. The

local comment.   **9** UCD, Folklore Commission, tape recording of the reminiscences of Robert Polke, 1966.   **10** NAI, Tithe applotment book for Ballycastle, parish of Doonfeeny, 1834, p. 21, TAB 21/3, microfilm no. 73.

house was not plastered or ceiled. A widow Madden is named in the tithe applot-ment book.[11] Daniel Madden is not listed in the 1901 census for Ballycastle.

Another surname which features prominently in the life of Ballycastle village is that of Polk[e]. When the Polks came to Ballycastle is not known but it is likely that they came from the North of Ireland sometime in the late eighteenth century. There was also a family of Polks living in the nearby Ballinglen town-land but they may have had no connection with the family of the same name living in the village of Ballycastle. The tithe applotment book of 1834 lists a Robert Polk with a real acreable value of £8.16s. 3d. and a composition for tithe holding of 17s. 2½d.[12] In the Ordnance Survey house books, the name of John Polk is listed for ground rent of house and offices. In the 1901 census, Robert Polk is shown as owning and residing in a public house with two stables, a cow house and a calf house. He is also shown as owning a shop with a cow house, a piggery and a turf house, with William Kneafsey as tenant. Robert Polk also owned a shop with Anne McDonnell as tenant. Other properties listed under his name were a private dwelling with a fowl house let to Annie Burns, and another private dwelling with a turf house let to Charles Brady, RIC. He also had the RIC barracks with a stable and two turf houses let to Edward Ardill. In 1966 Robert Polk recorded his reminiscences for the Folklore Commission.[13] An advertisement, dated 1884, gives some idea of Robert Polk's enterprise (Appendix 1). Polk's premises were in the Ballycastle townland part of the vil-lage on the same side as the Catholic chapel but farther down the street.

Mays' hotel was situated across the street from Robert Polk's premises. According to the 1901 census, it was owned by Bridget A. May. The hotel had two stables, a coach house, a cow house, a turf house and a shed. The post office was owned by Catherine May with Mary Kate May residing there. Bridget May also had a private dwelling, occupied by a John Cosgrove. The stables and coach house were at the back of the hotel as well as a very large two-storey building, the ruins of which can still be seen. It was believed to have been used for the storage of wool and grain before being taken to Killala for shipping to England.

LATER DEVELOPMENTS IN THE VILLAGE

The period between Griffith's Valuation of 1856 and 1900 saw the piecemeal development of the village. In 1856, the portion within Ballycastle townland had only two buildings of note – the church and a male national school a few doors down from the church. Daniel Madden held much of the property on the north side of the street while George Barrett and Richard Winters occupied new buildings – perhaps business premises – across the road separated by a group of

---

11 Ibid. **12** Ibid. **13** UCD, Folklore Commission, tape recording of the reminiscences of Robert Polke, 1966.

buildings in ruins. The remainder of the property in this townland was composed of very poor quality housing.[14]

Between 1856 and 1900, the development in this part of the village was virtually limited to the south side of the street with at least one public house occupied by the Winters family, while next door a large police barracks had been built on a site previously occupied by ruins. This site had been held by the Winters family but by 1900 Robert Polk was the lessor and he also held a house on a quarter-acre site next door to the barracks.[15]

In the Carrowkibbock section of the village, the small narrow-frontage houses with long narrow strips as back gardens, were being replaced piecemeal by better-quality buildings. In the 1870s, a female school replaced a few small cottages, and a male schoolhouse appeared a few years later. Polk had become a large lessor of property by 1880. The upgrading can be measured by the replacement of properties previously valued at 15s. and two of 12s. by new buildings valued at £3 15s., £6 and £12. The street frontages had also been straightened implying re-development. But much poor property remained. Some of the larger houses were now being described as shops or public houses.[16]

The Carrownisky section had previously been the most developed part of the village and in the latter half of the century the valuations remained much higher than elsewhere in the village. Yet the properties in Pound Street and the adjoining buildings on Main Street remained slum property. But progress was not continuous; the two main commercial properties, Madden's and May's were both re-valued downwards in the 1860s. By 1872, Madden's stores and kiln were 'unoccupied for years and going into ruin'. They were re-valued both upwards and downwards on a number of occasions before 1900 and had passed from Madden to Donoghue. Bridget May's property was re-valued downwards from £22 to £17 to £9 before 1875 but was restored to £17 by 1882 when it was described as 'house, shop, office, yard – licensed'. By 1886 it was roofless having been damaged by a storm. Further up the street the Petty Sessions house was abandoned by the Magistrates as untenantable in 1885. However, on the credit side the police barracks had been upgraded before 1880. By 1900, the main proprietors of Carrowniskey were Matilda S. Knox Gore, and the representatives of J. Madden.[17]

John Knox died in 1861, but before then, in the early 1850s, some parts of the estate were already being sold through the Encumbered Estates Court. Advertisements in the newspapers of the time show that other parts were placed in chancery, for instance, an advertisement in the *Tyrawley Herald* included the following: 'the lands of Ballyglass and Ballycastle and the several houses situate in the town of Ballycastle, and that part of the lands of Ballyknock, thereto

14 Griffith, *Valuation.* **15** OS County Mayo 25 inch sheets vii (13 and 14), surveyed 1896; VO cancellation books 1856–1900; annotated VO plan of Ballycastle dated 1900. **16** Ibid. **17** Ibid.

adjoining, containing about nineteen acres Irish plantation measure, in the barony of Tyrawley, and county of Mayo ... ' [18] Another advertisement containing a list of property in chancery included 'part of the lands of Ballycastle, containing 150 acres late Irish plantation measure, formerly in the possession of Thomas Palmer, esq.'[19] In 1853, the land on which the church was built in neighbouring Ballinglen, and which was leased from a Knox family in Ballina, was also sold through the Encumbered Estates Court.[20] It is likely that other parts of the Knox family estates were also sold around the same time. By 1901, only three shops, one public house and three private dwellings in the village of Ballycastle were listed in the census as being owned by persons of the name of Knox-Gore.

According to the census of 1901, the village of Ballycastle had a total of 76 buildings, consisting of 16 public houses, one of which was uninhabited, seven shops, 45 private dwellings (four uninhabited), a post office, hotel, church, Catholic chapel, two RIC barracks (one in chancery) and two schools. Three public houses and 7 private dwellings were held in chancery.[21] Among the occupations in the village by 1901, were three blacksmiths, two carpenters, two tailors, one shoemaker and one cobbler, a cooper making small tubs, usually for salting fish, a bakery and three butchers, as well as the sixteen public houses mentioned earlier.[22]

Ballycastle has been immortalised in the paintings and drawings of Jack B. Yeats who visited the village on at least two occasions. Maude Gonne MacBride also visited on two occasions. While staying at May's hotel in August 1910, she sent a letter to the poet W.B. Yeats in which she mentioned that his brother (Jack B. Yeats) and his wife had stayed there for two months the previous year, and that many of his sister's prints from the Cuala Press adorned the hotel.[23]

CONCLUSION

The village of Ballycastle stands at the crossroads between two very different types of landscape along the remote north Mayo coast. It grew rapidly in its first forty years, reaching an estimated population of 665 by the year 1841. It provided an administrative centre, with its churches, dispensary, petty session court, revenue-police and constabulary barracks, as well as a post office and a wide range of shops, serving its mainly agricultural hinterland. Its fairs and markets contributed to the social and economic development of the village. Like many other parts of county Mayo, Ballycastle never quite recovered from the effects

18 *Tyrawley Herald,* 1 March, 1850. **19** Ibid., 17 April 1851. **20** MacHale, *The parishes in the diocese of Killala,* ii, p.10. **21** NAI, Census of Ireland 1901, 94/20, Ballycastle town, parish of Doonfeeny, Form B1, House and Building Return. **22** *Census of Ireland, 1901,* Part I, Province of Connaught, table xxxiii. **23** Anna MacBride White and A. Norman Jeffares (eds), *Always your friend: the Gonne-Yeats letters 1893–1938* (London, 1993), pp 292–3.

of the Great Famine, its population having decreased by some 43 per cent in the following decade. Having explored some aspects of its history, one can agree with Synge that, like nearly all the 'towns' of its class, it was a trading centre kept up by the country people who lived around it.

APPENDIX I

Text of an advertisement displayed in Polke's premises in Ballycastle (courtesy of Brian Polke)

Family and commercial hotel, Ballycastle. This first class new family hotel and posting stablishment is now open for the accommodation of gentry, tourists, travellers and others and is in every respect fitted up as a first class hotel, possessing every modern comfort. The proprietor begs to assure the public that he has spared no expense in providing a hotel worthy of the name for Ballycastle and those visiting his establishment will find their wants carefully provided for.

Any number of traps with good horses and careful drivers, can be supplied on the shortest notice. Call for convenience and comfort at the family and commercial hotel, Ballycastle, Robert Polk [now spelt Polke], proprietor, Ballycastle.

13 December, 1884.

A history of Sixmilebridge, county Clare, 1603–1911

BRIAN Ó DÁLAIGH

The new motorway from Limerick to Shannon Airport travels through the undulating farmlands that fringe the northern shore of the Shannon estuary, carrying the traffic speedily to Ennis, Galway and the west country beyond. If, however, the motorist diverts at Cratloe, along a winding, secondary road, he will come eventually to the handsome, eighteenth-century village of Sixmilebridge. The settlement, sited at an important crossing point on the river Ogarney, was in centuries past one of the principal urban centres of county Clare. The main Limerick to Ennis road passed through the village. Sixmilebridge was noted for its fairs and markets and for its textile and milling industries. In the early nineteenth century the building of a new bridge over the Ogarney at Bunratty allowed the village to be bypassed and resulted in a steep decline in its fortunes. Following the Great Famine, economic decline accelerated and Sixmilebridge was overtaken in size by its nearest neighbours – the small towns of Tulla, Scariff and Newmarket-on-Fergus. Nevertheless Sixmilebridge retains much of its Old World charm with its ancient bridge forming the focal point of the village. The bridge connects two market squares of greatly varying size. The irregular layout is appealing and is indicative of the settlement's piecemeal development over the centuries.

Thomas Dinely, an English visitor to county Clare in 1681, in describing the routes from Bunratty to Limerick, explained how Sixmilebridge was named:

> From Bunratty castle, the chief seat of the earl of Thomond, unto the town of Sixmile-bridge, belonging also to that noble family, is three miles; from whence to the city of Limerick, to which there are two ways: by the Oyle Mills and the seat of the McNamaras beyond it, or over the high mountain, famous for its admirable prospect, hanging as it were over Sixmile-bridge town and commonly called by the name of Gallows-Hill; this is the upper, the other the lower way to Limerick and from the town to the city is six miles either way, whence the town hath its name.[1]

It should be understood that there were no standard miles in Ireland in the seventeenth century. Connacht miles, for instance, were held to be much longer than Clare miles.[2] Taking the two routes today, the lower way by Ballintlea and

1 Evelyn Philip Shirley (ed.), 'Extracts from the journal of Thomas Dineley, giving some account of his visit to Ireland in the reign of Charles II' in *JRSAI*, viii (1864–6), pp 42–3. 2 John Stevens, *A journal of my travels since the revolution containing a brief account of all the war in*

Cratloe, and the upper way by Gallows Hill and Meelick, the distance by both routes (from the bridge of Sixmilebridge to Thomondgate bridge in Limerick) is exactly 9.7 statute miles.[3] The 'Clare mile' therefore was approximately 1.6 statute miles or 2.6 kilometers, which was longer than the 'common Irish mile', defined by parliament in 1715 as twelve furlongs or one and a half statute miles.[4] Dinely consciously uses the word 'town' to describe Sixmilebridge, as he was anxious to compliment his benefactor, the earl of Thomond. Sixmilebridge in terms of its size was second only to the county capital, Ennis, and, while a town by Clare standards, by English standards of the period, it was a country village.

The Ogarney river gave access to the Shannon estuary and was an important channel of communication. Inhabitants could travel by boat to Limerick or alternatively could sail westward along the Shannon estuary to Ennis and Kilrush, the other two urban centres being developed by the earls of Thomond. Shallow bottomed boats came up the Ogarney as far as Ballintlea, a mile or so below the village, where they discharged their cargoes. Apart from transportation, the river made another significant contribution to the development of Sixmilebridge. The Ogarney marked an important territorial boundary between townland and barony and between parish and diocese. On the west side of the river was the parish of Kilfinaghta in the diocese of Killaloe and on the east the parish of Kilfintenan in the diocese of Limerick. These divisions, as we shall see, were to have a crucial bearing on the siting of buildings and on the organisation of public spaces within the urban precinct.

EXPANSION IN THE EARLY SEVENTEENTH CENTURY

On the completion of the Nine Years War in 1603, Donough O'Brien, fourth earl of Thomond, turned his attention to developing the economic potential of his large estates in county Clare. The earl resided at Bunratty castle, four miles south of Sixmilebridge, and the settlement would initially develop as the village of his principal residence. Donough O'Brien was a committed Protestant, who had been the staunchest ally on the English side during the nine years of conflict. Consequently as he sought to develop his estates, he invited large numbers of English and Dutch Protestants to settle on his lands in the vicinity of Bunratty and Sixmilebridge. Settlers with capital and superior commercial skills would improve agriculture, hasten economic development and promote urban expansion. A lease he granted to the merchant, Maximilian Vandelure, a Dutchman, who had settled on the lands of Cappagh, adjacent to Sixmilebridge in 1615, provides an insight into the earl's strategy. Vandelure was to pay a yearly rent of

Ireland, ed. Revd R.H. Murray (Oxford, 1912), abstracted in Brian Ó Dálaigh (ed.), *The stranger's gaze: travels in county Clare* (Ennis, 1998), p. 76. **3** As measured by car mileometer. **4** J.H. Andrews, *Plantation acres* (Belfast, 1985), p. 219.

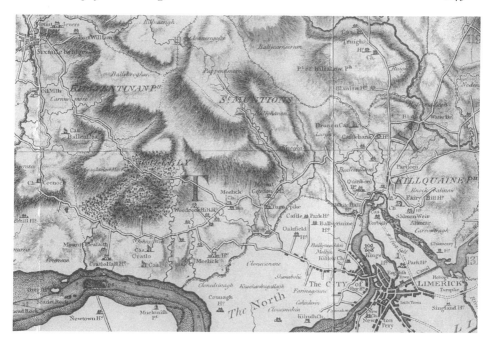

Figure 1. Abstract from Henry Pelham's map of county Clare, 1788, showing the two routes from Sixmilebridge to Limerick that gave the village its name. Both routes, the lower way by the Oil Mills and Cratloe and the upper way by Gallows Hill and Meelick, were six miles in length; thus the village was called Sixmilebridge

£28 'current money of England' for so long as he retained Irish tenants upon his lands. However, if he should introduce English or Dutch tenants in place of the Irish, his rent would be reduced.[5] Evidently O'Brien was seeking settlers not just as principal tenants but also as sub tenants. He was in addition following government policy where would-be settlers were required to reside in exclusive communities 'without interruption or intermixture of others'. It was the intention of the earl that a Protestant colony should be established at Sixmilebridge with the inhabitants holding land in the surrounding district. In 1621 James Vandelure, gentleman, leased two and a half quarters[6] of land in the parish of Kilfinaghta and a house and garden in Sixmilebridge. In 1623 the merchant Cornelius Johnson leased the house where he himself lived along with another house in the village and 'three score English acres joining to the bridge foot'. Edward Stacy, yeoman, leased three tenements, three gardens, 18 acres of arable

5 Bernadette Cunningham, 'Newcomers in the Thomond Lordship' in *Dál gCais,* xi (1993), pp 105–7. **6** A land unit nominally comprising of 120 acres, but quarters could vary considerably in size depending on the agricultural potential of the land. *Ceathrú* (a quarter) in its various anglicised forms prefixes some sixty townland names in county Clare.

land and 19 acres of moor and bog in the 'town and lands of Sixmilebridge' for
31 years.[7] All of these tenants were required to build:

> of lime and stone building, one substantial house two storeys and a half
> in height, and the same to contain a forty feet square measure in length
> between both pinions, and twenty foot in breadth, with convenient stone
> chimneys therein, and the same shall cover with stone tile or slate, and
> shall pave the street in front thereof … and shall enclose the said garden.[8]

By 1617 another important building project was coming to completion. A
stone bridge was in construction over the ford of the Ogarney river. In his will,
dated 28 November 1617, Donough O'Brien commanded his eldest son Henry
to 'finish the stone bridge by me built and made over the water of the Six Myle
Bridge, well caused at both ends thereof for the passage of carts and travelers'.[9]
The fact that the placename contained the element 'bridge' before the completion of the stone structure probably indicates that a timber bridge previously
spanned the river. Nonetheless the erection of the stone bridge marked an important milestone and ensured that all traffic proceeding from Limerick into county
Clare passed through the village.

The earl was also active in developing the commercial potential of the new
settlement. In 1618 O'Brien sought out a patent for the fairs and markets of Sixmilebridge. The patent permitted the holding of a Thursday market and two fairs
annually (25 April and 5 November). Fairs and markets brought substantial income
to landowners as tolls and customs could be levied on the produce and livestock
sold. A court of pie-powder (from the French *piepoudre,* dusty feet) was held to
maintain order and settle disputes arising at the annual fairs and weekly markets.[10]

Despite these developments and the favourable leases granted to the newcomers, not all settlers were successful or resided permanently. The lands of
Cappagh, which had been granted to Maximillian Vandelure in 1615 with conditions about the introduction of English and Dutch sub tenants, were in 1626
in the hands of James Tanner, merchant of Limerick. In 1635 the tenements of
Edward Stacy, who had been granted a lease in 1623, were re-leased to Donogh
McShane, a butcher of Sixmilebridge, at double the rent with the conditions to
build still included. A settler, who had more success, was Cornelius Johnson.
Johnson was granted a new lease of his houses and lands in 1637 at £26 per
annum instead of the original £9. He had increased the extent of his holdings
and since there was no new condition binding him to build, he probably had
complied with the building conditions of the original lease.[11]

7 Bernadette Cunningham, 'Newcomers' (1993), p. 105. 8 Ibid. 9 Brian Ó Dálaigh, 'A
comparative study of the wills of the first and fourth earls of Thomond, 1551–1617' in *North
Munster Antiquarian Journal,* xxxiv (1992), p. 61. 10 *Calendar of Irish patents rolls of James I*
(IMC, reprint, Dublin, 1966), p. 389. 11 Bernadette Cunningham, 'Newcomers', (1993), p.

What arrangements were made for the spiritual needs of the community? John Rider, the Church of Ireland bishop of Killaloe, appointed Andrew Chaplain vicar to Kilfinaghta parish in 1614. Chaplain was described as a 'minister and zealous preacher, a man of good life and conversation'.[12] He served the village community until 1633. Richard Fuller was made rector in 1617; the rector drew a sinecure of £12 per annum and was non-resident. In the bishop's visitation report of 1615 no place of worship is recorded. Villagers could have attended services at the re-edified church of Bunratty four miles off, or alternatively at the old parish church of Kilfinaghta. The church of Kilfinaghta was sited at Ballysheen in the townland of Sooreeny[13] a mile or so north of the village. In the normal course of events a settlement would have formed around the parish church. Ballysheen certainly continued in use as a burial ground. However, the decision of the earl to concentrate development at the ford of the Ogarney meant that the old parish centre decayed while the new settlement grew and prospered. It is likely that a church or meeting house was erected in Sixmilebridge prior to 1641. This judgement is based on the evidence of a single tombstone found during the recent renovation of the Protestant church.[14] The stone, which lay at the threshold of the western doorway, was dedicated to the memory of Mickil Clark and bore the date of 1640.[15] The new church was built on high ground on the western side of the river overlooking the bridge and market place. It is unlikely that the structure would have survived the military assaults on the village in the 1640s. By 1641 Sixmilebridge was reasonably prosperous and had made good progress since its inception. However, the rising of 1641 was to have a traumatic effect on its fortunes and much of the progress of the previous decades was undone.

UPRISING OF 1641

News of the rising in Ulster was announced at the great fair of Quin in November 1641. The inhabitants of Clare, fearful of the validity of their land titles under English law and incensed at the favourable treatment meted out to the newcomers, who now farmed some of the most fertile lands of the county,

107. **12** Philip Dwyer, *The diocese of Killaloe from the Reformation to the close of the eighteenth century* (Dublin, 1876), pp 105, 161. **13** Two-thirds the tithes of the lands of Sooreeny (*Siúríní*, little sisters) and Ballysheen (*Baile Oisín*, Oisin's town) in the medieval period were paid to the nunnery of Killone. After the closure of Killone Abbey in 1543, the tithes came into the possession of Murrough, first earl of Thomond and through him to the O'Briens, barons of Inchiquin. See John O'Donovan and Eugene O'Curry, *The antiquities of county Clare* (Ennis, 1997), p. 167. **14** The refurbished building functions as the new public lending library of Sixmilebridge. **15** Personal comments of Michael McNamara, Jamaica Inn, Sixmilebridge. See also Dwyer, *Diocese of Killaloe*, pp 473, 537–8.

joined in the uprising. In Sixmilebridge, as in many other places, settlers were despoiled of their goods and had to flee their houses. Some went to Limerick but many sought refuge with the earl of Thomond in Bunratty castle. The depositions of the Protestant settlers made at the end of 1642 list the injuries and losses they suffered. The depositions contain a degree of exaggeration and untruth and need to be treated with caution. Nonetheless, as testimony of contemporary witnesses, they provide valuable insights into the events of the period. We learn of the names, occupations and locations of the many individuals, who had come to colonise southeast Clare.[16]

James Vandelure of Sixmilebridge, a Dutch Protestant, declared that he was robbed of property worth £1,836 part of which consisted of debts due to him. His goods consisted of farming stock, tanned hides, malt and corn. Evidently Vandelure transacted business with fellow settlers and native Irish alike. He lost debts due by Jacques Graniere, late of Kilrush, a Dutch Protestant, and by George Hoff, William Cragg, Roger King and the Widow Bellamy, all Protestants of Sixmilebridge and 'now impoverished by the rebellion'. He also lost money he lent to Irishmen, then in open rebellion. Included in this list were Bartholomew Stritch and Nicholas Wolf, merchants of Limerick, and Thomas and William Creagh, merchants of Sixmilebridge. The record of his lost properties is impressive and shows the kind of industrial processes that were present in the village. Vandelure was expelled from his house, his two water mills, his mill for bark, a malt house, a tanyard and many other tenements, together with four quarters of land. The steep inclines and rapid flows of the Ogarney made it particularly suitable for mills. Tree bark was used in the tanning of leather; however, the stripping of bark quickly denuded the countryside of its tree cover. Included in Vandelure's deposition was a list of local landowners, mainly O'Briens and McNamaras, who, he claimed, despoiled him of his property.[17] Dispossessed settlers were encouraged to accuse leading landowners in order to provide the justification for the confiscation of Irish land. The confiscation of lands had already been legislated for by the English parliament and approved by the king. Consequently accusations against large landowners are a feature of the depositions.

The Revd Andrew Chaplain, former vicar of Sixmilebridge, swore he lost goods to the value of £520, together with church livings worth £105. Dermot O'Brien of Dromore stole his possessions and drove away his stock with the aid of certain yeomen. Meeting O'Brien subsequently at Sixmilebridge, he demanded by what authority the rebels despoiled Protestants. O'Brien produced the written authority of the earl of Thomond, authorising him and his agents to take into their custody the goods of Protestants, as a means of preserving them from destruction. Chaplain went on to state his conviction that the earl of Thomond had colluded with the Irish in plundering Protestants.[18]

16 Máire Mac Neill, *Máire Rua Lady of Leamaneh* (Whitegate, 1990), pp 25–6. 17 James Frost, *The history and topography of county Clare* (Dublin, 1893), pp 355–6. 18 Dwyer, *Diocese of*

Edward Mainwaring deposed that he was deprived of property worth £240. Dermot O'Brien aided by Donogh McNamara of Cratloe robbed him of his writings on his way from Limerick to Bunratty. James Lynch, a popish priest, turned him out of his house. His sheep were driven away by Conor Clune of Kilagurteen. According to Mainwaring Irish captains and soldiers were in a state of open rebellion, robbing the English of their goods and arms, and caring nothing for the earl of Thomond.[19]

As well as the principal tenants, the depositions record individuals of more modest means. The occupations of mason, miller, dyer, saddler, tailor, butcher and merchant are recorded showing the range of skills present in the village community. One of the more poignant depositions is that of Francis Ham, 'a poor glover of Sixmilebridge', who was robbed of his substance 'by the act of Rory Roe of that place, cottoner'.[20]

During the war-torn years that followed, settlers were absent from Sixmilebridge as the native population sought to reassert itself. Apart from one noted incident, little is known of what happened. In 1646 Barnabus O'Brien, sixth earl of Thomond, surrendered Bunratty castle to an English Parliamentary force. The Irish confederates under Lord Muskerry quickly besieged the castle, making Sixmilebridge their centre of operations. Muskerry set up extensive works around the village. In a surprise attack the English overcame his defences and drove the Irish out of Sixmilebridge. However, they were unable to pursue them 'by reason of the woods and a river near at hand'. The English set fire to the settlement, except for those buildings that contained provisions, and returned to Bunratty bearing 250 barrels of oatmeal.[21] Clearly the housing stock suffered extensive damage during the engagement. English control was not fully re-established in Sixmilebridge until after July 1651, when Cromwellian forces, under Henry Ireton, swept through the village on their way to besiege Clare Castle. The settlement again suffered damage on this occasion and in November of 1652 Captain Kyshe of the Parliamentarian army issued a warrant for the 'reparation' of Sixmilebridge.[22]

RESTORATION AND RECONSTRUCTION

In the post-Cromwellian period local circumstances were very different. The earl of Thomond no longer resided at Bunratty. He had become a permanent absentee living in England. The absence of the principal proprietor was to have severe long-term consequences. Much of the capital generated locally and paid in rent

Killaloe, pp 205–7; Frost, *History of Clare*, pp 365–6. **19** Frost, *History of Clare*, pp 367–9. **20** Ibid., p. 370; Dwyer, *Diocese of Killaloe* p. 224. **21** Granville Penn (ed.) *Memorials of the life and times of Sir William Penn, 1644–70* (2 vols., London, 1833), abstracted in Ó Dálaigh, *The stranger's gaze*, pp 20–1. **22** Dwyer, *Diocese of Killaloe*, p. 303.

would in future be spent abroad. Without the guiding hand of a resident proprietor, the reconstruction of Sixmilebridge would be piecemeal and haphazard. The
principal leaseholders rather than the earl would decide on the housetypes and on
the village layout. In the wake of the Cromwellian conquest there was an influx
of Limerick merchants into Sixmilebridge. Individuals with surnames like Arthur,
Bunch, Woulfe, Harrold, Roche and White appear as property holders.[23] Catholics
were prohibited from engaging in commerce in walled towns, so Sixmilebridge,
within easy reach of Limerick, was an ideal place for them to settle. The population grew to a considerable size. The poll-tax returns of 1660 record 259 taxpayers living in Sixmilebridge. The three most important inhabitants were Thomas
White, gent, Nicholas Harrold, apothecary and Edward Gould, gent.[24] There were
235 Irish and 24 English adults liable for tax or an excess of Irish over English of
nearly ten to one. To get an estimate of the total population one needs to multi-
ply the poll-tax return by a factor of three.[25] The population therefore for the village in 1660 was about 777 people. This is perhaps an over estimation but illustrates the extent to which the influx of Limerick people had temporarily swelled
the population. In terms of its size Sixmilebridge rivaled the county capital: while
259 taxpayers were recorded for Sixmilebridge, 267, just eight more, were registered for Ennis.[26] The price of property increased accordingly. The rent of a house
and shop was £10 a year, with a covenant to rebuild and £52 per annum was the
cost of a malt house. This was at a time when the best land in the area could be
had for as little as 5s. an acre, with a lease forever.[27] Few of the pre-1641 settlers
returned. One who did was Giles Vandelure, son of James, malthouse and tanyard owner, who had operated the mills of Sixmilebridge prior to 1641. In 1656
he leased the lands of Brickhill and Moyhill at a yearly rent of £70.[28] Giles was
to become the progenitor of the Vandelures of Ralahine[29] and by his will of 1701
left £10 for the 'Protestant poor' of Sixmilebridge.[30]

    As the local economy improved milling processes related to agricultural pro-
duction were revived. John Cooper obtained a lease of the lands of Cappagh in
1660 including 'the grist mill and the seat of the old oil mill'.[31] In 1664 Cooper
entered into articles with Thomas Greene to produce oil at Sixmilebridge. A
seed-crushing mill was built on the Ogarney at Ballintlea.[32] The oil mills became

---

23 NLI, Inchiquin Ms 14426, 'A scheme of Sixmilebridge'.   **24** Séamus Pender (ed.), *A census
of Ireland c. 1659* (IMC, Dublin, 1939), p. 171.   **25** Brian Gurrin, *Pre-census sources for Irish demography* (Dublin, 2002), pp 30–6, 74.   **26** *Census of Ireland c.1659*, p. 188.   **27** Frost, *History of
Clare*, pp 406–7.   **28** Ibid., p. 409.   **29** In 1831, John Scott Vandelure, a descendant of Giles,
applied the communistic ideas of Robert Owen on his estate and established Ireland's first
commune at Ralahine. See E.T. Craig, *An Irish commune* (Dublin, 1983).   **30** RIA, Ms 3A
39, Abstract of the will of Giles Vandelure, dated 25 April 1701, f. 212.   **31** West Sussex
Record Office, Chichester, Petworth House Archives [henceforth PHA], Ms C 27/7, f. 7;
NLI, microfilm pos. 4769.   **32** John Ainsworth (ed.), *The Inchiquin manuscripts* (IMC, Dublin
1963), p. 361, no. 1109.

synonymous with Sixmilebridge and continued in operation for over a hundred years. The industry was put on a firm footing in 1696 when George Pease of Amsterdam purchased a lease of the oil mills. Pease brought artisans from Holland who rebuilt the mills after the Dutch fashion. Rape seed was grown locally on marginal land in considerable quantities. The seed was then pressed into oil and shipped in bulk to Holland. Rape seed cakes, the residue of the milling process, were exported to England for manure at the rate of 45s. a ton. The extensive mill ruins together with the decayed quay, where boats carried away the seed oil, may still be seen at Ballintlea.[33]

Protestant settlers continued to be attracted to Sixmilebridge. One such individual was Henry Ievers, a man who had made a large fortune by speculating in forfeited estates following the Cromwellian land settlement. Ievers had accumulated an estate of nearly 12,000 acres, half of which were profitable Irish acres. He was reputed to have enjoyed an income of some £1,600 a year. By 1680 he had acquired the lands of Ballyarilla on the eastern bank of the Ogarney and was resident in Ballyarilla castle, whose name he promptly changed to Castle Ievers.[34] No other individual was to make a greater contribution to the development of Sixmilebridge than Henry Ievers. He set about with considerable energy developing his lands east of the river. By his patent, dated 21 June 1678, he obtained authority to hold a Saturday market and two annual fairs at Ballyliddane.[35] This name he altered to the more distinguished Ieverstown. Until then the village had clustered around the market place on the higher ground west of the river. Ievers was determined that he would establish his own settlement on the ground, leading to the bridge, east of the river. A square of ground was laid out on which fairs and markets could be held. It is a moot point whether a settlement the size of Sixmilebridge could have supported one, let alone two weekly markets. Ievers' patent therefore was more likely a speculation in the hope, that with expansion, the settlement would in future support two markets along with four annual fairs.

Little is known of what transpired in Sixmilebridge during the War of the Two Kings, 1689–91. Many Protestants again fled their properties as Catholics tried to overturn the Cromwellian settlement. Henry Ievers appears to have remained in Sixmilebridge, as his lands were not attainted by reason of his absence. Perhaps, because he was an old man, unfit for military service, he was not disturbed. Henry drew up his last will and testament in August 1690 and was dead by October of the following year. Having disinherited his eldest son for marrying 'a person of no fortune', he was succeeded by his second son John.[36]

In July of 1690 the Jacobite soldier, John Stevens, while marching with his regiment from Quin to Limerick, halted at the village on the Ogarney:

33 Hubert Roche-Kelly, 'The oil mills at Ballintlea' in *The Other Clare*, ii (1978), p. 19.   34 Ciarán Ó Murchadha, 'The scapegoat and the opportunist' in *The Other Clare*, x (1986), pp 19–22.   35 *Report of the commissioners appointed to inquire into the state of fairs and markets in Ireland*, HC 1852–3 (1674), xli, p. 66.   36 RIA, Ms 3A 39, ff 33, 209–10, Pedigree of Ievers

[Sixmilebridge] is an indifferent good town and takes its name from its distance from Limerick, and a small bridge over a little river that runs through it, and thence into the Shannon, yet we were quartered three or four companies in a house.[37]

The remarks of Stevens compare favourably with his comments on other settlements in the county. He described Scarriff and Tomgraney as 'villages not worth the naming' and Killaloe 'the meanest town I ever saw dignified with that character'. Clearly Sixmilebridge made a more positive impression on this critical observer. During the second siege of Limerick the Williamite army crossed the Shannon below Killaloe on a bridge of boats. Colonel Dominick Sheldon with his horse and foot was compelled to retreat to Sixmilebridge, 'a maneuver they executed with great difficulty'. The Jacobite cavalry, unable to find respite at Sixmilebridge, retreated further into Clare.[38] After the surrender of Limerick in October 1691 the Protestant Ascendancy was quickly re-established.

O'BRIENS OF DROMOLAND

Henry, seventh earl of Thomond, resided permanently in England. His agents, men who wielded considerable power, administered his Irish estates. Thomond found it difficult to find suitable agents. There was a succession of stewards on his lands and with virtually no supervision, his estates gradually became run down. Thus began a process whereby Thomond sold off large portions of his lands in county Clare on perpetual leases. In July of 1684 'a lease in reversion of the town of Sixmilebridge' was granted to Sir Donough O'Brien of Dromoland for the sum of £200. O'Brien was to pay a yearly rent of £118 and a fine of £5 on the death of each principal tenant.[39] Donough O'Brien was the largest resident landowner in Clare. Through inheritance and land dealing, he had acquired large estates and was considered the richest commoner in Ireland.[40] From now on the O'Briens of Dromoland would administer the portion of the village that lay west of the Ogarney in the barony of Tulla, while the Ievers' family managed that portion east of the river in the barony of Bunratty.

There is no evidence that O'Brien invested heavily in Sixmilebridge or set about developing its potential in any way. He was apparently satisfied to oversee the tenants and draw a rental income. In 1703, to facilitate the issuing of long-term leases to his tenants, the earl of Thomond commissioned Thomas Moland, the foremost mapmaker of the day, to carry out a major survey of his

family and abstract of the will of Henry Ievers, dated 9 August 1690. **37** Stevens, *A journal of my travels … in Ireland*, abstracted in Ó Dálaigh, *The stranger's gaze*, p. 76. **38** John D'Alton, *King James' Irish army list* (Dublin, 1855), p. 71. **39** PHA, Ms C 27/7, f. 7; NLI, microfilm pos. 4769. **40** Ciarán Ó Murchadha, 'The richest commoner in Clare' in *Dál gCais,* x (1991),

lands. In his survey Moland describes that portion of Sixmilebridge that lay on
the lands of Cappagh:

> On this land stands the town of Sixmilebridge on the south [*recte* west]
> side of the river, consisting of about 20 good tenements and about 32
> cabins; the tenements I compute to be worth about £5 per annum, taken
> one with another, valuing the cabins but at £1 per annum a piece, but
> the place improves everyday.[41]

Moland valued the village at £132. Bearing in mind that O'Brien was paying £118
a year in rent, that left a surplus of just £14 and shows that the settlement had not
increased in size since O'Brien first leased Sixmilebridge in 1684. In population
terms, if each dwelling contained five or six people, the population on the west
bank would have amounted to about 300 people; unfortunately we have no way
of knowing the number of houses that lay in Ieverstown east of the river.

Mills continued to operate on the Ogarney. On the lands of Lower Cappagh
south of the village. Moland records 'a dwelling house thatched, an orchard, two
corn mills, a tuck mill and about four cabins'.[42] Tuck mills were used for the
compacting of woven fabric. The reference shows that the textile industry had
already taken root in the locality. As early as 1675 John Reddan was granted a
lease of 'a tenement and a tucking mill in Sixmilebridge'.[43] Reddan later assigned
his lease without permission to John Ievers and the issue subsequently became
the source of a dispute between Ievers and Sir Donough O'Brien. In 1695
O'Brien ordered that 'the tucking mill, bridge and mill dam' be pulled down.
The day following, Ievers confronted O'Brien's agent 'swaggering and threatening what he would do to James McDonnell and those that broke down his
dam'.[44] The issue was still not settled by 1707 when the parties resorted to law.[45]
The Ogarney proved so convenient for milling there was no shortage of individuals willing to invest in the industry. Henry Bridgeman of Woodfield proposed to take the tuck mill in 1714. Complaining at the rent O'Brien was seeking, he pointed out that 'the house and mill races are at present of little value
and will require a great charge and time to render them tenantable'. Bridgeman
eventually offered £22 10s. rent with liberty to improve the premises and a war-
ranty against John Ievers.[46] In the same year Richard Lillis proposed to construct
a gristmill on the river. The building was to be 60 feet long by 18 feet broad.
Stone and timber with 55 labourers to serve the masons at 6d. per day, were estimated at a cost of £89.[47]

By 1717 Sir Edward O'Brien, grandson of Donough, had inherited the
Dromoland estate. Edward, a man who lived a lavish lifestyle, was anxious to

pp 7–13. **41** PHA, Ms 9342, abstracted in Ó Dálaigh, *The stranger's gaze*, p. 87. **42** Ibid.
43 Ainsworth, *Inchiquin manuscripts*, p. 642, no. 1890. **44** Ibid., p. 632, no. 1869. **45** Ibid.,
p. 642, no. 1890. **46** Ibid., p. 116, no. 375. **47** Ibid., p. 559, no. 1550.

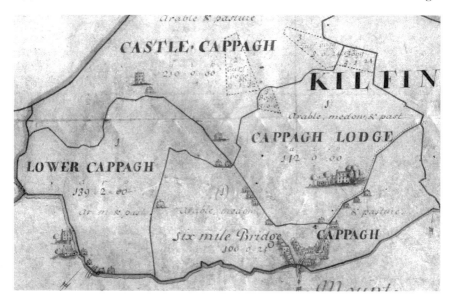

Figure 2 Thomas Moland's map of 1703, showing the portion of Sixmilebridge on the west bank of the Ogarney. No village church is recorded. However, note the buildings with mill wheels that front onto the river in Lower Cappagh. Cappagh Lodge was the residence of the Earl of Thomond on his rare visits to Ireland. (Photo: courtesy of Petworth House Archives, West Sussex.)

increase his rental income from Sixmilebridge. In 1726 a survey called 'A scheme of Sixmilebridge' was carried out.[48] The scheme records the properties of the village, the names of current and former tenants, the legal status of the occupiers and the amount of rent paid. It is a valuable survey and tells us much about what was happening in the village.

There were 50 lettings, comprising of 44 houses, seven parks and gardens and the fairs and markets of Sixmilebridge. The tolls of the fairs and markets, valued at £8 per annum, were unlet, signifying that the markets and perhaps the fairs also, did not operate. No less than nine tenements were waste or partly waste or not leased by anyone. Evidently the settlement was not prospering. The number of houses had decreased by eight since Thomas Moland's calculations of 1703. However, the rental income had grown as the value of property increased. The total value of the village was calculated at £180 per year, as opposed to £132 in 1703. With a rent of £124 being paid to the earl of Thomond, the leaseholder was left with a surplus of £56. This, however, represented the maximum rental the village could generate and clearly there were years when O'Brien's profit was much less.

---

48 NLI, Inchiquin MS 14426, 'A scheam of Sixmilebridge', 16 June 1726.

Table 1 Value of Houses in the 'Scheme of Sixmilebridge' 1726.

Values	Over £10	£10–£5	£5–£2	Under £2	Totals
No. of houses	5	6	11	22	44
	11%	14%	25%	50%	100%

The values of the properties are revealing. Five houses were valued at £10 or above per year. These were the most substantial buildings of the village and were leased by John Glew, John Hickie, John Creagh, Henry Bridgeman Esq. and William Fitzgerald Esq. It is unlikely that all these individuals lived in Sixmilebridge. The esquires in particular would have resided in the countryside, while sub-letting their properties in the village. Six tenements were valued at between £5 and £10; these were the better stone-walled slated houses. Eleven dwellings were valued at between £2 and £5; these were the good thatched houses referred to in the survey. And 22 habitations were valued at under £2 per year. These were the mud-walled cabins, sub rectangular or oval in plan, with thatched roofs and no chimneys, where the majority of the inhabitants lived.

Table 2 Racial composition of the tenants of Sixmilebridge 1726.

Race	Irish	Old English	New English	Totals
No. of tenants	40	7	6	53
	75%	13%	12%	100%

The majority of tenants bore the Gaelic surnames of the local hinterland – names like McNamara, McInerhiny, McMahon, Hickie, Henchy, Moloney, Reddan and Flynn. A much smaller group had names that originated with the Anglo-Normans in the twelfth century – Arthur, Roche, Arnold and Fitzgerald. These were families mainly of Limerick origin. The last group was those tenants who bore the surnames of families that had settled in Ireland in the seventeenth century – Spaight, Wilson, Shankey and Ievers. These individuals leased the more valuable properties and were the better off section of the community. Racial origins give a general indication of religious affiliation, Irish and Old English were largely Catholic while New English were Protestant.

A more accurate indicator of religious affiliation was the legal status of tenants. Whether, for example, they were leaseholders or tenants at will. Only Protestants could lease property for longer than 31 years. Protestants tended to lease property for the length of the lives of three named individuals, usually their children. Catholics were generally tenants at will or, if they could afford it, they leased for a period of years, usually 31, the maximum lease period.

Table 3 Legal status of Sixmilebridge tenants 1726.

	No. of tenants	Percentages
Leases for lives	18	36
Leases for years	7	14
Tenants at will	25	50
Totals	50	100

We may infer from the above table that in excess of one third of the tenants were of the Protestant religion and the remainder were Catholic. While Catholics made up the bulk of the population, there is no record of a Catholic place of worship. Maurice Mac Inerhiny, parish priest of Kilfinaghta, Kilmurry and Feenagh, is recorded as residing in Sixmilebridge in 1704.[49] However, it is not until 1734 that we have a reference to a mass house operating in the village. In the O'Brien rental of that year we find that Connor Halluran occupied John Henchy's tenement in 'Mass Lane'.[50] In the penal period Catholics erected simple mass houses where the liturgy was celebrated on Sundays. Mass houses were low, dark, damp buildings, which looked more like elongated cottages than places of Christian worship. It is possible, indeed probable, that Catholics had been allowed establish a mass house in the village prior to 1734, but there is no definite proof. The first Catholic church was not built in Sixmilebridge until 1812.[51]

IEVERSTOWN

John Ievers, the inheritor of Mount Ievers, was an accomplished individual. Appointed high sheriff of the county in 1710, he was elected member of parliament for Clare in 1715. The election, a most controversial one with an electorate of less than twenty voters, was held on his lands at Mount Ievers.[52] John maintained a house on St Stephen's Green, Dublin, and in 1719 was conferred with an honorary doctorate of laws (LLD) by Trinity College, Dublin.[53] John Ievers appears to have resided in the capital for much of the time and in a letter from his agent George Allen at Sixmilebridge, dated 27 September 1724, we gain an insight into the uncertain income of the non-resident landlord:

> I have paid your bill to Mr Davis of £30 5s. I was at Mr Mapleton's house [agent of Mr Disteare] but he was gone to Silver Grove. I sent the man

49 Ignatius Murphy, *The diocese of Killaloe in the eighteenth century* (Dublin, 1991), p. 275, no. 38. 50 NLI, Inchiquin Ms 14427, 'Sixmilebridge rent roll for Michaelmas Gale 1734', no. 51. 51 Ignatius Murphy, *The diocese of Killaloe, 1800–1850* (Dublin, 1992), p. 385. 52 Sheedy, *Clare elections*, pp 52–3. 53 RIA, Ms 3A 39, f. 33, Pedigree of Ievers family.

that was with me after him and this was his answer: Mr Disteare is not yet come home from the county of Cork. Miss Bow paid part of her arrears. I can't get anything from Will Bridgeman but promises. The tenants of Ballyliddane promise to pay next week. If they do not I believe there must be writs sent ... I received since of Dick Fitzgerald £10 11s.1d. on the account of grazing Mogohey. I have not in my hands above £20 so that you have no business to draw on me until after the sessions and Mr Disteare will be at home by that time.[54]

John Ievers failed in his attempt to get re-elected for the county in 1727 and by 1729 had been succeeded by his eldest son Henry.

Henry Ievers was a graduate of Trinity College Dublin. Unlike his father he took an active interest in the development of Ieverstown. One of his more innovative acts was to fix stone plaques on prominent buildings naming the streets and squares on the eastern bank of the Ogarney. His choice of nomenclature leaves us in no doubt as to where his political allegiances lay. The main road from the village towards Limerick, he called Orange Street after the saviour of the Protestant Ascendancy, King William of Orange. The large square of ground, where the fairs and markets were held, he called Hanover Square after the house of Hanover, who then occupied the throne of England. The road, leading north from the village, he named George's Street after the reigning monarch, King George II, and the open piece of ground around the entrance to the mills was labeled Frederick Square. Frederick was the son and heir of George II, who predeceased his father. The plaques, which may still be seen, all bear the date 1733.[55]

About the same time Henry embarked on an ambitious building project. He set about the construction of Mount Ievers Court, a magnificent new mansion, on the site of the old Castle Ievers. The house was built to the design of the Dublin architect John Rothery. Mount Ievers Court, which still stands, is described as the most perfect and the earliest of the tall Irish country houses. Four storeys high, the southern façade is of grey limestone ashlar while the northern façade is finished in faded pink brick. The brick was brought from Holland to Ballintlea by boat in return for rape seed oil. The roof timbers were cut in the oak-woods of Portumna, brought down the Shannon by boat to Killaloe, they were hauled overland to Sixmilebridge. John Rothery was dead by 1736 and the house appears to have been completed by his two sons Isaac and Jemmy.[56]

Near the gates of Mount Ievers, Henry commissioned the construction of an elegant markethouse in the style of Mount Ievers Court. The markethouse was a two-storey structure, arcaded on the ground floor with five windows overhead.[57] In a recent renovation of the building a stone plaque was exposed bear-

54 NAI, Ms M5992, Papers of the Ievers family of Sixmilebridge. **55** 'Sixmilebridge – Orange Street 1733' in *North Munster Antiquarian Journal,* ix (1965), p. 195. **56** Desmond Guinness and William Ryan, *Irish houses and castles* (London, 1971), pp 13–14. **57** RIA, Ms 3A 40A,

ing the inscription: 'Hanover Sq. John Rothery Builder 1733'.[58] The room over the markethouse was the venue for the law courts and in the evening time, when the legal business had been transacted, county balls and soirees were held there for the gentry of the district.[59] Henry was also responsible for the laying out of the enormous square of ground that stretched from the markethouse to the river. The square was perhaps four times the size of the marketplace on the western bank. The fairs and markets of Ieverstown would be held here but, as we shall see, it was also intended that the square would be put to other uses. As occasion required it would function as a parade ground for the parading and marshalling of troops of dragoons![60]

Despite having the finest markethouse in the county, the markets of Ieverstown-Sixmilebridge met with only limited success. The size of the settlement was never sufficient to generate the volume necessary for a regular market. The proximity of Limerick always left Sixmilebridge at a disadvantage. The higher prices available in the city meant that farmers preferred to sell their produce there than under the less attractive conditions at Sixmilebridge. In 1757 Mr Francis Kent was employed as clerk of the Ieverstown markets. The tolls, he collected, were paid in kind rather than money and appear to have been quite small. The tolls taken between October 1757 and January 1758 were two barrels of potatoes, one bushel of barley, 22 pottles of oats[61] and a box of seed potatoes.[62] For a market to succeed it needed the constant and energetic supervision of its owner. We get the impression that this was not the case at Mount Ievers. In February of 1757 as Henry Ievers was leaving for Dublin, he left a list of duties for his steward Mr Ryan to carry out. Included in the list was the instruction that the housemaids were to have the toll of the market every Saturday, the milk of the cow and whatever sustenance was necessary for their support. On his return Henry was informed that Ryan was continually drunk, that he sat beside the kitchen fire all day and took not the least care of the eight men he had working about the house.[63]

Fairs were more easily organised than markets. While markets required infrastructure and regularity, fairs were seasonal and required little by way of organisation. Some of the largest fairs in the county were held in Sixmilebridge. The most successful was the one held annually on 5 December, which was noted as an end-of-year sale for fat cattle. The Ievers, however, did not own this fair. It was held under the patent issued in 1618 to Donough, fourth earl of Thomond, and was the property of the O'Briens of Dromoland.[64]

ff 252–3, Map of Sixmilebridge, *circa* 1760.   **58** Personal comments of Michael McNamara, Jamaica Inn, Sixmilebridge.   **59** M.S.I., *Glimpses of Mount Ievers past* (Limerick, 1929), p. 11. **60** Ibid., p. 15.   **61** Half gallon measure for liquid and grain, equal to 2.273 litres.   **62** NAI, Ms M5992, Markethouse tolls taken by Francis Kent, 29 January 1758.   **63** NAI, Ms M5992, Instructions to Ryan, 3 February 1757.   **64** *Report of the commissioners appointed to inquire into the state of fairs and markets in Ireland*, HC 1852–3 (1674), xli, p. 66.

HENRY IEVERS AND THE CLARE DRAGOONS

The Ievers' family was noted for its interest in soldiering and military affairs. As early as January 1715 John Ievers sent a letter to Sir Donough O'Brien concerning proposals to be conveyed to government about the building of a barracks for soldiers at Sixmilebridge: 'The barracksmaster would have no difficulty in getting hay, straw and firing; the district is convenient and healthy.'[65] The plan appears to have come to nothing but his son Henry Ievers in the course of building Mount Ievers Court, included accommodation for the billeting of two troops of dragoons.[66] Henry was colonel in chief of the Clare Dragoons and in 1744 was appointed commissioner of array for county Clare.[67] The Clare Dragoons were a cavalry regiment raised to maintain the security of the Protestant Ascendancy of the county. As commissioner of array, Colonel Ievers was required to record the number of Protestants, between the ages of sixteen and sixty, fit to carry arms in the several baronies of the county. The Protestants of the barony of Bunratty assembled at Ieverstown. On such occasions the huge market square became a parade ground where the male Protestants of the barony were arrayed and regimented.[68] In times of tension the regiment was called upon to do its duty. As, for example, during the Jacobite scare of 1744 when a French invasion seemed imminent, the houses of Catholics were searched for arms and priests – and the mass houses were locked and nailed up.[69]

Henry Ievers overspent his inheritance not just on building projects, but on election campaigns and playing at soldiers. The interior of Mount Ievers Court was never completed. One can still see on the first landing where the money ran out and windows were left unpanelled and walls unplastered. The building has been called 'a tall house with tall notions'.[70] Henry furthered encumbered the estate with a sum of £3,000, which he left as a legacy to his second son Henry Morton and his two daughters Jane and Anna.[71] His eldest son, Colonel John Augustine Ievers, succeeded only to a remnant of the inheritance that should have been his. John Ievers did not reside at Mount Ievers. He was colonel of the 30th Regiment of Foot and served for thirty-eight years in the British army. He fought in the American War of Independence and in 1775 was badly wounded at the battle of Bunker Hill.[72] While recuperating in England, Ievers issued a recruiting poster inviting volunteers to join his regiment, which was soon to be quartered in 'the plentiful and flourishing Kingdom of Ireland'. Recruits were assured that provisions in Ireland were extremely cheap: beef and mutton at 2*d*. a pound and

65 Ainsworth, *Inchiquin manuscripts*, p.124, no. 396.   **66** M.S.I., *Glimpses of Mount Ievers past*, p. 7.   **67** RIA, Ms 3A 39, f. 33, Pedigree of Ievers family.   **68** NAI, Ms M5992, Newspaper advertisement for Co. Clare Commissioners of Array, 7 November 1756.   **69** William P. Burke, *Irish priests in the penal times* (Waterford, 1914), p. 409.   **70** Frank O'Connor, *Leinster, Munster and Connaught* (London, 1950), p. 219.   **71** RIA, Ms 3A 39, f. 241, Abstract of the will of Henry Ievers, dated 9 March 1752.   **72** Ibid., f. 33.

vegetables of all kinds, 'in such profusion that for one penny as much may be bought as will serve six men'. Young men would be encouraged to exercise their respective trades and when discharged would be entitled to set up as manufacturers and artificers in any town in Britain or Ireland.[73] There is, as we shall see, evidence to suggest that old soldiers, when they were discharged from Ievers' regiment may have settled in Ieverstown and Sixmilebridge.

Without investment and with the near permanent absence of the proprietor, the settlement of Ieverstown went into rapid and long-term decline. The markets were abandoned and by 1807 the markethouse had been unroofed.[74] Unoccupied for long periods of time, the upkeep of Mount Ievers Court proved to be beyond the family's resources. In 1806 the Revd Daniel A. Beaufort in one of his tours through Munster refers to Sixmilebridge: 'a small and very poor village, near which is a fine but now ruinous seat of Mr Ievers called Mount Ievers'.[75]

SIR EDWARD O'BRIEN, TENANTS AND RENTAL INCOME

The O'Briens made nothing like the investment of the Ievers in Sixmilebridge. No markethouse was ever built or grand scheme laid out on the west bank of the Ogarney. Perhaps motivated by the developments taking place in Ieverstown, Sir Edward O'Brien appointed William Spaight his new agent in Sixmilebridge in 1749. O'Brien expressed the hope that together they would be able 'to new model this town and if not make it equal to Westminster, we will to Tumgrany'. He directed Spaight to advertise the lettings of tenements and gardens and to 'be sure to have an eye to Protestant tenants and the linen manufacture, which nature designed this town for'.[76] Spaight apparently had only limited success in attracting tenants and building new houses. In 1761 Sir Edward accused him of committing 'depredations' and that by his actions, he had been 'the bane and destruction' of Sixmilebridge. In reply Spaight pointed out that under his management several new houses had been built and the rents had increased by over £30 pounds a year.[77] Nevertheless O'Brien was clearly unhappy with the progress of the settlement. The rental income was insufficient to cover his expenses and pay the £124 due yearly to the earl of Thomond. His account with the Thomond estate was then over £1,000 in arrears.[78] O'Brien's rent from the village depended on harvests and good weather and tended to vary from year to year. In 1737 he received £167 in rent, this had fallen to £142 by 1748 before rising to £164 in 1757 and to £185 in 1764. Thereafter it fell back to £166 in 1767 before rising substantially again in the final decades of the cen-

73 M.S.I., *Glimpses of Mount Ievers past*, p. 33. **74** Hely Dutton, *Statistical survey of county Clare* (Dublin, 1808), p. 173. **75** RCB Library, Ms 49, f 22, Daniel A. Beaufort, Irish travels, Galway to Clare, 1806. **76** Ainsworth, *Inchiquin manuscripts*, p. 161, no. 536. **77** Ibid., pp 176–7, no. 591. **78** Ibid.

tury.[79] An examination of the rentals for selected years shows that, while the size of the village was slowly increasing, there was a large turnover of tenants.

Table 4 Rents of Sixmilebridge, 1726–1823.[80]

Year	No. of tenants	Yearly rent		
		£	s.	d.
1726	50	18	1	6
1737	57	167	5	2
1795	46	264	17	8
1823	79	440	0	10

It is not until the 1790s that the village began to show a significant profit in terms of rental income. By then the value of property had increase several fold. The number of tenants actually decreased in 1795, but it should be borne in mind that only the names of the principal tenants appear in the rentals and several of these would have sublet to under tenants. Thirty-six different surnames are recorded in the 1726 rental and 47 in the rent roll of 1823. However, only 16 of the surnames of 1726 re-occur in the 1823 rental, showing that in the near one hundred year period, there was almost a 60 per cent turnover of tenants. The surnames that re-occur are Carthy, Creagh, Farrell, Fitzgerald, Griffy, Henchy, Hickey, Hogan, Ievers, McInerney, McMahon, McNamara, Moloney, Reddan, Spaight and Wilson. These were the quintessential names of Sixmilebridge. Why did so many people leave? Lack of economic opportunity is the most likely answer. With Limerick and Ennis having undergone economic transformation, there were clearly better opportunities at these centres than in rural Sixmilebridge.

Table 5 Ethnic origins of O'Brien tenants, 1726–1823.[81]

Race	Irish	Old English	New English	Totals
No. of tenants: 1726	40	7	6	53
Percentages	75	13	12	100
No. of tenants: 1823	50	11	18	79
Percentages	63	14	23	100

The racial composition of the tenants changed over the hundred-year period. The number of tenants with Irish names increased in real terms but decreased proportionally. The number of tenants with Limerick names decreased but were

79 Ibid., p. 567, no. 1563.   **80** NLI, Inchiquin Mss 14426 (1724), 14430 (1737), 14800 (1795–1823).   **81** NLI, Inchiquin Mss 14426, 14800.

replaced by the Old English surnames of Morris, Purcell and Russell. What, perhaps, is most surprising was the large increase in tenants with New English surnames. Names like Adlam, Gurnell, Huggart, Miller, Steele and Stenson appear.
In Ieverstown Bethel, Dalton, Hamilton, Hardgrove and Howard are recorded.[82]
Many of these were individuals of modest means some renting properties of £2
and less per year. In all likelihood what we have here are descendants of men
who served in the British army under Colonel John Ievers and who on their
discharge settled in Sixmilebridge.

TEXTILES AND THE LINEN MANUFACTURE

Linen was Ireland's most important manufacturing industry in the eighteenth
century. It was an industry of intensive labour rather than intensive capital. The
cultivation of flax, the spinning of yarn and the weaving of cloth were activities
well suited to rural small holders. The linen manufacture never really prospered
in county Clare and what limited success it achieved was centred on
Sixmilebridge. A spinning school under the Linen Board operated at Mount
Ievers. In 1732 ten looms from Mr Usher of Dublin were delivered to Henry
Ievers. A record of attendance was kept and in June of 1752 four spinners,
Catherine Collins, Honour Shaughnessy, Mary Keating and Anne Brasil successfully completed their courses.[83] Unlike spinning and weaving, bleaching and
finishing linen required mechanisation and capital investment. Consequently
these processes were located in urban centres. Robert Stephenson of the Linen
Board reported in 1760 that 'there is a little being done in the bleaching way by
Thomas Gurnell of Sixmilebridge, who seems to be very industrious'. Gurnell
requested seals of quality from the Linen Board to enable him to make up linens
for inland sale and export.[84] Thomas Gurnell had been one of the tenants introduced to the village by Thomas Spaight. In 1761 Gurnell leased five acres of
ground near the Catholic chapel, which became known as the Bleach Green.[85]
The Gurnells were to be involved in the bleaching of linen for nearly sixty years
and became one of the leading families of Sixmilebridge. Thomas Gurnell died
in 1771 but his widow Mary advertised that she would carry on the business in
his place.[86] James Gurnell succeeded to the concern and in 1782 he married Miss
Hastings of Killaloe.[87] In March of 1801 a Thomas Gurnell announced in the
Ennis Chronicle, that he had surrendered himself for trial for the alleged rape of
Mary McNamara, spinster of Sixmilebridge.[88] Unfortunately, our sources are
silent regarding the verdict of the court. Nevertheless the family business did

82 M.S.I., *Glimpses of Mount Ievers past*, p. 15.   **83** NAI, Ms M5992, Spinning school at
Ieverstown.   **84** Robert Stephenson, *The reports and observations of Robert Stephenson to the
trustees of the Linen Manufacture* (Dublin, 1762), p. 49.   **85** Ainsworth, *Inchiquin manuscripts*, p.
608, no. 1778.   **86** *Waterford Chronicle*, 29 October 1771; *Limerick Chronicle*, 7 May 1772.   **87**
Dublin Hibernian Journal, 19 August 1782.   **88** *Ennis Chronicle*, 5 March 1801.

continue and in 1803 James Gurnell of the Bleach Green, Sixmilebridge, advertised that he would receive linens for processing both at Limerick and Ennis: 'The utmost care (with good hands and best materials) will be taken to finish linens etc. in a proper manner, for all which I will be accountable.'[89]

However, all was not well in Sixmilebridge. Hely Dutton pointed out that while tuck mills operated at Ennis, Killaloe and Ardsollus among other places, not a single mill for the processing of cloth operated on the Ogarney. Linen was woven in bands 27 inches wide (69 centimeters). A piece of cloth might shorten by as much as a third in the milling process. Impressed by the potential he observed at Sixmilebridge, Dutton declared:

> The river Ougarnee... is one of the best calculated I have seen for extensive manufactures; the supply is equal to any expenditure of water, in the mist of a fine corn country ... From Ballymacastle to Six-mile-bridge the fall is so rapid, that there could be a mill erected at every hundred yards.[90]

Economic conditions continued to dis-improve and by 1816 the Sixmilebridge bleach green had ceased to operate. In March of the following year the bleaching business of James Gurnell was totally consumed by a fire, which had been maliciously set.[91] Thus was largely brought to an end the linen manufacture of Sixmilebridge. However, the industry continues to be remembered in the village, because the large open piece of ground in front of the Catholic church is still called the Bleach Green.

TRANSPORT AND COMMUNICATIONS

Being sited on the main road from Limerick into county Clare, many travelers visited Sixmilebridge. Some of these, particularly Protestant clergymen, have left written accounts. The Quaker, William Edmundson, on one of his preaching expeditions, held a large meeting in the village in 1707. Edmundson, who had been jailed a number of times for non-payment of tithes, attracted many people of note, including the parish priest. After the meeting the priest sought out the preacher at the inn, where his horses had been left, to offer his kind regards.[92] Jonathan Swift on his tour of Munster in 1723 is reputed to have stopped at Sixmilebridge. His alleged altercation with the village landlady is too well known to need repeating here and in any event, is more the stuff of legend than of history.[93] The founder of Methodism, John Wesley, rode through the village in 1756 on his way to Ennis. He did not preach himself, but he left his helper, Mr Walsh, to preach to the villagers in Irish.[94]

89 *Clare Journal*, 28 February 1803. **90** Hely Dutton, *Statistical Survey of county Clare* (Dublin, 1808), p. 268. **91** *Clare Journal,* 6 March 1817. **92** William Edmundson, *A journal of the life, travels, sufferings and labours of love in the work of the ministry etc.* (London, 1774), p. 285. **93** See Joseph McMinn, *Jonathan's travels* (Belfast, 1994), p. 82. **94** *The works of the Rev. John Wesley*

Because of its pivotal position in the communications network of the county, Sixmilebridge was the second centre after Ennis to open a post office. Lott McNamara was operating the post in 1734.[95] A letter sent on behalf of Sir Edward O'Brien to the postmistress Mary McNamara in 1752 gives an indication of how postal communications functioned. Miss McNamara was advised that if the bearer of the letters did not overtake the postman in the village that she should immediately send a man and horse away with the letters to Limerick as they were of great consequence.[96] Joseph Miller was appointed postmaster of Sixmilebridge in 1785, the authorities 'having received good testimony of [his] fidelity and loyalty to his Majesty'.[97]

In the 1730s the government, in an effort to improve the quality of the communications between the major urban centres, established a network of turnpike roads. Toll was to be levied on all passenger traffic, except on election days and the money so raised to be used for the upkeep of the roads. In 1733 a Road Act was introduced into the Irish House of Commons for the erecting of toll gates on the road 'from the Galway border at Tubber as far as Ennis and from thence to the towns of Ardsollus, Sixmilebridge and Mount Ievers to the Northern Liberties of Limerick city'.[98] Sir Edward O'Brien along with the other Clare members saw the bill through the House of Commons and Henry Ievers was one of the many trustees appointed to oversee the collection of tolls and the proper maintenance of the road. On the rare occasions that Sixmilebridge was mentioned in the national press it was invariably in connection with the bridge and the road network. In January of 1754 the *Belfast Newsletter,* reporting on the floods that had disrupted the mails from Munster, informed its readers that 'Six-mile-bridge near Limerick and several other bridges in Munster had been carried away or very much damaged'. Similarly in 1763 it was reported that the posts of Limerick, Sixmilebridge and Ennis had not arrived in Belfast 'being delayed by the late great floods in Munster'.[99]

In 1784 a construction project was completed that was to radically alter the course of history of Sixmilebridge. A local landowner, Henry D'Esterre, built a new bridge over the Ogarney at Rossmanagher, about two miles below the village. The bridge, for the first time, allowed Sixmilebridge to be bypassed. By this single act the very reason for the existence of the village had been undermined. The building of the bridge was a defining moment and was to have severe long-term consequences. It was a point well understood by the villagers themselves. In January of 1785, on the ringing of the church bell, three hundred or so people gathered and marched on Rossmanagher bridge. The crowd led by James Gurnell, bleacher, Walter Reddin, butcher and William Connors, publi-

(4 vols., London, 1872), abstracted in Ó Dálaigh, *The stranger's gaze,* p. 110.   **95** NLI, Inchiquin MS 14430.   **96** Ainsworth, *Inchiquin manuscripts,* p. 163, no. 541.   **97** John Mackey and Tony Cassidy, *Introduction to the post offices of county Clare* (Germany, 1989), p. 32.   **98** Sheedy, *Clare elections,* pp 58–9.   **99** *Belfast Newsletter,* 4 January 1754, p. 2; 11 October 1763, p. 2.

can, carried crowbars and sledgehammers to smash down the new bridge. At Rossmanagher, Henry D'Esterre and his brother Cornet D'Esterre of the Light Dragoons confronted the villagers. A number of shots were exchanged before the crowd had to retreat to Sixmilebridge, leaving the bridge intact. Henry D'Esterre subsequently offered a reward of £50 each for the apprehension of the principal ringleaders.[1] The construction of the new bridge was a double blow for the village as it came in the wake of the closing down of the oil mills. The mills were never likely to re-open because the new bridge so restricted the river that boats could no longer reach Ballintlea to discharge their cargoes as they had previously done. D'Esterre built a tollhouse at Rossmanagher bridge, which still stands, and levied toll on all horse and pedestrian traffic.

However, his monopoly did not last for long, because another landowner, Thomas Studdert Esq., at his own expense in 1804, erected a large, single span bridge over the Ogarney at Bunratty. Studdert installed a turnpike and levied a penny on foot passengers crossing the bridge.[2] Bunratty was the most southerly crossing point on the river and this new bridge was to make an even greater impact than the one at Rossmanagher. The journey from Limerick to Ennis was considerably shortened. The public traffic generally abandoned the circuitous route by Cratloe and Sixmilebridge and used the Bunratty-Newmarket route instead – the one that is still in use today.

Sixmilebridge had been bypassed for some twenty years when Hely Dutton visited the place in 1807. Not surprisingly he found the village disheartened and in general decline:

> Sixmilebridge was formerly of some note, but is now in a rapid decline; it has the skeleton of a beautiful market-house, the ruins of an oil mill and an extensive flour-mill almost in ruins and quite idle, but I understand it is likely to be at work soon.[3]

The first horse-drawn public transport service opened between Limerick and Ennis in 1809. The coaches, drawn by four horses, initially went via Cratloe and Sixmilebridge and took five hours to complete the relatively short journey. The service was carrying the mail by 1815. It is not possible to say exactly when the mailcoach ceased calling at Sixmilebridge. But in 1834 when the Limerick-Ennis Mail Coach Service was extended to Galway, a service inaugurated by Charles Bianconi, the coach ran by Bunratty and Newmarket-on-Fergus only, and by then the Sixmilebridge route had long been abandoned.[4]

1 *Limerick Chronicle*, 17 January 1785, see also David Lee and Christine Gonzalez, *Georgian Limerick, 1714–1845* (Limerick, 2000), p. 288.   2 Paul Duffy and Etienne Rynne, 'Studdert's Bridge, Bunratty' in *North Munster Antiquarian Journal*, xxxvii (1996), pp 107–11.   3 Hely Dutton, *Statistical Survey of county Clare* (Dublin, 1808), p. 173.   4 Patrick F. Wallace, 'The organisation of pre-railway transport in counties Limerick and Clare' in *North Munster*

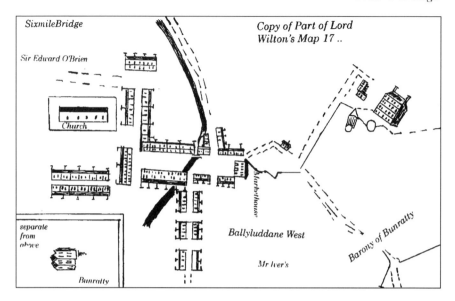

Figure 3. Lord Wilton's map of Sixmilebridge, *c.*1760 as drawn by T.J. Westropp in 1911. The village centre is depicted much as it is today. Note the church without bell tower and the arcaded markethouse. A sentry box stands in the grounds of Mount Ievers Court. Portion of the house-block that obstructs the road to Bunratty has since been removed. (Photo: courtesy of Royal Irish Academy.)

In marked contrast with the eighteenth century very few visitors came to the village in the nineteenth century. One of the few who did was the English member of parliament, John Manners, who attended the Sixmilebridge Petty Sessions in 1846. According to Manners every other house in the village was in ruin.[5] The settlement by then had become a backwater and was to remain so for much of the nineteenth century.

RELIGION AND EDUCATION

As he journeyed through Sixmilebridge in 1752, Bishop Pococke noted the 'handsome new church' that had been built for the Protestant community.[6] The church was a plain rectangular stone structure without a bell tower. It had round headed windows and a slated roof. A glebe house for the minister was located

Antiquarian Journal, xv (1972), pp 44–5. **5** Lord John Manor MP, *Notes of an Irish tour in 1846* (Edinburgh, 1881), abstracted in Ó Dálaigh, *The stranger's gaze*, p. 210. **6** John McVeagh (ed.), *Richard Popcocke's Irish tours* (Dublin, 1995), abstracted in Ó Dálaigh, *The stranger's gaze*, p. 107.

on the Kilkishen road.[7] The Catholic place of worship had been upgraded from a mass house to a chapel. Both Protestant church and Catholic chapel were said in 1764 to be in good repair.[8] About 1780 another Catholic chapel with thatched roof was built on the east side of the river.[9] This building was to cater for the Catholics of the parish of Kilfintenan, which formed part of the diocese of Limerick. A new parish priest, Cornelius Clune, was appointed to Sixmilebridge in 1808, in succession to Patrick Davin, who had been made parish priest of Ennis.[10] It was Father Clune who, in 1812 on a new site, built the Catholic church that is still in use in the village today. Reflecting the poverty of the congregation, the structure was thatched with a mud floor and small windows with brick surrounds.[11]

In the religious census of 1764 the parish of Kilfinaghta was recorded as having 175 Protestants and 952 Catholics or a ratio of Catholics over Protestants of 5:1.[12] The census was carried out by the Protestant clergy and is likely to have understated the number of Catholics in the parish. In 1820 the incumbent clergyman, William Miller, estimated the number of Protestants in the union of Kilfinaghta and Kilseily at 260 and the overall population at 6,000 or a ratio of Catholics over Protestants of 22:1, which was a considerable increase on the 1764 figure.[13] It was not until 1835, after the government census of 1831, that the actual numbers of both congregations could be accurately established. There were then in the parish of Kilfinaghta 99 Protestants and 4,032 Catholics or a ratio of Catholics over Protestants of 41:1.[14] There was one service in the Protestant church every Sunday with an average attendance of 50. By contrast there was an average weekly attendance of 800 at the Catholic church.[15] Nonetheless, the Church of Ireland clergy still entertained the hope that the Catholic population could be converted to the Established Church. Reporting to his bishop in 1820 that the numbers of his congregation had fluctuated, the Revd Miller expressed his belief that the rising generation would greatly increase Protestant numbers. His optimism was based on what he perceived to be the potential of the educational system. 'No project, he declared, 'can be so conducive to the welfare of the country as the establishment of schools for the gratuitous education of the children of the lower orders, under the care of Protestant teachers and the inspection of Protestant clergymen'.[16]

The report of Mr Miller to his bishop, the newly appointed Dr Walter Mant in 1820, provides much information on the organisation of the parish. Services

7 RIA, Ms 3A 40A, ff. 252–3, Map of Sixmilebridge, *circa* 1760.   **8** British Museum, Add. Ms 39269, f. 270, Materials for a history of Clann Cuilein; NLI, microfilm pos. 1061.   **9** OS, Placename books of county Clare, parish of Kilfintenan, townland of Ballyliddane West; NLI, microfilm pos. 1017.   **10** Murphy, *Diocese of Killaloe, 1800–50*, pp 429–30.   **11** Ibid., p. 385. **12** British Museum, Add. Ms 39269, f. 270; NLI, microfilm pos. 1061.   **13** NLI, MS 352, Bishop Walter Mant, Abstract of information in answer to queries concerning parishes in the diocese of Killaloe and Kilfenora, 1820.   **14** *First report of commissioners of public instruction, Ireland*, HC 1835 (45), xxxiii, p. 224c.   **15** Ibid., pp 224c–5c.   **16** NLI, MS 352, Vicarages of

were held on Sunday mornings, on Christmas day and at noon on Good Friday. Attendance at church was regular. The congregation consisted largely of landed gentry and 'a few decent trades people'. The Book of Common Prayer was in use, the parishioners were able to read the prayers, but they did not join in the service. Communion was provided once a month and at festivals when there were about thirty communicants. The catechism was taught to 27 children in the church after divine service during the summer months and once a week through the year at the schoolhouse. The annual average of baptisms was two, burials one or two and marriages one. No confirmations had been held in the parish since 1802 and no record kept of the persons confirmed. The old parish register was missing, but the minister promised to procure and retain it. A new register had been commenced in 1800 and was kept in the glebe house. All the Protestants spoke English. The Revd Miller did not know any Irish nor, he said, did any other clergyman in the county.[17]

However, it was in the area of education that Mr Miller's exertions most impressed the new bishop. The parish school was under the patronage of the Association for Discountenancing Vice and Protestant and Catholic children were educated together. Sir Edward O'Brien paid the £3 annual rent. The Protestant teachers James and Eleanor Healy received an income of £26 per year. Twenty-seven Protestant and 24 Catholic children attended. The Protestant children received religious instruction whereas the 'popish' pupils only read the scriptures, though opposed by the parish priest. The progress of the children was great. However, pupil numbers had fallen from 89 to 51 through the opposition of the priest. The minister added that the institution, while acceptable to the lower orders, was not patronised by the gentry.[18]

It is not until the publication of the report of the Irish Education Inquiry of 1824 that the full picture of the education provision becomes apparent. In Sixmilebridge there were 364 children receiving instruction in six schools. Substantially more boys than girls attended classes. The Protestant population had clearly declined. Only nine per cent of the school children were Protestant, which means that Protestants represented only about a tenth of the village inhabitants. This represented a considerable decline in the 100-year period from 1726 when Protestants had made up over a third of the village tenants.

The largest school was held in the Catholic church under the patronage of Father Cornelius Clune. The teacher, Dennis Woulfe, was a well-known Gaelic poet and scholar. Several of his compositions are extant. Perhaps his most famous work was his translation into English of Brian Merriman's masterpiece, *Cúirt an Mheon-Oíche*. In one of his poems Dennis expressed his desire to emigrate to Canada and perhaps he did, because after 1826 his pen falls silent.[19] By contrast Patrick Slattery remained in Sixmilebridge. He established a considerable repu-

Kilfinaghty and Kilseily. **17** Ibid. **18** Ibid. **19** Brian Merriman, *Cúirt an Mheon-Oíche*, ed. Liam P. Ó Murchú (Dublin, 1982), pp 84–105.

Table 6 Sixmilebridge schools, 1824.[20]

Teacher	Religion	Income	Building	Value	Pupils	M	F	Protestant
Dennis Woulfe	Catholic	£12	Sixmilebridge chapel	–	110	80	30	00
Patrick Hamilton	Catholic	£10	Ballyliddane chapel	–	90	60	30	01
Ann Armstrong	Catholic	£08	Thatched house	£07	54	00	54	00
James Healy	Protestant	£26	Thatched house	£30	53	32	21	29
Patrick Slattery	Catholic	£15	Thatched house	£14	45	35	10	02
Bridget Carmody	Catholic	£02	Thatched cabin	£09	12	05	07	00
			Totals		364	212	152	32
					100%	58%	42%	9%

tation as a teacher and attracted pupils from far and wide. One of his pupils, Patrick McMahon, who emigrated to Australia, rose to the rank of a colonial magistrate. Returning on a visit to his native village in 1888, he expressed his deep appreciation of the education he had received from Pat Slattery.[21] It should be borne in mind that teachers' income depended on the number and quality of pupils they could attract to their schools. Apart from the Protestant, James Healy, Pat Slattery earned the highest income of any teacher in the village. The girls were catered for in the schools run by Ann Armstrong and Bridget Carmody, but female teachers earned far less than their male counterparts. The school in Ballyliddane chapel was under the patronage of Father James Ryan, priest of the Diocese of Limerick.[22]

LAND UNITS AND THE ORDNANCE SURVEY

With the Ordnance Survey in 1839 we get our most complete picture of the state of affairs in Sixmilebridge. The settlement was spread across three town-lands. The principal part of the village was sited on the townland of Sixmilebridge. This was a newly created unit of 294 acres carved out of the old land division of Cappagh (*Ceapach*, tillage ground). East of the river the name Ballyarilla (*Baile Uí Fhearaile*, Farrell's town) had long been changed to Mount Ievers a townland of 60 acres. South of Mount Ievers lay Ballyliddane (*Baile Uí Roideáin*, Reddan's town) a parcel of 64 acres.[23] The Ordnance Survey abolished the old baronies of Bunratty and Tulla and the three townlands with their respec-tive parishes were placed in the new division of the barony of Bunratty Lower.[24]

20 *Appendix to the second report of the commissioners of Irish education inquiry* (Parocial Abstracts), HC 1826–7 (12), xii, pt. 2, pp 892–5. **21** Bill McInerney, 'A Sixmilebridge emigrant' in *The Other Clare*, viii (1984), pp 7–12. **22** John Begley, *The diocese of Limerick from 1691 to the pre-sent time* (Dublin, 1938), p. 616. **23** OS, Placename books for county Clare, under parishes of Kilfinaghta and Kilfintenan; NLI, microfilm pos. 1017. **24** *Index to the townlands, parishes and baronies of Ireland 1851* (HMSO, Dublin, 1861).

The surveyors described Sixmilebridge townland as follows:

> Proprietor Sir Lucius O'Brien, Dromoland, Newmarket. Agent Robert
> O'Brien Esq. Limerick. Let to 56 tenants, who all have leases of years and
> lives, at the yearly rent of from 40s. to 60s. per acre. County cess from
> 3s. to 4s. per acre yearly. Tithe 10d. to 12d. per acre. Soil loamy, heavy
> clay. Size of farm from 1 rood to 3 acres. Usual crops wheat, oats, pota-
> toes and vegetables. Fuel scarce. Prevailing names Gormans. Two schools
> containing 196 boys and 80 girls, all Roman Catholic. One paid by the
> scholars, the other by Board of Education. Schoolhouse built in 1809 by
> Mr Clune P.P. Chapel slated, built in 1812, can contain 600 persons.
> Church built 1812 [recte, circa 1752] can contain 200 persons. Sessions'
> house built in 1820. A police barracks, a sergeant and 7 sub constables.
> Fair held on the 5 December. No market, no weighing crane here. Milk
> sold daily. A post office in this town, a daily post, no post car runs from
> here. The bridge over the river O Garney in the centre of the town, bat-
> tlements 6 foot in height from road. The river O Garney waters this town-
> land north and east, contains salmon, pike, trout and eels. 125 houses.[25]

Although there were only 56 tenants there were 125 houses showing that a considerable amount of sub-division had occurred. The schoolhouse, built by Father
Clune, accommodated the boys on the ground floor and the girls on the upper
floor.[26] The village had also acquired the instruments of law enforcement; a courthouse had been built and a sergeant and seven constables maintained the peace.
Significantly there was no market or public scales for the weighing of farm produce and while one of the largest fairs in the county was held on 5 December,
there was no public transport to or from the village. On the far side of the river,
Ieverstown contained a much smaller portion of the settlement:

> Proprietor John A. Ievers Esq. Sixmilebridge. Agent none. Let to 42 ten-
> ants whom have leases of years and lives. Yearly rent from £2 to £3 per
> acre ... Size of farm from one half to 18 acres ... Prevailing names Brenans
> ... Paper Mills of Brenan and Company, no paper but lapping manufac-
> tured in it. Mansion house of the proprietor in the east of Sixmilebridge,
> built a hundred years since. 35 houses.[27]

The mills had for a period manufactured paper but this had ceased by 1839 and
the enterprise had switched to the production of textiles. Lapping was fabric

25 OS, Placename books for county Clare, parish of Kilfinaghta, townland of Sixmilebridge;
NLI, microfilm pos. 1017. 26 Murphy, Diocese of Killaloe, 1800–50, p. 314. 27 OS, Placename
books for county Clare, parish of Kilfintenan, townland of Mount Ievers; NLI, microfilm
pos. 1017.

being prepared for further processing. The landowner, John A. Ievers, did not reside in Sixmilebridge but at Killmallock in county Limerick. His agent occupied Mount Ievers Court:

> Mount Ievers House: The residence of William Ievers, agent to James A. Ievers Esq. proprietor. It is 4 storeys high in bad repair, the offices are in a state of dilapidation, an orchard and garden badly kept.[28]

Evidently the condition of the house had not improved since the Revd Beaufort's description of it in 1806. The third portion of Sixmilebridge lay in the townland of Ballyliddane:

> Proprietor John A. Ievers Esq. Agent none. Let to 8 occupying tenants who have leases of years. Rent from 20s. to 30s. per acre yearly ... Size of farm from 1 to 14 acres ... Prevailing names Kinvanes. A Roman Catholic chapel, which could contain about 200 persons, built about 60 years ago, thatched. A school, paid by the scholars of 40 boys and 20 girls all Roman Catholics, established in 1836. Burying lands at Kilavoher for children. Contains ruin of market house of Sixmilebridge. 20 houses.[29]

It is noticeable that the lands on the Ievers' estate, east of the river, were let twenty to thirty shillings per acre less than the lands west of the river. As the land quality is similar, it probably indicates better estate management on the part of the O'Briens. According to the Ordnance Survey there were 180 houses in the village. Allowing between five and six people per house, the overall population was about 1,000 people.

POLITICISING THE COMMUNITY

The long process which familiarised the people with the methods of parliamentary politics commenced with the setting up of the Catholic Association in 1824. By organising the collection of the Catholic rent at church doors, the Catholic clergy were to play a new and vital role in the politicisation process. The first public meeting in Clare to forward a petition in favour of Catholic Emancipation was held in Sixmilebridge in 1826 under the chairmanship of Fatherr Cornelius Clune.[30] The potential of popular parliamentary politics was impressed upon the people with the election of Daniel O'Connell as member of parliament for Clare and the final granting of Catholic Emancipation in 1829. Meetings for the repeal of the union between Ireland and Britain drew vast

28 Ibid. 29 Ibid., townland of Ballyliddane West. 30 Murphy, *Diocese of Killaloe, 1800–50*, p. 72.

crowds in east Clare. In 1841 Fatherr Clune at the head of 10,000 of his parishioners and fortified by the strains of the Sixmilebridge Temperance Band,
marched to the monster meeting at Ardsollus where Daniel O'Connell himself
addressed the crowds.[31] The failure of Repeal did not dint the people's enthusiasm for popular politics. In the aftermath of the Great Famine tenant protection societies were formed to protect tenants against excessive rents and landlord eviction. Supported and organised by the priests, tenant-right organisations
were particularly strong in the Sixmilebridge area. Cornelius Clune, who had
always striven to raise the political awareness of his congregation, passed away
in May 1849 after serving the parish community for forty-one years. Michael
Clune succeeded him.[32]

The extent to which the common people participated in the political process
is observable in an incident that occurred in Sixmilebridge at the general election of 1852. As voting was restricted to those with the required property qualifications, most people could only influence the outcome by persuading or intim-
idating those who could vote. Voters cast their ballot in open court.
Pro-tenant-right voters were wildly cheered, whereas anti-tenant-right voters
were booed and jeered. A group of soldiers was employed to escort eighteen
voters to the Sixmilebridge courthouse, where they were expected to vote for
Crofton Vandelure, the conservative anti-tenant-right candidate. As the party
approached the courthouse they were hissed at and pelted with stones by a hostile crowd. An attempt was made to drag some of the voters away. Under orders
from a magistrate, the soldiers opened fire on the people, killing six and wound-
ing several others, one of whom subsequently died. The incident propelled
Sixmilebridge onto the national stage. Father Clune, who was standing between
the soldiers and the crowd trying to calm the situation, had a narrow escape,
when a bullet went through his hat and grazed his temple. Vandelure lost the
election by only two votes. A subsequent parliamentary inquiry in London
declared the election null and void. A new election was held the following year
when Vandelure again lost by a slender margin.[33]

During the land war of the 1880s priests were to the fore once more in
leading the people. The activities of the Land League under Michael Davitt
received strong support in Sixmilebridge. During the attempted eviction of
the Frost family from their holding at Rossmanagher in 1887, Father Robert
Little, alerted his parishioners by having the church bells of Sixmilebridge,
Kilmurry and Cratloe rung. When the soldiers and police arrived they found
a crowd of 2,000 people waiting and Father Little securely chained to a gate
fixed across the doorway of the house. Eventually negotiations took place
between the priest and the landlord, Mr Henry D'Esterre, which resulted in

31 Ibid., p. 175. 32 Ibid., p. 429. 33 Ibid., pp 236–8; see also Sheedy, *Clare elections*, pp
208–10.

Figure 4. Sixmilebridge, *c.*1900. The photo shows the streetscape west of the river leading to the bridge. The river was unenclosed to allow cattle access to water on fair days.

an agreement and the end of the eviction to the delight of the crowd.[34] Circumstances had changed a great deal from the previous century, when the people had no political voice and when the presence of church and priest were barely tolerated in the village.

POPULATION DECLINE

Between 1821 and 1911 censuses were taken at regular ten-year intervals. Sixmilebridge provided special problems for the enumerators. Because the settlement was spread across three townlands in separate parishes, there was confusion as to what areas should be included in the urban precinct. Added to this was the problem of the absence of a settlement boundary. In some counts both the urban and rural dwellers of the townlands were included in the village population and in others the urban only.

This confusion can be seen in the census returns when, for example, an increase is recorded in the village population in 1891 (see Table 7), when all other indicators show that the population was falling. For the purpose of this survey, therefore, the village of Sixmilebridge will include the urban and rural populations of the townlands of Sixmilebridge, Mount Ievers and Ballyliddane, an area of 415 acres.

34 Ignatius Murphy, *The diocese of Killaloe, 1850–1904* (Dublin 1995), pp 240–1.

Table 7 Population of Sixmilebridge (unadjusted figures), 1841–1911.[35]

Years	1841	1851	1861	1871	1881	1891	1901	1911
Sixmilebridge	1,107	762	637	517	446	454	374	325
Percentages	100	69	58	47	40	41	34	29

What strikes one immediately is the enormity of the fall in the number of people. From a high of 1,491 in 1831 the Sixmilebridge population had fallen to less than a third of that number by 1911. The proportional fall recorded for the parish of Kilfinaghta was even greater and both village and parish recorded declines greater than the county Clare average.

Table 8 Population of Sixmilebridge (adjusted figures), parish of Kilfinaghta and county of Clare, 1821–1911, and population numbers expressed as a percentage of the census of 1821.[36]

	1821	1831	1841	1851	1861	1871	1881	1891	1901	1911
Sixmilebridge	1,092	1,491	1,388	1,107	909	676	597	557	458	444
Kilfinaghta	2,906	4,132	3,801	2,395	1,859	1,590	1,478	1,317	1,172	999
Clare Co. (1000s)	208	258	286	212	166	148	142	125	111	104
Sixmilebridge	100%	137%	127%	101%	83%	62%	55%	51%	42%	40%
Kilfinaghta	100%	142%	131%	82%	64%	55%	51%	45%	40%	34%
Clare county	100%	124%	137%	102%	80%	71%	68%	60%	53%	50%

While the county population declined by 64 per cent, based on the 1841 figure, the decline in the village and parish populations was 68 per cent and 74 per cent respectively. Why Sixmilebridge should have suffered more that the rest of the county is difficult to say. The village is set among some of the most fertile lands in county Clare. A general malaise appears to have settled on the village in the second half of the century and while the proximity of Limerick and the bypassing of the settlement contributed to the decay, a lack of industry on behalf of the inhabitants must also have played a part.

Table 9 Sixmilebridge, number of houses and average number of persons per house.[37]

Years	1821	1831	1841	1851	1861	1871	1881	1891	1901	1911
Population	1,092	1,491	1,388	1,107	909	676	597	557	458	444
Houses	193	229	255	245	217	162	154	142	109	113
Persons per house	5.7	6.5	5.4	4.5	4.2	4.2	3.9	3.9	4.2	3.9

35 *Censuses of Ireland, 1841–1911.* **36** *Censuses of Ireland, 1821–1911.* **37** Ibid.

The number of houses in the village was 193 in 1821; this had risen to 255 by 1841 before falling gradually to 113 by 1911. The housing stock certainly improved over the period with the disappearance of the worst of the mud cabins and the concentration of the majority of people in stone-walled, slated houses. With the decreasing population, the occupancy rate of dwellings also fell, from an average of six persons per house in the 1830s to less than four per house by 1911.

However, it is not until one compares Sixmilebridge with the other urban centres of the county that the full extent of its deterioration becomes apparent. In 1821 the settlement, in terms of its size, was ranked fourth in the county behind the towns of Ennis, Kilrush and Ennistymon. By 1841 Sixmilebridge had been overtaken by Killaloe, Newmarket-on-Fergus, Miltown Malbay, Tulla and Kilkee. Ten years later Corrofin, Scarriff and Clarecastle had larger populations than Sixmilebridge. In 1871 it was overtaken by Kiladysert and was ranked thirteenth in the county. In fact of the fifteen most populous settlements in county Clare, the only two not to overtake Sixmilebridge in the course of the nineteenth century were Kilfenora and Liscannor.[38] The Sixmilebridge experience was unique; no other centre in the county suffered the severity of the demographic decline experienced by Sixmilebridge.

RAILWAYS AND TRADE DIRECTORIES

The Limerick to Ennis railway line, which had been six years in building, opened for business in 1859. To facilitate the laying of the railway line, three high stone bridges were built over the main Limerick road between Sixmilebridge and Cratloe. The bridges constricted the road by forming three difficult bends for traffic to negotiate. Six trains, four passenger and two goods trains, stopped daily at the Sixmilebridge railway station. In 1868 the railway company introduced a 'market class' ticket, which was one and a half times the price of the single third-class fare. The purpose of the ticket was to encourage country people to sell their produce and purchase goods at the Limerick markets. The Sixmilebridge station prospered and in 1872 the siding was extended and a goods store erected.[39] On fair days special cattle trains operated from the village, which ended the drudgery of driving animals over long distances by road. However, the railway was also to have an effect unintended by its originators. In the wake of the Famine, as people fled farmland and abandoned agriculture, there was a staggering fall in population levels. The coming of the railway merely accelerated the emptying of Sixmilebridge. The daily trains carried the people to the emigrant ships at Limerick, Galway, Dublin and Queenstown.[40]

The trade directories that were published at the time provide, perhaps, the best picture of what was happening in the village. Trade directories are impor-

38 See appendix 1. **39** Michael McNamara, 'The Ennis and Limerick Railway' in *Sixmilebridge Parish Magazine*, 4 (1994), pp 3–8. **40** Ibid., p.7.

Figure 5. Sixmilebridge railway station in the 1950s. The sidings were for parking
rolling stock to enable trains to pass on the mainline. (Photo: courtesy of National
Library of Ireland.)

tant because they list the skills that were concentrated in a particular settlement.
They show the trends over a period, whether trade was expanding or contract-
ing and they allow comparisons to be made between one centre and another.
Viewing the trades and services, there was not in Sixmilebridge, with the single
exception of the woollen manufacture, any specialised skills that were not available in most other centres of the county (see Table 10).

The precipitous fall in the number of village enterprises is immediately apparent, from a high of sixty-nine in 1839 the number had fallen to twenty-two by
1905. The decrease reflects not only a diminishing skill pool, but also the serious drop in population levels. The appearance of an emigration agent in the village in 1886 shows that migration was then at its height. However, on the positive side, over the seventy-six-year period of the survey, the fall in population
corresponded with an improvement in the quality of village life. The reduction
in the numbers of weavers, the most common occupation in 1839, is allied in
subsequent years with an increase in tailors and dressmakers, showing that the
quality of village dress improved. In 1870 the first draper is recorded in the village. Similarly the increase in the number of butchers from one in 1839 to four
in 1870 shows that meat became a much more significant element in the village
diet. The drop in the number of shoemakers from twelve in 1839 to just one in

Table 10 Trade directories of Sixmilebridge, 1839–1905.

	1839[41]	1870[42]	1886[43]	1905[44]
Bakers	0	1	0	1
Blacksmiths	7	5	3	2
Butchers	1	4	4	1
Car owners	0	2	0	0
Carpenters	3	4	5	1
Coopers	3	1	0	0
Draper	0	1	0	0
Dressmakers	0	3	0	0
Emigration agent	0	0	1	0
Grocers	5	6	15	3
Lodging houses	3	0	0	0
Mason	1	0	0	0
Nailers	1	1	0	0
Painter	0	1	0	0
Publicans	11	6	3	9
Sawyer	1	0	0	0
Shoemakers	12	9	7	1
Shopkeepers	6	3	0	2
Tailors	1	3	4	0
Weavers	13	3	0	0
Wheelwright	1	0	0	0
Woollen manufacturers	0	2	2	2
Totals	69	55	44	22
	100%	80%	64%	32%

1905 probably reflects the penetration of factory made footwear into the village. The survey, if anything, overstates the number of individuals engaged in commerce as several traders engaged in more than one activity. In 1870, for instance, John O'Halloran is recorded as being both a grocer and a shoemaker. Similarly in 1870 James Flynn was a grocer, draper, corn miller and woollen manufacturer. The recording of fifteen general grocers in Sixmilebridge in 1886 is clearly an over-statement. In previous surveys they are entered as either shopkeepers or publicans. In 1905 many shopkeepers combined the trade of grocer with that of publican. Indeed by 1905, with nine public houses in the village, the trade of publican was the most numerous occupation of Sixmilebridge.

41 OS, Placename books for county Clare, under parishes of Kilfinaghta and Kilfintenan; NLI, microfilm pos. 1017. **42** *Slater's Royal National Commercial Directory of Ireland* (1870), pp 209–10. **43** *Guy's Postal Directory of Munster* (Cork, 1886), pp 828–9. **44** *Kelly's directory of Ireland* (London, 1905), ii, p. 381.

CONCLUSION

Today's visitor to Sixmilebridge is immediately struck by the open spaces and the dispersed nature of the settlement. The houses spread unevenly from the high ground in the west, across the river, to the low ground in the east. Few of the street frontages are regular and there are many voids. The pattern is the legacy of the particular history of the village. Largely neglected by its proprietors, the house building was haphazard and disorganised. Even when there was direct intervention by the landlord, as when Henry Ievers built the markethouse and laid out the parade ground, the scale was altogether too large, the village was never likely to attain the levels of prosperity envisaged. Measured against the grandiose schemes of its landlord, the village, even when it was doing well, always appeared to be under-achieving.

The original site, while it suited the purposes of the founders in the early seventeenth century, was not well chosen. The settlement was set too far back from the Shannon to take advantage of the trading opportunities presented by the estuary and it would always be vulnerable to being bypassed. Moreover, being in the shadow of Limerick, the larger centre would invariably prosper at the expense of its smaller neighbour.

Nevertheless Sixmilebridge is one of the few centres in Clare that can boast of an industrial heritage. Mills operated on the Ogarney from the early seventeenth century right up until the twentieth century. But they rarely flourished. Operations on the river were erratic. They were of small scale and with one notable exception, rarely amounted to anything more that short lived family enterprises.

The railway has left the village with a strange legacy. Between Sixmilebridge and Cratloe, three railway bridges constrict the road. Objected to at the time of their building for their narrowness, the bridges have restricted traffic on the main Limerick road for more than a century. With the burgeoning motor traffic of recent years, the problem has become particularly acute. The principal route out of the village remains a narrow, winding, secondary road and has done much to impede economic progress.

In the first half of the twentieth century the Sixmilebridge Woollen Mills, under the proprietorship of the O'Flynn family, was the only bright spot in an otherwise bleak landscape. Eighty people were employed during World War I producing blankets and khaki for the British army. One hundred and fifty workers with a weekly payroll of £350 were employed during World War II. Unfortunately the introduction of synthetic fibers in the post-war era put the plant under increasing pressure and the mills finally closed in 1959.[45] By then

45 Clare County Library, 'Sixmilebridge history, 1659–1995' (source book compiled by Linda Commane, Tina Talty, Mary McNamara and Brid O'Gorman in association with FÁS, 1996), pp 220–8.

the Shannon Free Airport industrial zone was in operation and many villagers found employment there.

Today Sixmilebridge is a vibrant and prosperous place. A large influx of people in recent decades has transformed the village. The most recent census recorded a population of 1,751 people, the highest ever achieved.[46] Sixmilebridge has become part of the commuter belt between Shannon Airport and Limerick city. The village, in addition, is known nationally for its prowess in hurling. Having won many county championships over the years, the Sixmilebridge hurling team won the All Ireland Senior Hurling Club Championship in 1996, a notable achievement. Much of the social and cultural life of the village today revolves around the hurling club. Sixmilebridge is a village with an interesting past, but more importantly, it is a place that has a bright and promising future.

APPENDIX I

Ranking of Clare towns and villages according to population, 1821–1911[47]

Population	1821	1831	1841	1851	1861	1871	1881	1891	1901	1911
Ennis	6701	7711	9319	8623	7175	6503	6307	5460	5093	5472
Kilrush	3465	3996	5071	9267	4902	4424	3805	4095	4179	3666
Ennistymon	1369	1430	2089	1741	1454	1411	1331	1200	1223	1204
Sixmilebridge	1092	1491	1107	762	639	517	446	454	374	325
Killaloe	1002	1411	2009	1830	1395	1207	1112	1079	885	821
Newmarket	999	1118	1771	1216	1137	750	618	456	504	521
Corrofin	771	900	909	994	741	639	579	495	393	381
Miltown	600	726	1295	1452	1330	1362	1400	1267	1013	995
Tulla	581	874	1217	1226	1198	861	758	644	592	478
Kilfenora	552	558	621	387	343	294	307	236	219	199
Clarecastle	505	1021	879	892	495	876	790	624	591	538
Kilkee	409	1051	1481	1869	1856	1605	1652	1839	1762	1688
Liscannor	315	506	562	429	394	415	331	286	251	242
Killadysert	293	337	604	440	534	573	560	346	354	340
Scarriff	221	761	656	954	694	734	785	599	593	478

46 *Census of Ireland, 2002*, information supplied by Central Statistics Office, Dublin. **47** *Censuses of Ireland, 1821–1911*.

Ranking	1821	1831	1841	1851	1861	1871	1881	1891	1901	1911	A[48]
Ennis	1	1	1	2	1	1	1	1	1	1	1st
Kilrush	2	2	2	1	2	2	2	2	2	2	2nd
Ennistymon	3	4	3	5	4	4	5	5	4	4	3rd
Sixmilebridge	4	3	9	12	11	13	13	12	12	13	11th
Killaloe	5	5	4	4	5	6	6	6	6	6	5th
Newmarket	6	6	5	8	8	9	10	11	10	8	7th
Corrofin	7	9	10	9	9	11	11	10	11	11	10th
Miltown	8	12	7	6	6	5	4	4	5	5	6th
Tulla	9	10	8	7	7	8	9	7	8	9	8th
Kilfenora	10	13	13	15	15	15	15	15	15	15	15th
Clarecastle	11	8	11	11	13	7	7	8	9	7	9th
Kilkee	12	7	6	3	3	3	3	3	3	3	4th
Liscannor	13	14	15	14	14	14	14	14	14	14	14th
Killadysert	14	15	14	13	12	12	12	13	13	12	13th
Scarriff	15	11	12	10	10	10	8	9	7	10	12th

48 Aggregate ranking of settlements over the survey period.

Pomeroy, county Tyrone, 1800–1960: 'A village perched on an elevation'[1]

AUSTIN STEWART

The origins of Pomeroy village in county Tyrone are uncertain. So too is the early history of many an Irish hamlet, but Pomeroy, more than most, rewards closer consideration. It is renowned as the village with the highest elevation in Ulster and its railway station was the highest in Ireland. Its sense of place differs from most others insofar as it was not built in the townland of Pomeroy. The Protestant parish did not include either the village or the townland of Pomeroy and the Catholic parish of Pomeroy did not include the townland of the same name.[2] It is uniquely a place apart, tucked away in the mountainous terrain of county Tyrone. For generations the village environs have been linked to Rapparee history. The term Rapparee comes from the Gaelic *rapaire*, a sort of pike. It referred to a robber acting alone or as part of an outlaw band who came down from his mountain hideout on a raiding mission. The original Rapparees in south Ulster in the late eighteenth century were dispossessed Catholics who waged a war of attrition against the settlers benefiting from the land confiscations following the 1641 Uprising and the Cromwellian plantation in the 1650s. There are questions about later Rapparee activity, especially that which continued into the early eighteenth century, and whether it ought to be seen as 'representing banditry of the kind found in remote and unpoliced regions throughout early modern Europe'.[3] Nevertheless, the mountains around Pomeroy village were home to many a gallant Rapparee, the most famous of which was Shane Bernagh O Donnelly from Altmore. Two geographical features in the area, namely Shane Bernagh's Chair and Shane Bernagh's Sentry Box are called after him, affirming his dominant place in local folklore.[4]

The village probably did not exist until the end of the eighteenth century, when folk memory recalls that in the late 1780s potatoes were gathered in the

<hr />

1 Quote is taken from the poem, *Sweet Pomeroy*, by P.J. Fox. Fox was a local poet who left Pomeroy for America at the height of the Land League agitation in the 1880s. In the poem Sweet Pomeroy the description of the village in the late nineteenth century remained the reality down to the middle of the twentieth century. **2** *Féach: essays on local history, 1987–1993* (Monaghan, 1999), Introduction. Hereafter *Féach*. The essays originally appeared in the Pomeroy parish newsletter. From the essays, I am grateful to the editor of *Féach*, Séamus Mac Giolla Phádraig, for permission to reproduce in this work two photographs – Pomeroy House and the railway station. **3** S.J. Connolly (ed.), *The Oxford companion to Irish history* (Oxford, 1998), p. 545. **4** Féach, p. 9.

Figure 1 Pomeroy House

field, now the centre of the village, where the Church of Ireland stands.[5] In the seventeenth century a family named Pomeroy acquired an estate of eighteen townlands in the area.[6] These were the first landlords and gave their name to the place. Later the Pomeroys sold their estate to another planter, John Lowry of Fintona. At the end of the eighteenth century the Lowrys built the 'Big House' (Figure 1) and began a major scheme of tree plantation around it. In 1928 a land act enabled the tenants to buy out the estate, and today the Lowrys are long gone. The village of Pomeroy, then, was largely the creation of the Lowry family. This essay traces its development from the uncertain settlement of the early nineteenth century through to the mid-twentieth, when the village assumed the physical and social fabric present today.

LOCATION

Pomeroy village is located in east Tyone (Figure 2) in the townland of Cavanakeeran (*Cábhan an Chaorthain*, hollow of the mountain). The townland of Pomeroy lies a short distance to the east, mostly in the neighbouring parish of Desertcreat. In 1845 the village of Pomeroy was located in the civil parish of Pomeroy.[7] The census returns for the parish in 1831 recorded a population of 7,183, which rose to 8,527 in 1841. They were accommodated in 1,562 houses. The parish consisted of almost 16,000 acres, half of which were described as

5 Ibid.   **6** Ibid.   **7** Samuel Lewis, *The Parliamentary Gazetteer of Ireland*, iii, 1844–45, p. 78.

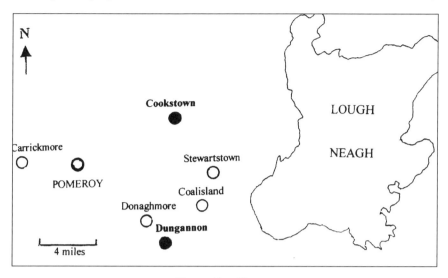

Figure 2 East Tyrone

unprofitable. The village was located on the northwest border of the parish on the Dungannon to Newtownstewart road, lying seven miles west-southwest of Cookstown. The Lowry domain adjoined the village and was officially in the neighbouring parish of Desertcreat. The English traveller, Arthur Young, commented at the end of the eighteenth century on the excellent state of Irish by-roads and how superior they were to their English equivalent.[8] At the beginning of the nineteenth century John McEvoy wrote that very few counties in Ireland could boast of better or more convenient roads than Tyrone.[9] The excellence of the road network did not favour Pomeroy sited on the outskirts of an isolated tract of moor, bog and mountain, which comprised the central region of the county. The environment there was 'wild and repulsive'.[10] An Ordnance Survey memoir in 1834 had already observed that its general appearance was 'bleak and miserable in the extreme'.[11] The same memoir commented that the village consisted of one small street. The houses were built with a 'species of sandstone' available locally and while there were a few slated houses most were thatched. All accommodation was considered 'very bad and dirty'. The memoir pointed out that the village was not likely to improve as the 'tenements are mostly

---

8 A.W. Hutton, *Arthur Young's Tour in Ireland (1776–1779)*, (2 vols. London, 1892), ii, p. 77. **9** John McEvoy, *A statistical survey of county Tyrone 1802*, p. 118. **10** Lewis, *Gazetteer*, p. 78. **11** *Ordnance Survey Memoir*, p. 70. The *Ordnance Survey Memoirs* form a detailed source for the history of northern Ireland just before the Great Famine. They were written in the 1830s to accompany the 6" Ordnance Survey maps and form a veritable nineteenth-century Domesday book offering valuable insights into community life at the time. They document landscape, buildings, antiquities, land holdings, population and employment.

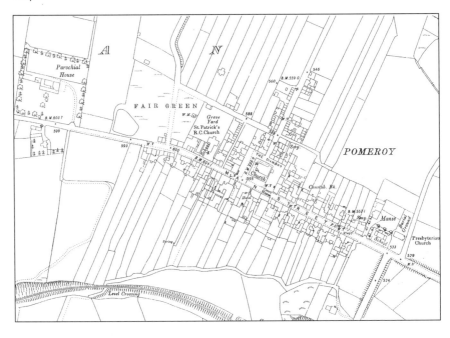

Figure 3 Pomeroy village

held under perpetuity leases by a very poor class of people'. To maintain law and order at this time, four policemen were stationed in the village and petty sessions were held there every fortnight. The heavy police presence did not deter a huge illicit distilling business from thriving in the ten years prior to the Famine. Ready sales of 6*s.* per gallon were the order of the day.[12] To escape the obvious hardship of a rural backwater and a failing cottage linen industry there was huge emigration to America.[13] Many in the village were involved in subsistence farming where the wages of farm labourers ranged from 8*d.* to 1*s.* per day. The hills on the western side of Pomeroy parish had a height above sea level between 570 and 946 feet and formed part of the Altmore mountain range, which included Cappagh mountain, Crannogue, Altmore (great hillock), and Gortnagarn (field of the heaped stones). The derivative meaning of these hills particulary Cappagh (land abundant in tree stumps) and Crannogue (a place covered in trees) convey that they were once densely wooded.[14] Pomeroy nestled in this mountain range giving it the highest elevation of any village in Ulster and the second highest in Ireland after Roundwood in county Wicklow. The village area consisted of twenty-one acres with a population in 1841 of 491 (Figure 3).

12 Ibid., p. 71.   13 Charles Dillon and Henry A. Jefferies (eds), *Tyrone, history and society* (Dublin, 2000), p. 446.   14 P. McAleer, *Townland names of county Tyrone* (Portadown, 1936), p. 31.

There were ninety-one houses. Later in the century Griffith's Valuation in 1859 described the ownership of property in Pomeroy and confirmed that R.W. Lowry was a significant and propertied landlord. Most of the substantial properties in the village were located in The Diamond and ranged in valuation from £8 to £17 and, with one exception, belonged to Lowry. The highest valued building in the village was the Catholic chapel and graveyard on Main Street, valued at £20. Over 90 per cent of houses in the village contained a yard and at least a small garden. There was a Presbyterian meeting-house. The dispensary of the Cookstown Board of Guardians was located in The Diamond as also was the petty-sessions-house. The police-barrack with an office, yard and garden was on Main Street. There were four houses on the Cookstown Old Road that reputedly took in lodgers and another three houses on the back-road. The Protestant church on The Diamond was valued at just over-half that of the Catholic chapel.

LOWRY FAMILY

The coming of the Lowry family to the area was the catalyst that enabled Pomeroy village to develop. In the early part of the seventeenth century the land around Pomeroy was densely forested until 1641 when it was nearly stripped of timber by an absentee landlord who had acquired it from Sir Arthur Chichester during the plantations.[15] Around 1770 the Revd James Lowry (b. 1707), rector of the parish of Desertcreat, decided to replant a great portion of the 556 acres of the domain and his son Robert was the first of the Lowrys to live there.[16] He also bequeathed a sum of money for the building of Pomeroy House, which became known locally as 'Lowry's castle'.[17] In 1750 the Revd James Lowry was granted the right to hold several yearly fairs in Pomeroy and to hold and toll a weekly market in the area every Tuesday.[18] Lowry spent forty-two years as rector of Desertcreat parish and he died in 1786. His eldest son Robert succeeded him at Pomeroy House. Robert (b. 1748) married Elizabeth, daughter of Major William Tighe of Ballyshannon. In his role as landlord he had responsibility for the maintenance of law and order and during the uprising of the United Irishmen he was in charge of a company of sixty-three yeomanry. The inception of the yeomanry had initially the 'happy effect in forcing in the arms' but Lowry was under no illusions that the yeomanry were in effect a 'licentious and undisciplined set of men'. They caused havoc in the county and as a magistrate and Protestant landowner he protested strongly against their activities.[19]

15 *Féach*, p. 101. **16** Ibid. **17** Mona Wylie, 'The Lowrys of Castlecoole and Caledon, a settler family', pp 114–31, in *Dúiche Néill (Journal of the O'Neill Country Historical Society)*, 1992. Wylie gives an excellent survey of the Lowry family pedigree in this article. **18** Ibid., p. 126. **19** Brendan McEvoy, *The United Irishmen in country Tyrone* (Armagh, 1998), p. 61. Originally published as a series of articles in *Seanchas Ard Mhacha* in 1959, 1960–1, and 1969.

Figure 4 Church of Ireland parish church, Pomeroy

Robert and Elizabeth reared a large family of five sons and four daughters. Their second son was Robert William JP, and appointed Tyrone high sheriff in 1812. Born in 1787 he married Anna, eldest daughter of Admiral Samuel Graves and they lived in Pomeroy House. In the early nineteenth century the Church of Ireland parish, Altedesert, was created for the village and Robert William was the first to be interred in the new family vault at Pomeroy. His uncle Armar was made a peer and took the title of Lord Belmore. In the early 1900s the two hotels in the village were called the Lowry Arms and the Belmore Arms.[20] The last named Lowry to live in Pomeroy House was Robert Thomas Graves Lowry, grandson of Robert William. He joined the army and was known locally as the 'Colonel', an honorary title. He never married and on his death in 1947 his sister Mary (Mrs Alexander) succeeded him in the house. When she died in 1951 Pomeroy estate passed to her son, Major Charles Adam Murray Alexander JP, Royal Inniskilling Fusiliers. He died in the early 1950s. In 1958 the Department

20 *Féach*, p. 102.

of Agriculture bought the estate and the house became a forestry school. The maintenance of the house became so costly that it was demolished in 1971, but the forestry school continued.[21]

From the eighteenth century through to the middle of the twentieth century the Lowry family made a vital contribution to the village life of Pomeroy in social, religious and educational matters. The family was responsible for the erection of many buildings in the village and Lt. Col. Lowry reconstructed the old Pomeroy Public Elementary School No. 2 in 1916. John and Armar Lowry built the tower on the Protestant church in The Diamond (Figure 4). Earlier in the century the Lowry family spearheaded an appeal for funds to complete the building of the parish church in 1839. In particular, Robert William Lowry put up £100 to match the contribution of the lord primate so that a church with 200 seats could be roofed.[22] This contribution from Lowry was not insignificant when it is considered that an estimate for the cost of repairs to the roof of Pomeroy House in 1815 came to £100. When the estimate was presented by the builder, William Harloe of Killyman, to Lowry it caused certain dismay because of the expense of a 'new roofing on top of everything else and so many things to do here'.[23] On another occasion when the miller left Mundery mill on the estate, Lowry was relieved when Andrew Trimble came forward to work the mill, and was prepared to repair the miller's house at his own expense.[24] It was also a Trimble who allegedly built the first house in Pomeroy, and this is recorded on his headstone in the Presbyterian churchyard at the bottom of the village.[25] One of the outstanding aspects of the nineteenth century engraving of Pomeroy House is the configuration of the tree-line around the house.[26] Robert William Lowry made concerted efforts to plant new trees on the estate. In 1811 16,200 new trees were planted including larch, scotch, and spruce fir, birch and alder trees.[27] Half that number was again planted in 1815 costing over £15.[28]

Robert William Lowry (called after his father) was the landlord in Pomeroy at the time of the Famine and he was high sheriff of Tyrone in 1849. Like many of his class he did not fully understand the initial distress of local people with the onset of famine. Pomeroy was part of the Cookstown poor law union, an area that extended from the town of Cookstown in the north to Stewartstown in the south, and from Lough Neagh in the east to Pomeroy in the west. When public works commenced in March 1846, mainly in the south and west of the country, there were none in Tyrone. In August 1846 there was almost complete failure of the potato crop and in October that year Pomeroy had its own Famine relief committee. This committee drew up 'lists of distressed persons eligible for employment'.[29] On 2 November an extraordinary presentment sessions of the

21 Ibid., p. 127. **22** PRONI, D/4121/E/2/G/1/3. Papers of Robert William Lowry, 1787–1869. **23** PRONI, D/4121/E/2/C/1/2. **24** PRONI, D/4121/E/2/C/1/1. **25** Féach, p. 9. **26** PRONI, D/4121/E/2/G/1/5. **27** PRONI, D/4121/E/2/B/1/2. Papers of Robert William Lowry 1787–1869. **28** PRONI, D/4121/E/2/B/1/4. **29** Frank Mayes and Aidan

grand jury for the barony of Upper Dungannon met to agree a sum of money to put these 'distressed persons' to work. A crowd gathered outside the Cookstown courthouse thinking that work was going to be disbursed there and then. When it became clear that that was not the case a riot ensued. Robert Lowry found himself in the thick of it. Two men assaulted him and when he tried to escape by a back staircase he came face to face with an old woman 'who with a tremendous oath cursed him for an old villain' accusing him of saying that 'cabbages and turnips were good enough for feeding them and if they did not like that, they must eat grass'.[30] Lowry escaped but no doubt lessons were learned. The following week the presentment sessions agreed that £4,000 would be spent in the barony of Upper Dungannon, which was roughly co-terminous with the Cookstown poor law union. Significantly, Pomeroy's ability to avail of this money was severely curtailed because out of fifteen electoral divisions in the upper barony it had the lowest poor rate valuation, and so received the lowest proportion of the £4,000, less than £100.[31] Early in 1847 matters gravely dis-improved in the parish of Pomeroy. The local clergyman, Alex Stuart wrote '... much distress is now prevailing in the district of the parish of Pomeroy ... every-day presents scenes of distress and misery and the misfortune is the poor not having the money to give for the price of provisions ever so small'.[32] The village itself seemed to cope better than the surrounding countryside as more and more people sought refuge there. During the Famine period the village was one of two (the other being The Grange) small urban settlements in the Cookstown union that actually increased its population.[33]

When Robert William Lowry JP, died in November 1869 it was indeed the end of an era. In a sermon delivered on the occasion of his death, the Revd Thomas Twigg denounced in sorrow the impending disestablishment of the Irish Church by the British government. In contrast, accolades of praise were heaped on the deceased Robert William Lowry. Not alone was he a resident landlord but he was a 'firm supporter of our Protestant religion'. The preacher remembered the time when there was no church in the village and when services were only occasionally celebrated in the schoolhouse. Lowry was truly 'Protestant in his politics and his religion' and neither patronised 'Romish or semi-Romish doctrines and practices'.[34] To the end, this sense of being Protestant both in politics and religion was found in the last male Lowry incumbent in Pomeroy House in the person of Lt. Col. R.T.G. Lowry. In 1935 he opened the new Orange Hall at Donaghmore and proclaimed that the great thing the Orange Institution had done was to bind the Protestant churches together in defence of their lib-

Fee, 'Making sense of the Famine' in *The Bell* no. 6 (Coleraine, 1996), p. 6.   **30** James Glendinning and Frank Mayes 'Public works during the Famine', in *The Bell* no. 6 (Coleraine 1996), p. 39.   **31** Ibid., p. 40.   **32** Quoted by Aidan Fee 'Local Relief Committees', in *The Bell* no 6., p. 56.   **33** Frank Mayes 'The Famine – local population changes', in *The Bell* no 6., p. 82.   **34** PRONI, D/4121/E/2/G/1/11. Lowry Papers 1787–1869.

Table 1 Pomeroy population structure. *Source: Census of Ireland, 1841–1937*

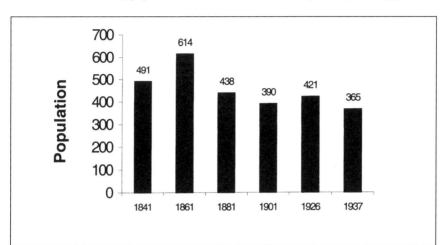

erties and that the present advance of new Orange halls throughout the country was 'a pleasure to behold'. Ending his address he gratified all present by declaring that he would have no truck with de Valera or his rebels.[35] Whatever about this public affirmation of his Protestant tradition R.T.G. Lowry will probably be best remembered in Dublin and at home for his great successes at the Ballsbridge show and sales where it was widely accepted that he made a name for himself and for Pomeroy in the cattle breeding world.[36] It was also during his time that Pomeroy House underwent elegant and extensive renovations and electric light was installed throughout the entire building. The place became a great attraction to the locals with its 'gigantic trees' and beautiful approaches.[37]

POPULATION AND EDUCATION

Despite the Lowry family's commitment to the area as improving and resident landlords, population declined between 1861 and 1937 (Table 1). The population increased by 20 per cent between 1841 and 1861 peaking at 614, a figure that was not to be surpassed until the late twentieth century. Between 1841 and 1901 the population dropped by 21 per cent. Early century saw it increase only to drop down to an all-time low of 349 in 1961 reflecting a 43 per cent fall in population between 1861 and 1961. The 1901 census gives us a snapshot of Pomeroy at the turn of the century. The population then was 390 comprising ninety-two families living in ninety-one houses. The largest percentage of the

---

35 *Tyrone Courier*, 25 April 1935. **36** Ibid., 12 March 1931, 14 March 1935. **37** Ibid., 9 April 1931.

working population (25 per cent) were involved in farming either as farmers, sons and daughters of farmers, farm servants and agricultural labourers. Significant work categories were entrepreneurial/business enterprise (14 per cent), domestic labour (14 per cent), dress makers and seamstress (15 per cent). Skilled workers (13 per cent) comprised mainly tailors, blacksmiths, carpenters and shoemakers. Other work categories, mainly unskilled, comprised 19 per cent. There were seven public houses, three lodging houses and two hotels. There were sixteen shops most of which supplied groceries and provisions. There were three postmen, two drapery merchants, two timber merchants and two bakers. Professions included three national school teachers, one doctor and a creamery manager. Six people out of ten of the village population were under thirty years of age. The dominant religion was Catholic (82 per cent). The Church of Ireland congregation represented 7 per cent, and the Presbyterian community was 10 per cent of the population. There were no Methodists or Baptists.

By the turn of the century 80 per cent of the population of Pomeroy could read and write. Only 10 per cent were illiterate and 10 per cent could read only. Given Pomeroy's location away in the mountainous terrain of Tyrone this was a remarkable high level of literacy. It reflected an exceptional level of school attendance that affected literacy rates resulting in high reading levels reached on school exit. It also reflected the high premium Pomeroy people put on education from early in the nineteenth century. Being literate, regettably, too often meant neglect of the native tongue. Between 1851 and 1911 the number of Irish speakers in Tyrone fell by 25 per cent.[38] The census returns for the Pomeroy area in 1911 recorded 52 resident native speakers of Irish. Altmore, two and a half miles from Pomeroy and celebrated for its Rapparee history, recorded 18 native speakers of Irish out of a total population of 1,200 (less than 2 per cent).[39]

The Commissioners of Irish Education reported in 1824 that there were six 'pay schools' in the vicinity of Pomeroy at Glenbeg, Galbally, Mullinagore, The Rock, Corracroar and Pomeroy itself. Four of the schools had Catholic schoolmasters, even when supported by the proselytising London Hibernian Association and the Kildare Place Society.[40] Of the children who attended these schools over two-thirds were Catholic. In Pomeroy, at the bottom of the village on the Lowry estate a Protestant called Alexander Lemon held his school in a 'thatched cabin'. With a little help from R.W. Lowry and the Revd Graham his annual wages came to £11.14s.1d. There were more than a hundred children on the rolls, half of them Catholic. While Pomeroy National School opened in 1914, Pomeroy Public Elementary School No. 2 had already been enlarged in 1867 and reconstructed in 1916, when John Topping became the longest serving principal in the first half of the twentieth century.[41] He was 32 years old when he came to the

---

38 *Féach*, p. 110. 39 Ibid. 40 *Féach*, p. 25. 41 Master Anderson was appointed principal of the Pomeroy National School in 1930 and had a longer term of office as principal. He retired

village in 1921 and retired thirty-three years later in 1954. During his time in Pomeroy the report books of the school inspectors give us some idea about the care and dedicated tuition offered to the children.[42] Remarks ranged from how pleased the inspectors were to find that the children were supplied with cocoa at lunchtime[43] to repeated comments over the years on how shy the children were, failing to do themselves justice in oral English.[44] The school was well run, though the work and discipline of the teachers was somewhat marred by the lack of self-reliance among the pupils.[45] One report remarked that the headmaster was probably doing too much for the children without demanding a similar effort on their part.[46] Reports of unruly children were rare but it was noted that at times children in the senior division lacked self-discipline and that more could be done to bring them into line suggesting that the threat of the rod was not particularly invoked in the school. By the early 1950s the school catered for 150 pupils.

NEW SOCIAL ORDER

The first third of the twentieth century saw Pomeroy develop its essential character that has remained with it to the present day. During the period Pomeroy grappled with a new social and administrative order. The Local Government Act in 1898 abolished the existing system of county government that depended on grand juries and poor law boards to maintain local infrastructure in rural areas.[47] In principle, this new system augured well for the systematic and equitable delivery of services to the community. In practice, the replacement of the landlord and grand jury system by a democratic system of rural and county councils was no guarantee that services would be delivered. This was the case for Pomeroy in the early 1930s when the citizens became alarmed at the physical neglect of their village. By the late 1920s major repairs were made to dwelling houses and buildings in the area but the infrastructural needs of the village itself were overlooked.[48] There was vital need for a new water supply, a dependable sewage system and footpaths were in urgent need of repair. Matters were considered serious enough to warrant a call in March 1930 for a 'Town Improvement Committee'.[49] By late summer housing had greatly improved in the rural districts of Pomeroy with labourers' cottages mushrooming all over the place but again little appeared to be done for the 'quaint little village of Pomeroy' despite the best efforts of J.F. Grimes, local councillor, who sat on both the rural and the county council.[50] By early 1931 there were still no improvements.[51] The

in 1966. **42** PRONI, SCH 896/5/1. **43** *Tyrone Courier*, 15 December 1933. **44** Ibid., 13 February 1935, 17 February 1936, 22 March 1937, 30 June 46, 31 July 1949. **45** Ibid., 13 February 1935. **46** Ibid., 30 June 1940. **47** S.J. Connolly (ed.), *The Oxford companion to Irish history* (Oxford, 1998), p. 326. **48** *Tyrone Courier*, 9 January 1930. **49** Ibid., 27 March 1930. **50** Ibid., 7 August 1930. **51** Ibid., 8 January 1931.

absence of a sufficient water supply was particularly detrimental for two of the village businesses in 1929–30. Two days before Christmas the shop window of Mary Conway, a draper in Main Street, caught fire. It was successfully put out but the inadequacy of the water supply was a great handicap with damage from the fire amounting to £100. [52] More serious was the fire in Frank O'Neill's public house in The Diamond when a considerable amount of damage was done by fire. It would have been worse except that O'Neill had the foresight to have in the yard two 40-gallon barrels of water, which were used to quench the fire. The loss to O'Neill was substantial and nine months later he left the village for Ballyshannon town in county Donegal. O'Neill's business acumen was a loss to the village as he was well known and respected as far away as Coalisland, Stewartstown, Donaghmore, Carrickmore, and Cookstown. [53] He was a prominent member of the local St Mary's flute band. Another prominent figure in business life in Pomeroy was also to leave the village later that year. This was Peter Malone who helped Albert Smyth build up the progressive Pomeroy Creamery. He was appointed manager of Killeenan Co-operative Dairy Society.[54] With the village so badly maintained – footpaths in a very bad way, streets covered in rough stones especially around the courthouse area and the sidewalks a continual source of complaint – some business people couldn't wait for the council to act. [55] They went ahead with the permission of the county surveyor and carried out their own repairs. A case in point was Mrs O'Neill of the Belmore Arms Hotel who had the sidewalks to her premises repaired at her own expense. By the mid-1930s the quality and extent of housing in the village had greatly improved and Cookstown rural council did much to develop housing for farm labourers. Thatched roofs and old hearth fires began to disappear to be replaced with roofs of galvanised iron and the installation of the latest type of American stove.[56] Yet many still had to leave Pomeroy because the place lacked suitable living accommodation.[57] In 1934 a new water scheme came to the town after a campaign of nine years. Apparently, the board of guardians in Cookstown had to be convinced of the necessity for a new water supply as they alleged huge sums of money had been spent on an existing well. On top of that, the farmers of Cavanakeeran were not at all pleased to help pay for a scheme when they received no direct benefit from it.

EMIGRATION

As the village struggled to maintain basic amenities, the young people were voting with their feet. Emigration was rife during the late 1920s and Pomeroy

52 Ibid., 30 January 1931. 53 Ibid., 11 September 1931. 54 Ibid., 6 March 1929. 55 Ibid., 5 March 1931. 56 Ibid., 14 March 1935. 57 Ibid., 31 August 1933.

celebrated many a farewell party in the AOH hall as young people emigrated every month of the year,[58] with the late summer of 1930 being particularly bad.[59] Incoming mails that Christmas were the heaviest for years. The American post broke all records with money orders from abroad bringing great benefits to the area.[60] Economic factors of 'push and pull' were both at work in fuelling the emigration trail. In 1930 a Mr Heap, the colonisation representative of the White Star Line in Northern Ireland, gave an impressive lantern-presentation (precursor of the slide projector) in the village, and no doubt this focused the minds of many young people in the area. Heap gave astounding figures of the acreage still awaiting cultivation in Canada and detailed the various government schemes that were there to assist new settlers. Heap had emigrated himself and now owned and farmed 1,000 acres in Canada.[61]

The shipping lines had local agents competing with one another for potential emigrants. On the eve of the First World War the Cunard Line agent in Pomeroy was Terrence McGlone. Cunard boasted the fastest vessels in the world especially to New York and Canada.[62] Not to be outdone, the agent for the Allen Royal Mail Line in Pomeroy, S.C. Colhoun, boasted that their shipping line had the most direct, the cheapest and shortest routes to all parts of Canada. To further entice, the Allen Line guaranteed 'unsurpassed accommodation and attention' to second-class and third-class passengers.[63]

Whatever the choice of shipping line, we are accustomed to think that the transportation costs for most people at that time meant that they did not return home for some time, if at all. Yet, for some the criss-crossing of the Atlantic by ship was not all that different to modern jet-setting, if a little slower. Consider the case of Father Toner of Pittsburg. In 1906 when Tom Kettle, 'frequently described as the greatest mind of his generation of Irish men',[64] stood for election as MP in East Tyrone, Father Toner came 'hotfoot' from Pittsburg. He arrived by ship on a Tuesday at Derry and travelled direct to Pomeroy to vote on the Wednesday. He then left at once for Queenstown (Cobh) where he just caught the White Star liner, *Majestic*, which took him immediately back to New York. Such were the demands on his time he regretted that he had to leave before the result was declared, but he made arrangements to receive it by Marconigram.[65]

Returning emigrants had a purchasing power, which in a real way reinforced the merits of emigration. An example of this was the sale of a valuable farm at

---

58 Ibid., 9 January 1930, 20 February 1930.   **59** Ibid., 28 August 1930.   **60** Ibid., 31 January 1931.   **61** Ibid., 30 January 1930.   **62** Irish Emigration Database (hereafter IED), American Folk Park, Omagh, serial 8816032, Linenhall library, Belfast. *Dungannon News and County Tyrone Advertiser*, vol xvi, no. 1021, 23 January 1913.   **63** IED, serial 8816035, Linenhall Library, Belfast. *Dungannon News*, vol. xx, no. 1226, 28 December 1916.   **64** Senia Paseta, 'Thomas Kettle: an Irish soldier in the army of Europe?' in Adrian Gregory and Senia Paseta (eds), *Ireland and the Great War* (Manchester, 2002), p. 9.   **65** IED, serial 9502183, Linenhall Library, Belfast. *Belfast Evening Telegraph*, 26 July 1906.

Limehill, Pomeroy. It was known as Tottan's farm and was sold to Thomas McAleer, USA. When William Mullan from North Street died at the age of sixty-two years in May 1930 it was reported that he spent forty years of his life in America and had crossed the Atlantic seven or eight times before settling in Pomeroy in 1928.[66] Undoubtably, the most famous son to emigrate to the USA from Pomeroy was General James Shields (1806–67). He was born at Altmore in 1806, two and a half miles south west of the village. As a young man he challenged Abraham Lincoln to a duel and had to be persuaded otherwise by his friends. In 1864 he fought in the United States/Mexican war, and he was the only American general to defeat Stonewall Jackson. After the American civil war he became governor of the state of Oregon and in that capacity played a major role in facilitating the passage of Irish immigrants to the American north west. Many Ulster names were given to towns and townships there.[67]

THE RAILWAY

Many people who left Pomeroy to emigrate probably did so via the local railway station at the bottom of the town. Ironically, it was the coming of the Great Northern Railway (hereafter GNR) in 1861 that had the greatest impact on the business and commercial life of the village and kept many rooted to the area. The GNR itself was an amalgamation of a number of smaller companies, which coalesced in 1876. Two of these companies were responsible for the building of the railway in Tyrone and transformed transport in the county. The GNR was the second largest rail network in Ireland and one of the great levellers of the sectarian/political divide when Protestant and Catholic shared a footplate in propelling the 'iron horse' through the countryside. In its heyday the GNR had a rolling stock of 200 locomotives and 500 carriages and in the late 1930s employed 5,330, which expanded during the war years to 7,000. It had a maximum route mileage of 560, which was one fifth of Ireland's total railway track.[68] One benefit that the GNR brought to the county was a through-route from Derry to Belfast known to GNR men as the 'Derry Road'. It was a difficult line to work because of the tunnel at Dungannon which was followed just after by Donaghmore stone overbridge and the first of seven restricted curves. Once past Donaghmore the long slow climb to Pomeroy began. Here, the countryside became increasingly barren in the approach to Ireland's highest railway station. Because the northbound train was ascending most of the curves were of no consequence but coming south they were a test of a driver's nerve and endurance. At Pomeroy all a passenger could hope to see of the village were the backs of

66 *Tyrone Courier*, 29 May 1930.   **67** Lord Killanin and M.V. Duignan (eds), *The Shell guide to Ireland* (London, 1967), p. 265.   **68** R.M. Arnold, *The golden years of the Great Northern Railway* (Belfast, 1976), p. viii.

Figure 5 Pomeroy railway station

houses high above (Figure 5). Trains often stopped here to take on water. Beyond the village the countryside opened out into the most scenic part of the whole line.[69] This part of the GNR line was very busy during World War Two carrying stone foundation for the Northern Ireland airfields from the siding at Carrickmore beyond Pomeroy. During World War One while in Britain railways deteriorated the GNR went from strength to strength. In 1931 it had such a sophisticated system that the timetable had expanded to no less than 159 pages and by 1941 it operated the fastest trains in these islands.[70]

In its heyday the rail connection greatly assisted the fairs and markets held in the village. Pomeroy had the reputation of hosting one of Tyrone's leading fairs. The great November Hiring Fair in the village was particularly well trumpeted. By the early 1930s there was practically no hiring of servants as all this was done before the fair started, and it was not uncommon for many farmers to dismiss servants owing to poor prices for cattle and farm produce.[71] Wages for able-bodied men ranged from £11 to £14 for the half-year with board, and boys and girls £7 to £10. From the early hours on fair days, streets were thronged with people from near and far, many having arrived by train. The Diamond in the centre of the village was an area of great teeming activity with the omnipresent carts and creels of young squealing pigs. The usual sideshows were there in abun-

69 Ibid., p. 40. **70** Ibid., p. ix. **71** *Tyrone Courier*, 16 November 1933.

Figure 6 Outline of Pomeroy railway track today

dance with hawkers attracting huge crowds. The traffic tended to become congested as the morning moved on. When eventually the cattle trek towards
Pomeroy station started, the thoroughfare became exceedingly busy.[72]

After the war Pomeroy railway suffered with increased use of bus and lorry
transport and in the 1950s more and more people were able to buy their own
motor. By 1956 it was clear that the days of the GNR were numbered and its
eventual closure in 1965 was a body blow to the rural district. At the time there
was genuine concern that the roads would be unable to carry the traffic then
being carried by the railway. During the night up to 12 goods trains passed
through Pomeroy station with 30 to 40 wagons on each.[73] At the end of the day
the problem besetting the rail closure was a problem of vision when government policies in the 1950s and 1960s shortsightedly argued that it was cheaper
to deploy buses than to invest in the proper upgrading of the rail network.[74]
Today, Pomeroy is one of the few places in Northern Ireland where the actual
site of the station is identifiable and traces of the line are distinctly visible on the
way north to Omagh (Figure 6).

72 Ibid., 15 November 1934. **73** *Dungannon Observer*, 21 April 1956. **74** Norman Johnson,
The Great Northern Railway in county Tyrone (Omagh, 1991), p. 13.

BUSINESS IN POMEROY

For half a century the local creamery was a major employer and by far the most successful business to flourish in Pomeroy. It came into existence around the turn of the twentieth century beside the Great Northern railway station, close to a spring used by Pomeroy Mineral Water Company.[75] The location was ideal, close to an unpolluted water source and through the GNR it had easy access to markets countrywide. The Pomeroy Co-Operative Society owned the creamery with an auxiliary outlet at Mulnagore. During the troubles of the early 1920s the Society faced financial ruin and it was put up for sale. A former manager of the Doons Creamery, Kildress, bought it and radical changes to its operation were put in place.[76] One important change was to reduce the dependence on a water supply from the GNR by sinking a new artesian well. In 1933 a new forty-four horsepower, oil-burning Blackstock engine was used to supply electricity not alone to the Creamery but to the village for the first time. Another welcome change was the installation of a Sabro refrigerator, which did away with the buying in of blocks of ice wrapped in hessian, which used to arrive by midnight train from the Belfast Ice Company. The number of suppliers to the creamery was large and they came from long distances.[77] The farming community saw the benefits as the creamery paid much better returns than did churning at home and selling their butter in the market. The management by Albert Smyth was considered progressive and enlightened. The balance sheet for 1930 showed that 333,885 gallons of milk were received during the year with an average price of 5s. 2d. paid per gallon representing a major increase on the previous year.[78] By mid-1933 there was a further 6 per cent increase. Total sales of butter and cream amounted to £20,396.[79] So long as Smyth was there to guide the fortunes of the creamery, times were good, but a major blow to this thriving enterprise was his tragic death on 29 March 1935. He was found dead with a bullet wound in his forehead.[80] The police ruled out foul play. He was a widower, his wife having died in the first year of their marriage when she was in confinement. He had 'cut his teeth' as a manager of Doons Co-Operative Society in Cookstown before he took over Pomeroy Creamery. He proved a shrewd businessman and before his death he had taken over the Tamnaskinney and Mulnagone Creameries and was instrumental in forming the Mulnagone Milk Recording Association of which he was chairman. After his death a receiver was called in and the books examined where it was revealed that the employees had not been paid for the previous three months. Smyth was declared a bankrupt and the days of the Creamery as a central creamery were over.[81] Killyman Creamery bought it and it became an auxiliary creamery supplying cream to Killyman by rail for a further seven years. A genial and generous man, Smyth initiated and installed, free

---

75 *Féach*, p. 94. **76** Ibid., p. 96. **77** *Tyrone Courier*, 5 March 1931. **78** Ibid., 2 April 1931.
79 Ibid., 6 April 1933. **80** Ibid., 4 April 1935. **81** *Féach*, p. 97.

of charge, an electric light scheme for the public lighting of the village streets in the early 1930s. He continued to support this venture until the lighting of the village was taken over by the Electricity Board of Northern Ireland. Through erecting poles the Electricity Board gave much employment to the village during the mid 1930s and consequently a large number of workmen had lodgings in the town.[82] The poles were initially put up at the northeast side of the town from Dungannon crossroads, through Mr Henry's land, to the foot of North Street via Cavanakeeran. Other work that gave much needed local employment was that at Cappagh reservoir.[83]

There were always business opportunities in the village to attract in new entrepreneurs.[84] In 1931 Patrick McGrath from Omagh opened up in the spirit business at the premises of Frank Quinn. R.T. Johnston opened a draper's shop in the village having spent five years working in William Alexander's draper shop in Cookstown.[85] There was also business movement out of the place in the same period as when M. Johnston saw greater opportunities for an extensive tailoring business in the market town of Dungannon, eight miles away, and he subsequently moved his business there.[86] By the mid 1930s the village was apparently doing so well that revaluation in the village business premises caused huge dismay. Valuation of business premises increased five fold with the license trade being hit particularly hard.

CATHOLIC CHURCH AND POMEROY

While the ways of Mammon were not foreign to the citizens of Pomeroy it is equally true that the business of religion also exercised the minds and heart of the community. The first Catholic church in Pomeroy was built in 1824. Parishioners before this attended mass in the Mass Garden at Munderrydoe. Members of the Orange Order saw it as an invasion of territory by the Catholic community and initially threatened to wreck it, as part of their July Twelfth demonstrations. It didn't happen. At this time the village of Pomeroy was on the outer edge of the parish of Donaghmore, where Donaghmore and Termonmaguirc parishes bordered each other. St Patrick's was built as a chapel of ease to enable the inhabitants to hear Mass without having to trek the whole way down to Donaghmore. The growing economic importance of Pomeroy was a major factor in siting the new church in the village. Folk tradition suggests that a local man, Arthur O'Neill, donated a bell to the new church and that it was the first bell on a Catholic church to be rung in the dioceses of Armagh after the Reformation.[87]

As was common in Catholic rural communities, the clergy played a major role in the life of the people in late nineteenth and early twentieth century. The

82 *Tyrone Courier*, 16 August 1934.   83 Ibid., 26 February 1932.   84 Ibid., 27 August 1931.
85 Ibid., 30 June 1932.   86 Ibid., 7 September 1933.   87 *Féach*, p. 42.

Figure 7 Remains of St Patrick's RC church

life of Father Michael McDermott (1883–1973) in Pomeroy, offers an outstanding exemplar of the important pastoral and spiritual concerns of the Church for its people.[88] First as curate, and later as parish priest, Father McDermott affected the lives of at least four generations of parishioners. He served in the parish between 1910 and 1918 and came back as parish priest in 1940 until his retirement in 1972. He had been a priest in the Armagh Archdiocese for sixty-three years, forty of which were spent in Pomeroy. He spent thirty-two years as parish priest and had no compunction about instilling the fear of God into his parishioners and 'although he frightened many people by his strict attitude to many of their actions, he was for the most part well loved in the parish'.[89] McDermott's first appointment was as a curate in Pomeroy in November 1910. He replaced Father Peter Cush. At that time Pomeroy was still a relatively new Catholic parish. It had been set up in 1836, carved out from the larger parish of Donaghmore. In 1891 the then parish priest, Peter Slevin, with the backing of Archbishop Logue and the negotiating skills of Father Peter Byrne of Dungannon managed to agree with William and Robert Lowry on the purchase of eight acres of land on the Cavanakeeran Road at the western end of the village, to build a new church. The existing church, St Patrick's on Main Street, was in disrepair and too small to accommodate the increased attendances. The land purchased cost £138 with a yearly rental of £5 15s.[90] In 1905 the parish priest, Charles McDonald, built the present parochial house. When Father McDermott arrived in the village a new parish priest was appointed and together the two

88 Vincent Campbell, *Fr Michael McDermott, 1883–1973* (Monaghan, 2001).   **89** Ibid., p. 32.
90 Ibid., p. 6.

Figure 8 The Grotto, Main Street

priests set about building the long-anticipated new church. The church was able to accommodate 700 and cost approximately £6,000. Folk memory recalls Father McDermott wearing putters – long strips of cloth wrapped around the legs from knee to ankle – as he worked at the church. Folk memory also recalls both priests travelling throughout the parish on foot collecting money for the church. On 15 August 1913, Cardinal Logue solemnly dedicated the new church of the Assumption. When the new church opened, the old church, St Patrick's on Main Street closed and the roof and walls had to be dismantled for safety reasons (Figure 8). The cemetery adjoining continued in use. In 1963 a grotto was built to the front of the old church facing onto the street (Figure 8).

Father McDermott left Pomeroy in 1918 and returned as parish priest in 1940. One of his first initiatives was to build a parochial hall on the site of a shed at the back of the parochial house. Up to this most entertainment in the parish found an outlet in the AOH hall on Main Street but local politics regarding the shared use of the premises led to a dispute that nearly split the parish. Father McDermott and his curate promptly decided to provide a neutral venue and subsequently a new hall was built.[91] A tennis court was constructed alongside. This hall became the focal point of entertainment in the parish down to the 1970s. It was used for céilís, drama productions, whist drives, concerts, and as a cinema. So popular was cinema that a 'picture house' was in full swing in the early 1930s hosting James Cagney in *Taxi*, Mary Astor in the biggest box-office

91 Ibid., p. 18.

thriller of the day, *The Lost Squadron* and of course the enduring *Tarzan, The Ape Man*.[92] When St Mary's school became too small to accommodate its pupils classes were held in the hall. Like most clerics of his time Father McDermott was a staunch supporter of the Gaelic Athletic Association. On his arrival in 1940 a major initiative was to seek a permanent playing pitch for the local club who played their games in whatever field was available. Four acres of land were bought on the Cavanakeeran Road and the curate, Father Hughes, travelled to America where he raised a large sum for the development fund for the new grounds.[93] In August 1948 Father McDermott's cousin, Frank Aiken, a leading southern politician in the departments of Defence, Finance, and later Foreign Affairs, and 'the closest person in the cabinet to de Valera' in the Dublin government, opened the pitch.[94] Like many of his generation Father McDermott zealously guarded his flock against the influence of what he perceived to be non-Irish forms of entertainment. Parishioners were increasingly going to dances rather than céilís. The parish priest disapproved. On one occasion when some of his parishioners attended a dance in the local courthouse on Main Street in aid of the local firemen, he denounced them from the altar at Sunday Mass.[95]

The role of the clergy did not end at the church door. In common with Catholic clergy in other rural communities their leadership role found expression in marching bands, amateur drama, and the Gaelic Athletic Association. Father McCooey, a parish curate, established a brass band that was much in demand at Land League meetings in the final decades of the nineteenth century. Another local curate, Father O'Loughlin set up a fife and drum band in the area in the early 1900s.[96] In 1935 an accordian band formed and was instrumental in setting up a dramatic society, which put on plays in the old parochial hall on the Fair Hill. The tradition of amateur drama in Pomeroy flourished in the early part of the century when a dramatic club put on melodramas like *The Shaughran*. The fabulous thing about such plays was that they required large casts so involving a lot of members of the community, and they helped to foster acting talent that might have otherwise have gone unnoticed. In the 1930s and the 1940s the plays of George Sheils were popular with many productions of *Moodie in Manitoba*, and Louis D'Alton's *They Got What They Wanted*.[97] Parish clergy led the way in encouraging this form of recreation. Father Patrick Brady was for a number of years a driving force. Father Peter Hughes and Father Kieran MacKeone followed him. Father Hughes was reputedly a stickler for rendering an authentic interpretation of the dramatist's work and long remembered productions of his were *The Rugged Path* and *The Summit*.[98] He handpicked his actors and actresses to achieve standards, unlike earlier days when there was a more *laissez-faire* approach to staging productions. Father MacKeone followed this

92 *Tyrone Courier*, 5 January 1933. **93** Ibid., p. 19. **94** Joseph Lee, *Ireland, 1912–1985* (Cambridge, 1989), p. 239. **95** Ibid., p. 21. **96** Féach, p. 79. **97** Ibid., p. 82. **98** Ibid., p. 83.

practice with his most successful production being that of *Professor Tim* by George Sheils in the mid-1950s.

Besides amateur drama the clergy also actively encouraged Irish cultural pursuits. Irish classes were set up, and Gaelic football encouraged. Céilís were very popular and were held in the Hibernian Hall until over time their attraction waned in the face of fierce competition from local dance promoters J.P. Dynes and P.J. Casey. These 'impresarios' were adept at organising the 'dance of the season' in the courthouse, when upwards of 150 could attend. The Coalisland Dance Orchestra provided the music and Mr and Mrs Gobain of the Café, Pomeroy, provided the catering.[99]

THE GAA

Pomeroy played a pivotal role in the early formation of the Gaelic Athletic Association in Tyrone. It is not clear if there was a GAA club in Pomeroy prior to 1908 but in late summer of that year a team, the Pomeroy Emmets, were entered in the Dungannon District league. Their first game against Sixmilecross Wolfe Tones saw Pomeroy emerge as victors.[1] The role of Pomeroy in helping to promote Gaelic games at this time is particularly significant. All was not well with the GAA in Tyrone. Soccer, 'the game of the oppressor', was played everywhere and between 1909 and 1916 and in 1920–23 there was no organised GAA in Tyrone. In 1910 a meeting planned for McAleers' Hotel in Pomeroy to rectify matters never materialised. No competitions were played in Tyrone after 1910, except in one small corner for a brief period in 1911. It was another three years before the GAA was to become active again and a structure put in place to promote Gaelic games. Ironically, it was during this fallow period that in 1911, a Strabane man, Dr George Sigerson, made a significant contribution to the Association by way of the Sigerson Cup, for competition between the universities.[2] Pomeroy continued to be the centre of GAA negotiations in an attempt to establish a county board in 1913. A meeting was held in the AOH Hall and J. McAleer of Pomeroy was elected county treasurer. This board did not last very long and went out of existence until a fresh administration was established on 17 September 1916.[3] The town hall in Pomeroy hosted the meeting that put the new administration in place and a convention took place in the village the following month when a total of eleven clubs affiliated. For the first time we hear mention of a local team, the Pomeroy Plunketts. In the years following, F. Corr and J. Grimes of Pomeroy refereed many matches and made a significant

99 *Tyrone Courier*, 8 May 1930. **1** Joseph Martin, *The GAA in Tyrone, 1884–1984* (Omagh, 1984), p. 89. **2** *Féach*, p. 7. In celebration of Pomeroy's rapparee history Sigerson also composed the song *The Mountains of Pomeroy*, a tragic love story about a fictional rapparee called Reynardine and a young woman of Planter stock. **3** Ibid., p. 123.

contribution to the ongoing development of the game.[4] During the troubled political period after 1918 and the early 1920s there was again no organised structure in the county and Tyrone shared this lack of organised administration with counties Fermanagh and Down. In 1923 there was a revival in East Tyrone again with Pomeroy to the fore. A Pomeroy District league was set up consisting of five teams – Pomeroy itself, Donaghmore, Beragh, Dungannon and Edendork. In the following season Pomeroy Plunketts was one of ten clubs that took part in the East Tyrone league and again to emphasise the pivotal role of Pomeroy in GAA affairs the annual convention was held there on 4 January 1925. It was during these years in Pomeroy that a county organisation was established which served the local needs of the GAA for the rest of the century. Pomeroy, along with a small number of other clubs in East Tyrone attempted to spread the organisation to the west of the county. During the 1930s and 1940s the Catholic clergy took an ever-increasing interest in the work of the GAA and were a decisive influence in the expansion of the Association in rural areas. Father Peter Hughes CC, Pomeroy, seconded a proposal by Father Eamon Devlin CC, Donaghmore, on behalf of the Tyrone County Board, that the Ulster Council should conduct its business through the medium of the Irish language.[5] Later in the decade between 1947 and 1949 Father Hughes served as chairman of the county board. John Anderson, a primary school teacher from Pomeroy, was secretary to the county board in 1936 when he succeeded the long-serving secretary Michael Coney from Arboe. Pomeroy also featured in important developments in the GAA during the 1940s as it saw the opening of three county grounds – Dungannon opened in 1947, Pomeroy in 1948 and Coalisland in 1949. The opening of Plunkett Park in Pomeroy was probably the most significant achievement following several years of hard work and fund-raising in Ireland and the USA. It became Tyrone's second county grounds.[6]

POLITICS

Besides the GAA, politics in the mainly nationalist village centred around the Ancient Order of Hibernians. It too was caught up in internal wrangling. The Ancient Order of Hibernians was established in New York in 1836 drawing much of its inspiration from the Irish secret society tradition. By 1900 it had 100,000 members. A benevolent society, it was Catholic and broadly nationalist in outlook. Membership in Ireland shot up six-fold between 1905 and 1909 to 60,000 mainly in the north of Ireland and Dublin. It had a broad appeal 'attractive to businessmen for its freemason-style, to workers for its benevolent activities, and to young Ulster Catholics as a rival to the Orange Order'.[7] Under Joe

4 Ibid., p. 134.   5 Ibid., p. 234.   6 Ibid., p. 244.   7 Connolly, *The Oxford companion to Irish history*, p. 13.

Devlin MP, national president 1905–35, 'it provided a direct link to Irish
American influence and money; it harnessed the Catholic content of Irish nationalism to lay leadership; and it provided new dynamism to replace the fading issue
of land tenure'.[8] The local branch of the AOH in Pomeroy was linked to the
national movement but an examination of the minute books of its meetings
between 1932 and 1959 show little reference to the great political questions of
the day.[9] Rather, an examination of the monthly business in Pomeroy estab-
lishes that it concerned itself with the day-to-day use of the Hibernian Hall by
the various local groups, as the hall became the centre of social activity in the
parish.[10] On the surface this was a sharing of a non-problematic scarce community resource but in reality it led to extraordinary friction. The GAA organised
céilís there on a regular basis but insisted on referring to the premises as Pomeroy
Hall without reference to the Ancient Order, while such was the influence of
the clergy that the hall might only be available for a GAA céilí subject to clerical approval. The hall was the venue for the Pomeroy Dramatic Society and
travelling companies from Cookstown and Omagh. In the late 1930s dance bands,
the Rhythm Boys from Omagh and the Melody Makers from Beragh entertained there, not always with the approval of the local clergy, particularly Father
McDermott, who perceived such entertainment as encroaching on traditional
values and culture.

The failure to address the political questions of the day led in the late 1940s
to a growing politicisation and clear Republican stance in the Pomeroy community. In 1950 Pomeroy people were very annoyed when Anthony Mulvey
was elected to the Westminister Parliament as an Abstentionist MP. Once elected
he publicly declared himself to be free from any obligation to remain abstentionist. A meeting was called in St Mary's Hall whereupon he was called on to
resign his seat as he had insulted 97 per cent of the parish that had elected him.[11]
Later in the year a torchlight mile-long procession to celebrate the Fenian
memory of the Manchester Martyrs Allen, Larkin, and O'Brien entered the village with a car draped in a massive tricolour followed by three bands. Police
from elsewhere were drafted in to line the footpaths in twos and threes. From
the speakers' platform, people were reminded that the Pomeroy Mountains in
troubled times provided a safe refuge for many a fleeting rebel and was a haunt
of the Rapparees. In Penal times many a priest hid from the Redcoats there.

Later in the decade a renewed IRA campaign saw Pomeroy the centre of
security operations in January 1957 when the new Territorial Army barracks in
Dungannon was blown up. Many Pomeroy people had their first close-up view
of a helicopter when two naval machines hovered low over the village in the
search for the cars abandoned by the raiders. Pomeroy police barracks then
became the headquarters for an intensive search of houses and outhouses in the

---

8 Ibid., p. 14.   **9** *Féach*, p. 86.   **10** Ibid., p. 87.   **11** *Dungannon Observer*, 13 May 1950.

mountainous districts around Cappagh, Galbally, and Altmore.[12] Pomeroy men had been prominent officers of the Sinn Féin Constituency Committee at the recent elections in Mid-Ulster.[13] Joseph Begley, a bread server, from The Diamond was chairman of the Sinn Féin election committee in the Mid-Tyrone area and Brendan Casey from North Street was director of publicity.

A LAW–ABIDING COMMUNITY

Politics aside, Pomeroy was a model of a law-abiding community in the early twentieth century. Up to 1931 Pomeroy had its own district inspector of police until the police stations in Pomeroy and Carrickmore were transferred from the Dungannon to the Cookstown district. Losing the district inspector was a downgrading of the police presence in Pomeroy. The chief officer in the village was now Sergeant Purdy who with six other local constables controlled law and order in the area.[14] For services rendered to the community Purdy himself was awarded the King's Silver Jubilee Medal in May 1935.[15] Judging by the matters coming before the Pomeroy petty sessions the job of the local constabulary cannot have been too onerous. The typical roll call of misdemeanors encompassed a large number of bicycle offences, a plague of unlicensed dogs (633 were licensed in the district in 1931),[16] a chronic list of summonses for school non-attendance, and the occasional alleged assault of a man on a woman.[17] The local constabulary worked very closely with the local community in crime detection to the extent that, on occasion, local civilian help was gratuitously given. Once when a postman's pushbike went missing from the hall of his home the local schoolmaster in his Austin Seven was enlisted to solve the crime. Along with a local constable he travelled out of the village in hot pursuit of the bicycle thief. They caught up with the miscreant and brought him back to barracks where he was brought to justice the next day. The poor unfortunate received two months hard labour in Derry gaol and had to spend Christmas in a prison cell.[18] By modern standards such justice might appear draconian, but it certainly made for the quiet of the area. On one occasion the petty sessions lasted but five minutes, drawing the comment from the magistrate that Pomeroy was living up to its record of peace and orderliness.[19] On the rare occasion a hint of more nefarious crime was glimpsed in a report of a car packed full with passengers that came down from Pomeroy to Dungannon town. On a 'tip-off' it was held up there while police searched the car for arms.[20]

Amid all this peace and tranquillity a few of the local constabulary found time to indulge their passion for motor cars. Constable Hall in 1932 attracted con-

12 Ibid., 26 January 1957. **13** Ibid., 2 March 1957. **14** *Tyrone Courier*, 16 April 1931. **15** Ibid., 16 May 1935. **16** Ibid., 9 April 1931. **17** Ibid., 20 July 1933. **18** Ibid., 22 November 1934. **19** Ibid., 19 July 1934. **20** Ibid., 19 January 1933.

siderable attention when he did a 'splendid remodelling' of his motor car which
was the talk of the village. Sergeant Purdy himself purchased a magnificent new
'Rover' motor car.[21] Unfortunately, this motor was badly damaged a short time
later when involved in an accident with a lady cyclist at the foot of Blackhill.
One of the more memorable events from these days in Pomeroy was the 1932
Ulster International Motor Rally motor trials, in which the police barracks played
a major role.[22] All eighty cars ranging from the mammoth Isotta-Fraschini down
to Austin Sevens and Riley Nines had to stop at the police barracks to be checked
in on their way through the village. The cars came from England, Scotland and
Ireland. From the villagers' point of view there was great novelty in the participation of a few young enterprising lady drivers. One of these who turned quite
a few heads was a Miss Paddie Naismith of London. She drove a Standard Avon,
1933 model, and attracted a lot of attention because she was the official chauf-
feur to Ramsey Macdonald, the British prime minister.

CONCLUSION

Samuel Lewis and the OS memoirs variously described Pomeroy in the early
nineteenth century as an inhospitable place, with poor accommodation, frequented by a poor class of people, who spent an inordinate amount of time distilling illegal whiskey.[23] Yet, they were not a feckless people. The 1841 Census
recorded that 26 per cent of families were involved in agriculture and a further
41 per cent in manufacture and trade. As the century progressed the Pomeroy
community placed great importance on the value of education as the way forward. The 1901 Census bears testimony to the exceptionally high level of literacy found in this remote village in east Tyrone. 'Have education, will travel'
was the 'driving force' for many, who saw it as facilitating an *entré* to the New
World. Pomeroy, along with other Tyrone settlements, benefited greatly from
the transformation of the world economy, in the final quarter of the nineteenth
century.[24] This period saw the coming of the mass market and in Pomeroy this
was reflected in the high number of shopkeepers recorded in the 1901 Census.
The arrival of the railway link in 1861 to the village opened up new exciting
horizons. The closure of the railway one hundred years later, despite the increased
road transport, marked a return to remoteness. Religious practice in Pomeroy
reflected the experience of other small Northern communities, particularly in
the all-embracing leadership roles entered into by the Catholic clergy. These
roles facilitated the inculcation of Catholic values, and helped to exercise a pervasive social control in a community that was over 80 per cent Catholic. There

21 Ibid., 28 January 1932.   **22** Ibid., 25 August 1932.   **23** Lewis, *Parliamentary Gazetteer,*
1844–5; A. Day and P. McWilliams (eds), *OS Memoir*, x, pp 70–2.   **24** Austin Stewart,
Coalisland, county Tyrone, in the industrial revolution (Dublin, 2002).

is no doubt that at times this overweening pastoral concern did lead to fright and even flight on the part of some parishioners. When the GAA was failing in Tyrone, Pomeroy played a gallant part in helping to establish a lasting administrative structure. The early twentieth century saw the village emerge as a peaceful haven, where newsworthy reports concerned the motor car fanaticism of the local constabulary. However, by mid-century, Pomeroy experienced a growing politicisation and unease regarding the outstanding political questions of the day. The expectations of a Catholic, Nationalist people found a strong resonance within a community whose physical remoteness and sense of Rapparee history allowed them to understand better than most, what it was to be outsiders, and the importance of doing something about it.

Illustrations

TABLES

Index